BRAZIL SINCE 1985:
POLITICS, ECONOMY AND SOCIETY

Brazil since 1985:
Politics, Economy and Society

Edited by
Maria D'Alva Kinzo and James Dunkerley

Institute of Latin American Studies
31 Tavistock Square, London WC1H 9HA
http://www.sas.ac.uk/ilas/publicat.htm

Institute of Latin American Studies
School of Advanced Study
University of London

British Library Cataloguing-in-Publication Data
A catalogue record for this book is available
from the British Library

ISBN   1 900039 53 2

Institute of Latin American Studies
University of London, 2003

TABLE OF CONTENTS

PART III: DEMOCRACY AND SOCIETY

LIST OF CONTRIBUTORS

Edmund Amann is a Lecturer in the School of Economic Studies at the University of Manchester. He specialises in the economics of technical change and the impacts of trade and market liberalisation on developing countries; the economies of Latin America, especially Brazil. He is the co-editor, with Ha-Joon Chang, of *Brazil and South Korea: Economic Crisis and Restructuring* (London, 2003).

Leslie Bethell is Director of the Centre for Brazilian Studies, University of Oxford. He is Emeritus Professor of Latin American History in the University of London and Professorial Fellow of St Antony's College, Oxford. He is the author of numerous publications on nineteenth-and twentieth-century Latin America, and is the editor of *The Cambridge History of Latin America*.

Leandro Piquet Carneiro is Assistant Professor of Political Science at the Universidade de São Paulo. He specialises in the quantitative analysis of data, particularly politics and criminality. He participated in the Violence, Public Safety and Human Rights programme at the Instituto de Estudos da Religião and is a consultant to the World Bank regarding 'Crime in Latin American Cities'.

Carlos A. Costa-Ribeiro is Assistant Professor of Sociology at the Universidade Estadual do Rio de Janeiro. He is also a fellow of the Center for the Study of Wealth and Inequality at Columbia University. His research encompasses several sub-disciplines within sociology, from social stratification, race relations and economic development, to quantitative methodology and criminal justice. He is the author of *Cor e criminalidade: estudo e análise da justiça no Rio de Janeiro* (Rio de Janeiro, 1996) and has published widely on criminal justice, social inequality and social mobility.

Mauricio C. Coutinho is Professor of the Institute of Economics, Universidade Estadual de Campinas (UNICAMP), Brazil. His research interests include public sector economics and the economics of social security. His publications include '100 grandes economistas,' in D. Berni (ed.), *Técnicas de pesquisa em economia* (Florianópolis, 2002) and 'The Brazilian Fiscal System in the 1990s: Equity and Efficiency under Inflationary Conditions,' *ILAS Research Paper no. 41* (London, 1996).

James Dunkerley is Professor of Politics and Director of the Institute of Latin American Studies, University of London, and Professor of Politics at Queen Mary, University of London. He is an editor of the *Journal of Latin American Studies*. His recent publications include *Americana: The*

Americas in the World around 1850 and *Warriors and Scribes: Essays in the History and Politics of South America* (both London, 2000). He is the editor of *Studies in the Formation of the Nation-State in Latin America* (London, 2002).

Argelina Cheibub Figueiredo is Professor at the Universidade Estadual de Campinas (UNICAMP) and Senior Researcher at the Centro Brasileiro de Análise e Planejamento (CEBRAP). Her main research interest is the comparative study of political institutions, decision-making processes and public policies in democratic polities. Recent publications include, 'The Role of Congress as an Agency of Horizontal Accountability: Lessons from the Brazilian Experience,' in Scott Mainwaring and Christopher Welna (eds.), *Democratic Accountability in Latin America* (Oxford, 2003), and, with Fernando Limongi, *Executivo e legislativo na nova ordem constitucional* (Rio de Janeiro, 1999).

Antonio Sérgio Alfredo Guimarães is Professor in the Department of Sociology, Universidade de São Paulo. His most recent publications are *Beyond Racism. Race and Inequality in Brazil, South Africa, and the United States* (Boulder and London, 2001) and *Classes, raças e democracia* (São Paulo, 2002).

Anthony Hall is Reader in Social Planning in Developing Countries in the Social Policy Department at the London School of Economics. He is the editor of *Amazonia at the Crossroads: The Challenge of Sustainable Development* (London, 2000) and of *Global Impact, Local Action: New Environmental Policy in Latin America* (forthcoming).

Maria D'Alva G. Kinzo is Professor in the Department of Political Science, Universidade de São Paulo. She was a Research Fellow (1991–92) at the Institute of Latin American Studies, University of London, where she also worked as part-time Senior Lecturer in 1997–98. Her publications include the books *Legal Opposition Politics under Authoritarian Rule in Brazil* (Basingstoke, 1988) and *Radiografia do quadro partidário brasileiro* (Rio de Janeiro, 1993). She has published widely on political parties, elections and democratisation.

Fernando Limongi is Professor of Political Science at the Universidade de São Paulo and President of the Centro Brasileiro de Análise e Planejamento (CEBRAP). He is co-author, with Adam Prezeworski, José Antonio Cheibub and Michael Alvarez, of *Democracy and Development* (Cambridge, 2000) and, with Argelina Figueiredo, of *Executivo e legislativo na nova ordem constitucional* (Rio de Janeiro, 1999).

Fiona Macaulay is Lecturer in Political Sociology at the Institute of Latin American Studies, University of London, and Research Associate at the Centre for Brazilian Studies, University of Oxford. Her research interests include human rights, gendered aspects of political and justice institutions, local government and the Brazilian Workers' Party. She is the author of *Gender Politics in Brazil and Chile: The Role of Political Parties in Local and*

National Policy-making (forthcoming) and 'Taking the Law into their Own Hands: Women, Legal Reform and Legal Literacy in Latin America,' in Maxine Molyneux and Nikki Craske (eds.), *Gender, Rights and Justice in Latin America* (Basingstoke, 2002).

Celso L. Martone is Professor of Economics, Department of Economics, Universidade de São Paulo. His recent publications include 'Recent Economic Policy in Brazil: Before and After the Mexican Peso Crisis,' in Riordan Roett (ed.), *The Paradoxes of Mexican Development* (Boulder, 1996), 'Os déficits gêmeos como desafios ao desenvolvimento,' in Ives G. da Silva Martins (ed.), *Brasil: desafios do século XXI* (São Paulo, 1998) and *A herança de FHC e os desafios econômicos do próximo governo, Bolsa de Valores de São Paulo* (São Paulo, 2002).

Mauro Porto is Assistant Professor of Communication at the Universidade de Brasília (UnB), where he is also the Head of the Research Center on Media and Politics. He is the Chair of the Political Communication Division of the National Association of Graduate Programs in Communication (COMPOS). His main research area is political communication, especially the study of the role of television in Brazilian politics, on which he has published widely.

Brasilio Sallum Jr is Professor of Sociology at the Universidade de São Paulo where he received his PhD in Political Sociology. Currently, he is working on comparative research on Brazilian and Mexican economic liberalisation and a research project on the new Brazilian State form. Recent publications include 'Crise économique et changement politique au Brèsil et au Mexique: une critique de l'analyse comparative des heritages institutionnels,' in Bruno Lautier and Jaime Marques-Pereira (eds.), *Brésil et Mexique, entre libéralisme et démocratie* (Paris, 2003) and 'Le libéralisme à la croisée des chemins au Brèsil,' *Revue Tiers Monde no. 167*, vol. XLII, juillet-septembre 2001.

Maria Celi Scalon is Assistant Professor and Coordinator of the Sociology Programme at Instituto Universitario de Pesquisas do Rio de Janeiro. She is currently working on social stratification, mobility and perceptions of inequality. Her publications include, *Mobilidade social no Brasil: padrões e tendências* (Rio de Janerio, 1999) and *Imagens da desigualdade* (forthcoming).

List of Tables

LIST OF FIGURES

Introduction

How should we assess Brazil's recent experience of democracy? To what extent has the emergence of a democratic regime in one of the world's largest nation-states actually improved Brazilians' social, economic and political life? Has democracy been consolidated to the point of making a political breakdown unthinkable or improbable? These are questions that any student of Brazilian public life has to address. The answers to them, however, are increasingly recognised to be far from simple. Contrasting evaluations abound, stressing either the positive or negative aspects of a period of democracy that is still decidedly short.

None of the chapters in this book seeks to deny the starkness of Brazilian reality past and present — almost all lay stress on the exceptional inequalities of wealth and widespread poverty — but, equally, all the authors resist recycling simplistic accounts or received beliefs. Most, whether working from primary or secondary sources and data, present revisionist interpretations. It is, indeed, unsurprising that a polity, economy and society of almost continental dimensions should manifest highly complex — sometimes openly contradictory — qualities, especially over a period when external conditions were so dynamic.

Immediate Political Background

Controversy over the nature of Brazilian democracy starts with the simple definition of its duration. Brazil has been governed by a civilian president since 1985. But only from 1990 has it been ruled by a president elected by universal suffrage, and those analysts for whom popular election of the president is the crucial criterion of democracy identify the new regime as being born only in 1989, when the presidential election was held. However, these two different dates serve as more than mere starting-points, showing that democracy in Brazil was the product of a long-lasting experience of political transition. This started as early as 1974, and it took eleven years for the military to return to the barracks. In that sense, no matter how positive or negative the assessment that could be made about 17 (or 13) years of democracy, it has to be recognised that such a long transition affected the conformation of the new order.[1] Accordingly, we open this introduction with a brief account of the political process in the years

---

1   It is worth noting here the concept of *path dependence*, which stresses the notion that political options in a given conjuncture are the product of preceding decisions made by political actors; that is, those decisions which affected the course of the political process to the extent that they constrain the range of options in the following conjuncture.

leading up to 1985, whilst the following chapter by Leslie Bethell provides an expansive treatment of the national electoral and democratic experience since independence.

Brazil's present regime was preceded by a gradual and controlled process of liberalisation conducted by the military, the starting-point of which was General Geisel's announcement — at the inauguration of his presidential term in 1974 — of a project of 'gradual and secure' political relaxation. The fact that the president was committed to a project of some liberalisation was made clear by the partial revocation of press censorship as well as the less tight conditions under which the 1974 legislative elections were held. However, the manner in which the liberalisation was directed by the president and the dynamics of the political process that led to democracy were very complex and prolonged. At no moment did the military lose control of the political process, being able throughout to establish the pace and scope of the liberalisation.

In all events, the more relaxed political climate obliged the democratic opposition to expand the scope of its action and become more effective. This became clear with the surprisingly successful 1974 election results of the opposition party (the MDB).[2] The military government, responsible for remarkable rates of economic growth, had little support at the polls. The 'tame' opposition party threatened to operate as a formal competitor to the government party, and to serve as an effective political instrument that could be used not only in the electoral arena but also in the political process at large. It was not by chance that the military government would make every effort to neutralise the impact of both the elections and the MDB.

This was not the only problem faced by the government. There was also the challenge of opposition within the armed forces, mainly of hard-line officers set against the slightest opening of the regime. President Geisel was quite successful in tackling the democratic and authoritarian oppositions by playing the game in both directions at the same time. On the one hand, he altered the electoral rules and legislative procedures several times, and purged some of the more outspoken MDB parliamentarians in order to appease the hard-line officers and reinforce his control over the democratic opposition. On the other, he acted promptly against the hard-liners, dismissing the army commander in São Paulo after the killing by torture of a journalist and a metal worker, and so demonstrating that the president was in full control of the political process. The president also dismissed the army minister — a hard-liner who aspired to replace him in the presidency — reinforcing his authority and control over the presiden-

---

2   The 1974 elections were to renew a third of the Senate, the Chamber of Deputies and the State Assemblies. The opposition won 16 out of 22 seats contested for the Senate, had an increase of 46 per cent in its representation in the House of Deputies and gained a majority in six State Assemblies.

tial succession. In the event, João Figueiredo — the general who succeeded Geisel in the presidency for the following six years — was nominated in strict accordance with Geisel's determination to impose his own choice.

If the military government proved to be very successful in controlling political liberalisation, it could not manage a comparable achievement in the economic realm. Early signs that the Brazilian 'economic miracle' was over were sharpened by the oil crisis and its worldwide consequences. Seeking to avoid the political damage of an economic contraction, Geisel responded to the oil crisis by promoting an ambitious programme of import substitution in the sectors of basic raw-materials and capital goods, involving significant state investment and high levels of external borrowing. This policy continued during the first years of Figueiredo's administration, with the result that the expansion of the economy was maintained at the expense of both the external accounts and inflation rates. The aggravation of the external problems finally forced Figueiredo's economic team to change policy course. An attempt at economic adjustment was carried out for the first time, leading to a sharp fall in the level of economic activity and a rise in unemployment. Another severe external shock in 1982 aggravated the conditions of an economy already extremely vulnerable to changes in the external environment.[3] Henceforth, economic crisis — meaning inflation and deterioration of the external and internal accounts — would accompany the political transition and the democratic governments that followed it.

Factors such as the government's electoral setbacks, internal conflict within the army and the emergence of serious problems in the economic front contributed to reinforce the gradual and controlled pattern of the liberalisation. Initiated in 1974, this liberalisation did not deepen substantially until 1978, when the military finally revoked the draconian Institutional Act No. 5. In 1979 — under Figueiredo's administration — Congress passed an amnesty bill, which, although limited, did allow the return from exile of most of the politicians and left-wing activists banned during the years of repression. A new political party law put an end to the two-party system compulsorily created in 1966. As a consequence, in addition to the established parties which were re-organised under new names (the ARENA became the PDS — Social Democratic Party — and the MDB became the PMDB — Party of the Brazilian Democratic Movement), three organisations were created in 1980: the PT (the Workers' Party), the PDT (Labour Democratic Party) and the PTB (Brazilian Labour Party).[4]

---

3   See Lamounier and Moura (1986).
4   Two other significant parties emerged later on: the PFL (Party of the Liberal Front, created in 1985) and the PSDB (Brazilian Social Democratic Party, created in 1988). On the political parties after democratisation, see Kinzo(1993), Jairo (1996) and Mainwaring (1999).

By the end of 1982 the process of liberalisation had reached a new phase, opened by the elections of that year: new political parties had been created and participated in the polls, politicians who had lost their rights in the 1960s had resumed political activity and, for the first time since 1965, state governors were elected by popular vote. The 1982 electoral contest certainly resulted in important gains for the military government, which enjoyed a guaranteed majority in the electoral college, that would choose the next president. But the opposition gains were also important, particularly for the PMDB, which kept its place as the main political force in opposition to the regime — a role that would prove to be important in the presidential succession.

In an attempt to change the rules of the presidential election, the PMDB proposed in 1984 a constitutional amendment for the reestablishment of elections by popular vote. In an effort to raise popular support for the bill, all the opposition parties joined together in the so-called 'Diretas-Já' campaign, which counted with the crucial organisational support of the governors of the three most important states — all in the hands of the opposition parties. This resulted in an impressive mobilisation with millions of people carrying banners and wearing T-shirts bearing the effective slogan 'Diretas-Já' at public rallies all over the country. The movement was devoid of violence but so forceful that even some PDS parliamentarians, concerned with the popular reaction if they sided with the government, voted in favour of the amendment. But the number of PDS dissidents was not large enough to enable the opposition to reach the two-thirds majority required for constitutional amendment bills.

Early Weaknesses

This key episode, once again, made clear the military's determination to maintain full control of the presidential succession. It was also evident that, in spite of its popular support, the opposition remained numerically too weak in congress to be able to defeat the regime. These factors pushed the moderate sectors of the opposition toward a policy of playing the political game according to the regime's own rules — to participate in the presidential election by presenting an opposition candidate at the electoral college, even though an opposition candidature could only win through a split within the government's parliamentary forces. The opportunity presented itself when a group of PDS politicians refused to support the government party's candidate. Negotiations between the PMDB and the regime's dissidents (who left to create the PFL)[5] led to the creation of the Democratic Alliance, the aim of which was simply to join forces to defeat

---

5   The Party of the Liberal Front became one of the largest parties of the new system. Apart from its centre-right ideological position, the PFL's main feature became its closeness to all governments since redemocratisation.

the government candidate. In return for the PFL support for Tancredo Neves — the PMDB's presidential candidate — Senator José Sarney, a dissident who had resigned the position of PDS national chairman, was nominated candidate for vice-president. They won the election in the electoral college on 15 January 1985.

However, the inauguration of the first civilian presidency after 19 years of military rule was shaken by an unexpected event: on the eve of the inauguration of the new government Tancredo Neves fell ill, and died a few months later, the office passing to the vice-president, José Sarney. In addition to the fact that the return to civilian rule had resulted from a compromise established between the moderate sectors of the opposition and the regime's dissidents, the death of the political figure who was supposed to lead the new government now made democratisation still more complicated. The president who was unexpectedly going to lead the New Republic — as the regime inaugurated in 1985 became known — would have to work under exceptionally precarious circumstances, particularly in the face of a mounting economic and social crisis.

In fact, Sarney inaugurated his government without any clear programme. His political weakness was evident: he was marked by his former links with the military regime, had not been elected by popular vote and was not attached to the party that was expected to lead the new government (the PMDB). His legitimacy was easily questioned, and the administration was vulnerable to all kinds of pressure, from the heterogeneous and competing political forces that composed his government to the opposition parties and organised sectors of civil society demanding social democracy.

Yet, the process of democratisation continued its course despite the fact that in the economic and social fields, very few improvements indeed were registered in either the official statistics or popular experience. Several economic plans and a variety of policy experiments were introduced in fruitless attempts to curb a persistent combination of high inflation and economic stagnation. The succession of failures resulted not only in the aggravation of the economic crisis and social problems, but also in the erosion of the state's capacity to govern.

In the political sphere improvements were much more tangible: free conditions of electoral participation and contestation were established (with the removal of all restrictions on the right to vote and to political organisation), and a new constitution was promulgated late in 1988. The result of almost two years' work, the Constitution represented a clear democratic advance despite many unintended (and some deliberate) consequences discussed in the chapters that follow. Apart from securing all the mechanisms of representative democracy, the new charter gave Brazilians the right to participate more directly in policy decisions through recourse to plebiscite, referendum and the initiation of a congressional bill. Power became less concentrated in all senses of the term — as a consequence of the strengthening of the legislature and the judiciary as well as the subnational spheres of the federation, and the guarantee of freedom of party organisation. In the social realm, important innovations included the widening of social security provisions and the introduction of rigorous penalties for discrimination against blacks and women.

The election of 1989 — when more than 72 million people went to the polls to choose a successor to Sarney — may, then, properly be seen as a critical chapter of Brazil's long and complex transition to a democratic system of governance.

Political developments after the inauguration of the 1989 victor, Fernando Collor de Mello, showed, nonetheless, that Brazil's emerging democracy had to pass severe tests before reaching a relatively stable situation. It had to survive acute popular disappointment provoked by the Collor Plan (1990) which, having confiscated savings and investments in its attempt to stabilise the economy, collapsed in complete failure. It had to face the popular frustration of the first popularly elected president of the country being impeached (1992) on charges of corruption. It had the provisions of its constitutional framework put in question both by a plebiscite (1993) about the adoption of parliamentarism or presidentialism and, indeed, by the endless constitutional revision that has been going on since 1994. It had to withstand several corruption scandals, the most impressive being that of the Congressional Budget Committee, which led to the creation of a parliamentary inquiry commission and the disclosure of massive levels of corruption. It had to confront, after brief calm resulting from the economic stabilisation of the Real Plan (1994), a succession of financial crises in the world — those emanating from Mexico in 1995, Asia in 1997 and Russia in 1998, in addition to the Argentine crisis of 2002 — the consequences of which were deeply felt by an economy such as Brazil's which still lacks consolidated stability and a sustained pattern of development.

These challenging (but increasingly familiar) experiences all occurred when management of the economy was under the direct or overall responsibility of Fernando Henrique Cardoso, first as author of the Real Plan as finance minister for Itamar Franco (1992–94), the vice-president who replaced the disgraced Collor, and thereafter as president himself for two terms (1994–98 and 1998–2002). Since much of the present book is devoted to analysis of the policy and performance of Brazil's government and economy under Cardoso's presidency we shall not dwell on its qualities here, except to note that he was one of the very few regional heads of state to be a social scientist, and that, having established an international reputation in political exile by refining dependency theory, he assumed office with a mandate to deliver economic stability of a type usually associated with those forces criticised in his academic publications. Much rather clumsy commentary was excited by this apparent anomaly although very few critics of the Real Plan were able convincingly to deny that it delivered some early relief to millions of impoverished Brazilians.

In the presidential polls of 1994 and 1998 Cardoso defeated Luiz Inacio Lula da Silva of the PT. In the first instance the victory was against the run of expectations and early poll findings, which, along with much of the character of the campaign, were overtaken by the decisive effects of the Real Plan. Nonetheless, both election campaigns, and the general competition between these two singular yet quite representative figures, underpin the particular consolidation of Brazilian democratic politics. There are few comparable cases elsewhere in the region of such a creative contestation between outwardly conservative and progressive leaders. Indeed, the qualities of the exchange between government and opposition throughout the late 1990s were not perhaps evident even in Brazil itself until the onset of the 2002 campaign, when recent economic crisis, depletion of administrative energy and originality, popular exasperation with the status quo, and simple insufficiency of the official candidate under such circumstances all combined to deliver to Lula and the PT a victory that defied early expectations and upset regional trends.

Lula, the PT and the Poll of 2002

Almost all the chapters of this book were drafted in 2000, in preparation for a conference held at the London Institute of Latin American Studies (ILAS) in February 2001. The authors had been asked to review the Brazilian experience of democracy in their field for the period 1985–2000. Their drafts were subsequently revised for publication and three further chapters (by Bethell, Amann and Hall) were added, all prior to the election of 2002. The collection was, then, ready to go into production at the time of the poll. Several authors understandably decided that their particular topic would register no short-term shift or did not require significant reconsideration as a consequence of the poll result. In some cases, such as social mobility, there is an entirely reasonable sense in which a single public event, however important, cannot be expected to register an immediate impact. However, the reader will find in some of the chapters a number of remarks that register the 2002 poll, and we must address it briefly here since it was undoubtedly one of the most important events in the consolidation of Brazilian democracy.

In the first place this was simply because of the environment for debate in which the campaign took place. There was wide information about the candidates, for which the role of the press and the mass media was fundamental in that it instilled through interview and debate a sharp popular interest in the political process. It is no coincidence that abstention rates fell compared to the previous presidential contest — 82 per cent of eligible voters went to the polls, against 78 per cent in 1998.

Secondly, the poll was held in a very competitive atmosphere, most of the electoral contests having no certain or probable outcome. This was evident not only in the great number of candidatures with a clear capacity to garner popular backing but also in the outcome of the gubernatorial elections, where many narrow results were registered in the first round and where there were a significant number of close victories in the second round.

However, as far as the overall consolidation of democracy is concerned, Lula's own victory was the most important feature of the election — not only for what his candidature represented in terms of the new president's social and political background but also for the left's simple capture of power. We could say that with this election Brazil has completed the cycle of democratic consolidation, in the sense of overcoming the obstacles to effective alternation in office and power. It is worth remembering that even during the 2002 campaign there were those who questioned the very fairness of the process. There were demands for the resignation of the president of the Supreme Electoral Tribunal, Nelson Jobim, on the grounds that he could not provide fair oversight of the election because of his friendship with one of the leading candidates. Equally, one should not forget the insinuations about the security of the electronic polling equipment or the claims about media manipulation. Such charges might well have cast doubt on the legitimacy of any defeat of the opposition, but the opposition won, and the accusations were rapidly forgotten.

Another important aspect relates to the possible impact of the 2002 elections on the strengthening of the party system, which is, of course, itself an essential component of a consolidated democracy. Here we should note the type of competition that took place in the second round of the presidential contest. After strong movement in the voters' first-round preferences for different candidates to compete against Lula in the second round, José Serra, from the PSDB, took the place of contender. As a result, the second round challenge to Lula came from a candidate who was closely tied to a party project (in this case that of the government), rather than from a politician whose linkage to a party was purely or primarily instrumental. Above all, it meant that the second round was a competition between two party platforms and projects, even though both Lula and Serra had accumulated the most diverse allies.[6]

The impact on the party political game of both the election of the PT's candidate for president and the growth of that party (and others of the left) in the legislature changed the entire correlation of national political forces.

6   This does not mean, though, that one should deny or ignore the strong electoral performance of populist and personalistic candidates, such as Garotinho and Ciro Gomes, whose connection with parties was very fragile.

With respect to the PT, there is no doubt that it is now benefiting from the prolonged construction of its distinctive profile. Indeed, even in the midst of sundry political and economic crises over the last two decades the PT has always given priority to its own institution-building.

It should also be noted that much of the PT's electoral success was due to the persistence of Lula's candidature for the presidency — in every poll since the transition — which helped serve as a catalyst of popular discontent with the incumbent administration. In fact, Lula's role was somewhat similar to that of the MDB in the 1974 legislative elections, and, as occurred in 1974, his electoral support was less programmatic than based on a diffuse demand for change. Neither was the 2002 contest essentially a personalistic dispute, because most voters knew full well whether they were for or against Lula in terms of the PT, which the electorate readily identified in the political spectrum. So, with respect to party consolidation, the inauguration of the Lula government could usher in a new phase in the Brazilian experience, where the principal protagonists will likely be the PT itself, the PSDB and the PFL. The first leads the new coalition in power and, as such, must take into account the various parties and social forces upon which it depends for staying in office. The PSDB and the PFL have now become the opposition, and so need to create new credentials for an authentic fulfilment of that role, particularly in developing far clearer public policies than they currently possess. These challenges are in themselves substantial, and they will be still more acute should — as seems highly likely — the coming period prove less stable than the eight years of the Cardoso government.

Thirdly, we should register the fact that the 2002 results confirmed the highly pluralist nature of the Brazilian party system. No less than 19 parties gained seats in the Chamber of Deputies — seven of them with a representation of over five per cent — 28 parties secured representatives to the state assemblies, and state governors were elected from eight different parties. If such pluralism is generally a positive factor, it also confirmed the high fragmentation of the current party system, which, in fact, increased in the 2002 poll.[7] The direct consequence of this is the difficulty of governments in obtaining a working majority in parliament. If the party coalition that supported Cardoso's government was already heterogeneous and fragmented, that supporting Lula's administration is still more so, because the PT is the only coalition member with a substantial parliamentary bloc.

The essential question to ask in the period immediately following the 2002 poll is: to what extent can Lula's government achieve its goals when faced with intense popular demands, high fragmentation in both the congress and the control of state governments, and the great diversity of social forces lending support to the new administration? This complex and

---

7   Measured by the effective number of parties, the fractionalisation index increased from 7.2 in 1998 to 8.5 in 2002.

challenging position plainly demands of the president an exceptional capacity simultaneously to lead and negotiate. Certainly, the expressive and popular endorsement he received at the ballot box is an invaluable asset in confronting the complications of the national political system and the globalised economy, but few doubt that such an early advantage will be subjected to severe test.

Brazil since 1985

The first chapter of the present volume, by Leslie Bethell, takes the claims made by Francis Fukuyama in the late 1980s about the triumph of liberal democracy as a most fitting reason for an historical survey of democratic forms in Brazil, which in key respects does not fit any 'end of history' prospectus. In a review that stretches back to 1822 Bethell demonstrates not only how a great 'sense of history' hung over the 2002 poll itself, but also that the record of political change since 1985 needs to be assessed against a background where elections 'had more to do with public demonstrations of personal loyalties, the offer and acceptance of patronage, the reduction of social and regional tensions, and, above all, control of the patrimonial state'. Providing copious statistical illustration of the simple but vital fact that there is 'more to democracy than elections', this expansive chapter simultaneously recalls the depth and partiality of the Brazilian electoral past.

Several core issues discussed in later chapters with respect to the tenuous nature of the rule of law, the institutional fragilities of federalism and presidentialism, and the country's exceptional social and economic disparities are introduced here in a long-run context that is more openly oligarchic, more strongly rural and much less related to mass or popular mobilisation than at the present time (whilst all are recognisably still present).

Maria D'Alva Kinzo shares Bethell's perspective on elections as a necessary but insufficient condition of democracy. For her treatment of the role and behaviour of political parties she draws on the conceptual legacy of Dahl and Sartori to strike a balance between minimalist and maximalist visions, particularly over issues of practicality and legitimacy during political transitions. Kinzo also notes the rural-urban divide, and she draws out the importance of sub-national actors, who, even in the case of Brazil, often get lost in studies that too readily rest on the nation-state as a natural unit of analysis. We have already noted the challenge of party fragmentation, which Kinzo links to the low intelligibility of the system in the eyes of the electorate. This, in turn, she associates with poor responsiveness to the populace, complicating representational links, and impeding the kinds of accountability that might fortify both legitimacy and partisanship. The result, at least until 2002, was exceptional electoral volatility in tandem with wider reliance upon coalition.

The following chapter by Argelina Cheibub Figueiredo and Fernando Limongi closes the focus more tightly still, subjecting the now substantial literature on executive-legislative relations to a sharp, and sometimes revisionist, appraisal. The authors directly question the view that, since 1988 in particular, Congress has 'rendered the country ungovernable', and they argue that it has been consistently responsive in policy formulation and implementation. In an exceptionally careful analysis of congressional voting patterns and forms of executive enactment, they build a strong case against the pertinence to Brazil of models of 'delegative democracy' or 'imperial presidentialism' that has been persuasively applied to other Latin American experiences. In Brazil, delegation comes about 'not as a direct and unconditional relationship between the electorate and the presidency but rather as a conditional delegation of institutional power to the president by Congress'. Figueirdo and Limongi persuasively claim that the Brazilian experience since 1985 provides no grounds for the view that its government has been immobilised by an excess of politically unmediated popular demands.

Fiona Macaulay's survey of the judiciary considers another institutional arena that has been subject to widespread criticism, not least internationally. She identifies two distinct phases of reform. The first took place in the late 1980s, immediately following the transition to civilian rule, when priority was given to establishing independence and the stable operation of judicial review. A second stage, in the 1990s, saw attention focused on internal management and accountability; the issue of differential access to (and treatment within) the judicial system; and the need for it to modernise and operate efficiently. Taking the salient features of each phase in turn, Macaulay shows that Brazil's judicial system, which combines elements of European and North American models, acquired autonomy at a substantial cost of overload, malpractice and sheer inefficiency. Independence, she reminds us, does not necessarily entail impartiality, especially at local level. Here, then, one finds the continued applicability of that traditional saying, 'for my enemies the law, for my friends, everything'. But Macaulay's chapter demonstrates that the challenge is as much about institutional design as probity and political culture. The extraordinary complexity of an institutional sphere which combines five parallel court systems at state and federal levels, including specialist electoral, military and labour tribunals, makes it unsurprising that the reform process has 'thickened' and remains very far from complete.

The second section of the volume does not relinquish concern for institutions but moves firmly into the domain of economics, which is at the core of understanding the political process in Brazil at the end of the twentieth century. In the first of three chapters that review that experience both internally and with regard to external factors of unprecedented consequence, Edmund Amann provides a synthetic but comprehensive review of the macroeconomic record since 1985. He shows how this was a period of 'unprecedented change' combining trade liberalisation and market deregulation, privatisation with fiscal reform and a major shift in exchange rate policy. This latter, revolving Fernando Henrique's Real Plan of 1994, is at the heart of Amann's analysis, which differentiates carefully between the (failed) policies of the governments up to 1994 and the distinct pressures and adjustments undergone thereafter. Although Amann stresses the 'impressive intensity' of changes in policy and performance, he, like other authors, notes the failure to secure significant alteration of either income distribution or the social security system.

Mauricio Coutinho's treatment of the internal constraints on policy and performance combines an institutional approach with that of political economy. This latter complements the analysis of Figuereido and Limongi but, in stressing how democratic policy-making differed from that under the military dictatorship, it necessarily draws out the challenges posed by federalism and congressional power. Coutinho also notes that high inflation, which prevailed for nine of the 15 years under survey, provided the executive with some scope for policy experimentation. After the Real Plan the taming of inflation was won at the expense of growth, through an overvalued currency, liberalised imports, and high interest rates. Moreover, although in its first phase the Plan was successful in detaining the impoverishment that derives from hyperinflation, that impact stalled and then stopped. The chapter's concern with the legacy of indexation and the operation of the fiscal system is pitched within the wider legal, and indeed cultural, context, where risk-averse practices and weak contractual custom are more consequential than any putative congressional impediment. Coutinho also brings out the degree to which the Cardoso administration vanquished the considerable financial autonomy of the states, but he, like Amann and others, notes the failure to deliver a significant improvement of income inequality or reduction in levels of poverty.

Celso Martone's chapter on external constraints on the economy pursues a rather more technical course but reaches a not dissimilar conclusion that Brazil has yet to enter any 'virtuous cycle' of growth and stability. Martone necessarily devotes early attention to the experience of the 1980s, noting that in 1985 Sarney inherited from the military a system in which very few of the targets agreed with the IMF since 1982 were met. He reminds us that after the failure of Sarney's Cruzado Plan, Brazil entered a two-year moratorium, and that between March 1989 and November 1998 the national economy 'lived without formal supervision of the Fund'. Martone distinguishes between the 'disastrous failure' of the Collor government to deal with inflation and the role that failure played in the laying the basis of the Real Plan. For Martone, the failure of anti-inflation policies between 1986 and 1992 was essentially political — and so internal —

in nature, but it was the lack of external funding that drove the net transfer of funds abroad and so closed down the last possibility of policy freedom. After the accumulated impact of the Mexican, Asian and Russian crises, the key moment comes with the floating of the Real in January 1999. It is not at all clear that investor confidence was thereby restored, but it is evident that fiscal adjustments have hitherto been insufficient to generate significant savings at home. Brazil, in this regard, is entirely of a piece with the rest of Latin America.

The third and final section of the book reviews the democratic experience from various social perspectives and experiences. Here, naturally, an element of selectivity has been required. We have opted not to include in the present collection studies of gender, the landless and environmental questions because — vital though they indisputably are — these are themes that have already attracted a broad and generally buoyant literature. Neither have we addressed here issues concerned with regional integration and culture because those are topics of other ILAS conferences, which have either been published or are under preparation.[8]

Brasílio Sallum's survey of state-society relations builds from an explicit concern to match in theoretical terms the challenge of changed practical circumstances. Thus, in a strikingly suggestive passage, he depicts the Real Plan as a 'Machiavellian Moment' in which, from a profusion of different experiences, the 'universality principle' came into effect, at least for a while. Sallum's perspective does not exclude institutions but is more concerned with the wider matrix of ideas and expectations within which those institutions take hold and acquire a 'natural' part of the collective landscape. Neither, does he overlook the inevitable consequences of an overvalued Real, the Russian moratorium of August 1998, or the inheritance of indexation, which are all discussed elsewhere in the book. To these now familiar features, though, he adds the additional interpretative elements of Collor as a Caesar-figure, and the entire process of his impeachment as a framework for relegitimating the 'New Republic' — a term that still stands rather unsteadily alongside that of the *Estado Novo*, which Sallum himself includes within the 'Vargas State' that effectively lasted from 1930 to 1985.

Carlos Antonio Costa Ribeiro and Celi Scalon are explicitly and purposefully less concerned with the nature of governmental composition and ideas in their clear-sighted analysis of social mobility. Departing from the interpretative scheme devised by Erickson, Goldthorpe and Portocarrero, they pose four questions: how did Brazilian class structure

---

8   See Bulmer-Thomas (ed.) (2001). David Treece and Nancy Naro are currently preparing a volume based upon two conferences: 'Fashioning Brazil: Behind Visitor's Eyes in the Nineteenth and Twentieth Centuries', and 'Brazil — Representing the Nation: Alternative Voices and Identities in the Year 2000'.

evolve over the different phases of growth and crisis during the last half of the twentieth century? What was the impact of rapid industrialisation on patterns of social mobility? Did class structure become more open or closed, or did it simply retain existing elements of rigidity? And how similar was the Brazilian experience to that of other countries?

In this latter case the authors find that, indeed, absolute mobility rates approximate to those registered by recently industrialised states such as Ireland, Hungary and Poland. However, in relative terms Brazil continues to manifest very great inequality of opportunity. Taking data from 1973, 1988 and 1996, Ribeiro and Scalon show that for the first 15 years there was a marked diminution in the profile of the rural upper class, that between 1988 and 1996 the national class structure remained practically unchanged, and that the presence of unskilled male manual workers remains high in both urban and rural spheres. Yet, they find great disparity between class origin and destination in all three sample years, and, perhaps most importantly, 'the total mobility index in Brazil is not very different from that in other countries. This obviously contradicts previous studies on social mobility in Brazil, which, through less accurate comparisons, tended to claim that the Brazilian rate was one of the highest in the world.' This, of course, is not to deny the 'incidence of exceptional inequality of wealth and income'. Rather, it is to place that condition in a much more dynamic social and economic experience than many are prepared to recognise.

There is much in the essay by Leandro Piquet Carneiro on civil rights that chimes with Macaulay's piece. Again, institutional design stands to the fore, and close attention is paid to the precise and practical determinants that lie behind the headlines. We are taken carefully through the efforts to deal with the individual and collective causes and consequences of the fact that the Rio police are responsible in one year for as many deaths as are the entire police forces of the USA. Together, the police of Rio and São Paulo, which form the empirical case studies at the heart of this chapter, account for up to ten per cent of the homicides in their cities. At the same time, though, what appear to be the 'common sense' origins and effects of official lawlessness are here coolly refracted through a conceptual requestioning that retrieves the contribution of Robert Dahl on the need to synchronise levels of participation with rules of competition. Piquet Carneiro also considers the problematic interface of political rights and civil liberties in the light of Guillermo O'Donnell's concerns for a 'second transition'. This is a socio-political space in which low political legitimacy prevails in combination with acute socio-economic differentiation, threatening not such an old-style military coup, but rather a distended erosion of the roots of consensus, leading to an arguably more dangerous political regression. As in Sallum's chapter, we encounter what some trained in the Anglo-Saxon academic firmament might find a disconcerting conjunction of political theory and quotidian considerations of 'improving police action', but, of course, neither realm can enjoy prolonged and healthy existence without the other.

Antonio Sergio Guimaraes' reconsideration of the 'race question' confronts the core received beliefs and easy assumptions associated with the politics of ethnicity in Brazil. Building on — but also questioning and refining — the work of Bolivar Lamounier and Amaury de Souza from the early years of the dictatorship, Guimaraes seeks answers to three questions: do black and white Brazilians display different political behaviour? Do all Brazilians display racial solidarity in their collective behaviour? And how has the political system acted to reduce the impact of any collective political behaviour? He treats the conventional notion of Brazil as a 'racial democracy' as not only problematic but also an active ideology of control. Moving eloquently and decisively beyond Freyre, Guimaraes picks up on Lamounier's perceived paradox between high racial inequality and low levels of protest, and reviews de Souza's explanation of this in the state's success in generating symbols of black integration, anticipating sources of racial tension, and coopting black leadership challenges. This, though, has not been a static scenario, and from the 1980s, Guimaraes argues, the black movement has expanded the range of its demands and deepened its radicalism, drawing opportunity from the international context and energy from the crises within the national arena. The ideological commitment at the heart of official propagation of 'racial democracy' has been effectively dismantled by force of circumstances, and the 1988 constitution raises the question whether, by contrast, the prospect is now one of a 'racialisation of politics'. This is not likely to take the form of a simple inversion of the Freyre-style 'melting pot', but it is still hard to see how any 'universal principle' of citizenship can be practically applied beyond ethnically-determined parameters.

Anthony Hall depicts a 'mixed but bleak' performance in the attempted reform of the educational system under democratic administration. This, he shows, is the case, even if we limit ourselves to the pattern of enrolment and completion from primary to tertiary sectors under the New Republic. The bleakness is disturbingly conveyed by the fact that, in 1997, 54 per cent of Brazil's primary teachers had themselves no qualifications beyond secondary level. On the other hand, reform of the entire educational apparatus of such a vast country poses an exceptional challenge and cannot sensibly be expected to yield radical and emphatic results overnight. Such evidence of change that is available cannot be dismissed as irrelevant: primary enrolments up from 91 to 95 per cent between 1996 and 1999; functional illiteracy down from 37 to 29 per cent over the same period; and average years of schooling up, from 4.9 to 5.9 years (with girls averaging a year more than boys).

Of course, in absolute terms these statistics reveal a dreadful failure to improve the human condition in Brazil as well as a depressing inability to harness its huge potential. In this respect Hall soberly comments that there is 'no evidence to support the view that wider access to schooling has reduced income disparities', and he likewise raises an unpopular issue in noting that Brazil's state universities are funded at twice the rate of those in the UK, France and Spain whereas far less is spent on the primary sector than in those states.

As with the judiciary, increased educational autonomy has not led to unalloyed efficiency, and it is has often involved further dispersion of traditional clientelistic practices. But Hall resists any precipitate judgement on the process of reform set in place in 1996 by Cardoso and Darcy Ribeiro. If it is easier to claim than it is to show that educational enhancement begets economic improvement, so is it misconceived to counterpose general economic improvement to continued policy innovation and institutional change. Both are plainly required, and some enclaves of middle-class privilege are unlikely to escape further scrutiny and reform, even in a better economic context than that which prevailed at the time of the 2002 victory for Lula and the PT.

The changes identified by Guimaraes in the realm of ethnicity constitute a submerged but perceptible influence in the response of the mass media to the new democratic framework that is surveyed in the final chapter by Mauro Porto. Here, of course, there exists a sharply truncated predemocratic legacy, but one should certainly not dismiss the fact that the dictatorship of 1964–85 was born and subsisted comfortably within the age of television and radio. Porto rightly insists that too little attention has been paid by the scholarly literature to the role of electronic communication technologies in political transition, whether in Brazil or elsewhere. His methodological hypothesis here is that, 'the more the process of democratisation advances in society, the more important become the approaches that go beyond instrumental views of the media'. In this light he considers the mass media not only as instruments but also as creators of culture, autonomous organisations, and dependent upon as well as mirrors of their audiences. The overlaps, tensions and outright contradictions implicit in such a perspective properly reflect the multiple refractions we find in practice — from Rubens Ricúpero's unwitting *lapsus linguae* on air about the *realpolitik* in promoting the Real Plan to the 'real life' appearances on *O Rei do Gado* of Darcy Ribeiro, Eduardo Suplicy and Benedita da Silva. If TV Globo did patently favour Cardoso in the 1994 election through simple scheduling and editing manipulation, the *telenovelas* of the selfsame company practically undermined much of the editorial thrust of its news programmes with respect both to Collor's presidency and the campaigns of the MST. Plainly, the era of 'electronic *coronelismo*' is not entirely finished — the pattern of ownership alone strongly suggests a more than vestigial presence — but this can no longer practised in any simple, uncontested fashion. Equally, the investigative skills built up by the press over the better part of two decades saturated in scandal have established a formidable instrument in favour of an authentic second transition. Insofar as the mass media help to 'shrink the world', so they encourage the application of civil and even familial ethical values upon those who hitherto had reposed with disdain — almost as if from another world — upon their state-sanctioned privileges and perquisites. Much here remains intangible, but it could yet prove to the sphere in which the consolidation of democracy is most decisively transformed into a democratic culture.

The editors thank all the authors for their work and diligent trans-Atlantic collaboration centred on the conference held by ILAS at the University of London's Senate House in February 2001. We are most grateful to the Hewlett Foundation and the British Council for support which made that event possible. Particular thanks go to Leslie Bethell, Edmund Amann and Anthony Hall, who generously provided material to a less than friendly schedule but with great goodwill towards a project that, by its very nature, cannot be risk-free. Victor Bulmer-Thomas, Edmund Amann, Joe Foweraker, Anthony Hall, Laurence Whitehead and Carlos Pereira acted as incisive and constructive commentators at the conference and study group that followed it. We are also much indebted to the labours of our colleagues Olga Jiménez, Tony Bell, Melanie Jones and John Maher, all of whom improved a collective effort with individual flair.

PART I
DEMOCRACY AND
POLITICAL INSTITUTIONS

CHAPTER 1

Politics in Brazil: From Elections without Democracy to Democracy without Citizenship*

Leslie Bethell

When in the late 1980s Francis Fukuyama first began to formulate his ideas on the late twentieth-century triumph of liberal democracy worldwide — 'the universalisation of Western liberal democracy as the final form of human government' — which he presented, first in a series of lectures at the University of Chicago, and then in an article published in *The National Interest*, China, the Soviet Union and much of Eastern and Central Europe were still under Communist rule. Equally, in the Western Hemisphere, besides the notoriously complex case of Mexico, Brazil — the fifth largest country in the world, with the fifth largest population (160 million) — was a not insignificant exception to Fukuyamian triumphalism. The painfully slow process of political liberalisation, then finally democratisation at the end of two decades of military dictatorship — part of Samuel Huntington's 'third wave' of global democratisation, which had started in southern Europe in the 1970s and spread to Latin America in the 1980s — was still by no means complete. And the Brazilian economy remained one of the most closed and state-regulated — with one of the largest public sectors — in the capitalist world.

By the time Fukuyama published his book *The End of History and the Last Man* in 1992, however, not only had momentous events taken place in Moscow and Berlin but, following the presidential elections of November-December 1989, Brazil could unquestionably be counted a fully-fledged democracy, with regular free, fair and competitive elections for both the executive and legislative branches of government, based on the principle of one person, one vote, for the first time in its history as an independent state. Brazil had become in fact, after India and the United States, the third largest democracy in the world. It was also in the late 1980s and more particularly the early 1990s that Brazil took the first steps towards the liberalisation and de-regulation of its economy — and the privatisation of its state industries and public utilities.

*   This is a revised version of an essay 'Politics in Brazil: From Elections without Democracy to Democracy without Citizenship' that first appeared in a special issue of *Daedalus*, Journal of the American Academy of Arts and Sciences, *Brazil. Burden of the Past, Promise of the Future* (Spring 2000), pp. 1-27, and in Leslie Bethell (ed.), *Brasil. Fardo do passado, promessa do futuro. Dez ensaios sobre política e sociedade brasileira* (Rio de Janeiro: Editora Record/Civilização Brasileira, 2002), pp. 9–43.

Brazil's new democracy, though like all democracies flawed, has so far survived, despite fears at the time that it might not and little in the past to justify much optimism that it would. More than this, it has been, as political scientists would say, consolidated. Whether more than a decade of democracy and neo-liberal economic reform has made Brazil significantly more prosperous and less socially unequal and divided, and what the implications are for the future of democracy in Brazil if it has not, are questions I will briefly address at the end of this chapter.

I

Elections in the Nineteenth and Twentieth Centuries

In contrast to the 13 Colonies in British North America, but like colonial Spanish America, Brazil served no significant apprenticeship in representative self-government under Portuguese colonial rule. For three centuries Brazil was governed by Crown-appointed governors-general (or viceroys), captains-general (or governors), high court judges, magistrates and other lesser bureaucrats.[1]

The first elections held in Brazil — the election of delegates to the *cortes* summoned to meet in Lisbon in the aftermath of the Portuguese Revolution of 1820 — did not take place until May–September 1821. By that time, as a consequence of the transfer of the Portuguese court from Lisbon to Rio de Janeiro in 1807–08 during the Napoleonic Wars, Brazil was already no longer strictly speaking a Portuguese colony but an equal partner in a dual monarchy. A year later, in June 1822, there followed elections — indirect elections on a strictly limited suffrage after the extreme liberals or radicals of the period (many of them republicans) failed to secure direct popular elections — to a Constituent Assembly in Rio de Janeiro as Brazil finally moved towards full separation from Portugal.

The Independence of Brazil in 1822 can be regarded as part of the so-called 'democratic revolution' of the Atlantic world in the late eighteenth and early nineteenth centuries in the sense that liberal democratic ideas were widely proclaimed in the struggle against Portuguese colonialism and absolutism. There was, however, never any intention of establishing in Brazil anything that, even at the time, looked remotely like liberal repre-

---

1   On colonial government, see Leslie Bethell (ed.), *Colonial Brazil* (Cambridge, 1987: chapters from *Cambridge History of Latin America*, vols. I and II), pp. 46, 129–35, 142, 257. It has been argued that the municipal *senados da camara*, like the *cabildos* in late colonial Spanish America, were rather more than simply self-perpetuating oligarchies: councilmen (*vereadores*) and some local judges were chosen or indirectly 'elected' by *homens bons*, men of wealth and good standing. However, the number of 'voters' was always small and the powers of the *camaras* severely restricted.

sentative democracy based, however theoretically, on the sovereignty of the people. (Brazil's population at the time, in a territory of three million square miles, was between four and five million, less than a third white, more than a third slave.) Unlike the newly independent Spanish American states, Brazil did not even become a republic. Uniquely, Brazil proclaimed itself an Empire, with Dom Pedro I, the son of King Joao VI of Portugal and heir to the Portuguese throne, becoming the independent country's first emperor (succeeded on his abdication in 1831 by his five-year-old son who eventually became Dom Pedro II).[2]

Brazil has had a long history of elections that compares favourably with most countries in the world. Under the Empire (1822–89), under the First Republic (1889–1930), in the aftermath of the Revolution of 1930, in the post war period (1945–64), even under the military dictatorship (1964–85), elections were regularly held in Brazil. There has in fact been only one period of more than a few years in the entire modern history of Brazil without elections: the Estado Novo (1937–45). Until ten years ago, however, Brazilian elections were not always for positions of political power, executive or legislative; they were rarely honest and usually not freely contested; and the level of participation always fell some way short of universal suffrage. Historically, elections in Brazil had more to do with public demonstrations of personal loyalties, the offer and acceptance of patronage, the reduction of social (and regional) tensions and conflict and, above all, control of a patrimonial state and the use of public power for private interests without resource to violence than it did with the exercise of power by the people in choosing and bringing to account those who govern them. Before 1989 Brazil was a case study in elections without democracy.

Under the political system of the Empire Brazil had an elected Chamber of Deputies. But governments were only to a limited extent responsible to it. Power was concentrated in the hands of the hereditary emperor himself, his chosen ministers, the counsellors of state he appointed (for life), the provincial presidents he also appointed, and a Senate (with senators appointed, also for life, by the emperor, though from lists of three submitted by each province). It was only when Brazil finally became a republic in 1889 that the executive (president, state governor, municipal *prefeito*) as well both houses of the legislature (the Senate and Chamber of Deputies), state assemblies and municipal councils were all elected. Presidential, congressional, state and municipal elections were a feature of both the First Republic and the period after the Second World War. During the military dictatorship presidents were 'elected' for a fixed term, which is unusual in military regimes, but they were indirectly elected by an Electoral

---

2   On Brazilian Independence, see Bethell (1985, reprinted in *Brazil: Empire and Republic, 1822–1930* (1989). See also two essays by Costa (1975 and 1985).

College in which (until 1984 at least) the regime could count on a majority. In practice all five military presidents were imposed by the military high command. State governors (until 1982) and mayors of state capitals and other cities of importance to 'national security' were appointed by the military. Congress and state legislatures, which continued to function under the military regime (apart from one or two brief closures), though with their powers much reduced, alone continued to be directly elected — on schedule every four years.

During the Empire voting in elections was open (and oral). Fraud, intimidation, violence and the exercise of patronage by local landowners and others and by agents of the Crown were widespread. Elections under the First Republic — a highly decentralised federal republic — were not much less dishonest, possibly more so, controlled as they were for the most part by state governments and *coroneis* (local political bosses) representing powerful landed oligarchies, especially in the more backward states of the north-east and north. Not until 1932 was the ballot made secret and a system of electoral supervision (*justiça eleitoral*) introduced. In practice, however, the new electoral legislation was not fully implemented until after the Second World War — and then for less than 20 years. Under the military dictatorship, electoral rules were frequently manipulated in the most arbitrary and blatant way to guarantee majorities for the pro-military ruling party.

There has always been some measure of contestation between different parties, programmes and candidates in Brazilian elections. In the parliamentary elections of the Empire the choice was between Liberals, Conservatives and, finally, Republicans. During the First Republic elections were contested by state parties only and in each state the Republican Party was dominant. The outcome of elections for president of the republic was pre-determined by agreements between state governors (*a política dos governadores*). No 'official' candidate backed by the governors and republican political machines of at least one (and it was usually both) of the two states with the largest electorates — São Paulo and Minas Gerais — and two or three of the largest second rank states (Rio Grande do Sul, Rio de Janeiro, Bahia, Pernambuco) ever lost, and no 'opposition' candidate ever won, a presidential election.

Apart from the Brazilian Communist Party (PCB), founded in 1922 and immediately declared illegal, and the fascist Ação Integralista Brasileira (AIB), founded in 1932 and declared illegal along with all other political parties during the Estado Novo there were no national political parties or political movements until 1945. In the post-war period more than a dozen parties for the first time competed for office. But in May 1947, at the beginning of the Cold War, the PCB, the only significant party of the Left, was once again declared illegal by Congress after 18 months of *de facto* legality. The PCB, which was not for its part fully committed to legal strategies and the electoral road to power, was effectively excluded from democratic politics — and remained so for the next 40 years. For most of the period of military rule — between the party 'reforms' of 1966 and 1979 — only two parties, the pro-government ARENA (later PDS) and the opposition Movimento Democratico Brasileiro (MDB, later PMDB) were permitted to contest elections.

In the middle decades of the nineteenth century, the golden age of the Empire, the level of political participation was surprisingly high: men (not women, of course) who were 25 years old (21 if married), Catholic, born free and with a quite low annual income from property, trade or employment had the right to vote in elections for the Chamber of Deputies. Richard Graham has calculated that in 1870 one million Brazilians out of a total population of a little under 10 million (i.e. half the free adult male population, including many of quite modest means, illiterate and even black) could vote.[3] (This is a far higher proportion of the population than in England, for example, after the Reform Act of 1832 and even after the Reform Act of 1867.) The elections, however, were indirect. The so-called *votantes* elected *eleitores* (who were required to have a higher annual income), and only *eleitores* — some 20,000 of them in 1870 — had the right to vote for *deputados*. Moreover, the turn out was generally low. This was hardly *democracia coroada*, crowned democracy, as the historian Joao Camillo de Oliveira Torres entitled a book published in 1957 on the political system of the Empire.

Moreover, the level of political participation under the Empire was severely reduced in 1881. During the last quarter of the nineteenth century, as the coffee economy expanded and the shift from slave to free labour finally gathered momentum, making the final abolition of slavery increasingly inevitable, there was a growing fear amongst the dominant political class — shared by many liberal reformers — that ex-slaves ('barbarians') — in the rural areas but more particularly in the rapidly expanding urban areas — would readily acquire the low income sufficient to secure the right to vote. Under the Saraiva Law of 1881 elections for the Chamber of Deputies were made direct; the property/income qualification to vote was removed; non-Catholics, naturalised citizens (though not resident foreign immigrants) and even ex-slaves (freedmen) were eligible to become voters. However, undermining somewhat these apparent liberal/democratic advances, a new requirement for voter registration was introduced for the first time: namely, education as measured by a literacy test — in a country in which 80–85 per cent of the population was illiterate. (In England, John Stuart Mill, the great apostle of liberal democracy, also argued against giving the vote to illiterates, but Mill at least believed in the rapid expansion

---

3   Graham (1990), p. 109, Table 2, and p. 332, note 41. On the political system of the Empire, see also Carvalho (1980, 1988).

of public education to reduce the level of illiteracy, not something advocated by many people in Brazil in the late nineteenth century.)

Thus, after 1881, while the number of *eleitores* increased (initially to around 150,000), the vast majority of Brazilians, even most free males, who had previously had the right to vote, albeit only as *votantes* in indirect elections, were consciously and deliberately excluded from political participation.[4] Liberalism may have been the dominant ideology in nineteenth century Brazil but, as in Spanish America, it was liberalism of a predominantly and increasingly conservative variety as it was forced to adjust to the realities of an authoritarian political culture, economic underdevelopment and, most of all, a society deeply stratified (and along racial lines).

The republican Constitution of 1891 reduced the minimum voting age from 25 to 21 but, like the Constitution of 1824, excluded from politics the great mass of adult Brazilians by continuing to deny the vote to women and illiterates. In the Constituent Assembly a greater effort was made to extend the suffrage to women than to illiterates. Not surprisingly it failed. And such was the neglect of public education during the First Republic that over 75 per cent of the population remained illiterate as late as 1920. Nevertheless, the presidential and congressional elections of the early republic did represent a substantial advance in direct popular political participation compared with the late Empire: in 1898, for example, almost half a million Brazilians voted, including sections of the emerging urban middle class and even some urban workers in Rio de Janeiro, São Paulo, Porto Alegre and elsewhere.[5] However, even in the city of Rio de Janeiro, the capital of the republic, with a population of half a million in the early part of this century, José Murilo de Carvalho has calculated that only about 100,000 people had the right to vote, that only 25 to 35 per cent of these ever registered to vote in national elections between 1890 and 1910, and that only between seven and 13 per cent (five to ten per cent of the adult population) actually voted.[6] In the country as a whole, in even the most competitive presidential elections with the greatest degree of political mobilisation — for example, the elections of 1910 and 1919 in which Rui Barbosa, the great liberal jurist, stood as a *civilista* opposition candidate (and lost) — less than five per cent of the adult population voted.[7] It was not until 1930 that more than ten per cent of the adult population voted in presidential elections. What has been called oligarchical democracy

---

4   Graham (1990), pp. 185–6, 200, 202.
5   Lamounier and Muszynski (1993), pp. 93–134, especially Table 2.1 'Evolucion del electorado 1933–1990 [in fact 1894–1990]' (p. 99) and Table 2.9 'Elecciones presidenciales 1894–1989' (pp. 125–30), contains valuable statistical information on all elections in Brazil down to 1990. For elections after 1982, Nicolau (ed.) (1998a) is indispensable.
6   de Carvalho (1987), chap. 3 'Cidadaos inativos: a abstenção eleitoral'.
7   Lamounier and Muszinski (1993), pp. 99 and 128.

(surely an oxymoron) is, as a description of the political system of the Old Republic, as hard to swallow as is crowned democracy for the Empire.

From the 1930s, wider sections of the Brazilian population were gradually incorporated into the political process. The 1932 electoral law lowered the voting age to 18 and, more importantly, for the first time gave women the vote (always provided they were literate).[8] Brazil was second to Ecuador in Latin America in extending the suffrage to women — ahead of, for example, France. Women were slow to register, however; only 15 per cent of those eligible to vote in the elections for a Constituent Assembly in May 1933 did so, and only one woman, Carlota Pereira de Queiróz from São Paulo, was elected.

As part of 'democratisation' in 1945 a new electoral law included automatic voter registration for employees, male and female, in public and private companies (many of whom were in fact illiterate) — a measure designed to extend the vote to wider sections of the urban working class while still excluding the rural population, around 60–70 per cent of the total. The elections of December 1945 were the first reasonably honest, competitive (even the Brazilian Communist party was allowed to take part), relatively popular elections ever held in Brazil. 7.5 million Brazilians registered to vote (more than half in the city of Rio de Janeiro, the Federal District and around a third in the states of São Paulo and Rio de Janeiro, by means of the ex-officio registration through the workplace). This was four or five times the number who had registered to vote only 15 years earlier and a substantial proportion (35 per cent) of the adult population. A little more than six million actually voted.[9] Under the 'democratic' Constitution of 1946, however, more than half the adult population of Brazil remained disenfranchised by its illiteracy. And Congress in 1950 restored individual responsibility for voter registration — on the face of it a liberal measure but in the circumstances of Brazil at the time a blow aimed at the political participation of the urban working class.

Nevertheless, as a result of a dramatic growth in the population (from 40 million in 1940 to 70 million in 1960 and 120 million in 1980), rapid urbanisation (35 per cent of the population was classified as urban in 1940, 45 per cent in 1960, 70 per cent in 1980), and in the 1960s and 1970s for the first time real progress in the direction of universal basic literacy, the electorate grew steadily. It reached 18 million in 1962 and, despite the breakdown of Brazil's post-war limited form of democracy in 1964, it grew to over 60 million in 1982 (which means that the electorate actually increased fourfold during the military dictatorship). However, not until the return to civilian rule in 1985, in one of a series of constitutional amendments passed

8   Hahner (1991), pp. 171–3.
9   Nohlen (1993), pp. 108, 113 and 128.

during the first months of the Sarney administration, were illiterates (still over 30 million of them, comprising between 20 and 25 per cent of the population, a large proportion of them black) finally enfranchised. The Constitution of 1988 then extended the vote to 16 and 17 year olds.

The municipal elections of November 1985 and the elections for Congress and state governor a year later were the first elections in Brazil based on universal suffrage, though few *analfabetos* had time to register to vote in the first and only half registered to vote in the second.[10] Nevertheless, the 1987–90 Congress not only had 26 women members, a small number but more than had been elected in the entire period 1932–86, but also 19 blacks, including the first black *deputada*, Benedita da Silva (Partido dos Trabalhadores — PT — Rio de Janeiro).

Finally, in 1989, the first direct presidential elections for 30 years were the first in the history of the republic based upon universal suffrage. They were held symbolically on the centenary of the Republic (15 November 1989). The electorate now numbered 82 million (in a population of almost 150 million) and, since voting has been mandatory in Brazil since 1945 (under the Constitution of 1988 for those over 18 and under 70 only), the turn out, as always, was extremely high (88 per cent). Candidates of 22 parties from across the political spectrum, far Right to far Left, contested the first round. In the second round Brazilians were offered a straight choice between Right (Fernando Collor de Mello, Partido da Renovação Nacional — PRN) and Left (Luiz Inacio 'Lula' da Silva, PT). By a narrow margin they chose Collor.[11]

Brazil's new democracy showed early signs of fragility and in September–December 1992 Brazilians suffered the trauma of the impeachment (on corruption charges) of their first democratically elected president less than halfway through his term of office. In the end, however, the successful impeachment of Collor can perhaps be seen to have demonstrated more the maturity than the fragility of Brazilian democracy.[12] Twice before the end of the decade Brazilians went to the polls — 78.2 million (82.3 per cent of the electorate) in 1994, 83.3 million (78.5 per cent) in 1998 — in remarkably free, honest and orderly *super-eleições, eleições casadas* (presidential, gubernatorial, Congressional and state assembly elections held on the same day). Both presidential elections were won handsomely by Fernando Henrique Cardoso, a distinguished sociologist with an international reputation and a politician with impeccable democratic credentials and advanced social democratic ideas, though on each occasion, as we

10   For an inteesting analysis of the 'black vote' in the elections of 1985 and 1986, see Berquo and de Alencastro (1992).

11   Nohlen (ed.) (1993), pp. 99 and 130, and Nicolau (ed.) (1998a), pp. 23–6, 29–36.

12   President Fernando Collor de Mello was impeached first in the Chamber of Deputies on 29 September (441 votes to 38) and then, definitively, in the Senate on 29 December 1992 (76 votes to 3), the day after he had in fact resigned.

shall see, the candidate of a Centre-Right coalition. (The defeated candidate in both elections, as in 1989, was Luiz Inacio 'Lula' da Silva.) Cardoso was only the third elected president in 70 years (since 1930) to serve a full term, the first since Juscelino Kubitschek (1956–61), the first elected under universal suffrage — and the first to be re-elected for a second term.

The international environment in the 1990s was uniquely favourable to the survival and consolidation of democracy in Latin America. In particular, the United States made support for democracy a central feature of its policy towards the region, as it had done in the past but this time with rather better results. Furthermore, with the end of the Cold War anti-communism was no longer available as the main justification for the overthrow of democratic (or semi-democratic) governments as it had been in Brazil in 1964 (and even in 1937). Like the Left, the Right — the traditional political class (rural and urban), the more powerful economic interest groups and the military itself — was, it seemed, now committed to peaceful democratic politics, as it had not always been in the past. The political crisis surrounding the impeachment of Collor in 1992 was the first in the history of the republic in which the military — whose privileges and prerogatives, including the right to intervene in the political process, are explicitly recognised in the 1988 Constitution — was not an active participant.

Of course, it could be argued that the 'propertied classes' (including broad sections of the middle class) were no more than fair weather democrats. When the costs of overthrowing democracy and resorting to authoritarianism are high and the costs of tolerating democracy low, democracy is likely to survive. But when their interests are threatened by forces favouring a significant distribution of wealth and power, as they were, or were believed to be, in 1964, there is always a possibility that they will look to the military to overthrow democracy. We shall never know whether Brazil's new democracy would have passed its supreme test — the acceptance of victory by Lula and the PT in the presidential elections of 1989 or 1994. As Adam Przeworski once remarked, only where the Left lost the first elections following a process of democratisation was democracy truly safe. It is a mark of the growing maturity of Brazilian democracy — and also of the PT's shift, whether temporary or permanent, from Left to Centre-Left — that the election of Lula to the presidency at the fourth attempt in October 2002 raised not the slightest doubt that he would be allowed to assume power in January 2003.

II

Democracy in the 1990s

There can be elections without democracy but there cannot be democracy, at least not liberal representative democracy, without elections. At the same time

there is, of course, more to democracy than elections, however honestly conducted and freely contested and whatever the level of popular participation.
The democratic exercise of power *between* elections is also important, and
democratic political systems vary in the degree to which they facilitate it.
Brazil's democratic institutions functioned relatively well in the 1990s. And at
least there remained no 'authoritarian enclaves', parts of the power apparatus
of the former military dictatorship not accountable to democratically elected
civilian governments. The military itself has steadfastly remained out of politics. But Brazilian democracy is not without its flaws.

Some political scientists would go so far as to claim that in Brazil, as in
the rest of Latin America, the presidential system itself is a major obstacle
to the proper functioning of representative democracy. It is an expression
of, and it reinforces, the personalism and authoritarianism deeply rooted in
the country's political culture. Moreover, however poor their performance,
however weak their support in Congress, however low their standing in the
country, presidents can only be removed in advance of the next scheduled
elections by extreme measures: for example, in the case of Brazil, suicide
(Vargas, 1954), resignation (Quadros, 1961), military coup (Goulart, 1964)
or impeachment (Collor, 1992). Brazil had two opportunities to change its
system of government during the process of democratisation: in March
1988, after prolonged debate on the issue, the Constituent Assembly voted
344 to 212 in favour of a presidential rather than a parliamentary system;
and five years later (April 1993), in the plebiscite required under the 1988
Constitution, 55 per cent of the electorate voted for presidentialism, 25
per cent for a parliamentary system of government, with 20 per cent of
the vote spoiled or blank. (In the same plebiscite Brazilians were also
offered the opportunity to restore the monarchy: 12 per cent voted in
favour compared to 66 per cent who supported the republic.)

Brazil's electoral system (elections for the Chamber of Deputies based
on proportional representation, but with large, state-wide electoral districts
and 'open' lists of candidates) and its 'underdeveloped' party system have
come in for a great deal of criticism.[13] Parties do not for the most part
have deep historical roots, nor ideological/programmatic consistency
(even the PT is deeply divided). Moreover, except for the PT and, until
recently, the PFL they are lacking in cohesion and discipline: almost a third
of the deputies elected in 1994 switched parties during the Congress of
1995–98 — some several times! — and those elected in 1998 were no less
volatile. Finally, there are, some would argue, too many parties. 76 put up
candidates in the nine elections between 1982 and 1996, though 39 of
them only once. 30 or so parties are currently registered. 18 had seats in

---

13   On the Brazilian party system, see in particular the work of Scott P. Mainwaring
      (1992, 1993 and 1999).

the 1999–2002 Congress, though it should be emphasised that only eight had more than ten seats in the Chamber of Deputies and at least one seat in the Senate. Nevertheless, the largest party (the PMDB after the 1994 election, the PFL after 1998 and, a major surprise, the PT after 2002) had no more than 20 per cent of the seats in Congress. President Cardoso's party, the PSDB, had only 12 per cent of the seats in the 1995–98 Congress. What has been called 'permanent minority presidentialism' – no popularly elected president since 1950 has in fact had a majority in Congress provided by his own party — leads inevitably to party alliances, coalition government and political bargaining in the endless search for majorities for every piece of legislation. Constitutional reform (and the 1988 Constitution is so detailed and all-embracing that almost any major reform has constitutional implications) requires the support of 60 per cent of the members of both legislative houses on two separate occasions, which is extremely difficult to achieve not least because of the high level of congressional absenteeism in Brasilia. This is all part of the game of democratic politics, no doubt, but it helps to explain why Brazilian presidents in the 1990s increasingly resorted to the (constitutional but undemocratic) use of *medidas provisorias* in order to bypass Congress.

The most undemocratic or, as political scientists would say, demos-constraining feature of Brazilian democracy — and the most difficult to reform — is a federal system which since the beginning of the republic has rewarded the less populated, less developed, more politically traditional and conservative (that is to say, clientalistic and corrupt) states, especially in the north, with extreme over-representation in Congress. The problem here is not simply that, as in the United States, all 27 of Brazil's states regardless of population have an equal number of seats in the Senate (three), but that the Senate in Brazil has wider powers than the US Senate and that representation in the lower house is also not proportional to population or electorate. Despite the enormous disparity in size and population (and wealth) between states in Brazil — much greater than in the United States — there is for the Chamber of Deputies currently a minimum 'floor' (eight seats) and a maximum 'ceiling' (70 seats). Thus, São Paulo with an electorate of over 22 million has 70 seats (only recently raised from 60), the former federal territory of Roraima with an electorate of 120,000 has eight. Brazil's seven smallest states (by population, not size), which together account for only four per cent of Brazil's population elect 25 per cent of the Senate and over ten per cent of the Chamber. The system also favours the parties that are strongest in the more backward states. With only two or three percentage points more of the popular vote nationwide than the PT in 1994 and 1998, the Centre-Right PFL elected three times as many senators and almost twice as many federal deputies.

An even greater cause for concern is the fragility of the rule of law in Brazil after more than a decade of democracy. Although no government in Brazilian history has been more supportive of civil and human rights than that of president Fernando Henrique Cardoso, for a large proportion of the population basic civil liberties remain inadequately protected and guaranteed by the courts, and there are frequent gross violations of human rights, many of them perpetrated by the state military police. Brazil is a democracy of voters, not yet a democracy of citizens.

Brazilian democracy has so far been broadly and deeply legitimated. Public opinion polls throughout the 1990s consistently indicated a widespread lack of trust not just in politicians, political parties and political institutions but in democracy itself. Equally noteworthy are the large numbers of Brazilians who failed to vote in elections, even though the vote is technically mandatory, and those who vote but vote *nulo* (spoiled ballot) or *em branco* (blank ballot) — practices common (and understandable) during a period of military rule but disturbing in a democracy. Abstentions rose from 11.9 per cent in 1989 to 17.7 per cent in 1994 and 21.5 per cent in 1998. In the presidential elections of 1994, 18.8 per cent of those who turned out voted *em branco* and *nulo*, 18.7 per cent in 1998. Thus, in 1998 38.4 million Brazilians either abstained or voted *nulo* or *em branco* — more than those who voted for Fernando Henrique Cardoso. The number voting *em branco* or *nulo* in congressional and gubernatorial elections was around 30 per cent (in some states — for example, Maranhao, Bahia and Pará — as high as 50 per cent), and even higher in State Assembly elections. These figures are extraordinarily high by the standards of any democracy in the world. In the first round of the presidential election of 2002, however, not only did the abstention rate fall to 17.8 per cent but the number of those voting *em branco* and *nulo* fell to 10.4 per cent — in part due to the fact that the vote was for the first time 100 per cent electronic.

Brazilian democracy may be imperfect and 'shallow', but democracy it is nonetheless. There may be no justification for indulging in end-of-history democratic triumphalism as far as Brazil is concerned, but there is at the same time no reason to dismiss, as some still do (especially on the Left), the establishment of democratic institutions, the extension of political rights to all Brazilians and even the slow but steady progress that has been made in the field of civil and human rights as merely constituting 'formal' democracy. Nevertheless, those who argue that Brazilian democracy is not yet 'substantive', that it neglects economic and social 'rights', have a serious point. Brazil is a country with remarkably few of the regional, nationalist, racial, ethnic, linguistic, religious divisions, tensions and conflicts that pose a threat to democracies, old and new, throughout most of the world. In this respect it is uniquely fortunate. But with the ninth or tenth largest economy in the world, Brazil is sixtieth or worse in interna-

tional league tables of human development and is a strong contender for the title of world champion in social inequality. Can democracy be healthy, can it properly function, can it even survive in the long run, when, as in Brazil, a third of the population (some would put it much higher) live in conditions of extreme poverty, ignorance and ill health and are treated at best as second class citizens?

Poverty, inequality, social exclusion (which despite Brazil's claim to be a racial democracy have a clear racial dimension) have their roots in Portuguese colonialism (especially the system of land ownership), in slavery (both colonial and post colonial), in (as some would still argue) post-colonial economic underdevelopment and 'dependency', in mass immigration in the late nineteenth and early twentieth centuries, in rapid urbanisation after 1940 — but also in past failures to address the 'social problem'. Brazil, as Eric Hobsbawm once said, is a monument to social neglect.

There was some reduction of poverty and exclusion (possibly even of inequality) as a consequence of economic growth, upward social mobility and social policy from the 1930s to the 1970s. But the situation worsened with the economic difficulties of the 1980s (the so called 'lost decade' in terms of economic growth) and the (albeit necessary) structural adjustment policies of the early 1990s. And despite the clear benefits to the poor of the anti-inflationary Real Plan, at least in its first years, and the rhetoric, and in some areas policies, of the Cardoso administrations, democratic government is perceived by many as having so far failed to promote a much needed social transformation in Brazil. In this respect it runs the risk of being considered no different from the non-democratic governments of the past.

III

Elites and people

Throughout modern Brazilian history every change of political regime — from the establishment of an independent empire in the early 1820s to the establishment of a modern representative democracy in the late 1980s — has demonstrated the extraordinary capacity of the Brazilian elites to defend the status quo and their own interests by controlling, co-opting and, if necessary, repressing the forces in favour of radical social change or, if you prefer, the extraordinary capacity of the Brazilian people for tolerating poverty, exclusion, inequality and injustice and thus collaborating in their own subordination. Not only has there been no social revolution in Brazilian history comparable, for example, to those of Mexico, Russia or China, there has been remarkably little popular mobilisation of any kind for political and social change. On the rare occasions when popular forces were mobilised and organised to challenge the status quo, especially after

1930, whether through elections or on the streets, the Brazilian elites (always with the military) have been prepared to take the necessary measures to contain them and even to support and maintain long periods of anti-popular, authoritarian government, as in 1937–45 and 1964–85.

Brazilian Independence in 1822 was more the outcome of political and military developments in Europe and their repercussions in the New World than some kind of 'general crisis' — economic, political, ideological — of the old colonial system producing an anti-colonial political movement. As late as 1820 there was no widespread desire in Brazil for total separation from Portugal. The main aim of the leaders and supporters of Brazilian independence in 1821–22 — *fazendeiros* (plantation owners), especially in the province of Rio de Janeiro but to a lesser extent also Bahia and Pernambuco, merchants in the principal cities and some bureaucrats — was to achieve political and economic autonomy without sacrificing the stability so crucial for the maintenance of Brazil's territorial unity and existing socioeconomic structures built, above all, on African slavery. (Brazil's population at the time, in a vast territory of three million square miles, was between four and five million, less than a third white, more than a third slave.) But once decided upon independence was secured quickly and peacefully — without a long and bloody war with the colonial power or civil war (in sharp contrast to events in Spanish America), and without significant social mobilisation or social upheaval. The popular forces were in any case weak — and divided by class, colour and legal status; no significant concessions had to be made to the underprivileged groups in society. The transition from colony to independent empire was characterised by political, economic and social continuity. The existing Portuguese state apparatus never ceased to function. The economy suffered no major dislocation. Above all, as well as the existing pattern of land ownership, the institution of slavery survived — in all regions of the country and, while heavily concentrated in plantation agriculture, in all sections of the economy and society, rural and urban.[14]

No far-reaching land reform was ever effected. But Brazil did eventually abolish slavery — though not until 1888. The greatest threat to slavery in the nineteenth century, however, had come not from opposition within Brazil (which was always weak) but, given Brazil's dependence on massive annual imports of new slaves, from outside in the form of the unrelenting and finally successful pressure from Britain to end the transatlantic slave trade. From the middle of the nineteenth century slavery entered into decline, but there were still over one and a half million slaves in Brazil in 1870 (more than at Independence) and over a million in 1880. The Brazilian abolitionist movement of the 1880s represented the highest

---

14   On the independence of Brazil, see note 2.

control of organised labour, continued restrictions on political participation (no extension of the vote to the illiterate half of the population), and repression of the communist Left (after the PCB had polled half a million votes — ten per cent of the vote — in both the presidential and congressional elections of December 1945 and in the gubernatorial, State Assembly and municipal elections of January 1947). The distribution of seats in Congress under the 'democratic' Constitution of 1946 ensured that the more conservative states of the north and northeast were overwhelmingly over-represented at the expense of the states of the south and southeast, especially São Paulo. Finally, and most important of all, the military retained its independent political power. It remained largely beyond civilian control, and without its support it was impossible for any elected president to remain in power.[19]

Underpinned by the rapid economic growth of the post-war period, this limited form of democracy survived several political crises, notably those surrounding the suicide in August 1954 of Getúlio Vargas (who had been elected to the presidency in the second post-war elections in 1950) under pressure from the military to resign, and the resignation in August 1961 of President Janio Quadros, whose many problems included his relations with the military, after only eight months in office. In the early 1960s, however, with by now a much higher level of popular participation in politics, a number of factors, principally a sharp economic downturn but also including the impact of the Cuban Revolution, combined to radicalise the popular forces in Brazil. Labour and the Left demanded radical social and economic change. The 'Right' (including by now large sections of the urban middle class) was prepared to support (indeed encourage) a military coup if this was the only way of preventing the kind of radical change sought by the Left. Overestimating the strength of the forces for change and underestimating the strength of the existing power structure, civilian and military, and its unity and decisiveness when its interests came under threat, President Joao Goulart (1961–64) attempted to create an opening to the Left. The result was his overthrow by the military on 31 March 1964, bringing to an end Brazil's post-war 'experiment with democracy'. There was little popular resistance.[20]

The process of political liberalisation leading finally to democratisation in the 1970s and 1980s was, like that at the end of the Estado Novo in 1945–46, initiated and controlled from above. It was not primarily a response by the military to opposition MDB/PMDB victories in elections (as in the congressional elections of 1974 or the gubernatorial elections of 1982), nor the unexpectedly strong emergence of civil society in the form of new unionism in 1978–79 and the formation of the Workers' Party (PT) in 1979–82, nor even

19   On the 'democratisation' of Brazil at the end of the Second World War, see Bethell (1992).
20   On the collapse of post-war democracy in 1964, see dos Santos (1986), and Argelina Figueiredo (1993).

the extraordinary mass mobilisation in favour of Diretas Já (immediate direct presidential elections) in 1984 (which after all failed) — although these all played their part. Rather, the regime sought to consolidate and advance its own institutionalisation and reduce the costs of repression. It is not even clear that democracy was ever the intended outcome. Only when it lost control of the presidential succession process, being no longer able to count on a majority in the Electoral College, did the military to throw its weight behind a deal struck between PDS dissidents (who later formed the Partido da Frente Liberal — PFL) and the opposition PMDB under which the 75 year old liberal-conservative opposition politician Tancredo Neves became the 'official' presidential candidate. Tancredo was duly 'elected', but as is well known never took office. He was taken ill on the eve of his inauguration and died a few weeks later. The presidency went to the vice-president-elect José Sarney who was, though a civilian (and therefore the first civilian president of Brazil in more than two decades), the former president of the ruling party under the military regime.

In 1985 a transition from military to civilian rule (but not yet to democracy) was peacefully effected. It was a *transição pactuada*, a transition *sem ruptura*. The Nova República, like the limited form of democracy established in 1945–46, was thus compromised by its origins. It was built on the institutional foundations of the authoritarian regime it replaced.[21] Those who were anticipating simply a continuation of military rule by other means were, however, confounded. Sarney, despite some delaying tactics, presided over a genuine transition to democracy, culminating in the presidential elections of 1989 based on universal suffrage.

The 1989 presidential election was not, however, as we have seen, won by the PMDB, the main opposition movement for over 20 years and by far the biggest and broadest party in Brazil, as might have been expected; nor by the PDT, the party of Leonel Brizola, the heir to Getúlio Vargas and João Goulart; nor by the PT, the new grassroots opposition party, whose leader, Lula, reached the second round; but by Fernando Collor de Mello — young, energetic, psychologically unstable and corrupt (as we know now), a hitherto virtually unknown politician from the poor northeast state of Alagoas with no significant party behind him. He proved attractive to the dominant class, which, after the 21-year military dictatorship, had no credible candidate of its own; to the poor who were susceptible to his populist appeal; to some sections of the middle class; and, to their lasting shame, to some intellectuals.[22]

The 1994 election was again won by neither the PMDB, nor the PDT, nor the PT, but by Fernando Henrique Cardoso and the small Centre-

21   On the process of liberalisation/democratisation in the 1970s and 1980s there is a vast literature. See, in particular, Martins (1986), also Stepan (ed.)(1989).

22   In the first round Collor secured 30.5 per cent of the *votos válidos* (i.e. excluding the blank and spoiled ballots), Lula 17.2 per cent and Brizola 16.5 per cent. In the second round Collor had 53 per cent, Lula 47 per cent.

Left/Centre PSDB, which had split from the PMDB in 1988, backed by the parties of the Centre-Right/Right, especially the PFL. In 1994, even more than in 1989, the principal aim of the conservative forces in Brazil, which again, after the Collor debacle, had no candidate of their own, was to defeat Lula, who six months before the election had a considerable lead in the opinion polls and was apparently heading for victory. It was the Real Plan, of course, with its promise of a final end to runaway inflation, that guaranteed victory for Cardoso and in particular secured the support of the poorest sections of Brazilian society.[23] Above all, the 1989 and 1994 (and 1998) elections in Brazil, like most mass democratic presidential elections in the late twentieth century, were won not so much by the candidates and certainly not by their parties, but by serious money, modern campaign organisation and methods and the influence of the media, especially television.

In each of these elections Lula, the defeated candidate, had had to battle against deep-rooted prejudice: the majority of Brazilians (of all classes) found it hard to imagine as president a São Paulo *metalúrgico* from a poor rural northeastern background with only a modest primary education. But the PT also contributed to its own defeat: it was internally divided; many of its policies were unconvincing; its social base in the industrial working class was too narrow; it could never decide whether to bid for the support of the very poor and underprivileged or to look for alliances in the Centre ground (which were in any case probably unavailable).

In the light of Brazil's political history, political culture and political system as described in this chapter (and the defeat of the socialist Left almost everywhere in the world in this period), the growth of the PT in the 1990s was therefore a remarkable story. Lula increased his personal vote from 17 per cent in 1989 (first round) to 27 per cent in 1994 and 32 per cent in 1998. Moreover, in every election — 1990, 1994, 1998 — the PT increased its seats in both the Senate and the Chamber of Deputies, as well as the number of states it controlled (including the Federal District in 1994 and Rio Grande do Sul in 1998). In the municipal elections the PT also won control of major cities like São Paulo (1988 and 2000) and Porto Alegre (1988, 1992, 1996 and 2000). The party's triumph in the elections of 2002 was even more remarkable — and, it has to be said, until the final stages of the campaign, largely unexpected. The PT became overnight the largest party in the Chamber of Deputies (although with only 91 of 513 seats) and the third largest in the Senate. More importantly, Luiz Inacio 'Lula' da Silva finally won the presidency, securing 46.4 per cent of the *votos validos* in the first round (39.4 million votes) and 61.3 per cent in the second round (52.8 million votes). It will be interesting to see when research on the 2002 elec-

---

23   Cardoso won in the first round with 54 per cent of the *votos validos*. In 1998 he won re-election in the first round with 53 per cent.

tions is complete whether, as seems probable, the poorest sections of
Brazilian society for the first time in Brazilian history voted in significant
numbers for the Left, that is to say, for the PT and Lula – and why.

IV

Democracy, Citizenship and Social Justice

Since the three Brazilian administrations democratically elected in 1989, 1994
and 1998 all depended for support in Congress on the parties of the Right,
Centre-Right and Centre which, except in a rhetorical sense, do not put social
issues high on their agendas, since these administrations were in any case constrained in their capacity to focus on the 'social question' by the demands of
macroeconomic stability, especially the need to reduce the fiscal deficit, by
low economic grothw, and by the realities of Brazil's position in the international economy, and since Brazil's social problems are intractable and not susceptible to short-term solutions, it is not surprising that progress in this area
has been slow. However, it does matter that democratic governments are seen
to make a difference. And democracy does offer more possibilities for fundamental social change — and peaceful change — than other political systems. All Brazilians, even the indigent, the poor, the illiterate and semi literate
(tens of millions of them), now have the vote. Despite all the obstacles put
in their way, not least by the unreformed political system itself, they can use
it effectively in their own interests — or not.

Education is perhaps the key. 'We must educate our masters', famously declared Robert Lowe in the House of Commons on the passage of the
Reform Act of 1867. (What he actually said was, 'I believe it will be necessary that you should prevail on our future masters to learn their letters'.)
Almost a century later Anisio Teixeira, one of Brazil's greatest educators,
declared, 'There will only be democracy in Brazil the day the machine
(*maquina*) that prepares people for democracy — the public school — is
assembled in Brazil.' Primary education is an area in which considerable
improvements have been made in recent years, though reform has too
often seemed to have been driven more by the needs of the economy in
the twenty-first century than by the requirements of education in citizenship (building a democracy of citizens, not just voters), and it remains
woefully inadequate.

Organisation is also important. Civil society is now highly mobilised in
Brazil, offering new forms of participation and 'empowerment', but it is perhaps less *politically* combative than in the recent past. Its connections to political parties, even the PT, are relatively weak. And it is still working out how
to make the democratic state 'useable'. The elected Centre/Centre-Right
Brazilian governments of the 1990s could have been more effectively pres-

sured into engaging in more meaningful dialogue with the representatives of civil society and with leaders of opposition political parties and, without resorting to 'populist economics', could have been made more responsive to the economic and social needs of the mass of the population, more willing to give priority to compensatory, redistributive social policies.

If Brazil's still relatively new democracy fails to deliver not only economic benefits to the population as a whole but at least the beginnings of a more equitable distribution of wealth and power, it will always be fragile and will always struggle to command popular support. And there are dangers to democracy — not so much from social revolution (there is nothing in Brazilian history or political culture to suggest this as a real possibility, as we have seen, and any resort to more violent ways of demanding economic and social change outside democratic institutions would, as always, meet powerful resistance), or from military coup as from self-destruction. Like electorates in many other Latin American countries, the Brazilian electorate — overwhelmingly young (almost 50 per cent under 35), poorly educated (70 per cent with no more than seven years in primary school) and extremely poor (60 per cent of the economically active living on less than two minimum wages, not much more than US$100 per month) — could in certain circumstances be persuaded to support populist, authoritarian solutions to their problems. Besides maintaining hard-won economic stability and restoring healthier levels of economic growth (in a most difficult economic climate, both domestic and international), the principal challenge (and opportunity) for the Lula administration which came to power in January 2003 is to demonstrate that Brazil can successfully combine 'formal' liberal representative democracy with a significant extension of citizens' rights and a much greater measure of social justice.

CHAPTER 2

Parties and Elections:
Brazil's Democratic Experience since 1985

Maria D'Alva G. Kinzo

Introduction

It is a widespread assumption that political parties and elections are necessary components of a democratic regime. Free and fair elections in which the parties compete for public positions are a crucial criterion in identifying whether a political system is a democracy. Nevertheless, while the effective presence of parties and elections indicates the existence of a democratic regime, it is the continuous existence of a democratic situation that makes possible the consolidation of institutions such as parties and elections. Though obvious, this observation is relevant when considering the Brazilian political experience, as the military-authoritarian regime — which lasted from 1964 to 1985 — did not abolish either parties or elections. That is, even with the interruption in 1964 of the democratic experience initiated in 1945, election and party activities were not interrupted. Obviously, the existence of parties and elections under a regime that imposes strict limits on public contestation is not an indication of the effective functioning of these mechanisms of representation, just as their presence in a post-authoritarian regime does not in itself guarantee the democratic nature of this regime.

The concern of this chapter is, therefore, to reflect on the relationship between parties, elections and democracy in the present Brazilian context. Thus, the main aspect to be discussed is the extent that the democratic setting in place since 1985 has contributed, in a significant way, to the consolidation of the parties and the party system and, consequently, to the consolidation of democracy in Brazil. To deal with this subject fully would require a discussion of several issues — such as the degree to which Brazil's democracy has participatory traits, and even the extent to which the party system, as a typical institution of representative democracy, is central to the Brazilian polity — which go beyond the scope of this analysis. Thus, in order to set the parameters of this work, it is important to start by making clear the meaning of the terms — parties, elections and democracy — as they will be used here. This will be dealt with in the first section. The second will focus on the election and its role to secure minimal conditions of a democratic polity. In the third section the analysis will concentrate on party experience,

its main features and problems. Finally, I will comment on the prospects for consolidation of Brazil's Democratic Party politics.

Democracy, Elections and Political Parties: A Conceptual Note

Democracy, as so often with themes analysed in the social sciences, is a very complex term. Volumes have been produced debating its various meanings and their theoretical and empirical implications. It is not my intention to go through the complexity of this debate, which would involve giving an overview of a vast literature. It is necessary, nonetheless, to clarify the definition employed in this chapter. The meaning of democracy used here is limited to its procedural mode, derived from Schumpeter's conceptualisation.[1] This prioritises the concept's analytical and empirical capacity to identify, in the political system, a distinct method of organisation based on rules and procedures that guarantee the selection of leaders through political competition and free participation of the people. In other words, it refers to Dahl's two dimensions of a polyarchy — public contestation and participation — the operation of which depends on free conditions for expression and organisation.[2] To stress the political dimensions of democracy does not imply ignoring the social aspect that is part of a democratic setting. In other words, it does not deny that high levels of social inequalities are a serious obstacle to the realisation of democracy.[3] As Dahl properly observes, inequalities in a society affect the chances of effective public contestation, not only because of the imbalances in the distribution of political resources and skills, but also because of the emergence of resentments and frustrations that erode the population's allegiance to democracy.[4]

---

1   In Schumpeter's words, 'the democratic method is that institutional arrangement for arriving at political decisions in which individuals acquire the power to decide by means of a competitive struggle for the people's vote' (Schumpeter, 1976).

2   Dahl (1971).

3   The controversy between political democracy and social democracy is well known. It was largely debated during the first years of redemocratisation in Brazil (see especially the work edited by Reis and O'Donnell (eds.)1988). Yet, it often emerges whenever the current experience of the so-called emerging democracies is assessed. Without entering into the arguments and implications of this controversy, it is worth making a simple observation: it is true that the narrow concept of democracy based on procedural rules leaves aside the issue of social inequality and the consequent unequal access to the so-called political market. But it is also true that to conceive democracy in comprehensive terms as that invoked by the advocates of social democracy deprives the concept of its property of distinguishing a democratic from an authoritarian or totalitarian regime. It is for this characteristic that Sartori formulates his definition of democracy as, first of all, 'a system in which no one can choose himself, no one can invest himself with the power to rule and, therefore, no one can arrogate to himself unconditional and unlimited power' (Sartori, 1987, p. 206).

4   Dahl (1971).

To take as parameters the minimal definition of democracy allows us readily to differentiate between a democratic and a non-democratic regime; it also allows us to recognise as important, in countries such as Brazil, what has been achieved since redemocratisation, even if it is limited to the political realm. And it is within the scope of this meaning of democracy that elections and political parties are fundamental elements in a democratic polity.

The role of elections in the political system is here considered (1) a crucial element in the representative government provided that participation or, in Dahl's terminology, political inclusion, is assured to the members of the polity; and (2) as a means through which the correlation of forces of the different groups have expression, to the extent that competition between those groups organised in political parties is secured (Dahl's dimension of peaceful contestation).[5] Elections make possible not only the replacement of one majority by another majority, but also the realisation of two requirements of a representative government. First, representativity, that is, that Parliament reflects the diversity of the polity; and second, responsiveness, which involves as much the notion of a government acting in response to the people as the notion of a government acting in an efficient and competent way on the basis of which it is accounted to the people.[6] Though representativeness may be secured by establishing an electoral system that enables the electorate's social, and political, diversity to be expressed in a collective representative arena, responsiveness is much more complex. Its effectiveness depends largely on the conditions for participation as well as on the intelligibility of the electoral competition. This will be discussed later in the chapter.

As regards the concept of political parties, in spite of several meanings, we could agree on several of their characteristic features. These are related, first, to the context in which political parties operate and, second, to the activities they perform in this context.[7] Political parties have a distinct place in two arenas of the political system: the electoral and the decision-making. In the latter, its activity is associated with the formulation, planning and implementation of public policies, participating as legitimate actors in the power game and in the process of political negotiation. Parties present themselves as legitimate actors and fundamental agents in the representative democratic process because they have the support of the popular vote. Indeed, it is only based on this criterion — electoral support — that it is possible, in the context of mass democracies, to talk about parties as channels of expression and representation of interests, as

5   Ibid.
6   Sartori (1987).
7   I am following here the structural definition of parties, such as that found in Panebianco's work. (See Panebianco, 1988).

a linkage, even though weak, between society and the state. In the electoral arena, their specific role is to compete for the voters' support in order to gain positions of power. It is through this mechanism that the chain of political representation is formed in representative democracies, a chain which connects the citizens to the arenas of public decision-making. Thus, if on the one hand the gaining of legitimate power in the context of mass politics became feasible through the organisation of political parties, on the other, the system of democratic representation became viable because modern parties, by establishing themselves, assumed the tasks of (1) structuring electoral competition, that is, defining and differentiating the options to be offered to the voter, thus making the act of voting easier while enabling the formation of political identities; and (2) mobilising the electorate, that is, by looking for popular support, encouraging voters both to participate and to choose one of the options offered, options which consist of aggregation of preferences, that is, interests to be represented. To the extent that parties are critical to the question of democracy, electoral activity is their most important activity. Therefore my examination of the performance of party politics in Brazil's democracy will focus particularly on the electoral arena.

Elections in a Democratic Setting

A rapid glance at the Brazilian political picture would allow one to affirm that the current regime has gained clear features of a political democracy. If Dahl's two dimensions of polyarchy are taken as a reference point, Brazil has certainly improved its conditions for participation and public contestation.

Figure 2.1: The Brazilian Electorate 1960–2002

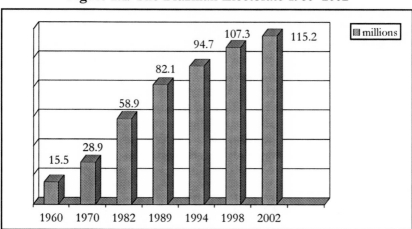

As regards the first dimension — inclusiveness — political participation has improved significantly. First, there has been a remarkable increase in the number of potential voters as a result of universal franchise established in 1985, when illiterates acquired the right to vote. Franchise was expanded further in 1988 when the age limit for voting was reduced to 16. As shown in Figure 2.1, Brazil's electorate jumped from 15.5 million in 1960 to 94.7 million in 1994, reaching over 115 million in 2002.

Second, political uncertainty has become a clear feature of the political system due not only to the size of the electorate — whose large numbers make it less controllable — but also to significant improvement in the conditions for freedom of voting. For this reason, the effective role played by the Electoral Court, an institution that has guaranteed that electoral fraud is kept under control, was very important. It is worth noting that since the municipal elections held in 2000, electronic polling machines have been used in 100 per cent of voting stations. In those elections 345,000 electronic polling machines were used to register the vote. This means a considerable reduction in the possibility of electoral fraud.

Electoral uncertainty is also ensured by the fact that elections have taken place in a predominantly urban society, where political weight is given to a mass electorate living in large cities. Just to give an idea of the significance of this change: in the 1960s at least 55 per cent of the population lived in the countryside while in the 1990s more than 80 per cent of the population were living in urban areas. It is true that the majority of the Brazilian electorate has very low levels of schooling, but they no longer live in rural villages where voters could be easily manipulated by local bosses and electoral corruption was widespread.

In this respect, it is worth noting some trends that marked Brazil over the last three or four decades.[8] I am referring to the social and economic transformations resulting from economic development. It is true that the economic path taken by the military governments was responsible for serious distortions, which resulted in the aggravation of poverty and social and regional inequalities in Brazil. But that path was also responsible for a rapid process of industrialisation and urbanisation that resulted in the emergence of a mass society with all its complexities. Several consequences followed from this shift. One was the large number of dispossessed people who are not entirely integrated into society,[9] but are part of the electoral arena,[10] having considerable weight in elections (sometimes taking them as a means to protest against all sorts of deprivation). Another

---

8   The following two paragraphs rely on Kinzo (2001).
9   In the sense that their citizenship rights are not fully guaranteed. On the problems of citizenship in Brazil see Carvalho (2001) .
10   It is worth noting that in Brazil voting is compulsory.

was the substantial increase in the numbers of industrial and urban workers who have become the basis for the emergence of social movements and progressive parties. Although they are less prominent than during the first years of democratisation, urban social movements are an important element of the new democratic polity. In fact they have gone through a redefinition of their methods of action in response both to recent changes undergone by the state and to the political opportunities opened by decentralisation and participation at the local level. Referring to the impact on society produced by post-authoritarian decentralisation, Martins suggests that 'the municipalisation of social policies has opened ample space for participation of civil society through state delegation'.[11] In several places, he continues, social movements have made use of the new possibilities of social intervention to expand the capacity of the State's response to social demands.[12]

Also, in the rural areas, there have been important changes over the agriculture sector in the last three decades. There, the amalgamation of rural capitalism with old forms of land property and production characterising that process of transformation certainly had the effect of aggravating the problem of social exclusion; but it also produced the social cement for the intensification of the land reform movement which, led by the strongly organised MST (Movement for the Landless), has become the most important manifestation of social disobedience in Brazil.[13] All these social and political transformations are important indications of the revitalisation of civil society and certainly have an impact on the degree of inclusiveness of the Brazilian democratic polity.

With regard to Dahl's second dimension — public contestation — improvement has also been significant, if the current regime is compared to Brazil's previous experience of democratic rule (1945–64). In that experience, political competition was limited not only by the low level of acceptance of the rules of the game — the most visible signs were the military's several attempts to intervene in politics[14] — but also by the limitations to the opposition's right to compete. It is worth remembering that the Communist Party, which, in the elections of 1945 and 1947 performed

11   Martins (1999).
12   Ibid.
13   In spite of its radical positions and questionable means of action – such as occupations of government offices — the MST mobilisation not only has kept the agrarian reform issue in the government agenda but has also established a different kind of relationship with the State. According to Martins' excellent analysis on the MST and the agrarian reform issue, the innovation in the MST's relationship with the State is the fact that the State is not acting preventively to neutralise social tensions, but as a response to initiatives and pressures coming from society. Martins concludes: '[this is] a politically important change that has inverted the typical process that, here in Brazil, made the State the creator of civil society' (Ibid., p. 121).
14   On this see especially Stepan (1973).

well in the industrial areas of the country, was outlawed in 1947, being banned from party politics until 1985.[15]

In contrast, nowadays, there is much wider acceptance of democratic rules and procedures as well as toleration of opposition. Since the re-establishment of civilian rule in 1985, Brazil was confronted with a succession of serious economic and political problems — such as hyperinflation, economic shocks, high unemployment, corruption scandals of several sorts and, above all, the impeachment of a president — events that could have threatened the new regime's survival. The absence of any attempt to respond to those crises by surpassing the limits of a democratic order is a sign of wider acceptance of democratic rules.

Table 2.1: Number of Mayorships won by the PT, by Region, 1992–2000

	Number of Mayorships		
Regions	1992	1996	2000
North	8	12	18
North-east	8	11	22
Centre-west	3	5	16
South-east	26	48	73
South	9	39	58
Total	54	115	187

Source: Tribunal Superior Eleitoral.

No doubt that there are better conditions for opposition's participation and contestation. This is indicated by the existence of all kinds of political organisations, unions and social movements, irrespective of their ideological orientation or social basis. This is also shown by the place held in the system by the left-wing opposition which has become a real contender in elections and an effective participant of decision making. The most significant example is the emergence of the PT (the Workers' Party) as a real competitor in national as well as regional and local elections. In this respect, Brazil's democratisation was quite an innovation. The reestablishment of competitive party politics brought about the creation of a political organisation with typical features of a mass party and whose collective identity was built through its association with both the salaried workers and the organised sectors of civil society, stressing, therefore, the principle of participatory democracy. In this respect,

15   On this see Skidmore (1967), Chilcote (1982) and Brandão (1997).

the results of the 2000 municipal elections were very significant, as were those of the 2002 national elections. In the former, the PT won the mayorship in six state capitals and in 29 cities with populations of over 200,000. As shown in Table 2.1, it has considerably expanded its presence in the country as a whole: in the north-east, apart from winning in two state capitals, the PT doubled in relation to 1996 the number of municipalities under its control; in the centre west region this tripled from the last election.

More remarkable was the PT's electoral performance in 2002. As shown in tables 2.2 and 2.3, that party not only won the presidential office with the election of Luis Ignacio Lula da Silva (who had contested the presidency in the three previous elections), but also its representation in the legislative houses expanded considerably.

Table 2.2: Results of Presidential Elections 1989–2002 (per cent)

Candidates and Parties	1989 1st R	1989 2nd R	1994	1998	2002 1st R	2002 2nd R
PT (Lula)*	17	47	27	32	46	61
PDT (Brizola)	16	*	3	*	***	*
PPS ***	1	*	*	11	12	*
PSDB **	11	-	54	53	23	39
PMDB	5	-	4	**	**	**
PFL	1	-	**	**	-	-
PPB (Maluf)	9	-	3	**	-	-
PRN (Collor)	31	53	1	-	-	-
Others***	9	-	8	4	18	-

Source: Tribunal Superior Eleitoral.

* In 1994 five parties (PSB-PV-PPS-PCdoB-PSTU) allied with the PT candidate Lula; in 1998 the PDT was also included in this alliance. In 2002 the PT was allied with PcdoB, PMN and expanded its alliance to the right by integrating the Liberal Party (PL).

** In 1989 the PSDB's candidate was Mario Covas and in both 1994 and 1998 this party allied with the PFL and the PTB to elect Fernando H.Cardoso. In 1998 two other parties — the PPB and PMDB — integrated Cardoso's electoral alliance. In 2002 the PSDB candidate, José Serra, was allied only with the PMDB.

*** The PPS is Ciro Gomes' party, through which he contested the 1998 and 2002 elections. In the latter the PDT and PTB integrated the PPS's alliance. In 2002 there was also another candidate — Antony Garotinho (PSB), whose percentage of the vote is included in Others.

Table 2.3: The PT's Representation in the Legislative Houses, 1990–2002

Elected offices (No. and %)	1990	1994	1998	2002
Senate No.	1	5	8	14
%	1.2	6.2	9.9	17.3
Chamber of Deputies No.	35	49	58	91
%	7.0	9.6	11.3	17.7
State Assemblies No.	83	92	91	147
%	7.9	8.8	8.6	13.9

Source: Tribunal Superior Eleitoral.

In sum, the fundamental conditions for the operation of a representative democratic system are set, and it has been in operation. The next question to be answered regards the extent to which the functioning of this system has ensured two important components of a democratic government: representativeness and responsiveness. In other words, that the body of representatives, to some extent, resembles society, and that elected government officials are accountable to the governed as well as responsible and efficient in their actions.[16]

In terms of representativeness, one could say that Brazil's political system meets its main requirement, namely, the guarantee of representation for minorities provided by the system of proportional representation used in the election for the Chamber of Deputies as well as for the state assemblies and municipal councils. In fact, if one looks at the level of party pluralism in the Brazilian Congress, one would conclude that the system is quite representative in so far as it apparently allows, through its fragmented party system, all sectors of the Brazilian society to be represented.

Even though proportional representation forms, *grosso modo*, the basis of Brazil's system, this principle, however, has not been respected. This is due mainly to malapportionment in Congress. In the Senate, whose representatives are elected by the plurality system, the federalist principle of equal representation for each state has prevailed regardless of sharp differences in population between states. In the Chamber of Deputies malapportionment results from the fact that, by law, no state may have fewer than eight or more than 70 representatives in the House. This means that

16   See Sartori (1987).

the less populous states are over represented while the more populous — that is, São Paulo which happens to be the most developed state — are underrepresented.[17] The disproportionate share of seats per state means that party representation in Congress does not accurately reflect the voting balance between the parties because their electoral support is not evenly distributed among the states. Thus, parties such as the PT and the PSDB, whose electoral support is more concentrated in the highly urbanised and industrialised southern and south-eastern regions, end up having proportionately fewer seats than if the proportional criteria were fairly respected.[18]

But, it is in relation to *responsiveness* that Brazil's democracy has problems to overcome. The political system is far from having mechanisms capable of securing a reasonable degree of accountability.[19] This could happen if the system had conditions to make voters (1) choose between clear policy and/or party options; and (2) be able to keep a representational link with their representatives. None of these conditions is entirely present in Brazil's polity.

With regard to the first — that is the system's capability to be intelligible to the ordinary citizen by presenting clear options to the voters — Brazil's institutions are far from contributing to enhanced intelligibility in the election process. As it is a federation, Brazil has a system of representation which operates on different levels of power — national, state and local. And, even though elections for national and state levels are simultaneous, both for executive and legislative offices, they are based on different voting methods: proportional representation for the Chamber of Deputies, state assemblies and municipal councils, plurality for the Senate, and two-round majority system for president and governors (as well as for mayors in cities with more than 200,000 inhabitants). Besides, as it is a system of proportional representation with open list, election for federal and state deputies, rather than a contest between parties, is a competition between individual candidates. Moreover, due to the presence of a large number of parties trying their electoral luck in state districts of high magnitude,[20] there are many candidates, making voters' electoral options less clear in the face of the large number of competitors campaigning for their support. On top of that, the electoral rules have encouraged the formation of party coalitions for all kinds of elections, including the ones run according to proportional representation (PR). This means that electoral options presented to voters are based either on individual candidates (who are so

17   Lamounier (1980); Kinzo (1980); Mainwaring (1991) and Lima Júnior (1993).
18   See Nicolau (1997).
19   I am referring to vertical rather than horizontal accountability. On this see especially O'Donnell (1998).
20   In eight states it is over 20 and in two states it is over 50.

numerous that voters are unable to gather enough information to differentiate between them and to make an informed choice) or on electoral alliances, which are made up of a diversity of parties.

With regard to the second — the system's capability to provide a representational link — problems are largely related to the size and magnitude of the electoral districts. As constituencies' boundaries are those of the states, whose number of representatives (or district magnitude) varies according to population, it is not possible to identify a constituency of supporters to whom representatives are supposed to respond. In other words, constituents do not bind representatives. This does not mean to say that deputies who have a clear link either with a specific group (e.g. professional, religious) or a region (such as those typical electoral strongholds based on clientelism) do not exist in Brazil. But, generally speaking, deputies tend to enjoy a great deal of autonomy in their parliamentary activity — which is particularly common among those whose votes come from large cities. The fact that most of the voters do not remember who their deputy is, or for whom they voted in the last legislative elections, is a good indication of the absence of a clear representational link between legislators and voters.

All these features combine to prevent vertical accountability from being effective. They produce a situation that tends to distance voters and representatives from each other, thereby making it extremely difficult for people to assess responsibility for governmental performance. This is, perhaps, one of the factors contributing to a widening of the gap between party politics in the electorate and party politics in Congress or in government,[21] a trait that had already characterised party politics during the 1945–64 democratic period.[22] This leads me to focus the analysis on the party issue.

Parties, Party System and Democracy in Brazil

The assessment of Brazil's experience of party politics since 1985 requires that at least three questions be answered. First, to what extent have Brazilian parties played a relevant role in integrating the electorate into the political system by mobilising them to participate in elections and to vote for one of the options (parties and/or candidates) presented by the electoral contest? Second, to what extent have Brazilian parties offered distinct and visible options to the voter, in other words, have they properly served to frame electoral choices and to create political identities? And third, have these 17 years of party politics resulted in the emergence of a pattern that will be consolidated in the future? Let us deal with each one of these questions.

---

21   On this see especially the important remarks made by Lima Jr (1993).
22   See Lavareda (1991).

Party Mobilisation

One of the main roles of political parties is to get votes. In fact, they became organisations due to the need to encourage voters to go to the polls. Thus, a good indication of the capacity of the party system to perform this function is electoral turnout. A high turnout indicates high capacity of the parties to persuade voters to participate in elections. In the case of Brazil, however, turnout is not a good indication of participation, because voting is compulsory. Thus, it is not impossible to find situations in which the turnout rate is high while voting results show a considerable number of blank or spoiled ballots.[23] This means that in order to measure the parties' capacity to mobilise voters, we should redefine electoral participation. This will be understood as the portion of the voters who expressed their preference for one of the options offered in the election, that is, the percentage of the franchised population who went to the polls and effectively voted for a candidate or a party. Thus, a low degree of electoral participation would mean that the parties are not competently performing one of their main functions, that is, to mobilise their electoral base.

Table 2.4 presents the percentage of the electorate to cast a valid vote in three kinds of electoral contests — elections for president, for state governors and for the Chamber of Deputies — for the period of 1986–2002. In general terms, electoral participation rates in Brazil are not so different from those found in established democracies, where the average was around 78 per cent in the 1950s, dropping to 70 per cent in late 1990s.[24] In Brazil, the average rate in the presidential elections held since redemocratisation is 73 per cent.[25] The numbers presented in the table show, however, three important aspects: first, much lower participation rates, especially in the 1990 and 1994 elections, for governor and for the Chamber of Deputies (the averages for the period are, respectively, 66 and 59 per cent); second, a significant decline in the rates occurring in the elections held in the period up to 1998: in the presidential elections, between 1989 and 1998, the rate dropped by 19 per cent, a similar decline (17 per cent) occurring in the elections for state governor between 1986 and

---

23   This was particularly the case in the elections held under military rule. For example, in the 1970 elections the percentages of blank and null ballots surpassed those of the opposition party (See Kinzo, 1988).

24   See Dalton, Flanagan and Beck (eds.) (1984); Wattenberg (1998); and Dalton, McAllister and Wattenberg (2000) .

25   I opted for taking as franchised the portion of the population over 18 instead of over 16 years old, given the fact that between the ages of 16 and 18 registration and voting are not compulsory. The numbers for the population over 18 are estimates for the years 1986, 1994, 1998 and 2002 produced by IBGE–Instituto Brasileiro de Geografia e Estatística.

1998;[26] and, third, a considerable increase in the participation rate between 1998 and 2002 in all three kind of elections.

Table 2.4: Electoral Participation in Brazil, 1986–2002 *

	Presidential Elections	Gubernatorial Elections	Chamber of Deputies Elections
1986	-	71	60
1990	80/78**	63	47
1994	66	60	48
1998	64	63	63
2002	75/76**	74	77

Source: Nicolau (1998a), Tribunal Superior Eleitoral and IBGE-Instituto Brasileiro de Geografia e Estatística.

* As measured by the percentage of the valid ballots on the population over 18 years old.
** The presidential elections of 1989 and 2002 had two rounds. The figures refer to the first and second rounds.

If these data are taken as an indicator of party mobilisation, one could say that instead of a gradual increase in political mobilisation, Brazil's democratisation was followed by demobilisation, at least up to 1998. Nonetheless, this would be a misleading conclusion, if one takes into consideration the fact that election mobilisation started long before 1985. In fact, this was a feature characterising the Brazilian transition to democracy during which the opposition managed to mobilise voters against the regime. Because of that previous mobilisation, the inauguration of the new regime in 1985 was not followed by a continuous engagement of the population in electoral politics. Instead, the peak of mobilisation was achieved in the first presidential election in 1989. From then on, mobilisation declined. The same process occurred in the elections for governor. For the first event that was held in a highly democratic context (1986), participation rates were very high, dropping considerably afterwards. This declining trend was, however, reversed in 2002 when participation rates increased more than ten percentage points. It is also worth noting the levels for the Chamber of Deputies: they used to be much lower than those for the gubernatorial and presidential elections (as shown in the first three election years). This is

26   Marked differences between regions and states also indicate that the capacity of the parties to mobilise voters varies considerably from one state to another. In any case, electoral participation rates have dropped in all parts of the country.

certainly related to the fact that, in Brazil, executive offices have been at the core of the political system, making voters pay much more attention to presidents, governors and mayors than to their representatives in Parliament, and therefore, predisposing them to participate less in legislative elections. It is also related to the fact that for the voters it is more complicated to make up their minds in an electoral contest in which there are many candidates competing for their support. As a consequence, the proportions of blank and nullified votes were much higher in legislative elections. This pattern, however, has changed since the 1998 elections, as indicated by the substantial increase in participation rates in 1998 and 2002 (Table 2.4). This change has to do not only with the use of the electronic polling machine, but mainly, with the fact that the electoral court, in order to reduce absenteeism in the legislative election, established a different voting sequence in the electronic polling machine: voters had to choose first the candidate for the legislative houses (under proportional representation) and then the candidates for president and for governor (under the majority system). Because of this change in the sequence of voting, a substantial portion of voters may have pressed the number of their governor candidate when the machine was displaying the choice related to the legislative elections, pressing it again when the machine displayed the choice for the gubernatorial and presidential elections.

A second aspect to assess in the party issue in Brazil is related to the system's capacity to offer different options for the voters, that is to frame electoral choices and to create party identities. This leads us to the examination of the dynamics of party competition and the intelligibility of the system for the electorate.

High Fragmentation and Low Intelligibility of the Party System

It is common sense to state that the Brazilian party system is highly fragmented and the parties as organisations are weak. In spite of much of the controversy on this matter I would have no doubt to confirm this 'common sense',[27] for it is a fact that Brazil's party system is one of the most fragmented in the world. As Table 2.5 shows, the degree of fractionalisation in the federal Chamber of Deputies, as measured by Laakso's and Taagepera's 'effective-number-of-parties' index (N),[28] was about three in 1986, rose to nine in 1990, fell to eight in 1994 and to seven in 1998 and rose again to 8.5 in the last election.

27 See Lamounier and Meneguello (1986); Kinzo (1993); and Mainwaring (1995 and 1999). A contrasting view is espoused by Figueiredo and Limongi (1999).
28 Laakso and Taagepera (1979). Effective number of parties is calculated by $N = 1/(1 - \text{åpi2})$, p is the proportion of votes obtained by each party for the Chamber of Deputies. See also Rae (1975).

Table 2.5: Number of Effective Parties by Region — Federal Chamber of Deputies, 1986–2002[29]

Regions	Federal Chamber of Deputies				
	1986	1990	1994	1998	2002
Rondônia	1.8	1.2	4.0	4.4	5.3
Acre	2.0	1.9	2.5	4.0	4.0
Amazonas	2.5	4.5	3.2	3.2	3.2
Roraima	2.0	3.9	3.2	2.9	4.0
Pará	1.6	4.1	4.0	5.5	5.3
Amapá	1.6	3.1	4.0	4.0	5.3
Tocantins	-	2.8	4.0	3.5	4.0
North	**1.7**	**6.4**	**6.4**	**4.9**	**8.8**
Maranhão	2.5	5.5	3.9	5.5	4.6
Piaui	2.6	2.9	3.3	2.8	3.8
Ceará	2.5	5.1	3.1	1.7	4.7
R.G.Norte	2.4	3.1	2.2	2.5	4.0
Paraiba	2.2	4.2	2.4	3.8	6.5
Pernambuco	2.1	3.6	3.4	4.4	7.2
Alagoas	2.5	3.5	7.5	7.5	5.4
Sergipe	2.4	2.8	4.6	6.3	6.4
Bahia	2.2	6.6	4.6	3.3	3.5
North-east	**2.4**	**6.2**	**5.3**	**5.7**	**6.5**
Minas Gerais	2.0	7.4	6.8	6.5	8.6
Espirito Santo	1.8	2.1	5.0	4.5	7.1
Rio de Janeiro	5.0	4.9	9.9	6.7	9.5
São Paulo	3.6	7.4	6.8	7.1	7.8
South-east	**3.4**	**9.4**	**8.9**	**7.4**	**9.4**
Parana	1.4	5.5	7.1	6.0	6.8
Santa Catarina	2.4	4.1	4.4	5.0	4.1
Rio Grande do Sul	2.7	4.1	5.4	5.7	6.4
South	**2.1**	**6.0**	**7.4**	**7.2**	**6.4**
Mato Grosso Sul	2.4	3.9	4.6	5.2	4.0
Mato Grosso	2.0	3.5	8.0	4.0	4.6
Goias	1.8	4.5	4.6	3.7	4.6
Distrito Federal	2.4	5.2	4.0	5.2	4.0
Centre-west	**2.2**	**8.7**	**7.2**	**6.0**	**5.9**
Brazil	**2.9**	**9.0**	**8.2**	**7.2**	**8.5**

Source: LEEX – IUPERJ.

It is true that the three-party dynamics in operation in 1986 did not represent the most likely context for consolidation, because in those early years of

29   I would like to thank Maria do Socorro Braga for having provided the data for this table.

democratisation the two-party politics inherited from the previous regime was still alive. But it is also true that the slight decrease in the 'effective-number-of-parties' index between 1990 and 1998 — a trend that was in fact reversed in 2002 — is not sufficient to draw the conclusion that the format of the Brazilian party system will be one of moderate fragmentation. As can be seen in the table, high fractionalisation is also present — even though, in some cases, to a lesser degree — at the state level. Besides, if we take as a reference the year 1990, which registered the highest index at national level, we can observe that in 22 out of 27 states the indices of fractionalisation have increased, rather than declined, between 1990 and 2002.

Fragmentation of the party system would not be a problem for the functioning of democracy if it did not affect the intelligibility of the electoral process — the capacity of the system to produce clear options for the voters who would choose according to their knowledge about them or identity with them. The problem in Brazil is that there is a combination of high fragmentation and low intelligibility of the competition. In fact, in a fragmented party system one would expect to have parties with clearer contours, based on some social, regional or political cleavage. This would mean that voters had clearly defined options to choose in the electoral competition. This assumption does not apply to the Brazilian situation, because, in spite of the presence of ideological differentiation between the parties — broadly a continuum from left to right — most of the parties, individually, have no clear boundaries.[30]

This is illustrated by the common practice among elected office-holders of shifting party allegiance[31] — which is, by the way, a sign of fragility of the parties as organisations. Much stronger evidence, however, is the fact that parties rarely compete in elections as single actors; most of the time they make alliances. This means that the contenders in the elections are not single parties; rather, they are coalitions formed by several parties sometimes of different ideological orientations.

One could argue that it is natural that parties form electoral alliances when they have to contest a nationwide election under a multiparty system in a country as large as Brazil. This is true in the case of presidential elections in which the electoral district is the country as a whole. But the use of coalitions extends both to state and to local elections. For example, in the gubernatorial elections all parties, no matter their size or their ideological coloration, have resorted to electoral coalitions. Figures for 1998[32] show that in 17 out of 19 states where the PMDB ran for governor, this party was supported by a coalition. The cases of the PFL and the PSDB are

30   On this see, Kinzo (1993) and Figueiredo and Limongi (1999).
31   On the changing party allegiance see especially Melo (2000); on party discipline see Mainwaring and Liñan (1998).
32   Tribunal Superior Eleitoral

still more striking: in none of the states did they contest the gubernatorial elections as a single actor; they were in alliance with other parties in every one of them. This coalitionist practice is less common among left-wing parties, but this strategy is used and has recently increased among them also. For example, the PT, which was very reluctant in the past to form electoral alliances, ran in the gubernatorial election of 1998 as a single competitor in only three out of the 15 states in which it had a candidate for governor.

As mentioned before, elections for state governor are based on the system of two round majority, which makes it possible for all parties to try their luck in the first round and then, in the second, to join together around the two strongest contenders in a coalition. Nonetheless, out of necessity, parties build coalitions even for the first round election. Obviously, if a party wants to increase its chances of electoral success in the context of multi-party politics and election by majority, it has to follow this strategy. What is remarkable in Brazil, however, is the use of coalitions even in the legislative elections based on the system of proportional representation, which is a system designed to secure representation for minorities willing to differentiate themselves from the large parties.

Therefore, coalitions, which have various different compositions in different localities and states, are frequent not only in elections based on the majority system (for the executive offices and the Senate) but also in those based on the system of proportional representation. Obviously this is a necessity because the party system is fragmented. And it continues to be fragmented because politicians and parties are allowed to make coalitions. Thus politicians' electoral strategies are devised to obtain the best results under the institutional structure in which they operate. To form a coalition is the best strategy not only for the major parties but also for the small ones. By allying with the big party that puts forward the candidate for governor, for example, the small parties guarantee a partnership in the coalition for the legislative elections and increase their chance of gaining a seat in the house of deputies or in the state assembly. In turn, by allying with the small parties, the large ones increase their chances (which include a larger portion of the free radio and television time for electoral campaign) of winning the election for the executive office. The trade-off will be felt in the legislative elections: by running in the legislative election on a coalition list of candidates, the large parties, while giving space to the small partners in the coalition, reduce their chances of gaining a larger number of seats in the legislative house.

Though this may be the most rational strategy for both the politicians and the parties, it is harmful for the voters, because voters can hardly distinguish between the parties as distinct actors, that is, as entities framing electoral choices and identities. In other words, in such a situation voters have difficulty in identifying and separating the parties that are contesting the elections: so many parties, so many electoral alliances, which are different from one place to the other, from one election to the other. In addition, the competition is centred much more around individual candidates than on parties. In sum, high fragmentation and the lack of clarity of the party system make it difficult for the voters to fix the parties, to distinguish who is who, and to create party identities.[33]

Electoral Volatility

A visible consequence of weak partisan attachments on the part of the electorate has been electoral volatility, which is an important dimension of party system stabilisation.[34] The lower it is, the more likely that in the electoral arena the established party labels have some role in determining preferences independent from the appeal of a party's particular candidate, issue positions or unexpected events. Institutionalisation will hardly take place if electoral volatility is very high. Is this the case in Brazil?

Brazilian electoral volatility, from a comparative perspective, is among the highest in the world. Among the established democracies volatility scores, as measured by Pedersen's index, vary from country to country, but they rarely reached as high a score as Brazil's.[35] Figures in Nicolau (1998) indicate that, in the period 1982–98, on average about 30 per cent of the electorate shifted their votes from one party to another in consecutive elections. A more detailed analysis of that electoral volatility is found in Braga (2003) who calculates the index for the Federal Chamber and State Assemblies using the election results by municipality for the period 1990-2002. The figures are still more striking: the average for the whole country, taking the three pairs of elections, is 38.3 in the Federal Chamber and 36.7 in the State Assemblies. Is this volatility a national phenomenon or is it concentrated in some localities? Braga's work as well as that of Peres (2002), who calculated electoral volatility by state, show a stark variation in the indices, not only between different groups of municipalities[36] but also between states.[37]

---

33   It is worth noting, however, that there are at least two factors that may be contributing to fix the parties' identity: the first is related to the fact that candidates and parties are identified by a number which voters can use to vote in the electronic polls. As in the case of the parties their number is permanent, it ends up fixing an association between the party and the number, which always prevails over the coalition. Second, parties are granted free television time twice a year to publicise their programme and their achievements. This is an occasion when it is the party and its main leaders that are in focus.

34   See Pedersen (1990); and Bartolini and Mair (1990).

35   Pedersen's index average for the European countries, between 1985–96, were 11.0 (See Nicolau, 1998b). On electoral volatility see especially Bartolini and Mair (1990) and Mair (1997).

36   Braga (2003) established that the indices are higher in the categories of small and medium size towns than for either large cities or state-capitals.

37   Variation among states, for the period 1982–98, ranges from 16.4 to 54.0 according to data analysed by Peres (2002).

It should be noted, however, that although electoral volatility has stopped growing, and has even shown, in large cities, a downward trend.[38] In fact, the level of instability of the party system reached its peak in 1990, a trend that reflected significant party changes during the period of elaboration of the Constituent Assembly works (1987–88) — for example, the creation of the PSDB out of the PMDB's split and the reorganisation of the PDS after a fusion with two other parties. The upward tendency found in some states as well as in towns of medium and small sizes[39] may be explained by the fact that some parties have managed to establish themselves in a larger number of states, thus changing the election dynamics in some states. The nationwide establishment of the main parties, that is, their nationalisation, is still in process, which means that volatility will continue to be high in Brazil.

Final Remarks

The party picture depicted here — showing a party system marked by high fractionalisation, ample use of electoral coalitions, low party identification and high electoral volatility — could lead us to the conclusion that over these 17 years of democracy Brazil has achieved very little in terms of the institutionalisation of its party system, and prospects for the future are not very promising. In fact, the evidence presented here makes it very difficult to support the different view that the party system has consolidated. However, if we take into account the short period of existence of the present party configuration as well as the inhospitable conditions for party development characterising the Brazilian institutional framework, then the achievements have not been so insignificant.

Although slowly, a pattern of party dynamics has been in process of consolidation. As stated above, indices of volatility are high, but they have stopped growing. Fractionalisation continues to be high, but there is a chance that it will decrease in the future, because the party system is largely shaped by intra-elite disputes, rather than by sharp divisions in society. This means that there are not, either between parties on the left or on the right, insuperable differences of positions that could be real impediments for party merging, which would consequently reduce fragmentation. As pointed out earlier, most of the parties have worked together in coalitions either for electoral purposes or in government. And if left-wing parties such as the PT continue to grow, as occurred both in the 2000 municipal elections and in 2002 — when this party achieved the supreme electoral success, the presidency of the Republic — there is good reason to expect that party re-grouping will occur. The more the main parties in the Left expand their organisation over the country the greater the likelihood that fractionalisation

---

38   Peres (2002), Braga (2003).
39   See Braga (2003)

will increase in localities previously controlled by traditional conservative parties, fractionalisation which eventually would become costly for the main competitors. This in turn will make a process of party re-aggregation more likely. It should also be noted that, according to the current Party Organisation Law,[40] after the present legislature, no party will be entitled to have representation and, therefore, to function as a party in the Chamber of Deputies, unless it gets five per cent of the valid votes nationwide, distributed over one-third of the states with two per cent of the vote in each. Moreover, political reform, so much debated over the last decade, is still on the agenda. Nobody can predict how wide-ranging and comprehensive it will be, but the possibility of further party developments is still open.

Contemporary democracies have been under scrutiny all over the world. The debate about the emergence of new trends in political attitudes and behaviour, creating alternative forms of political participation, has been intense in the last three or four decades. This has put in question the centrality of the traditional institutions of representation — that is, parties and elections. Low rates of mobilisation and participation, decreasing partisan attachments, and negative assessments of the political institutions, are features that can no longer be associated only with the so-called politically underdeveloped world. Are these symptoms of something wrong with western democracies? Or are they simply an indication of some changes in election trends and in the role of parties, changes easily processed by consolidated democratic systems? No matter where the truth lies, the fact is that these new trends have become part of the problematic of contemporary democracy. By referring to this issue, I do not intend to reflect on the prospects of contemporary democracy in general, but rather to place my assessment of the prospect of party politics in democratic Brazil in the context of the significant transformations undergone by the institutions of representation in the established democracies. In fact, over these17 years of democratic experiment, Brazil has faced a paradoxical situation: to consolidate institutions — such as parties or elections — which, notwithstanding the fundamental role they played in the consolidation of Western democracies, political parties no longer enjoy the central position they used to have in the political system. In spite of that, they continue to be central to the political debate and crucial for the consolidation of democracy in Brazil. For the simple reason that, either in theory or in practice, there are no alternative means of building and consolidating a democratic form of political cohabitation that can replace the institutional mechanisms that were the foundations of the established Western democracies.

---

40   Law 9.096, 19/09/1995.

CHAPTER 3

Congress and Decision-Making in Democratic Brazil

Argelina Cheibub Figueiredo
Fernando Limongi

Introduction

Unlike most analyses, this chapter will make a positive assessment of the role performed by Congress in these 15 years of democratic rule in Brazil. Evaluations of the Brazilian Congress are usually contradictory. Congress has been regarded both as an institutional obstacle to effective government and a mere rubber stamp to executive initiatives. Considerable energy and creativity have been devoted to conciliating these two views.

The success rates of recent presidents in achieving their legislative agenda and in guaranteeing their dominance in law-making hardly support the claim that Congress hinders executive action. On the other hand, the image of subservience is also far from the actual congressional action. Government performance has relied on the stable parliamentary support from the parties participating in the ministries. Congress has not been either subservient or conflicting. It is possible to observe changes in congressional action that can be traced to the shift in the political agenda. But on balance, throughout these 15 years, Congress has played a consistent and responsive role in policy-making.

One of the most widespread opinions after the enactment of the 1988 Constitution is that 'its provisions have rendered the country ungovernable'. This statement is usually made with regard to the rules organising the polity or to the rules regulating the economy and extending social entitlements, or both. The first set of rules allegedly precludes policy change while the latter inhibits economic development.

The diagnosis of ungovernability, however, completely disregards two facts. First, the 1988 Constitution endowed the Executive with broad legislative powers as a consequence of the constitutional delegates' concern with guaranteeing the Executive with instruments for an effective government. Thus, the decision-making system designed by the constitution favours governability, narrowly defined as the Executive's capacity to enact its legislative agenda.[1] The constitutional delegates' main concern was to prevent decisional paralysis derived from Congress's veto or incapacity.

---

1 The concept of governability is very imprecisely used. Here it means that there is no decisional paralysis.

The institutional powers the constitution endowed the Executive neutralise incentives provided by the electoral and party legislation. Most analysts did not recognise the importance of this institutional change and stressed the continuity between the 1946 and the 1988 institutional frameworks expressed by the option for presidentialism and proportional open list system. Our main argument is that comparative institutional analysis must go beyond forms of government and electoral laws.

Secondly, this diagnosis also ignores the shift in the country's political agenda. During the democratisation process, two issues dominated the political agenda: the struggle against social and economic inequalities and the need for increased political participation and decentralisation of state action. Many social provisions embedded in the new constitution can be seen as the Constituent Assembly's responses to these general demands. To rescue the so-called 'social debt' left by the military, constitutional delegates guaranteed an extensive range of egalitarian and universal social rights. Thus, they not only conferred constitutional status to the legal entitlements that various interest groups had acquired during authoritarian rule, as they are usually blamed, but they also sought to compensate large social segments that had been excluded from distorted social policies implemented during the military regime.

It is worth noting that the need to rescue the 'social debt' was not created by the politicians who wrote the constitution. First, it was an integral part of the opposition discourse to the military regime, i.e. it was the keystone of PMDB's political programme. Second, it was buttressed by social scientists' concern with democratic consolidation. According to this view, democracy would not endure without a substantive component. Democracy would not secure the popular support if it did not bring direct and immediate material benefits to the poorest sectors of society. The prevalent poverty and social inequality conspired against the survival of democracy. Paradoxically, most provisions incorporated in the constitution to guarantee democracy came later to be considered as obstacles to development and to democratic governance itself.

Responding to a more general claim, the constitutional delegates also established new forms of political participation, such as the population's right to initiate legislation, popular referendum and participation in policy implementation, and strengthened federalism by assigning greater political, fiscal and administrative autonomy to the federal units. As for the organisation of the polity, they kept unchanged the system of government and the rules organising the system of representation, i.e. bicameral legislature, proportional representation and multiparty system. They thus maintained the institutional basis for political fragmentation and for multiple veto players in the political system.[2]

2   For the concept of veto players and their role in policy change see Tsebelis (1995).

Therefore, the idea that the constitution made the country ungovernable disregards the immense and rapid transformation in the priorities of the political agenda during this period. At the time the constitution was promulgated it expressed the dominant opinion that the consolidation of democracy required concrete social policies and increased political participation.

On the contrary, the agenda of the governments that followed the 1988 constitution has been to a great extent conditioned by changes in the international economy and the aggravation of the fiscal crisis. The new agenda comprised monetary stabilisation measures, adjustment of public accounts, as well as social and economic reforms to integrate the country in the new economic environment. Social inequality and redistributive policies were no longer at the heart of the new political agenda. In fact, monetary stabilisation and market-oriented reforms came to the fore.

Although Congress has not rejected the changes in the new agenda altogether, it did put up considerable resistance. Indeed, Congress sought to guarantee higher income for the lower classes. During the implementation of the stabilisation plans by Verão and Collor the PMDB led the parties' attempt to protect wages. In other words, the PMDB and the PSDB did not bestow immediate support to the shift in the political agenda. During the Franco government, however, the PSDB, with Cardoso in the Ministry of Finance, commanded a shift of the centre parties' position on the issue. The launching of the new stabilisation plan in 1994, the Real Plan, marks the centre's acceptance of monetary stabilisation and market-oriented reforms. This acceptance was facilitated by the electoral returns of the plan.

The success of the Real Plan attests that the institutional framework created by the 1988 Constitution did not produce structural obstacles to executive action. Brazilian presidents are not weak. The 1988 Constitution preserved the legislative powers with which the Executive was endowed during the military regime, the most important of which was the power of decree. These legislative powers, as will be argued in the next section, grant the Executive control over the legislative agenda with clear effects on legislative outcomes.

Control over the agenda, however, does not place Brazilian presidents above the fray. Their powers rely on institutional prerogatives that do not allow them to dispense with the support of political parties. Our objective in the third section of this chapter is to show that political support is necessary to translate control over the legislative agenda into control over the legal output. In other words, executive legislative powers do not grant the president the capacity to govern against the will of the majority in the legislature. However, if the presidents have majority support, agenda powers are powerful weapons to render their action effective.

Institutional Mechanisms and Policy Outcomes: Executive Success and Dominance

The Brazilian decision-making process entails high levels of delegation from the legislature to the executive branch of the government and, within Congress, from Congress members to party leaders.

The constitutional rules regulating Executive-Legislative relations assign to the former extensive legislative powers that enables the Executive to control the legislative agenda. The Executive in Brazil has the monopoly of legal initiative in three fundamental areas: public administration, taxation and the budget. It also has the power to request 'urgency' for its bills, a device that determines a bill's priority and time limit for discussion. However, the most powerful legal instrument in the Executives' hand is the provisional decrees (*medidas provisórias*). According to Article 62 of the 1988 Constitution the president can issue decrees with the force of law in situations he deems urgent and important. Thus, the Executive is able to change the status quo unilaterally, creating a consummated situation that, in certain cases, makes the rejection of the decree practically impossible.

The issuing of a provisional decree (PD) modifies the structure of the parliamentary choice. A vote takes place under the new status quo created by the PD. Hence, even if Congress's first preference is the status quo prior to the issuing of the provisional decree, it can approve the decree if it prefers the situation created by the provisional decree to the one that would obtain with its rejection. In this case, if the same measure had been introduced as an ordinary bill, it would have been rejected. Besides that, if Congress fails to vote on a decree within the 30 days required by the constitution, non-constitutional regulation allows the reissue of a PD for an indefinite period. The original act is thereby kept in force without being voted on. The costs of forming a majority are then transferred to the opposition. Therefore, the executive act has a direct and immediate effect on the definition of the legislative agenda. Moreover, it also allows the Executive to influence the outcomes of the decision-making process.

The internal rules that distribute power within the Congress, in its turn, favour party leaders. The speaker and the party leaders exercise tight control over the legislative agenda. Leaders have the prerogative to represent their party members. Because of this prerogative, party leaders can control the requests of roll-calls, the presentation and consideration of amendments and the requests for 'urgency'. The latter is a quite important device because this urgent procedure allows bills to be discharged from the standing committees and restricts the rights to propose amendments on the floor. The leaders can also nominate the members of the standing committees and replace them at any time during their mandate. Through these instruments the leaders can, and in fact do, exert control over both the legislative process and the behaviour of the representatives on the floor.

The extensive legislative powers held by the president and the distribution of legislative rights within the legislature in favour of party leaders resulted in a highly centralised decision-making process. The impact of these rules upon the decisional capacity of recent governments becomes obvious through a detailed analysis of Table 3.1.

Table 3.1: Laws Enacted by Government: Initiator, Dominance and Success of the Executive — 1989–2000

Government	Sarney	Collor	Franco	Cardoso I	Cardoso II	Total
Laws enacted by type and initiator (monthly average)						
Executive Initiative						
Budgetary*	7.4	7.1	7.1	8.0	9.5	7.8
Provisional Decree	6.4	2.2	2.7	2.7	1.7	2.8
Others	2.9	4.4	3.1	2.4	1.3	2.8
Sub total (Executive)	16.7	13.7	12.9	13.1	12.5	13.4
Legislature	4.3	4.0	1.3	1.7	0.8	2.2
Total	21.0	17.7	14.3	14.8	13.3	15.7
Executive dominance and success (per cent)						
Dominance **	81	77	90	89	94	86
Success ***	72	66	73	76	74	73

Source: PRODASEN; Banco de Dados Legislativos, Cebrap.
* In addition to the laws regulating the annual budget, this figure includes also the requests for supplementary credits that change previously approved items of the budget.
** Proportion of enacted laws initiated by the Executive.
*** Proportion of bills initiated by the Executive that are approved.

The Executive clearly dominates the legal output and obtains a high rate of success for its legislative proposals. All the administrations show high rates of success and dominance, although the only president to form a minority cabinet, Collor de Mello, indeed obtained the lowest rates. On average, Congress enacted a monthly average of 13.4 bills introduced by the Executive, against only 2.2 of its own initiative. This difference is due to the agenda powers — exclusive initiative and decree power — held by the Executive. These institutional powers assured executive dominance in legislation.

The highest average (7.8 laws per month) among the laws introduced by the Executive refers to the budgetary laws, an area in which the Executive retains the constitutional right to exclusive initiative. The budgetary laws comprise the annual budget and laws concerning modifications of the previously voted budget through additional, special and extraordinary transfers of resources from one budget item to another. These laws are important instruments for reallocation of public resources and thus, for the definition of public policies. The monopoly of initiative allows the strategic use of time by the Executive and, for this reason, becomes an effective instrument of pressure on the legislature. Only four proposals of budgetary changes were rejected. In general they are approved quickly (50 days on average) and without modifications.

Congress participation in the budget process is usually seen as an example of its incapacity to act in a timely and responsible fashion. Most delays in the approval of the annual budget law, however, are due to the following: the constitution has no provision regarding the consequences of the failure to approve the budget in due time and the laws regulating the annual budget process authorise the Executive to implement the budget bill by appropriating one twelfth per month of any budget item. Therefore, failure to approve the budget on time is not necessarily bad for the Executive. Presidents have in fact taken advantage of the existing legal procedures to delay the approval of the annual budget bill. In 1994, for instance, the government sent the budget bill to Congress but withdrew it many times to introduce modifications which, according to the existing rules, forced the budget committee to re-open the whole process of consideration at each modification. Recent changes in this legislation and in the rules regulating the implementation of the budget were approved to induce both branches of government to ensure that the budget bill was approved on time. Furthermore, as a consequence of the 1993 budget scandal, Congress by its own initiative has approved a whole set of legislation reforming the budget process in order to increase its transparency and the predictability of implementation of the approved budget law.[3]

The provisional decree (PD) also accounts for a significant proportion of the enacted laws, an average equivalent to the laws introduced as ordinary bills for the whole period.[4] The analysis of their content shows that the PDs were the Executive's privileged instrument for the implementation of economic policy, especially the monetary stabilisation plans: more than 50 per cent of the decrees issued related to economic matters. This proportion reached about 60 per cent during the Cardoso administration. Most PDs concerning social and administrative issues consisted of measures complementary to these economic plans as, for example, the legislation regulating

3　For the provisions and the results they produced see Figueiredo and Limongi (2000).
4　Note that Table 6.1 considers decrees that were approved by Congress and transformed into law. The monthly average was calculated based on the date the decree was issued. Hence a decree issued by Franco, and approved during the Cardoso administration after several reissues, was credited to Franco. The figures do not consider reissuing. Reissuing and alternative count methods are discussed below.

constitutional rules for social security, which included an increase in contributions to cope with deficits. Administrative laws comprised the reorganisation of the state apparatus and the privatisation of state companies.

Since provisional decrees grant the president the power to alter the status quo unilaterally, it is not surprising that all presidents have used them extensively. It is the Executive's most powerful legislative weapon. For this reason most analysts associate the use of decree with minority governments. It is usually considered a weapon to bypass or circumvent the legislature. However, if one assumes that the Executive acts constitutionally, this legislative instrument is limited when there is a clear opposing majority. Decree power does not allow the Executive to circumvent partisan majorities. Disregarding this fact leads analysts to overestimate the power of decree and to blur the distinction between its constitutional and non-constitutional use.

These views also neglect the role that this institutional instrument can play in the hands of executives holding majority support in the legislature, especially in coalition governments. The institutional strength of the provisional decree interacts with the partisan power of the Executive in ways not anticipated by analysts who perceive them as sheer instruments to confront Congress resistance. Following Huber's analysis of the 'package vote', established by the 1958 French constitution, we can see provisional decrees as valuable instruments for solving problems of 'horizontal bargaining' between the government and its supporting majority rather than means of solving 'vertical conflict' between the government and the legislature.[5] This kind of institutional mechanism — rather than establishing a hierarchical relationship between the Executive and the Legislature, in which the former suppress the majority's will and subjugates the latter — can in fact play an important role in protecting majorities in coalition governments. According to what Huber labels the 'political cover hypothesis', this institutional device can be used to protect the government majority from debates and votes about sensitive issues made prominent by a minority and to preserve policy agreements between the government and its supporting coalition.[6] In this sense, the use of provisional decree does not imply conflict, but rather concerted action between the government and its supporting majority in the legislature.

The analysis of the use different governments made of provisional decrees and of Congress' responses to it show that this interpretation finds strong empirical support. The relevant information is summarised in Table 3.2. The first row presents the monthly average of original PDs issued irrespective of the final outcome (such as approval, rejection or loss of effectiveness due to the fact a PD was not approved but it was not reissued either). The second row presents the monthly average of provisional

5   Huber (1996), pp. 90–91.
6   *Ibid.* (1996), p. 76.

decrees reissued and the third sum up the previous ones. The figures in the fourth row are calculated on the basis of total bills introduced by the Executive, regardless of the result. It represents the use of PDs as compared to the use of ordinary bills, that is to say that the complement of the figures shown in the table corresponds to the proportion introduced as ordinary bills.[7] The two following rows represent the proportion of PDs enacted and rejected. The last row represents the modifications made by Congress on the original decree by means of conversion bills (CB), i.e. amendments approved at the Congress floor.

Table 3.2: Provisional Decree by Government — 1989–2000

Governments	Sarney	Collor	Franco	Cardoso I	Cardoso II
PDs issued (monthly average)	7.6	2.9	5.2	3.3	3.0
PDs reissued (monthly average)	0.9	2.3	13.5	50.9	88.4
Total (monthly average)	8.5	5.2	18.7	54.2	91.4
Percentage executive bills introduced as PDs	68.9	32.3	46.1	53.0	55.5
Percentage PDs enacted into laws	87.3	74.2	83.0	67.7	37.5
Percentage PDs rejected	6.4	7.9	-	0.6	-
Percentage CB/ total PDs enacted into laws	44.8	69.7	35.9	33.0	33.3

Source: PRODASEN; Banco de Dados Legislativos, Cebrap.

As we can see, the relationship between political support — whether a minority or a majority government is formed — and the use of PDs departs from the direction usually predicted by the literature.[8] Collor, the only president to form a minority government in the period, presents the lowest average of original PDs.[9] In addition, the distribution of PDs in each administration shows that they are concentrated around the implementation of monetary stabilisation plans, except for Cardoso's where they are spread along the whole period. On the other hand, Collor was the president who exploited the least the strategy of relying on decree power. His government presents on average the lowest proportion — 32.3 per cent — of bills intro-

---

7   Due to their specificity, the budgetary bills were excluded.
8   Carey and Shugart (1995); Cox and Morgenstern (1998).
9   These figures in Table 3.1 are different because they include only the decrees enacted as laws.

duced as provisional decrees. The higher proportions of legislation introduced as PDs in the other administrations indicate the importance of the
PDs for the implementation of the government legislative agenda.

The last three rows in Table 3.2 indicate that Congress participation
decreased over time. The proportion of PDs enacted into laws fell from
87.3 per cent, during the Sarney administration, to 37.5 per cent in
Cardoso's second term. This change did not result from rejection as we can
see from the rejection rates. On the contrary, at the time of writing only
one decree had been rejected since 1994. Therefore, congressional opposition does not explain the decline in the rate of provisional decrees enacted into laws. In fact, since the implementation of the Real stabilisation
plan, launched by Cardoso in the Finance Ministry, and especially during
his administration as president of the republic, a new pattern of relationship with the legislature was inaugurated. The lower rate of enactment is
due to the constant reissuing of decrees.

A consideration of the rates of the conversion bill (CB) — the formal
means by which the legislature can present an alternative to the PD issued
— shows that Congress exercised its power to amend decrees more
intensely during the Collor administration when 69.7 per cent of provisional decrees were modified through conversion bills. In comparison, during the Cardoso administrations the legislature Congress introduced modified only one third of the PDs issued.

The Cardoso government consolidated the practice, initiated during the
implementation of the Real Plan in the previous government, of continuously reissuing PDs. In his administration the number of reissues escalated: from a monthly average of two reissues in Collor's government to over
50. That is to say, the issuing and reissuing of PDs became part of the
ordinary implementation of public policy.

On the other hand, the reissued decrees introduce modifications in the
original text. These modifications are not formally presented as conversion
bills by the special committees that, according to procedural rules, should
be formed to consider the PDs issued. In fact, these committees do not
meet regularly and the Congress member appointed to report on the PD
proceeds with great autonomy and conducts the negotiations with the government for the introduction of the changes to the original text. These
modifications may or may not involve the participation of other members
of Congress, but since it does not take place on the floor of Congress, as
would be the case if they were introduced as conversion bills, the role of
the opposition is necessarily reduced.

Thus, the greater number of PDs reissued reflected a less active and
oppositional stand by Congress. The reissuing of decrees does not seem
to be a weapon used by the president to avoid Congress altogether.
Reissues can have majority support.

Let us examine the point in depth. The reissuing of a PD means that the legislative has not made a decision on it within the 30 days stipulated in the constitution. The president can prevent a PD from being voted on, if he is not sure about the possibilities of approval, through denying quorum on the vote, a strategy that has often been used. Nevertheless if the opposition in the legislature musters a majority against the PD, the Executive has no means of preventing the vote from taking place. Hence, presidents cannot govern against the will of the majority, even with power of decree. In fact, Congress has rejected PDs during the Sarney and Collor governments. If Congress can muster this majority, why would it prefer the continuous reissuing of the PDs?

A simplistic explanation given for the inaction of Congress is a lack of 'political will', as if not voting was exclusively determined by inertia, as if not voting was not in itself a result of concrete actions that demand further explanations. A more general explanation, suggested by Shugart and Carey, sees congressional inaction as the result of delegation from the legislature majority pursuing particularistic interests to the Executive. For these authors, this situation would take place in political systems such as Brazil's, where we can observe the operation of the 'inefficient secret' deriving from the combination of strong legislative powers with a Congress elected on clientelistic bases. This interpretation assumes that the interests of Congress members are necessarily in conflict with the interests of the Executive. For this reason, it predicts a turbulent relationship between these two branches, as strong presidents are encouraged to govern unilaterally and have no incentives to negotiate.[10]

The evidence, nevertheless, reinforces the interpretation that takes into account the interests of the parties that form the coalition supporting the president. Everything indicates that the continuous reissuing of PDs relied on the collaboration of these party leaders, who controlled the process of discussion of the PDs and influenced their frequent alterations. The *relatores* (the Congress members responsible for reviewing the PD) played an important role in the modifications introduced. During the Cardoso administration, the PSDB and the PFL, the two main parties of the coalition, controlled the position of *relatores*, with the PFL supplying the majority. The special committees formed for the discussion of the PDs did not even assemble together and aimed, primarily, to nominate the *relator*. Therefore, they have functioned as a focus for bargaining and decisions between the government and its supporting parties rather than as loci for deliberation and discussion. The costs of reissuing a PD are lower than the costs involved in its approval.

Based on the same reasons, i.e. cost-benefit analysis, the majority may prefer a PD over an ordinary bill. As Huber has argued with regard to

10   See Shugart and Carey (1992), pp. 37–8, 165.

France, agenda powers are weapons for protecting the cohesion of the coalition. They neutralise incentives for opportunistic behaviour by the coalition members.

Executive sway consequently relies heavily on decree power. But, as argued above, this does not mean that the president governs against or without Congress. In fact, the actions of party leaders make the non-voting of a PD and its subsequent reissuing possible. Presidents, even with all legislative power they may bring to bear, cannot govern against the majority, as Collor learned when he faced the PMDB's opposition. On the other hand, agenda powers and a centralised decision-making process make the action of the majority that supports the president — if one exists — much easier. Hence presidential action is constrained — as it should be under a democracy — by the distribution of seats in the Legislative.

Up to this point we have analysed proposals whose outcomes derive directly from the Executive's institutional position. The Executive has the exclusive right to initiate budgetary bills and to issue PDs. But, even in the areas in which the initiative is open to the Legislature as well as to the Executive, i.e., on ordinary bills, the decision-making process is highly centralised. In general, bills are approved under urgent procedures requested by party leaders. Deliberation under urgency means that bills are passed on from the committees and voted on by the floor in a few days.

Urgency procedures restrict Congress members' capacity to have a bearing on the policy-making process since they reduce the time for debate on the matter and restrict the possibility of presenting amendments. That means that urgent procedure heightens the control of party leaders over the policy-making process. Voting under urgent procedure increases the leaders' control over the issues at stake, therefore making the approval of the proposal much easier.

Party leaders can also shape policy outcomes in the committees by appointing and replacing their members. They have often made use of these prerogatives to save representatives from voting on policies that are harmful to their constituencies. This practice, usually considered an expression of the shortcomings or the weaknesses of the Brazilian parties, in reality, denotes an effective partisan strategy. At the same time this guarantees the party's interests at the expense of the representatives' immediate aim to please their constituency, it protects the representatives from electoral retaliation. For this reason, these practices have the support of Congress members.

The control over the voting process by the government leaders acquired an even greater importance during the approval of the amendments to the constitution proposed by Cardoso. In this case, the Executive could not count on the legislative powers available for the implementation of ordinary bills. As is well known, constitutional changes require quite demanding conditions for the proponents: every proposed alteration has to be approved twice by both houses. Besides, one cannot avoid a roll-call. Those opposing the constitutional changes could count on an additional device to expose parliamentary decisions to public scrutiny: they could request parts of the text, usually the most unpopular ones, to be voted on separately. Using this device, during the process of voting for the constitutional amendments, the opposition could multiply the number of times that a topic was submitted to vote. In this way the opposition was able to increase the costs of approving these topics for the government supporters. Thus, the opposition's main strategy was to increase the number of roll-calls via amendments to the voting on parts of the text. The government, on the other hand, tried to prevent these votes. In the end, the supporters of the government altered the standing orders establishing a cap on the number of times separate parts of the text could be voted on separately.[11]

As a consequence of all these legislative battles, the number of roll-calls in this period was significant, especially during Cardoso's administration due to the amount of constitutional amendments introduced. Between January 1989 and the end of the 50th legislature (February 1999), 675 roll-calls took place in the Brazilian house of representatives. Usually, representatives vote by standing up or remaining seated according to the speaker's command, a procedure called symbolic voting. Recorded votes are mandatory for constitutional amendments and for legislation that is supplementary to constitutional norms (*leis complementares*). Otherwise it takes place only when requested by party leaders.[12]

Evidently, leaders will force a roll-call based on political calculations. They may hope to reverse decisions and or to increase their adversaries' political costs through the recording of their votes.[13] For this reason it is unlikely that party leaders will require a roll-call on non-controversial matters. They would not do so because their right to call for a recorded vote is limited: the standing orders dictate a period of one hour between the end of a roll-call and a new request.[14] In the case of constitutional amendments the number of votes can be multiplied through the request for a separate vote, which is an opposition strategy. Thus, roll-calls represent the most important and controversial issues considered by Congress as selected by the political process itself.[15] The table below shows the distribution of roll-calls by government and subject matter under consideration.

11 On the social security reform, see Figueiredo and Limongi (1998).
12 Leaders of micro parties do not have this right.
13 This is why opposition parties requested two thirds of the roll-calls.
14 This provision intends to curb the use of successive roll-calls as means to obstruct the decision-making process.
15 We excluded the cases in which the minority assembled less than ten per cent of the votes. For methodological details, see Limongi and Figueiredo (1995).

**Table 3.3: Distribution of Roll-Call Votes According to
Government and Subject Matter, 1989–99 (monthly average)**

Subject matter	Sarney	Collor	Franco	Cardoso	Total
Constitutional	-	0.26	0.40	3.80	1.90
Provisional Measure	0.89	1.37	0.18	0.36	0.62
Budget Bills	0.34	0.29	0.11	0.01	0.13
Ordinary Bills	0.75	2.13	1.60	3.40	2.45
Total	2.0	4.1	2.3	7.6	5.1

Source: Banco de Dados Legislativos, Cebrap.

As can be seen, the average number of decisions made by recorded vote is not irrelevant: five per month. However, their distribution by government and subject matter varies considerably. This variation reflects the nature of the legislative agenda of these governments and the role played by the opposition parties. Roll-calls on constitutional matters are concentrated on Cardoso's government. On the other hand, during Collor's administration, consistent with the pattern described above, provisional measures were more frequently decided by roll-call than during Cardoso's. Budgetary legislation does not seem to create legislative disputes. Peculiarities of the budgetary process explain the low degree of conflict identified in this area.[16] Ordinary legislation, on the other hand, gave rise to an increasing number of roll-calls. In sum, government's support in the legislature has been frequently tested.

Government Coalitions and Party Support for the Executive Agenda

The previous section has argued that the Executive is the main legislator in post-1988 Brazil. The Executive dominates the law-making process and legislative outcomes: it introduces the great majority of the laws enacted and its bills are rarely rejected. The analysis of the type and number of roll-calls shows that the Executive upper hand did not come about without political conflicts and changing priorities in the public policy agenda. In this section we seek to show that the Executive pre-eminence rested on disciplined political support from the parties included in the presidential coalition. Most bills presented by the president were approved because he could count on the support of a party coalition that participated in the var-

---

16   On the subject see Figueiredo and Limongi (2000).

ious cabinets formed during this period. The process of building government coalitions in the Brazilian presidential system does not differ greatly from the way prime ministers act under parliamentary systems.

The comparative literature takes for granted that government formation assumes diametrically different logics under presidential and parliamentary systems. Coalition government is the norm in several parliamentary regimes and this fact does not seem to cause any analytical problem.[17] However, in spite of evidence to the contrary, coalition governments are regarded as unfeasible under presidentialism. The president's prerogative of selecting the cabinet is usually taken as if presidents could — and, in fact, would — form a government without any political constraint.

The popular origins of the presidential mandate, according to this view, would induce presidents to overestimate their power and to resist sharing government control with parties. All non-presidential parties, on the other hand, would not choose to join a coalition since the failure of a president provides prospects for winning the presidency at the next election. The argument assumes that participation in a presidential cabinet would not bring electoral payoffs.[18] Hence, a president must rely exclusively on the support of his own party or on his personal power.

In the Brazilian presidential system, multiparty coalition governments were the rule rather than the exception: they corresponded to two thirds of the cabinets formed under democracy (in the 1945–64 and post 1985 period).[19] For the current period, the pattern has been for the formation of majority coalition cabinets on the basis of an alliance of ideologically contiguous parties, mostly at the centre and the right of the ideological spectrum. This pattern of coalition formation is a direct consequence of electoral results.

The distribution of seats in the Chamber of Deputies and the Senate shows that none of the three ideological blocs (left, centre or right) could have governed alone in this period. The right-wing parties, in reality, controlled just over 50 per cent of the seats throughout the 1991–94 legislative term, but their scant majority in the Senate did not allow Collor to govern with the exclusive support of the right-wing parties. Anyway, under Collor the right registered its best electoral performance. In the last two congressional elections, right-wing parties controlled around 40 per cent of the seats in the lower house.

17 Studies on government formation revolve around the definition of the parties that will form the coalition and the duration of the coalition. The possibility that a coalition will fail to materialise is rarely considered.
18 Jones sums up all these considerations (1995, p. 6).
19 Studies on Brazil include Abranches (1988); Amorim Neto (1995); and Meneguello (1998). For Latin America, see Deheza (1997).

From 1982 up to the 1990 election the left-wing parties considerably increased their share of seats in the chamber. But, since then electoral support for the leftist parties in congressional elections has been stable. The share of seats controlled by the leftist parties in the lower chamber in the last three legislatures stabilised at around 20 per cent. In the Senate the left-wing parties hold a very small percentage of seats.

Therefore, the parties in the centre (PMDB and PSDB) were in a very advantageous situation, controlling about one third of the lower chamber. Given this share of seats they became the pivots for the formation of any ideologically-connected majority. Table 3.4 presents information regarding the composition of the cabinets and the number of seats held by the coalition parties in the post-1985 period. As can be seen, most presidential coalitions were structured around the right and centre parties. Collor was the only president to dispense with the support of the centre parties.

Table 3.4: Government Coalitions, 1985–2000

Cabinets	Parties	Average Percentage of Seats*		Initial Date
		House	Senate	
Sarney I	PFL – PMDB	57.9	50.7	03/85
Sarney II	PFL – PMDB	56.5	64.0	10/88
Collor I	PFL – PDS – PTB (BLOCO)	47.9	36.0	03/90
Collor II	PFL – PDS – PTB (BLOCO)	52.6	45.9	04/92
Franco I	PFL – PMDB – PTB – PSDB – PSB	52.8	76.5	10/92
Franco II	PFL – PMDB – PTB – PSDB – PP	60.3	75.3	08/93
Cardoso I	PFL – PMDB – PTB – PSDB – PPB	58.0	76.5	01/95
Cardoso II	PFL – PMDB – PTB –PSDB – PPB	74.3	82.7	05/96

Sources: Banco de Dados Legislativos, Cebrap; Amorim Neto (1995) and Rachel Meneguello (1998) and *Relatórios da Presidência do Senado Federal* (different years).

* Cardoso's second term; the PTB is not represented in cabinet but is a member of the government coalition in Congress.

The first civilian government formed a two-party cabinet while subsequent governments built up multiparty cabinets. Fernando Collor, the first directly elected president, formed the only minority cabinet in the period. Despite his strategy of departing from the established parties, Collor did not completely disregard them. In fact, he organised a coalition of right-wing parties to support him in Parliament. In the lower house, the PFL led a parliamentary coalition, the so-called Parliamentary Bloc, that included the PTB, the PRN (the president's newly-formed party) and almost all small right-wing parties represented in the house. His first cabinet included few politicians from the PFL and PDS. His second cabinet included a greater number of politicians recruited from the same parties. Despite being supported by the same parties, this cabinet controlled a larger share of seats as a result of the 1990 congressional election.

From the beginning of his term Collor had a tense and conflictive relationship with the largest party in the legislature, the centrist PMDB. This relationship explains most political difficulties faced by his government. Before the 1990 election neither Collor nor the PMDB could benefit from mutual cooperation. Collor's campaign assumed an anti-establishment and anti-party stance. Moreover, the policies he intended to promote clashed with the PMDB's programme. Collor completed the changes to the political agenda already announced by Sarney's Plan Verão. The priority shifted from 'rescuing the social debt' to cutting the public debt via state reform. Given its political history, the PMPD could not back such a shift.

The 1990 election did not change the structure of the situation. The PMDB remained the largest party in the lower chamber. Hence this party was in a position to ask for greater concessions from Collor. The president, however, was not willing to concede and tried to outflank the PMDB by seeking support from the PSDB or PDT. The PSDB hesitated but decided not to join the government. A PDT–Collor agreement worked out for a while but it could not count on the unconditional support of the PDT's representatives on the floor. Neither the centre nor the centre-left accepted the idea that stabilisation and streamlining the state should have precedence over social measures.

Franco took up the government in the aftermath of Collor's impeachment and formed a coalition that represented a move towards the left. His second cabinet was more centrist. Fernando Henrique Cardoso was the first president to form a cabinet based on an electoral alliance (PSDB–PFL–PTB). However, compelled by an agenda that required constitutional reforms and, consequently, the support of a qualified majority, Cardoso included the PMDB in his first cabinet, and in the following year, during the voting on the social security reform, he also incorporated the PPB, the party farthest to the right of Brazil's ideological spectrum. Under Cardoso the PSDB and the PMDB endorsed the programme they were not willing to accept under Collor. The electoral success of the Real Plan made this shift easier.

In sum, over the whole period the relative strength of the right-wing parties was always superior to the strength of the parties on the left, therefore the centre-right coalition has been dominant on the floor. A typical conflict on the floor has been one in which the left-wing parties confront the centre-right parties. It is worth noting that even when the PSDB leaned-towards the Left, the Centre-Right coalition always controlled enough seats to form a comfortable majority. Divisions in which a centre-left coalition confronted the right-wing parties were rare and tended to occur exclusively during the Collor government. This type of conflict did not occur during the Cardoso administration.

So far, we have traced the existence of a presidential coalition from the distribution of portfolios. We now turn to the behaviour of the members of the coalition based on the voting record of the parties and the governmental leaders for the roll-call votes in the lower chamber. Evidently, not all roll-calls involved matters of executive interest. For this reason, from now on our analysis will be restricted to the recorded votes on what we call the executive agenda.

We considered part of the executive agenda those roll-calls referring to the bills introduced by the government or to those bills on which the government leader announced the position of the government. In both cases we identified the government interest and position on the matter. With this information, we verified whether or not the Executive received the backing of its coalition on the floor.

Applying these criteria, 474 out of the 675 valid roll-calls that took place in the lower chamber were considered part of the executive agenda. The government coalition was defined as 'unified' when all leaders followed the government orientation and 'not unified' when at least one party leader announced a position opposed to the government. Table 3.5 presents the votes of the members of the coalition in these two situations.

Table 3.5: Average Percentage of Votes from the Members of the Government Coalition Parties to the Presidential Agenda According to Party Leaders' Announced Position Roll-call votes — 1989–99*

Cabinets	Unified coalition		Non-Unified Coalition		Total	
	N	Per cent disc.	N	Per cent disc.	N	Per cent disc.
Sarney	7	88.1	1	19.2	8	79.5
Collor I	49	89.6	15	49.4	64	79.9
Collor II	10	92.7	-	-	10	92.7
Franco I	24	82.0	7	67.1	31	79.9
Franco II	5	96.5	2	73.9	7	90.0
FHC I	89	90.6	7	49.0	96	67.2
FHC II	245	89.7	13	67.0	258	87.5
Total	429	89.7	45	57.8	474	86.7

Source: PRODASEN; Banco de Dados Legislativos, Cebrap.
* Until February 1999, the end of the 50th legislature and corresponding to Cardoso's first term.

The data show that the members of the parties with portfolio — the members of the government coalition — do provide support for the executive agenda. Explicit opposition from a party included in the government coalition amounts to less than ten per cent of the cases, 45 out of 474.

Congress members that belong to the parties included in the government coalition vote with their leaders, i.e., they give political support to the executive's agenda. On average 86.7 per cent vote in accordance with the president's position. It is worth noting that support from the coalition did not vary across presidencies. The observed variation depends on the support given by the coalition parties. When these parties are unified the average support is around 90.0 per cent. The members' vote for the government falls to 57.8 per cent when the government loses the support of at least one of the parties from the coalition. Thus, the support provided by the members of the parties in the coalition to the government agenda is not unconditional. When party leaders oppose the government position, representatives vote according to their position and not according to the position of the government leader.

The data on roll-calls allow us to conclude that political parties are decisive players in the legislature. The decision-making process is far from chaotic. On the contrary, we can predict voting outcomes from the announced position of party leaders. Floor behaviour is rarely surprising. Government support thus depends on the position taken by coalition parties. Under Collor, the presidential coalition collected the highest percentage of defeats in the presidential agenda: 16 defeats for 72 non-constitutional roll calls, i.e. 22 per cent of the cases. Cardoso, on the other hand, lost only ten out of the 188 non-constitutional roll calls. Cardoso's coalition was further tested on 168 constitutional matters that require a 3/5 quorum, and it was defeated 15 times, only 8.9 per cent of the cases. Since, as we saw, the coalition discipline showed little variation, the difference between Collor and Cardoso rests on the size of the coalition they were able to put and keep together.

The pattern of party alliances on the floor obeys the principle of ideological contiguity. Based upon the indications of party leaders' orientation, we classified no less than 75.8 per cent of the roll-calls for the whole period as ideologically connected. Unmistakably non-contiguousroll-calls, the ones in which *ad hoc* alliances were formed, represent only 11.3 per cent of the cases. The remaining 13.5 per cent could not be classified because some leaders did not announce the party position on the vote.

When these cases are broken down according to government, one observes that the parties proved to be able to change their strategic alliances, which is just to say that they behaved as collective actors. The most conspicuous case concerns the alignment of the PFL with the PSDB. During the Collor administration the leaders of these two parties indicated similar votes in 42.5 per cent of the cases. Agreement between these parties rose to 92.1 per cent during Cardoso's first term.

The role of federalism deserves a special mention since it has been frequently cited as one of the obstacles to presidential action. More specifically, Abrucio (1998) and Samuels (1998) have stressed the importance of the
bancadas estaduais, organised around state governors, as obstacles to the executive capacity to implement its agenda. Analysis of roll-calls shows no significant variation per state. Applying an index of party similarity, it was
found that members of a given party from different states are much more
likely to vote in the same way than members of the same state from different parties. It would not be surprising that this is so for, say, the PFL and the
PT. However, what is more striking is that it is also true for the parties in the
same ideological bloc, the PFL and the PPB for instance. In other words:
Brazilian congressional parties behave as national parties. Representatives
vote as members of parties irrespective of the state they come from.[20]

These results contradict current interpretations regarding the existence
of institutional obstacles to executive action. The executive may have
problems forming majorities to implement some specific policies but the
origins of these problems are not institutional. They are political in the
sense that they depend on the distribution of votes and the positions of
the parties on the issues at stake.

Final Considerations

The concentration of institutional power and the centralisation of the
decision-making process are based on institutional prerogatives that are
attached to the office of the chief executive and/or party leaders.
Consequently this decision-making system differs sharply from models
that emphasise personal attributes and styles of leadership, such as the so-
called 'imperial presidentialism' seen as peculiar to Latin America. It also
differs from the model of 'delegative democracy'. In the policy-making
model identified here delegation does not come about as a direct and
unconditional relationship between the electorate and the president but
rather as a conditional delegation of institutional power to the president by
Congress. Today one can find similar institutional designs in other new
democracies in Latin America as well as in southern and eastern Europe.
These trends, referred to as 'rationalisation of parliaments', can also be
identified in the post-World War II European parliamentary democracies.[21] Agenda power and control over the legislative work is usually considered peculiar to parliamentary systems.[22] However, as the Brazilian
experience suggests, they can produce similar effects in presidential sys-

20   See Limongi and Figueiredo (2000) for details and further elaboration of the point.
21   On this phenomenon in various countries see Lauvaux (1993) and, on France, see
     Huber (1996)
22   Tsebelis (1995), p. 325.

tems. This institutional arrangement, regardless of the system of government, constrains parliamentary rights and thereby neutralises the so-called personal vote deriving from incentives in the electoral arena.

The centralisation of the decision-making process reduces the influence Congress members could exert individually by limiting their access to resources that could guarantee benefits to their clientele. In this way, the possibility of Congress behaving as an institutional obstacle to the government agenda as a consequence of the interest divergences between them is eliminated. That is to say, it affects directly the source of what is identified by the literature as the origins of 'governability crisis'. Agenda control contributes to prevent the occurrence of the latent institutional conflict that stem from the separation of powers. In short, it enhances governability understood as the government ability to pass its agenda.

The federalism and the consociative structure of the polity, the partisan fragmentation, the absence of partisan control in the electoral arena, in other words, all the institutional bases of political representation kept unchanged in the 1988 Constitution, did not inhibit the approval of highly unpopular constitutional amendments that went against the interests of a considerable part of the population as well as highly organised social groups. Similarly, in spite of the alleged weight of state and municipal interests in Congress, the government could also achieve the balance of federal revenues changing the fiscal decentralising measures set up by the constitution. Finally, inflationary control was implemented by an adjustment policy that managed to reduce government expenditure substantially, even though the results were lower than the governments hoped. Recessive measures with perverse social effects also received congressional approval. In sum, what is stressed here is that all these policy changes were achieved without the use of any extraordinary or unconstitutional measures, in spite of the controversies concerning the abuse of some of these powers, especially the provisional decree.

However, it does not follow that Congress was excluded from national political decisions nor that the Executive was able to impose its will against a majority in Congress. As we argued before, executive agenda powers can work as instruments for 'horizontal bargaining' between the government and its majority and not only as a means to overcome a 'vertical conflict' between the Executive and the Legislature, considered as separate branches of the government. Agenda power and control over the legislative process may be important mechanisms to protect the majority supporting the government against individual motivations to seek short-term and particularistic benefits. They may also help to preserve agreements between the government and its supporting parties on public policies.

Institutional instruments that give control over the agenda and the legislative process facilitate concerted action between the Executive and those party leaders who are members of a government coalition. They function as a constraint on the processing of the demands that, given the Brazilian representation system, are channelled into the National Congress. In other words, they enhance government efficiency.

As argued previously, the concentration of decision-making power is an institutional arrangement. It is the result of the choices made by con-stitution makers and Congress members and, for many of them, it was a question of guaranteeing precisely that 'governability'. That is to say, they sought to avoid Congress becoming a hindrance to executive action. Based on the evidence presented here it seems that the desired effect has been produced. Therefore, it would be unnecessary to change the system of government or to restrict parliamentary rights even more in the name of 'governability' and even more so to establish barriers to the political sys-tem. These sorts of decision can block the channelling of social demands through the legislature into the national decision-making process, unlike the present situation. There are no reasons to reduce the number of par-ties or to bestow more advantages on party leaders. It is simply not true that the Brazilian government finds itself immobilised as a result of exces-sive demands from society expressed directly in the political system.

The range of political reforms proposed with a view to fostering majoritarianism in the Brazilian policy-making system would further limit the role of Congress in the definition of the government's agenda and its autonomous influence in policy making. The decision-making pattern pre-vailing in Brazil today greatly increases the autonomous action of the Executive and the bureaucracy. Decisions are taken through negotiations among parliamentary party leaders, government experts and high-level bureaucrats at the expense of public debate on the floor of Congress, especially when discussing provisional measures. The visibility of public decisions is reduced as well as the flow of information to the public opin-ion. Consequently, the capacity of Congress to function as a countervail-ing power and a mechanism to control executive action also decreases, thereby affecting vertical control by citizens.

Nevertheless, Congress is an effective channel where different demands — stemming from local or corporatist interests but also from wider social sectors — can secure access to the political system. In a set-ting where the executive agenda was marked by economic priorities, Congress had an important role in the formulation of social policies. In this area, distributive policies with diffuse costs and concentrated gains were the exception rather than the rule. Congress approved social legisla-tion guaranteeing and expanding universal rights to citizens and establish-ing consumer and civil rights guarantees, environment protection, access to justice and punishments for discriminatory practices.[23] It is true that Congress has not been concerned with overseeing the Executive in a systematic and centralised way.[24] But it has established and improved a system of norms and procedures that regulates civil public action and the defence of collective rights to allow a decentralised control involving social movements, interest groups and citizens with regard to state actions. In this way, Congress defined its own agenda and contributed to diminishing the dissociation between the public and the government's agenda. With the proposed reforms this would hardly be possible.

23　Between 1989 and 1998, only 15 per cent of the social laws initiated by the legislature granted particularistic (group, local or personal) benefits, against 28 per cent of the laws initiated by the Executive (Figueiredo, 2000, p. 14)

24　On Congress oversight and parliamentary investigations see Figueiredo (2000).

CHAPTER 4

Democratisation and the Judiciary: Competing Reform Agendas

Fiona Macaulay

Introduction

The judiciary exercises multiple functions in a modern democratic society: upholding the rule of law, defusing social conflict, guaranteeing the collective and individual rights enshrined in the constitution and legal codes and creating a stable and predictable investment environment. Since the return to democratic civilian rule in 1985, interest groups, civil society and some politicians have acknowledged the Brazilian judiciary's role in relationship to political democracy, citizenship, equality and development and proposed a series of reform initiatives designed to improve the judiciary's performance in all these diverse dimensions. Consequently the question of the judiciary's contribution to the construction of the new democratic regime has appeared intermittently and insistently on the political agenda, but never at the top. Two waves of reform have occurred, the first during the Constituent Assembly of 1987–88, the second initiated in the latter part of the 1990s in an attempt to mend some of the perceived faults of the first. The reforms, both enacted and proposed, reveal underlying tensions and contradictions in government and society as to the proper role of the judiciary in a democratic, market-oriented society. Should the courts provide a stable and predictable investment environment to promote economic growth in an era of irreversible globalisation? Or is the judiciary's responsibility principally to provide an accessible channel through which citizens may exercise democratic control over the actions of the government? What impact do the relative inefficiency and inaccessibility of the courts have on the quality of civil liberties and citizenship? This chapter explores the dynamics of judicial reform in Brazil since 1985 and assesses the relative weight of political, economic and social considerations in the different mixes of reform proposals.

Democratisation in a mass society with civil society mobilisation brings with it heightened expectations with regard to the judiciary's ability to deliver over a very wide range of functions. The court system deals with civil, criminal, labour, electoral and military/policing issues, besides considering the legality and constitutionality of government laws and decrees. Its performance affects questions ranging from national economic policy right down to the micro level of facilitating and guaranteeing the citizenship of individuals. Establishing the rule of law within the national territory continues to be a challenge for the Brazilian criminal justice system, especially as the courts have been extremely slow and overburdened with cases. The judiciary's perceived, and real, inability to deal with rising levels of crime and new forms of social conflict, for example over land, generated by new social actors, leads some to adopt extralegal strategies. These may range from bribery or an avoidance of the courts on the one hand, to violence, vigilantism and death squad summary justice on the other. Continuing abuses of criminal suspects' human rights by the police, involving extrajudicial executions, torture and other forms of ill treatment and excessive force[1] are in part related to their mistrust of the justice system's capacity to deliver results.

Access to justice and the speed with which courts deal with cases has become an ever-more pressing issue, in order to tackle social demands on the courts and stem undesirable extralegal strategies, and also for broadly developmental/economic reasons. As market opening took hold in the 1990s, accompanied by privatisations of state sector enterprises and increased foreign direct investment, concern grew over the unstable investment environment in Brazil caused not only by inflation, but also by institutional arrangements, including the relics of the statist-corporatist framework, and the performance of the courts. Confidence in the courts on the part of business and the common citizen would be enhanced on the one hand by improving efficiency in terms of faster processing of cases, reduction of futile appeals and replica cases, and increased access, and on the other by removing the insulation and excessive autonomy of the courts. These broadly were the issues that emerged in the second wave of reform that followed on the heels of the first, problematic one.

Four broad aspects of the judiciary's contribution to democracy have occupied public debates and the agendas of reformers in this period: judicial independence and exercise of judicial review; internal management and accountability; differential access and treatment within the justice system; and modernisation and efficiency. The first issue dominated the 1980s, the other three framed the debates of the 1990s. These are now examined in turn, followed by an analysis of the political and institutional dynamic of attempts at reform over the last two decades.

The First Democratic Reforms

The reformers of the early democratisation period were concerned with the formal, procedural and institutional aspects of democracy, such as the proper separation of powers and protection of constitutional guarantees.

1   Amnesty International (1999) and Human Rights Watch (1998), São Paulo police ombudsman's office: www.ouvidoria-policia.sp.gov.br.

Democratic actors were acutely aware that the military government had reduced judicial independence[2] and wiped out powers of judicial review as the regime placed itself above the authority of the courts and above the 1946 Constitution.[3] That said, Brazilian courts had not remained completely supine in the face of repression, and did not suffer the same fate as other judiciaries in the region such as politicisation of the justice system, court packing and purges, progressive deprofessionalisation and the disappearance of the Public Ministry.[4] As a result, during the transition judicial independence became the overwhelming consideration, relegating to the back burner other matters such as access or efficiency.

During the *abertura* period in the early 1980s issues of court independence and efficiency briefly entered the political agenda as the major opposition party, the PMDB, pledged a judicial reform. However, prospects of such died along with its main proponent, Tancredo Neves, the PMDB president-elect. Vice-President Sarney, who assumed power, had no interest in such matters,[5] and spent his presidency battling with hyperinflation, ensuring he won an extra year in office, and attempting to rein in the more radical proposals of the Constituent Assembly of 1987–88. Reform was sidelined as neither the Executive nor the essentially conservative political class that remained in power through the regime change had any coherent project for the judiciary. The 43 articles of the 1988 Constitution that lay out the structure and powers of the courts and the public prosecution service bear the stamp of the chaotic process of drafting and the corporate interests of judges and lawyers groups whose influence shaped the final text. They accord the Brazilian courts more political and operational autonomy than anywhere else in Latin America. Arguably, the resultant hyper-autonomy and insulation created more problems than they solved.

---

2   Via the introduction of 17 institutional acts and 100 complementary acts.

3   Institutional Act (AI) No. 1 declared the military government's decrees the highest law in the land and acts of high command were excluded from judicial review. The number of judges in the Supreme Court was manipulated in order to get rid of uncooperative justices. The military could, on grounds of threat to national security, move cases from lower courts to the Supreme Court (with its approval). AI–5 gave the president power to remove or retire any sitting judge. In 1977 Congress was closed after opposing a bill to create an external oversight body for courts, a measure eventually appended to the Constitution.

4   Courts often challenged the government: the Supreme Federal Court kept ruling in favour of political detainees and in 1968 declared unconstitutional the National Security Law. See Pereira (1998) on the complex political role of the military courts, and Osiel (1995) for a comparison of the courts under military rule in Argentina and Brazil.

5   Indeed, as an ARENA (official government party) senator, he had supported a military government judicial reform bill that was opposed by the MDB.

Political Autonomy

The 1988 Constitution made Brazil's judiciary almost completely structurally independent of the Executive. The only exception is the Supreme Federal Court (Supremo Tribunal Federal — STF) whose members are appointed by the President of the Republic. However, the restoration of a classically republican separation of powers was accompanied by two other complicating developments. The first was the highly *dirigiste* and detailed nature of the Constitution, which effectively judicialised a vast range of social and economic as well as civil rights, shifting the terrain of social conflict from the government to the courts. The Constitution also required additional legislation to put its non-self-executing provisions into operation. Much of this legislation has not yet been drafted or passed, causing many mundane questions to be referred to the federal courts for them to rule on the legality of the government's action or inaction.[6] The second was the reprise of the long association in Brazil between democratisation and decentralisation. After the period of centralising authoritarian military rule, the pendulum swung back, granting Brazil's states, and especially the municipalities, an unprecedented level of political and fiscal autonomy. This tendency was reflected in the judicial apparatus, with lower court judges acquiring a high level of discretion untrammelled by interference from higher courts. Brazil is the only federal country in which the decisions of higher courts exert no power of binding precedent over lower courts with regard not only to civil and criminal matters, but also to constitutional questions. The lack of binding precedent (known in Brazil as the *súmula de efeito vinculante* or SEV) has profound implications for the operational efficiency of the courts, for the dynamic of executive–judicial relations and for the collective identity of the judiciary as a democratic actor.

The courts' power of judicial review is a crucial tool in countering the autocratic inclinations of many governments, military and civilian, and as such has been a chief concern in redemocratising polities in Latin America.[7] The particular form of judicial review in operation in Brazil lies at the heart of debates about the judiciary's democratic functions. It has been characterised as a 'hybrid' system: it contains elements of the *diffuse* model employed in the USA, by which any judge may rule on the constitutionality of a law as a matter *incidental* to any type of court case under consideration. These combine with aspects of the *concentrated* model of many European countries in which the power to assess *direct* challenges, to the constitutionality of a law in the abstract, is the monopoly of a specially designated constitutional court kept separate from the main body of the

---

6   The Constitution required 285 ordinary laws and 41 complementary laws (cited in Rosenn, 1998 footnote 13).
7   Domingo (1999).

judiciary.[8] The Brazilian STF took on judicial review as its chief — but not sole — responsibility when a new Supreme Court of Justice (Superior Tribunal de Justiça — STJ)[9] was formed in 1988 specifically to take away from the STF the burden of hearing routine appeals. This strategy failed as the STF ended up ruling on two types of cases. On the one hand, it handles cases and appeals passed on from the lower courts in which the constitutionality of an issue is incidental, not the main concern. However, as a quasi-constitutional court it also holds the concentrated power to adjudicate on Direct Actions of Unconstitutionality (*Ações Diretas de Inconstitucionalidade* — ADINs), a challenge against any federal or state law that may be brought by a wide variety of actors ranging from state governors to public prosecutors, to political parties and even, significantly, civil society organisations such as trade unions, professional groups and the Bar Association.

This hybrid arrangement has produced contradictory outcomes for governability and democratic accountability. The diffusion of judicial review potentially gives to the plaintiff and the judge extraordinary veto power over the democratically elected government. It has been a source of great frustration to successive governments, not simply because local court rulings nullify the effect, at least temporarily, of a law, directive or decree, but also because the sources of the challenge are multiple, sometimes contradictory, engage the government in expensive legal disputes and fail to settle the matter once and for all. Each lower-level federal court remains autonomous with regard to its interpretation of the law regardless of how the STF rules, whether on appeal or in the first hearing. This has produced what is referred to contemptuously as the *indústria dos liminares* (injunction industry), a free-for-all for lawyers when certain controversial government rulings create flurries of lawsuits and interim court rulings. When President Collor decreed in 1990 the notorious provisional decree 168, freezing everyone's bank accounts and assets, tens of thousands of legal challenges were unleashed in the federal courts of first and second instance, while the STF itself declined to rule directly of the legality of the decree. The number of cases entered in the federal justice system rocketed from 193,709 in 1988 to 725,993 in 1991, with a nearly threefold increase between 1990 and 1991.[10] Unsurprisingly, without a corresponding boost in resources and personnel the courts were unable to cope with the surge. Whilst in 1988 the federal courts were hearing as many cases as they received, by 1991 two-thirds of cases went unresolved, contributing to a huge backlog that amassed during the 1990s. The Collor government responded by entering an appeal in each of these thousands of cases until

8   Arantes (1997).
9   I shall refer to the STF and the highest courts of each branch of justice (*tribunais superiores*) as supreme courts or by their Portuguese acronym.
10   Arantes (1997), p.161.

they all reached the STF, completely paralysing it. It also attempted to restrict judicial review to the STF, which had indicated it would not rule against the government's anti-inflationary measures, and to eliminate the judicial review power of the lower courts. All subsequent governments have proposed the introduction of binding precedent. Thousands of the 60–70,000 cases that reach the STF every year are identical and at present the STJ receives 5,000 cases on appeal a week. The current system has led, in the view of many, to a clogging up of the court system, the creation of legal uncertainty, and a situation in which the Executive is constantly unsure which of its measures will survive without legal challenge. Consequently this question dominated the second round of judicial reform initiated in the 1990s.

The concentrated and direct form of judicial review, the ADIN, is a more manageable and less volatile instrument from a government perspective, although the STF's decisions do not constitute binding precedent in this case either.[11] Since 1988 some 175 ADINs have been submitted every year, with a peak of 255 in 1990 and 235 in 1991. Around a quarter have been submitted by, respectively, civic associations, particularly trade unions, state governors and state prosecutors. Political parties, overwhelmingly on the left, account for an eighth on average, although this rose sharply in the years 1995–98 under the Cardoso government.[12] This use of the ADIN by the opposition, both in Parliament and outside, has been identified with a 'judicialisation of politics' in Brazil in which the left, bereft of a viable national political alternative to the government's economic policies and marginalised within an already sidelined legislature, has chosen to take its battles with the government to the courts rather than to the floor of the chamber or the ballot-box. This is borne out by a breakdown of the legislation being challenged: the left-wing parties are concerned overwhelmingly with decrees issued by the Federal Executive in the economic area. This recourse to the courts by the opposition is due in part to increased executive dominance over the timing and content of the legislative agenda since 1985, exemplified in the steady rise in the issuing of provisional measures by the president of the republic, an executive prerogative that replaced the much-criticised Decree Law of the military government. In the period 1995–97 128 provisional decrees were issued, over 55 per cent of them on economic policy. Of all the bills enacted in

---

11 Curiously the only binding precedent wielded by the STF is in respect to Declaration of Constitutionality Actions, a tool created in 1993 allowing the President of the Republic, Senate, or Chamber of Deputies, or Attorney General of the Republic to head off the legal challenge of an ADIN by having a law declared constitutional in advance. However, it has been employed very rarely (Arantes and Nunes, 1999, Arantes, 2001).

12 Vianna (1999) and Castro (1997).

the Chamber of Deputies in this period, 80 per cent had been introduced by the Executive.[13] The Executive has retained this power since it acquired it under military rule.[14]

To what extent then does judicial review rein in the excessive political powers of the Executive, and how well do the courts arbitrate between Executive and Legislature? The evidence shows that the STF is rather parsimonious in upholding ADINs and tends, in general terms, to support the government's policies.[15] Very few provisional decrees have been defeated in the courts in this manner. This is due to two factors. The first is the inevitably political character of a constitutional court. The STF justices, in common with other countries, are appointed by the president after approval by the Senate. Indeed, two ex-ministers of justice sit in the court.[16] One would therefore suppose them to be selected for their sympathy with the broad aims of the government, particularly in the economic management field. One, Nelson Jobim, as a deputy then as minister, was responsible for submitting bills to Congress supporting binding precedent power for decisions of the STF, a position advocated by the STF and STJ contrary to the opinion of the majority of judges. The second factor is the over-detailed and inflexible character of the 1988 Constitution which, combined with the diffuse and incidental element of judicial review in Brazil, creates the potential for governability gridlock. The STF's caution in relation to ADINs would appear to offer a counterbalance.

The diffuse form of judicial review was adopted in 1981 along with a federal model of government at a time when enhancing the power of local courts permitted a necessary accommodation of regional political differences. With the current trend to devolve greater fiscal, administrative and political power to the states, a reconcentration of power in any realm is considered authoritarian. As the bulk of judicial activities falls under the aegis of the state governments, not of the federal government, diminution of the jurisdiction of the state level courts is viewed as an attack on the states' autonomy. Despite the strength of such feeling, the federal government has, in several areas, begun to rein in the excessive powers of the states and to re-establish federal restraints.[17] The current decentralised system has been robustly

13   See Pereira (2000), tables 4 and 6.
14   In the period 1946–63, the Executive was the author of, on average, 40 per cent of bills approved in Congress. Around 50 per cent were initiatives of the legislature and around ten per cent of the Judiciary. This reversed under the military, a pattern continued to the present day. See Figueiredo and Limongi (1999), figure 1, p. 49.
15   Castro (1997).
16   Maurício Corrêa, minister under Sarney, and Nelson Jobim, minister under Cardoso.
17   For example, the so-called Camata Law restricted state governments to spending no more than 60 per cent of its budget on the payroll (25 per cent for municipal governments) whilst the Law of Fiscal Responsibility punishes municipal and state officers for spending beyond their means.

defended by the lower ranks of the judiciary and, initially, by the Left, as a bulwark against the potential politicisation and capture of the STF by the Executive and as a means of democratising channels of dissent. However, in reality this 'citizen' power was a chimera. Courts ground to a halt under the mountain of cases, and the STF rarely ruled against the government on final appeal. The higher courts deal with the thousands of identical claims (which form 90 per cent of appeals to the STF) by automatically applying pre-determined judgments, making a mockery of the idea that every case is examined on its individual merits. Judges also tend to follow informally the rulings of higher courts for they know that a contrary ruling will be overturned on appeal.[18] This sort of access for all has become the wrong sort of access, and therefore results in access for none.[19] Moreover it embroils the government in expensive litigation.[20] Indeed, in 1996 the government agreed not to contest some 250,000 cases in the federal courts as it was simply not worth the cost. Many cases drag on, however, because the federal government contests them, appeals and delays making payments mandated by the court in order to save money.

The legal remedies suggested for this swamping of the courts have included the introduction of binding precedent and of a 'filter' system by which only cases of constitutional or legal relevance would be accepted by the higher courts. The latter would also have the power to take over such cases from the lower courts via a mechanism known as *incidente de inconstitucionalidade*, akin to *avocatória*, a tool introduced by the military regime. Opponents of such 'formalistic' measures maintain that these will increase Executive control over the judiciary while contributing little to clearing the backlog, as the problem lies more in the lack of resources (staff, infrastructure), procedural issues (endless appeals and delaying tactics are allowed by law), and the need for greater access to justice via small claims courts.

Operational Autonomy

While the independence of the judiciary is a *sine qua non* for a democratic regime, it potentially conflicts with the increasing consensus in Latin America as to the importance of democratic scrutiny and control of public institutions, including the courts. Since 1988 the Brazilian courts have wielded exclusive powers to manage their own financial, administrative and disciplinary matters when external oversight, imposed under the military, was removed. Budgets, approved by the state legislatures or National

18   Rosenn (1998), p. 27.
19   Prillamen (2000).
20   A survey carried by the STJ revealed that of 87,628 cases proceeding through the federal courts between January and August 2000, 74,438 (85 per cent) were cases contested by the federal government, treasury, national savings bank (Caixa Econômico Federal) or social security institute (INSS) *Estado de São Paulo*, 5 September 2000.

Congress, are regularly overspent, the shortfall made up by the treasury. As senior judges set their own salaries, pensions and staffing, resources are concentrated in the upper echelons. In the five highest courts 88 justices are serviced by 5,000 staff.[21] A judge in the STJ earns more than the president of the republic and enjoys 60 days' holiday, a free furnished apartment, car and driver and medical expenses. The new STJ headquarters cost $170 million, including a swimming pool and a ballroom, providing accommodation for 81 judges although there are currently only 33. The maldistribution of resources in the system results in the lower courts being desperately short of funds and of staff. By law there should be one judge per 25,000 inhabitants. Due to a 20 per cent shortfall of judges throughout the country in 2001, there were 31,000 inhabitants per judge.[22]

It was clear soon after the passing of the 1988 reforms that judicial autonomy had gone too far, leaving the door open to corruption and nepotism. The judiciary came to be viewed as excessively insulated from public scrutiny and from current concerns.

If the judicial branch could not keep its own house in order, the other branches would have to impose some form of external regulation. However, this suggestion was initially fiercely opposed. Judges threatened to strike over a 1996 law forbidding judges from employing unqualified relatives, and did strike in 1999 in protest at the Senate subcommission set up by Senator Antonio Carlos Magalhães to investigate evidence of graft in the judiciary. The new São Paulo regional labour appeals court (TRT) building had cost US$230 million to build, of which 75 per cent was embezzled by retired Labour Court Judge Nicolau dos Santos Neto via backhanders from constructors. This particular scandal provoked public outrage, firstly at the perceived lack of transparency and levels of profligacy, and secondly at the practice of impunity or special treatment for the privileged. Public opinion undermined corporativist resistance to external control[23] and the 2000 reform bill sent to the Senate proposed the establishment of a National Justice Council (Conselho Nacional de Justiça — CNJ), an idea put forward initially by the left and then supported by the Bar Association.[24] This would be composed of nine judges, two representatives of the prosecution service, two lawyers and two independent citizens appointed by Parliament with a remit to demand or oversee disciplinary inquiries into particular judges, as well as to monitor the management of the courts. The presence of the Bar Association and two lay people is a triumph for those who argued for civil society involve-

---

21 Each Supreme Court justice has 45 staff, while those in the labour courts have 65.
22 Data from 2001. Banco de Dados da Justiça: www.stf.gov.br.
23 A similar proposal was defeated by the judges' lobby in the 1987–88 Constituent Assembly.
24 Constitutional amendment put forward by federal deputy José Genoíno of the Workers' Party (PT).

ment.[25] A similar council was proposed to oversee the prosecution service. In addition, state appeals courts would acquire a 'special body' to deal with administrative issues as well as ombuds offices (*ouvidorias*). Other proposals for increasing internal democratisation and removing unjustifiable perks have also been aired, including changes to the system for promoting judges and to the guarantee of life tenure, restricting appointments to the STF and STJ to limited periods, eliminating the privileged forum for judges accused of common crimes, and an end to the long court recess.

Democratising Treatment and Access

If the Brazilian judiciary is independent, it is not necessarily impartial, particularly at a very local level, where informal relations between members of the judiciary, police and the local political and economic elite tend to form a power nexus that frequently ensures impunity for the powerful and an 'over-zealous' application of the law for socially marginal or disruptive groups such as rural trade unions. Differential access to the courts for dispute resolution and differential treatment by the justice system are two sides of the same coin. The old phrase 'for my enemies the law, for my friends, anything'[26] sums up the social stratification entrenched via both formal provisions and informal practices in the operation of the criminal justice system — courts, police and the prison system. Those without the power to exert influence on the system find themselves victims of the lack of accountability in the system, whereas the powerful find many legal and extralegal escape routes.[27] One survey found that 95.7 per cent of interviewees agreed that a poor person would be dealt with by the criminal justice system much more severely than a rich person.[28]

All reform efforts have sidestepped this inequality embedded in the justice system. Politicians in elected office and legal officials continue to enjoy the perk of *foro privilegiado*. If they face criminal charges, either for common crimes or offences linked to their office, they are tried in a higher court, rather than in the courts of first instance.[29] This leads to absurd sit-

25 The composition and remit of the CNJ has been much debated in the course of the proposed reforms of the 1990s, with gradual acceptance that some non-judges would sit on the council. For a full discussion see Sadek (2001b).

26 Attributed to President Getúlio Vargas.

27 For example, the number of appeals that the Criminal Procedure Code allows a defendant is regarded as excessive by many criminal justice experts. A good lawyer can delay the conclusion of a case for years.

28 CPDOC–FGV/ISER (1996).

29 The STF currently tries, for common crimes, the president, vice-president, members of Congress, its own justices and the Attorney General, and for common crimes and administrative ones the justices of the state appeals courts and diplomatic missions. The state appeals courts try mayors, state judges and prosecutors. Regional federal tribunals try judges of the federal, military and labour courts, and locally-based federal prosecutors for common and administrative crimes.

uations: in September 2000 the STJ was obliged to hear the case of a man whose dogs attacked his neighbour's parrots[30] because the dog-owner was a prosecutor in the supreme labour court. The bill submitted in 2000 even extended this right to two new categories, members of the armed forces and ministers of state, although it limits protection only to those still in office. Similarly, parliamentary immunity from prosecution for federal and state deputies and senators has been interpreted to include not only activities related to their public office,[31] but also to common crimes, with the result that several representatives have serious criminal charges pending, the cases suspended for as long as they hold office.[32]

Privilege does not end at the courtroom door. A decree passed in 1941 entitles federal cabinet members, state governors and secretaries, mayors, city councillors, chiefs of police, state and federal legislators, armed forces and police officers, judges and anyone who has ever served on a jury or has a university degree to *prisão especial*, namely, conditions of detention while awaiting trial that are greatly superior to the overcrowding, violence and lack of hygiene inflicted on the vast majority of the prison population. In essence, elite-class prisoners are guaranteed rights accorded, on paper, to all detainees under Brazil's domestic law and commitments to international human rights conventions. Public condemnation of such special treatment,[33] in violation of the constitutional principle of equality before the law, has been fired by a series of high level corruption scandals since 1985 and an increasingly active role by the media and prosecution service in exposing those who presume themselves above the law. The other side of the coin is the violation of the civil liberties of low-income or status criminal suspects and convicted prisoners.[34] Despite the constitutional guarantee of free legal aid to needy defendants, the service is understaffed, provoking long delays and provides such a cursory defence as to undermine the principle of a fair trial. The widespread practice of torture in police stations as a method of investigation,[35] the primacy of the confession over

---

30 He was charged under article 31 of the penal code ('lack of care in the handling of animals').

31 According to article 53 legislators may not be arrested, except when caught *in flagrante* committing an unbailable crime, or tried without the prior permission of their House.

32 In 1999 in high profile cases, two federal deputies were stripped by the Chamber of Deputies of their immunity for their clear involvement in murders. Proposals to remove immunity for criminal acts are currently under debate.

33 Collor abolished *prisão especial* in 1991 but, as he did not replace it with a new legal provision, it remained in place by default. In 2001, a reform introduced under Cardoso retained the status of 'special prisoner' but restricted special treatment to a separate cell and transport of the same standard given to other prisoners

34 See Amnesty International (1999) and Human Rights Watch (1998).

35 United Nations (2001).

other forms of evidence, and the effective presumption of guilt with regard to lower class suspects underscores the dualism inherent in the procedures and culture of the justice system.

Access to justice underpins any notion of civil rights. Carvalho (1995) argues that Brazil has reversed the Marshallian sequence in which different sorts of rights — civil, political and social — are acquired. Social rights, for certain sectors of the population,[36] were granted from the top down by Vargas during his authoritarian revolution of the 1930s and 1940s and the Labour courts continue to deliver those corporatist benefits. Political rights were completed with the return to democracy in 1985 and the extension of the franchise to illiterates[37] and are relatively well guaranteed by the electoral courts.[38] However, civil rights, most essentially the rights to physical integrity, to a fair trial and to adequate redress against abuses committed by the state, are still very insecure in Brazil for the majority of the population. For many even the most basic elements of legal existence and citizenship — birth, death and marriage certificates, ID and work cards — have been beyond their financial reach, obtainable only at expense through the notorious monopoly of the *cartórios*, the civil and land registry offices.[39]

A common theme among judicial reformers of the twentieth century has been the need to increase access to the courts via decentralisation of the court system,[40] bringing it closer to the population and reducing access costs, and through the installation of specialist courts equipped to use fast-track procedures. Provision to set up small claims courts (*juizados especiais*) to deal with minor civil and criminal cases was passed in law by the military in 1984, enshrined in the 1988 Constitution and regulated by law in 1995. These new courts are guided by the principles of speed, informality, self-representation, oral argumentation and direct plaintiff/defendant interaction with the judge. Judgements are unappealable, thus unburdening higher courts. In early 2001 a similar bill was put forward to create a similar provision in the federal justice system to handle cases involving claims to the value of six minimum wages. The small claims courts represent a

36   These rights were restricted to formal sector workers, both public and private, and were contingent on membership of recognised unions. For the 'outsiders' in this arrangement, that is those in the informal sector, there was no legal protection whatsoever.

37   Bethell (1994).

38   It is interesting that both the labour courts and electoral courts enjoy a much greater degree of public confidence than the civil courts; for example 80.8 per cent expressed medium to high approval of the labour courts in contrast to 64.5 per cent in reference to the civil courts (Pandolfi et al., 1999, p.104).

39   Even though the Constitution guarantees that these will be provided free of charge to the poor, it has required subsequent leigislation and action by local authorities to make this a reality.

40   Lins e Silva (1997).

trade-off in which speedy efficient resolution of a larger number of cases, possibly of small financial value overall, but of importance to the litigant, overrides the previously defended principle that democratic access had to guarantee every litigant's right to an appeal in every kind of case. The civil *juizados especiais* have been something of a success to date. By 1999 there were 2,564 such courts throughout Brazil and they handled 1,096,871 cases and resolved 988,937. However, there is evidence that even these courts are becoming oversubscribed as demand grows.[41] Other attempts to promote alternative dispute resolution include both government and NGO initiatives such as the Integrated Citizenship Centres in São Paulo, and Viva Rio's *Balcão de Direitos* (Legal Aid Counter) in Rio de Janeiro and elsewhere, both set up to offer free legal services to low-income communities.[42] It is a feature of the federal system in Brazil that the key legal and institutional frameworks affecting the performance of the justice system — constitutional provisions, legal codes of all descriptions — must be fought over at national level, while the actual provision of justice occurs largely at state level, where a wide variety of solutions to the issue of access is evident. That diversity reflects the history of the judicial apparatus and civil society of each state, but lies beyond the scope of this chapter.

Efficiency and Modernisation

A common element of judicial reform in Latin America has been a streamlining of the court system, removing redundant elements and adding new, specialist branches of justice in an attempt to allocate responsibility and resources more efficiently, speed the processing of cases and reduce transaction costs.[43] Survey and anecdotal evidence identifies an inefficient judiciary as a major institutional bottleneck restricting economic growth and development, as well as governability. A recent survey shows that small and medium Brazilian businesses tend to avoid the courts where possible, even at a loss to themselves.[44] The opportunity cost of judicial underperformance — lost contracts and investments — is estimated to be far greater than the actual costs of litigation. Recent reforms have proposed a horizontal and vertical redistribution of resources with certain branches being downsized, and new specialised courts being created, although there is no proposal as

41　Azevedo (2000). The 2000 reform proposed that each specialised branch of the Judiciary should set up 'mobile courts' (*justiça itinerante*) and decentralise its activities, setting up local courts if necessary. In Amapá boats and buses take the entire court to the population in remote areas.
42　Ribeiro and Strozenberg (2001). The scheme currently deals with 6,000 requests a year. In 2000 this was extended to Roraima, Pernambuco, Paraná and Rio Grande do Sul, and now to the Federal District.
43　Hammergren (1998).
44　Pinheiro (2000).

yet to create a small claims court to handle business litigation (only individ
uals, not companies, may use the other small claims courts).

Brazil sustains five parallel court systems, each of which supports lower
courts, state or regional appellate courts and supreme courts (see Figure
4.1). These are: the ordinary civil and criminal courts, organised at state
level; the federal courts which deal with any matters of federal or consti
tutional relevance; and the specialised federal justice system consisting of
the electoral courts,[45] the military courts and the labour courts, the latter
two having, for different reasons, attracted the attentions of reformers.[46]

Figure 4.1: Structure of the Judicial Branch

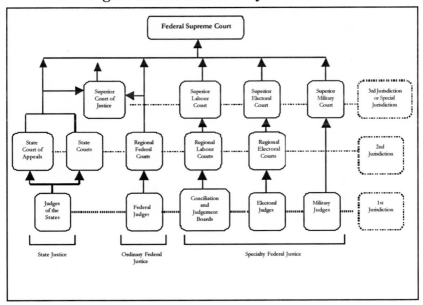

The Labour Courts were born of the corporatist system of state–labour rela
tions instituted by President Vargas during the Estado Novo, and oversee the
implementation of the labour legislation contained in the CLT (Consolidated
Labour Law of 1943).[47] They thus represent the apex of the statist bureau

---

45   The electoral courts are the cheapest to run, at around R$1 million, and least contro
      versial. They preside over a modernised electoral system (now 100 per cent electron
      ic voting) which has managed to eliminate the old practices of electoral fraud. See
      Sadek (1995).
46   The 1988 Constitution allowed states to set up specialist *varas agrárias* (land courts)
      whilst the 2000 reform proposed abolishing the Tribunais de Alçada, which were
      originally small claims courts and became effectively a parallel state courts of appeal.
47   www.tst.gov.br

cratic apparatus that President Cardoso intended to sweep away with his agenda of modernising institutional reforms. In the late 1990s, various proposals were made, such as abolishing the Labour Courts altogether,[48] eliminating the Supreme Labour Court (Tribunal Superior do Trabalho — TST)[49] by merging it with the STJ, or reducing its regional presence. These courts allegedly cost Brazil R$231 million a year, supporting 1,109 local arbitration councils, 24 regional appeals courts and the TST, with a typical labour suit costing R$1,800, compared to R$500 in the federal, civil and criminal courts. Scrutiny of the labour courts came to a head in 1999 with the TRT scandal. Nonetheless, the labour courts are also backed by substantial interest groups, namely the trade unions and employers' federations because they provide a functional mechanism of channelling labour-employer disputes. The amount of litigation increased exponentially from 164,179 cases initiated and 183,476 cases solved in the 1980s to 590,755 and 467,583 cases, respectively, in the 1990s. The 2000 reform proposed replacing one half of the labour judges, the so-called *juizes classistas*, who are laypeople without legal training, selected from employers associations and unions, with career judges. The *juntas de conciliação e julgamento* would be replaced by *varas de justiça de trabalho* and arbitration services would be offered to prevent so many cases coming to court. Both moves point in the direction of professionalisation, on the one hand, and the growing preference for alternative dispute resolution, on the other.

The military courts symbolise part of the 'authoritarian débris'[50] left over from the military regime, despite their long history.[51] They hold jurisdiction not only over strictly military crimes committed by the armed forces, but also over crimes committed against civilians by the state-level military police. The latter were central to the military regime's repressive project, and pursued both political dissidents and suspected criminals with the same violent zeal.[52] Since the return to civilian rule they have continued to commit grave human rights abuses against civilians. The military courts form a bulwark of institutional impunity as military prosecutors regularly shelve cases on spurious technical grounds and military judges generally acquit.[53] Human rights advo-

---

48   This was proposed in the report of the first rapporteur of the Special Commission, PSDB deputy Aloysio Nunes Ferreira, general secretary to President Cardoso.
49   A proposal put forward in 2000 by the President of the Bar Association, later voted down by the membership.
50   A term coined by Cardoso, when he was a Senator.
51   The Superior Military Court (Superior Tribunal Militar – STM) was founded in 1808 and as such is the oldest high court in the country. An account of its development may be found at www.stm.gov.br.
52   Pinheiro (1991); Barcellos (1992).
53   Ignacio Cano (1999). Most military prosecutors prior to 1996 accepted the police version of killings of civilians, namely that they died in armed confrontations or while resisting arrest. Another study (Cano, 1997) shows that the majority of civilians killed by the military police are victims of extrajudicial executions.

cates regard the demilitarisation of the police as fundamental to strengthening the rule of law and increasing the democratic accountability of law enforcement but attempts to bring the military police under civilian jurisdiction failed due to the powerful lobby of the military police in Congress.[54] The courts are also relatively overendowed with resources. Their budget for 1999 was R$94 million, close to that of the STF, allocated R$112 million. The Supreme Military Tribunal has 15 justices and in 1997 judged a mere 464 cases compared to the thousands dealt with in the other supreme courts. Given the delicacy of the matter, a sleight of hand was employed in the 2000 reform, which proposed a reduction in the number of judges from 15 to nine. Although abolition of the courts was not possible, all references to the 'military police' were removed, opening the way to a future constitutional amendment allowing states to abolish this controversial institution. Regional military courts would exist in states with more than 20,000 military personnel (*efetivo militar*) not 'military police', and would judge 'military crimes' (here the crime is defined, not the author).

Improving the efficiency of the criminal courts depends on the parallel reform of the other institutions of the criminal justice system and on improving cooperation between the three main elements, police, prosecution service and judges. The reform of the police has been the subject of much heated debate in recent years and is currently stalled, as the military police's allies in Congress resist its abolition or merger with the civil police.[55] The performance of the courts also depends on a revision of the substantive codes and procedures, principally the Penal Code, Procedural Code and the Law of Penal Execution. This revision initiated in 1999 under minister of justice José Carlos Dias, was designed to tackle the excessive formalism and irrational system of appeals.

Dynamics of Reform

Judicial reform in Brazil has been internally generated, in contrast to other countries in Latin America emerging from authoritarian rule or civil conflict over the last two decades where external assistance agencies, such as the World Bank, USAID or the IDB have strongly shaped the reform agenda. Brazil has excluded itself from their attentions for several reasons. Firstly, the

---

54   A bill by PT federal deputy Hélio Bicudo was eventually passed in 1996, but was watered down so that only intentional homicides of civilians committed by military police on duty would go to a civilian court. However, the police themselves investigate and determine 'intentionality'.

55   Most policing in Brazil is carried out under the remit of the two state-level police forces, the military police and civil police. The former are responsible for crime prevention on the streets, while the latter are responsible for crime investigation. There is very poor coordination between the two.

size and diversity of the country militate against institutional dynamics that dictate that 'pilot projects' are more manageable and measurable in smaller countries. Secondly, Brazil has a 180-year tradition of professionalisation of legal agents, dating back to the founding of the law schools in Recife and São Paulo, and the Brazilian judiciary has never been as politicised or sub-servient as in other countries in the region. Finally, nationalism at the high-est level of the judiciary has created an attitude of self-sufficiency and sus-picion of external reform blueprints, as well as a belief that the World Bank's model is essentially geared towards the interests of international capital. These elements, combined with a gradual and non-conflictive transition to democracy produced a confidence within the legal profession that it could put its own house in order in the new democracy.

Reform of the judiciary has been a stop-start process since 1985, fre-quently buffeted by external events and taken on by proponents of sharply differing priorities.[56] Organised interest groups took advantage of the tran-sition conjuncture and the absence of a strong executive project in the Constituent Assembly to acquire new, exclusive powers. Support for such hyper-autonomy quickly dissipated and in 1992 well-known human rights advocate, lawyer and Workers' Party (PT) federal deputy Hélio Bicudo sub-mitted a constitutional amendment proposing a series of fundamental reforms.[57] However, in a year in which President Collor was being impeached, and inflation rocketed, it was buried under more pressing par-liamentary business. In 1993 federal deputy Nelson Jobim attempted to introduce binding precedent for all the rulings of the supreme courts and the decisions on the merit of constitutional challenges. In 1995 a special parliamentary committee was set up and a draft bill prepared by PFL fed-eral deputy Jairo Carneiro. Although shelved in 1996, it did prompt debate and the formation of a group of progressive judges, the Association of Judges for Democracy. In March 1999 the judiciary hit the headlines once more when Senator Antonio Carlos Magalhães set up a Senate committee of inquiry to investigate the TRT embezzlement scandal. A powerful figure in the PFL, he had set his populist sights on the judiciary as an easy target, given the low level of public confidence in the courts. As he threatened to turn this into a full-blown inquiry into the judiciary as a whole, the govern-ment was forced to seize back the initiative by reviving the special commit-tee. Its first rapporteur, PSDB federal deputy Aloysio Nunes Ferreira, sub-mitted an initial report, followed by a substitute report of the subsequent rapporteur, PSDB federal deputy Zulaiê Cobra, published in September

---

56   For a full account of the differences between the various reform bill drafts, see Sadek (2000a)

57   PEC 96–A/92. To this a number of amendments were added: 112/95, 127/95, 215/95, 368/96 and 500/97.

1999. Finally approved with changes in November 1999, the Constitutional Amendment Bill was sent to await its final vote in the Senate in June 2001.[58]

In this second phase of reform the initiative came first from the left, lost steam in the Congress and was only revived by the government benches in order to head off another challenge, this time from the right. It has been hypothesised that the Executive will leave certain issues in the hands of a legislative committee rather than initiating legislation itself either when it agrees with the likely orientation of the committee, or when it has too little information on the subject and wishes to wait for the committee to fill that gap.[59] The internal momentum for reform was not directed by the Executive for a number of reasons. The Ministry of Justice in contemporary Brazil is essentially a political position, often filled by nominees selected to satisfy the ministerial quotas of the parties of the governing coalition backing the president. The quality of ministers has varied greatly, along with their background and interest in legal matters, and they have more often operated as political 'fixers' for the president than as legal reformers. Since 1994 reform initiatives were revived briefly under ministers of justice Nelson Jobim (1994–96), José Carlos Dias (1999–2000) and Miguel Reale Júnior, all committed reformers in their own manner, but ignored under the others. Turnover has also been a problem: between 1985–2002 Brazil had 17 ministers of justice, that is, one a year on average, even under Cardoso. The conservative character of the judiciary has rendered it reactive,[60] *qua* institution, to exogenously proposed reform. This stands in sharp contrast to the endogenously engendered proactive reform process within the prosecution service (*Ministério Público*) which has, in recent decades, forged a new identity for itself as guardian of civil liberties, protector of the *res publica*, and watchdog of the public authorities.[61] Finally the federal system of government in Brazil, originally designed to accommodate and preserve local elite power bases, has complicated central government influence over a justice system which is administered at state level, even when some of the proposed reforms fall within federal remit. Other key aspects, such as increasing access and efficiency, depend fundamentally on state-level initiatives and present an array of experience, both encouraging, where innovation has occurred, and discouraging, where reform efforts meet conservative resistance. The heated debate over binding precedent exemplifies this centre–local tension.

---

58   It went through two rounds of voting in the Chamber of Deputies on 12 April, and on 7 June 2000 and then passed to the Senate where it will have to go to a commission then through two votes requiring a two-thirds majority.
59   Pereira and Mueller (2000).
60   Sadek (1995b).
61   Arantes (2000b); Sadek (2000); Cavalcanti (1999).

The federal government did intermittently influence the process via the proposals put forward by Jobim, Carneiro and Ferreira. However, subsequent drafts of the report escaped its influence and shifted emphasis towards other, competing, models of reform. It is worth examining the main models propounded in order to understand the relative weight accorded by different reformers to the four main aspects of reform outlined above.[62] Koerner (1999) describes the three main positions as promoting, respectively, democratisation of the judiciary, a minimal judiciary and a corporatist-conservative status quo. The Bicudo model, supported by the PT and the lower ranks of the judiciary, advocated decentralisation, external control and internal democracy within the judiciary. The substitute report submitted by federal deputy Zulaiê Cobra and heavily influenced by the minister of justice, José Carlos Dias,[63] and STF Justice Celso de Mello, broadly reflected these concerns but was not supported by the government. The second model is an economistic one linking stable, predictable environments for investment and foreign capital to the rule of law à la the World Bank, broadly reflected in Ferreira's report.[64] This advocated elimination or downsizing of the Labour Courts and reconcentration of the power of judicial review and jurisprudence in the supreme courts via the effective reinstatement of *avocatória*, introduction of binding precedent,[65] and Supreme Court powers of jurisdictional and disciplinary control over the lower courts in each branch. It is notable for its verticalised conception of the judiciary and minimal civil society control over the judiciary. The third model, favoured by the professional bodies representing judges and prosecutors, especially those in the lower ranks,[66] would reinforce the institutional power of the judiciary and accord it a privileged status with respect to salary and working conditions. Technical solutions to court delays, such as computerisation, are acceptable but binding precedent has been strenuously opposed. The bill finally sent to the Senate in 2001 did contain this provision, suggesting a victory of government economic policy-makers over the corporativist interests of the judiciary.[67]

62   I am grateful to Oscar Vilhena Vieira for this insight.
63   A criminal lawyer and human rights advocate, his attempts at structural change in the justice system were thwarted by internal turf wars in the Ministry of Justice.
64   Arantes (2000a).
65   The Superior Labour Court (TST) also supports such efficiency/concentration measures. On its website it advocates more powers of the TST over the Regional Courts, better procedural laws to speed cases up, for TST cases to be filtered using the criterion of relevance and the *súmula vinculante* for rulings in which the position of the court is clear via repeated rulings on the same issue (www.tst.gov.br).
66   For example, the Associação de Magistrados Brasileiros, a professional body representing 14,700 federal, labour, state and military judges at all levels. For their views on the reform see their website www.amb.org.br.
67   Ballard (1999).

In the event, no vote was ever taken. In January 2003 minister of justice, Márcio Thomaz Bastos, appointed by the new PT administration, announced that he wished to restart from scratch the whole process of consultation over judicial reform. In his opinion, the final bill had been the result of so much haggling, horsetrading and compromise that it satisfied no clear aims and would be unworkable if approved in its current form. The proposal to set up a National Secretariat for the Modernisation of the judiciary indicates at least that the new government has placed justice reform at the heart of the justice ministry's remit and is concerned to develop a clear project of its own, in order to resist the multifarious pressures of lobby groups. It is to be hoped that this new phase of reform will be concluded rather more quickly than that initiated a decade ago.

Conclusion

In the first wave of reform that coincided with the democratic transition, the judiciary's macro-political role of judicial review and exercise of horizontal accountability predominated.[68] The lack of a coherent executive agenda for the judiciary resulted in a classic case of producer capture as the courts won an unprecedented degree of operational and juridical autonomy. However, as democracy began to consolidate in Brazil, more micro-political concerns emerged, in part related to the internationalised agenda of good governance, involving greater efficiency, modernisation, accountability and 'value-for-money' of judicial institutions, and in part to more substantive considerations regarding the quality of democracy such as social exclusion, access to justice and citizenship. These two reform agendas are not necessarily complementary. One was primarily economic in character, a response to the exigencies of the government's privatisation and market-opening policies, which increasingly met time- and resource-consuming, if temporary, obstacles in the local courts. The other addressed the accountability of the judiciary itself, and its potential in universalising the rule of law, equalising treatment of citizens before the law and opening access to justice to all. A shift of power occurred, with the corporatist interests of the legal professions losing ground to the overriding economic management concerns of the Executive. The area in which least progress has been made is that of universalising access to justice and equalising treatment under the law, precisely because the mass of 'consumers' is less organised and vocal than either of the two groups previously mentioned.

Brazilian reformers have been concerned with the key elements of judicial organisation and activity common to other democratising countries in Latin America: access, efficiency, independence and accountability. However,

---

68   Schedler et al. (1999).

these elements are not necessarily compatible and those advocating and designing judicial reform have clashed over the purpose and desired outcomes of such reforms. Institutional reform has inevitably been shaped by political realities — by the conjunctures of democratisation, by the particular balance of power between the three branches of government in Brazil, by the federal system of government and by corporativist interests within the judiciary. As the reform agenda has 'thickened', and the number of interested parties multiplied, it is clear that Brazil is still in the midst of an ongoing process of building an appropriate justice system for its new democracy.

PART II
THE ECONOMY IN A DEMOCRATIC SETTING

CHAPTER 5

Economic Policy and Performance in Brazil since 1985

Edmund Amann*

Introduction

Since 1985 the Brazilian economy has undergone change on an unprecedented scale, the nature of which has transformed its structural characteristics and position in the global economy. Breaking with the past, trade barriers have been lowered, markets deregulated, privatisations implemented and more orthodox fiscal and monetary policy put into practice. As these processes have unfolded, the performance characteristics of the economy have, in many senses, improved markedly. Most important of all, following a successful stabilisation programme in the mid-1990s, the near hyperinflation that characterised much of the 1980s has become a thing of the past. At the same time, there is little question but that supply-side competitiveness has improved out of all recognition with strong increases in productivity being registered and Brazilian business being ever more global in orientation. However, these undoubted achievements need to be set beside lingering long-term problems, especially the continued overdependence of Brazil on foreign savings and the persistence of a highly uneven distribution of income. These ingrained features of the economy have survived the switch from military to civilian rule, countless changes in currency and the reorientation of the economy away from import substitution and towards insertion in the global trading system.

In the course of this chapter an attempt is made to review in more detail these achievements and shortcomings, focusing in particular on the impact of trade and market liberalisation. The chapter begins with a brief review of economic policy and performance in 1985–90, a transitional period in Brazil's economic history that marked the end of military rule but in which attempts at large-scale systematic trade and market liberalisation proved absent. Having thus set the scene, the bulk of the chapter is then dedicated to a review of the evolution of the Brazilian economy over the 1990s. Beginning with a review of the radical shifts in economic poli-

*   Some of the material upon which this chapter is based appeared originally in a contribution the author made to *Investing in Latin American Growth: Unlocking Opportunities in Brazil, Mexico, Argentina and Chile* (Canberra: Department of Foreign Affairs and Trade, 2001)

cy which dominated the early 1990s, the chapter goes on to explore the implications these had for general macroeconomic performance, poverty and income distribution, the state of public finances, the external sector and financial market behaviour.

Setting the Scene: The Brazilian Economy in the Late 1980s

For much of the post-war period Brazil pursued a development strategy that had as its fundamental aim the structural transformation of the economy through the pursuit of import substituting industrialisation (ISI). Under the terms of ISI barriers to trade were intensified, the exchange rate was maintained at an artificially high rate while the state played an increasing role both as a direct producer and a regulator of economic activity. The results of this policy, whose implementation commenced just prior to World War II, were initially impressive. Between 1940 and 1960 Brazil was transformed from being a primarily agricultural and mineral based economy into a highly industrialised, urbanised society. Over this period the share of industry in GDP increased from 19.4 per cent to 25.2 per cent while the agricultural sector's share declined from 25.8 per cent to 22.6 per cent.[1] During these boom years GDP growth accelerated, inflation remained surprisingly restrained while FDI poured in. However, the success of ISI could not be sustained. By the mid-1960s the external deficit had reached worrying proportions while inflation, hitherto muted, had begun to spiral upwards. At the root of these difficulties was the fact that the policy of ISI had created inefficient industrial sectors whose survival depended on access to increasing quantities of imported inputs.

With the accession to power of the military in 1964 policy-makers attempted to address some of the most undesirable consequences of ISI through a programme of modest trade liberalisation, stepped currency devaluation and accelerated investment in transport, communications and energy infrastructure. For a while these policies proved highly successful with strong export and GDP growth achieved during the so-called 'miracle' years of 1967-73.[2] However, with the first oil crisis of 1973 Brazilian exports tapered off while oil import bills surged. As a result Brazil was once again plunged into crisis, the response to which was the readoption of ISI.[3] However, as before, ISI proved incapable of functioning without the accumulation of large deficits on the current account of the balance of payments.

By the early 1980s, with the debt default of Mexico and tightening monetary policy in the USA and Europe, the Brazilian authorities were no

---

1   Baer (1995).
2   Brum (1997).
3   Baer (1995).

longer able to finance cost-effectively the growing current account deficits with which ISI was associated. Consequently, policy-makers were forced to reappraise radically the basic economic strategies that had guided the development of Brazil since World War II.[4] The transition to civilian rule in 1985 marked an unprecedented opportunity in which such a reappraisal could take place. With the coming to office of President José Sarney in 1985 it appeared possible that Brazil might swiftly embark upon a path of rapid economic opening in which orthodox macroeconomic stabilisation would be accompanied by thoroughgoing microeconomic liberalisation. However, these hopes were to be disappointed. With inflation surging to worryingly high levels and the civilian government only beginning to find its feet, policy-makers instead embarked upon a series of ultimately fruitless attempts to reduce price pressures through the use of heterodox stabilisation plans.

Table 5.1a. Brazil: Key Economic Indicators, 1985-89

Year	GDP Change (per cent)	Industrial Production Change (per cent)	Price Index Change (per cent)	Exports (US$ billions)
1985	8.3	8.3	225.5	25.64
1986	8.0	12.4	124.3	22.38
1987	2.9	0.2	228.7	26.23
1988	0.0	-3.4	1061.5	33.78
1989	3.6	3.9	847.7	34.39

Source: Nogueira da Cruz and da Silva (1997), p. 46.

The first such plan to be implemented came to be known as the Cruzado Plan. Introduced in early 1986, the Plan sought to reduce inflation through the creation of a new currency, the cruzado, and the implementation of selective price and wage freezes. Initially, the results of the Plan proved highly impressive with inflation tumbling and economic activity accelerating. Unfortunately, the acceleration in growth — driven largely by the effects of lower inflation on real income levels — proved to be the ultimate undoing of the Plan. As demand expanded so the external accounts deteri-

4   Amann (2000).

orated while pressure on prices mounted. By the end of 1986 the government found itself forced to cede to pressure to allow the selective unfreezing of prices. Consequently, as 1987 commenced, inflation began to accelerate once more while real incomes began to fall, leading in time to reduced growth (see Table 5.1a). During the remainder of the decade various other stabilisation initiatives were put in place in an attempt to put inflation in check. To varying degrees, the Bresser Plan of 1987, the Rice and Beans Plan of 1988 and the Summer Plan of 1989 all employed price freeze measures. Without exception, all ultimately failed in their objectives despite instances of short-run success. As policy-makers came to recognise, a long-term solution to the problem of inflation was unlikely to derive from price freezes, currency changes or monetary squeezes no matter how cleverly or selectively implemented. Instead, the tackling of inflation was likely to require a broader range of measures embracing market reform, fiscal adjustment, the end of indexation and the pursuit of more orthodox monetary and fiscal policy. The first real hint of such a change in thinking came in 1988 with the implementation of a limited programme of privatisation and trade policy reforms. While insignificant in comparison with what was to follow, President Sarney's attempts at trade liberalisation — embracing selective tariff reductions — marked an important change in emphasis, as did the privatisation of some smaller state-owned enterprises.

The Brazilian Economy in the 1990s

Policy Reforms

By the end of President Sarney's term in 1989, a consensus of opinion had emerged within the political and business elite that the policies that had been associated with import substitution industrialisation were no longer sustainable. In common with other Latin American economies — especially Chile, Mexico and Argentina — a strategic decision was taken to break with the inward-orientated legacy of the past and to pursue a much more open, liberal and foreign investor friendly strategy which had as its core the insertion of Brazil into the global economy.[5] In 1990, with the accession to power of Fernando Collor de Melo, Brazil's first directly elected president for over 30 years, this change in consensus made itself felt in an ambitious programme of economic reform, the main elements of which remain in place to this day. The key features of this reform programme were as follows:

5   Bulmer-Thomas (1994).

Trade Liberalisation

Given the need to improve industrial efficiency and export performance after years of intense protection, President Collor's government adopted in 1990 a four-year rolling programme of trade reforms. Between 1990 and 1994 average tariff levels were more than halved from 32 per cent to 14 per cent.[6] The implementation of these reductions followed a limited programme of tariff reductions in 1988-90 instituted under President José Sarney. More significantly still, 1990 saw the abolition of the vast majority of non-tariff barriers (NTBs). Prior to 1990 these had, in practice, formed the most important protective barriers behind which Brazilian industry sheltered. The abolition of one NTB especially — The Law of Similars — constituted an enormous increase in competitive pressure on Brazilian business. While operational the law had effectively prohibited the import of a range of consumer durable and capital goods whose production took place in Brazil.

Table 5.1b: Nominal Tariff Reductions in Brazil (1990-2006)
Nominal Tariffs by Sector (per cent)

	1990	1991	1992	1993	1994	1995	2006 CET
Agriculture	14.8	9.8	7.8	4.5	4.1	4.7	4.7
Mechanical Equipment	39.5	30.4	25.9	19.1	18.9	18.2	13.9
Paper	23.1	12.9	10.1	9.3	8.3	10.5	11.9
Textiles	38.8	37.6	29.5	14.4	12.4	16.4	15.8
Electrical Equipment	39.6	34.3	30.6	18.8	18.4	21.5	16.0
Mineral Extraction	6.6	3.9	2.4	2.8	2.6	4.0	4.0

Source: Almeida and Pinheiro (1994); Kume (1996).
Note: CET = Mercosul Common External Tariff.

Table 5.1b above indicates the extent to which tariffs fell over the course of the 1990s for a number of key sectors. It can be noted that for some sectors tariffs increased slightly between 1994 and 1995 as the government attempted to keep import growth under control. Over the next few years the Brazilian government will be obliged in some cases to adjust tar-

6   Kume (1996).

iffs downwards in order to bring tariff levels into compliance with the Mercosul Common External Tariff. The deadline for such compliance is December 2006.

Privatisation

The process of privatisation began timidly under President Sarney in 1988. However, under President Collor its pace accelerated substantially. By the time of his impeachment in 1992 most of the state owned steel and petrochemical sectors had been transferred to the private sector.[7] President Collor also developed an ambitious programme known as the Programa Nacional de Desestatização (PND — National State Divestment Programme), in which he set out the government's plans to privatise further sectors, including telecommunications and electrical energy. However, the realisation of such plans depended on the passage of constitutional amendments permitting the entry of private investors (both foreign and domestic) into these sectors. After much debate, the necessary legislation was passed in 1995 under President Fernando Henrique Cardoso. In the years since the passing of the amendment the telecommunications sector has been entirely privatised and opened up to competition while the process of electricity privatisation has been virtually completed. The privatisation programme has also embraced other sectors, notably the state banking sector and the mining sector with the sale of CVRD, the state-owned resources enterprise in 1997. With few state enterprises remaining unsold, the pace of the PND is expected to slow markedly over the next two to three years.

A key feature explaining the relative success of the Brazilian privatisation programme has been the existence of a reasonably transparent (and recently developed) regulatory regime. Regulatory agencies now exist for the oil and gas, telecommunications and electrical energy sectors. In the event that a new mining code is introduced (this has not yet taken place) it appears likely that the mineral extraction sector will benefit from the establishment of its own regulator. Of the regulatory agencies already established, the most significant are the oil sector regulator (the Agência Nacional de Petroleo — National Petroleum Agency or ANP), the telecommunications regulator (The Agência Nacional de Telecommunicações — National Telecommunications Agency or ANATEL) and the electricity regulator (Agência Nacional de Energia Electrica — National Electrical Energy Agency or ANEEL).[8] All of these agencies perform the following functions:

---

7   President Collor was impeached following allegations that, together with associates, he had siphoned off large quantities of public funds for private gain.
8   Leite (1997).

i)   The administration of the granting of concessions to utility providers

ii)   The monitoring of service quality and the imposition of quality directives

iii)   The setting of tariffs

iv)   The provision of incentives for enterprises within their sectors to invest in technology

v)   The setting of long-term strategic priorities for their respective sectors.

As the state continues to withdraw from the role of direct producer, the power and influence of the regulatory agencies is likely to grow further.

Market Deregulation

President Collor's government committed itself from the start to a programme of far-reaching market deregulation designed to increase the competitiveness of domestic markets and to attract much needed foreign investment. Despite this commitment, relatively little progress in this area had been made by the time of President Collor's removal from office in 1992. However, under President Cardoso the pace of market deregulation has sharply accelerated. During his first year in office (1995) President Cardoso succeeded in securing the passage of legislation to open up the oil, gas and mining sectors to both domestic and foreign private sector investors.

Moreover, legislation accompanying the privatisation of the telecommunications and electricity distribution and generation sectors specifically allows for the entry of new market competitors to challenge the privatised incumbents. In addition, most of the privatised sectors now benefit from special regulatory agencies whose function is to ensure the existence of competitive markets and a level playing field for all investors, regardless of nationality. As a result of these developments, barriers to foreign investment are now a fraction of what they were at the beginning of the 1990s. Barriers to investment have been removed across a range of sectors including mining, oil exploration and production, telecommunications and electricity generation and distribution. In all sectors bar the media, air transport and coastal shipping 100 per cent foreign ownership of enterprises is now permitted. Even in the case of the remaining exceptions to this general rule, the government is actively considering a process of investment liberalisation which is likely to take effect in the next two to three years.

Fiscal Reform

Not all of the reform agenda over the past decade has been focused on microeconomic issues. For much of the post-war period successive governments encountered difficulties in restraining the growth of the public sector deficit. However, the persistence of high inflation enabled policy-makers to artificially contain the expansion of deficits through clever use of indexation mechanisms and the deliberate insertion of delays between receipt and disbursement of revenues. With the end of high inflation following the introduction of the *real* in July 1994, the weak state of public finances was thrown into sharper relief than ever. As a consequence, the government of Fernando Henrique Cardoso has been forced to redouble the efforts of earlier administrations to bring about substantial reductions in the fiscal deficit. This has involved a number of measures whose nature is discussed in greater detail in the section below on public finances. In brief, the key policies adopted have consisted of reducing the scale of capital spending, while clamping down on constitutionally mandated expenditures and personnel costs. On the revenue side the key policies have involved imposing increases in levels of indirect taxation while broadening the scope of public sector pension contributions. So far these measures have succeeded in converting a primary deficit (that is the balance of non-debt related expenditures and revenues) into a substantial surplus. Taken together with the impact of falling domestic interest rates, the result of this fiscal turnaround has been to bring about substantial reductions in the scale of the public sector borrowing requirement (PSBR).

Taking these policy developments together, there is no question but that Brazil has made strenuous efforts to embark upon a new era of global economic integration and orthodox macroeconomic policy. However desirable this change in policy direction may have been, however, the experience of the past decade has indicated that it did not always translate into greater macroeconomic stability. It is to this issue that the discussion now turns.

Macroeconomic Trends in the 1990s and Beyond

The Pre Real Plan Period (1990–93)

The evolution of the Brazilian macroeconomy since 1990 divides into two key phases; that encompassing the period up until the adoption of the Real Plan in late 1993 and that which has pertained subsequently. Prior to the advent of the Real Plan, the Brazilian economy, despite the rapid introduction of structural microeconomic reforms, was still very much constrained by the hyper-inflationary legacy of the 1970s and 1980s.[9]

---

9   Amann and Baer (2000).

Figure 5.1: Real GDP Growth (percentage) 1990–2000

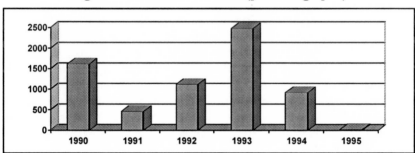

Source: Banco Central do Brasil (BCB) (2001) Fundação Getúlio Vargas (FGV) (2000).

Figure 5.2: Inflation 1990-95 (percentage p.a.)

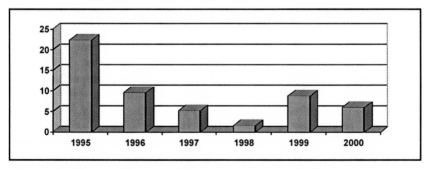

Figure 5.3: Inflation 1995-2000 (percentage p.a.)

Source for Figures 5.2 and 5.3: Brazilian Central Bank (2001) Inflation index used is IPCA (Indice dos Preços ao Consumidor Atacado — Consumer Wholesale Prices Index).

As the figures above indicate, between 1990 and 1994 average yearly consumer and producer price inflation never dipped below three digits while growth performance, at least up until early 1993, was profoundly disappointing. Put simply, by the early 1990s Brazil appeared to have entered a stagflationary phase in which contraction in output accompanied growing difficulties in restraining the acceleration in inflation. That the macro-economy had reached such a pass was the product of a number of factors. First, despite the government's achievements in trade and market reform, policy-makers under President de Melo failed to devise a stabilisation plan with sufficient credibility to halt the acceleration of inflation. In particular the two key stabilisation plans of the early 1990s, Collor I and II, emphasised short-term monetary freezes and drastic public spending cuts which both foreign and domestic economic agents knew to be unsustainable in the long run. As a result, the plans only temporarily acted to restrain inflation and then only at the cost of drastic reductions in output. Once the monetary freezes and shock fiscal measures inevitably unwound, inflation rapidly returned with the credibility of policy-makers further undermined.

In trying to effect macroeconomic stabilisation the efforts of policy-makers were further hampered by the fact that the implications of their trade and market reforms had yet to be fully absorbed by the private sector. Perhaps even more seriously, the fight against inflation was hindered by the fact that Brazil's elaborate system of wage and price indexation remained stubbornly intact.[10]

The Emergence of the Real Plan (1993–94)

The removal of President de Melo from office in September 1992 and his replacement by the mercurial Itamar Franco appeared at first to constitute yet another serious blow to policy-makers' continuing attempts to foster greater macroeconomic stability. However, Franco proved a more pragmatic and capable operator than most had imagined. Appointing a former academic sociologist and political exile, Fernando Henrique Cardoso, to the office of Finance Minister in May 1993, Mr. Franco granted the newest member of his cabinet a virtually free hand to assemble a new economic team and devise a radical new macroeconomic policy agenda.[11]

Drawing on the experience of such distinguished academic economists as Gustavo Franco and Pedro Malan (later to become respectively Central Bank governor and finance minister) Cardoso swiftly devised a comprehensive and innovative stabilisation plan whose success was to transform the fortunes of

10   The indexation system allowed for automatic price and wage increases to protect the
      real incomes of enterprises and workers. However, in propagating such increases on
      an automatic basis, the indexation system ensured that inflation was kept on the boil.
11   Baer (1995).

the Brazilian economy. The plan, introduced in late 1993, quickly became known as the Real Plan and comprised the following key elements:

1.   Across the board spending cuts of US$7.5bn allied (around two per cent of total expenditure) to a five per cent increase in tax rates, the latter delivering around a seven per cent increase in revenues.

2.   The progressive abolition of the indexation system. Between mid-1993 and late 1994 both wage and price-indexing systems were abolished. Generally speaking, progress on eliminating price index-ing moved ahead of efforts to eliminate wage indexing. However, by the end of 1994 both systems had been dismantled.

3.   The introduction of a new currency — the *real* — pegged to the US dollar at an initial rate of 1 to 1. The advent of a strong, dollar-pegged currency had a profound impact on price relativities in that prices in the tradeables sector were forced down by imported com-petition. Over time, the price moderation forced on the tradeables sector began to feed through into the non-tradeables sector as input costs for the latter sector fell.

4.   The pursuit of a tight monetary policy, both to restrain directly demand side inflationary pressures and to maintain the external value of the *real*.[12]

With the key elements of the Plan implemented by July 1994, their macro-economic effects had already begun to make themselves felt by the end of the year. With the indexation system dismantled and with a dollar-linked currency driving down import prices, inflation began a sharp descent with the result that between 1994 and 1995 accumulated annual consumer price inflation declined from 916.46 per cent to 22.41 per cent. At the same time, with real incomes buoyed by the fall in inflation, consumer spending rose sharply with the result that GDP growth accelerated from 4.9 per cent to 5.9 per cent between 1993 and 1994, declining somewhat the following year (see Figure 5.1).[13]

Thus, in its initial year of operation the Real Plan had succeeded where so many of its predecessors had failed. Not only had the plan managed to bring inflation under control but it had done so without bringing about a loss in output. Quite the contrary in fact: the Real Plan appeared to demonstrate that in the Brazilian context accelerated growth and declining inflation *could* be mutually compatible macroeconomic objectives.

---

12   Amann and Baer (2000).
13   Gambiagi et al (1999).

The Real Plan under Threat (1995–99)

With the successful introduction of the Real Plan, the stage appeared to be set for the continuation of strong, low-inflationary growth throughout the remainder of the decade. As the ongoing effects of trade and market liberalisation made themselves felt, so the theory went, the growing competitiveness of the economy allied to progressive fiscal adjustment would consolidate the early achievements of the Plan while insulating Brazil from the contagious effects of any external economic crisis. However, despite its achievements the Real Plan failed to address two long-standing structural weaknesses that had restrained economic growth in the past: recurrent fiscal and external imbalance.

The first significant challenge to be confronted by the Real Plan came in late 1994 and early 1995 with the Mexican peso crisis. The peso crisis, triggered in large part by the accumulation of an unsustainably large current account deficit, led to an upsurge in concern among international investors surrounding the sustainability of macroeconomic policy throughout the region. Brazil, despite its recent achievements, proved itself far from immune from these concerns. As a result, in order to maintain the external value of the *real*, the authorities were forced to maintain in place a much tighter monetary policy than would have otherwise been desirable.[14] The policy proved effective in containing the slide of the *real* whose value for 1995 averaged around 0.92 per dollar.[15] However, the tightness of monetary policy served only to magnify the growing disequilibrium on the public accounts. The operational deficit (the inflation adjusted balance of total public sector revenues and expenditures) rose sharply after 1994 as the real cost of debt servicing increased, tax reform initiatives faltered and the government failed to trim non-debt-related expenditures (see Table 5.1). Another partial consequence of the maintenance of a tight monetary policy was felt on the external balance.

The adoption of trade liberalisation measures in the early 1990s had opened the Brazilian market as never before to the import of goods and services. With positive growth and a strong exchange rate two key outcomes of the Real Plan, it is not surprising that the current account balance began to rapidly deteriorate after 1994. As the data indicate, between 1994 and 1998 the deficit on current account rose from US$1,689 million (0.3 per cent of GDP) to US$ 3,3611 million (4.1 per cent of GDP). Taken together with the rising public sector deficit, this development created a source of instability so enormous in its potential that it eventually brought the Real Plan to an effective end.

14   Amann and Baer (2000).
15   Gambiagi et al (1999). The exchange rate for the *real* was allowed to fluctuate within a target band set by the authorities. The Central Bank intervened if the exchange rate strayed outside these bands.

Table 5.2: Operational Public Deficit, External Imbalance, Exchange Rate and Interest Rate 1990–2000

	1990	1991	1992	1993	1994	1995	1996	1997	1998	1999	2000
Operational Public Sector Deficit (per cent GDP)	-1.3	-1.35	2.16	-0.25	-1.32	4.88	3.75	4.3	7.57	3.85	0.52*
Current Account Deficit (US$ million) Figures in parentheses – deficit as a per cent of GDP	-3,782	-1,407	6,144	-592	-1,689	17,972	24,347	33,054	33,611	24,375	15,933**
	(-0.8)	(0.3)	(1.6)	(-0.1)	(-0.3)	(-2.5)	(-3.0)	(-3.8)	(-4.3)	(-4.7)	(-4.1)
Average Exchange Rate – R$:US$***						0.9177	1.0052	1.0787	1.611	1.8158	1.9480****
Interest Rates (Selic Dec per cent p.a.)							23.94	42.04	31.24	18.99	15.75

*12 months to November
** First three quarters
***Selling rate average
****November
Source: Banco Central do Brasil (2001); Fundação Getúlio Vargas (FGV) (2000).

Despite the growing scale of the internal and external imbalance, policy-makers between 1995 and 1997 refrained from taking substantial remedial measures. Instead the key focus of the government during this period rested on an acceleration of microeconomic reform and the pursuit of a constitutional amendment granting President Cardoso the right to run for a second term. In the absence of any external financial crisis there is little doubt that the authorities' relatively sanguine attitude to macroeconomic policy would have persisted with the deficits increasing further in scale. However, such an attitude was not allowed to continue for long. With the eruption of the Asian Financial Crisis in July 1997 investors began to view the Brazilian macroeconomic stance with increasing concern. As a result, the *real* came under increasing pressure, pushing its value against the US dollar down to an average of R$1.07: US$1 for 1997 as a whole. Attempting to halt the slide in the value of the *real* interest rates were increased further while, in November 1997, a limited emergency package of fiscal cuts was implemented.[16]

As might have been expected, the consequences of these policy developments had some unfavourable implications. In first place, the tightening of monetary policy served to place a brake on growth, which dwindled in 1997 and 1998 (See Figure 5.1). In addition, the raised costs of servicing public debt imposed by higher interest rates drove the fiscal deficit up higher. With the Russian crisis of August 1998 the scale of the problems now facing Brazil assumed a higher priority still among the concerns of investors. With international reserves evaporating and the *real* under serious downward pressure, the Brazilian government in association with the IMF launched in November 1998 a package of fiscal cuts and tax increases aimed at generating a primary surplus of 2.6 per cent of GDP. To provide adequate liquidity over the period of the package's implementation — and to ensure the retention of the currency peg — the IMF in association with other institutions — provided an assistance package amounting to US$41.5billion.[17]

Unfortunately, however, even the provision of assistance on this scale, investors remained unconvinced as to the long-term sustainability of the currency peg. As a result, capital continued to flee Brazil while the Central Bank's reserves rapidly diminished.

16　Gambiagi et al (1999).
17　IMF (2000).

Figure 5.4: The Evolution of Brazil's International Reserves, 1990–2000 (US$ billion)

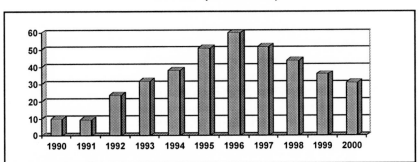

Note: Data for 2000 refer to August.
Source: Brazilian Central Bank (2001).

By the middle of January 1999 the authorities faced up to the inevitable and reluctantly allowed the *real* to float against the US dollar. Thus, a key element of the Real Plan — if not the plan itself — had come to an end with consequences that were to prove rather more favourable than many had expected.

Macroeconomic Performance, Population and Income Distribution over the Long Run

The growth performance of the Brazilian economy over the past decade, as the discussion has already emphasised, has been extremely uneven with real declines in output in 1990 and 1992, strong expansion in 1993–95 and stagnation in 1998–99. However, despite the magnitude of these short-term fluctuations — on which much of the literature concerning the Brazilian economy tends to dwell — it is possible to observe some longer-run, structural trends. Perhaps most encouragingly, the period since 1990 has been one in which labour productivity growth has been particularly and consistently strong. As Table 5.6 indicates, by October 2000 industrial labour productivity in São Paulo, Brazil's most industrialised state, stood some 68 per cent higher in absolute terms than it had a decade earlier. Driving this substantial improvement in performance have been a number of factors, not least improved training, investment in new machinery, the adoption of new working practices and — perhaps most significantly — the wholesale shedding of labour.[18] Not surprisingly, the latter factor has strongly contributed towards the development of higher rates of unemployment over the course of the 1990s. In the 1997–99 period unemployment escalated substantially, driven not only by structural change in industry but also by the impact of slowing growth and flagging business confidence.

18   See Posthuma (1999).

Despite the magnitude of the changes affecting the economy over the past few years, one long-standing structural characteristic — Brazil's famously skewed income distribution — has remained largely unaffected by the course of events (see Table 5.3). The most recent estimates put Brazil's Gini Coefficient (the most widely used measure of income inequality)[19] at 0.60, a level virtually unchanged from that of a decade ago. In international terms, the relative income share of the richer section of the population compared with the poorer is very substantial indeed as demonstrated in Table 5.4.

The stubbornness of Brazil's income inequalities has a number of causes. In first place, despite substantial structural change, the ownership of assets remains highly concentrated in relatively few hands. In addition, the process of labour market restructuring has also mitigated against improvements in the distributional pattern: the past decade has seen a general decline in the numbers of formally employed industrial employees and the rise of more casual forms of employment. As a result, average working class incomes have risen relatively little notwithstanding some of the beneficial effects of the decline in inflation. Finally, the privatisation of the public utility industries has coincided with a substantial upturn in prices for basic services such as electricity and telecommunications. This has had a negative impact upon the real incomes of the poorer members of society.[20]

More encouragingly however, while Brazil's income distribution may not have evened out, a combination of falling inflation and rising growth in the mid 1990s did prove sufficient to bring about a notable reduction of the proportion of the population classified as 'poor' (Table 5.3). Unfortunately, the economic downturn at the end of the 1990s served to undo some of the undoubted progress that had been made in the immediate wake of the launch of the Real Plan.

Despite the persistence of poverty and inequality, Brazil's population of around 165 million contains substantial numbers of affluent consumers, forming a ready market for both exporters and domestically based producers. There is no doubt though that the persistence of acute income inequality places a strong limits on the rapidity with which the economy may grow. Leaving considerations of social welfare and equity to one side, the existence of a substantial sector (around 25 per cent) of the population outside the formal sector and in acute poverty represents a considerable market foregone and a substantial under-utilisation of a valuable resource.[21]

---

19   The Gini coefficient provides an index of income inequality. A coefficient of zero indicates a perfectly even distribution of income while a coefficient of one indicates that all income is concentrated in the hands of one individual. Thus, the nearer one the value of the Gini is, the more uneven the distribution of income.

20   Amann and Baer (forthcoming).

21   Paes de Barros (2000).

Table 5.3: Indicators of Income Distribution and Poverty: 1990–1999

Year	Gini Coefficient	Gap between the richest 20 per cent and the poorest 20 per cent	Gap between the richest 40 per cent and the poorest 40 per cent	Poor as a percentage of the total population*
1990	0.62	31.2	26.9	43.8 (63.2)
1991	n.a.	n.a.	n.a	n.a.
1992	0.58	26.7	21.8	40.8 (57.3)
1993	0.60	28.8	24.5	41.7 (59.4)
1994	n.a.	n.a.	n.a.	n.a.
1995	0.60	28.0	24.1	33.9 (50.2)
1996	0.60	29.8	24.6	33.5 (50.1)
1997	0.60	29.2	24.5	33.9 (51.5)
1998	0.60	28.6	24.2	32.8 (50.3)
1999	0.60	27.2	23.3	34.1 (53.1)

* Figures in parentheses are absolute numbers of poor in millions. The poor are defined in terms of those whose incomes fall below a notional poverty line determined by IBGE, the National Statistical Agency.
Source: Paes de Barros, Enriques and Mendonça (2000).

Table 5.4: Gap Between the Income of the Richest 10 per cent and the Poorest 40 per cent of the Population

Low income countries		High income countries		Latin American countries	
China	1.6	United States	1.6	Brazil	5.6
Egypt	1.3	UK	1.9	Argentina	2.8
India	1.4	Sweden	1.0	Chile	4.4
Nigeria	2.4	Germany	1.3	Mexico	4.4
Pakistan	1.2	France	2.1	Peru	2.6

Source: Ramos and Vieira (2000).

Turning to more general demographic issues, a number of interesting trends emerge from Table 5.5. Most importantly, in contrast to many developed societies, the Brazilian population is still growing quite strongly in absolute terms. However, mirroring a long established trend in the West, the population structure is beginning to age with both birth and death rates in gradual decline.

Table 5.5: Population Trends

	1995	2000
Total population (millions)	155.32	165.93
Annual pop. growth rate	1.4%	1.32%
Age profile (percentage of Total population)		
0-14	31.3	28.3
15-64	63.5	66.4
65+	4.8	5.2

Source: Brazilian National Statistical Agency (IBGE) (2001).

An interesting trend to emerge from a longer-term examination of Brazilian macroeconomic performance concerns the sectoral pattern of growth. As the data indicate, there have been considerable fluctuations in the relative contributions of the main sectors to GDP growth since 1990. Whereas agricultural and industrial growth has been characterised by considerable volatility, that of the services sector has demonstrated a far greater degree of stability: over the course of the 1990s in only one year — 1990 — did services output contract. Resulting from this trend, the past decade has seen the services sector increase its share of national output at the expense of the industrial and agricultural sectors. As in most advanced nations, the services sector in Brazil now represents the largest single source of output in the economy.

In common with many other developing economies, Brazil has continued to suffer from a substantial savings gap. As Figure 5.5 indicates, in the 1990s, for every year bar 1996 and 1997, the level of investment consistently exceeded that of savings. The inevitable result of this long-established trend is that Brazil remains highly dependent on foreign investors to meet its domestic capital requirements. Aware of the potential hazards of this situation, the authorities have been trying to accelerate the development and modernisation of domestic capital markets.[22] However, so far, these efforts have met with no discernible response in terms of an improvement in rates of domestic saving.

Table 5.6: Key Macroeconomic Indicators

Year	Industrial Labour Productivity (1992=100)	Unemployment (% in December)	Real Rates of Growth by Sector		
			Agriculture	Industry	Services
1990	n.a	n.a	-3.7	-8.2	-0.8
1991	n.a	n.a	1.4	0.3	2.0
1992	100	4.5	4.9	-4.2	1.5
1993	108.13	4.39	-0.1	7.0	3.2
1994	118.73	3.42	5.5	6.7	4.7
1995	122.44	4.44	4.1	1.9	1.3
1996	132.36	3.82	3.1	3.3	2.3
1997	144.17	4.84	-0.8	4.7	2.6
1998	151.93	6.32	1.9	-1.5	1.1
1999	164.46	6.28	7.4	-1.6	1.9
2000	167.06	5.6	2.9	4.8	3.6

Source: BCB (2001); IBGE (2001) (Brazilian Statistical Agency).

Figure 5.5: Saving and Investment 1990–99 (per cent of GDP)

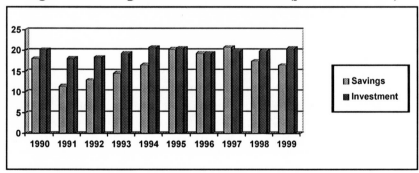

Source: Brazilian Central Bank (BCB) (2001).

22   One of the main efforts in this direction has been the authorities' establishment of a new corporate governance law – The Law of S.A.s – which aims at increasing the rights of minority shareholders and, by extension, encouraging wider share ownership. The São Paulo stock exchange has also established the Novo Mercado (the New Market) aimed at facilitating the swifter launch of share offerings in high-tech companies.

The Brazilian Macroeconomy since 1999

The effective abandonment of the real exchange rate anchor at the beginning of 1999 initially gave rise to concern that, besides further undermining international confidence in the Brazilian economy, the counter-inflationary achievements of the previous four years would be swiftly reversed.

In fact, despite a small initial upsurge, price pressures soon faded with the result that, for 1999 as a whole, consumer price inflation remained firmly in single digits, at just 8.94 per cent. Subsequently, price pressures abated further with consumer price inflation reaching just under six per cent for 2000.[23] Following an intensification of concern over the economic future of Argentina, the value of the *real* slipped sharply over the first ten months of 2001. Despite this, consumer price inflation for the year as a whole is not expected to exceed nine per cent. The experience of the past two years appears to demonstrate conclusively that the Brazilian economy has broken decisively with the habits of the past, despite the removal of the exchange rate anchor. Tight monetary policy, the abolition of indexation and a more competitive business environment have acted to shore up price stability. Price stability has also been particularly reinforced by the continuing deregulation of internal product markets and the success with which the government reversed the growth of the fiscal deficit.

Perhaps even more encouragingly, the counter-inflationary achievements of the past two years have been realised without falls in the level of real income. Contrary to expectations, GDP actually expanded slightly (by 0.54 per cent) in 1999, in what was originally forecast to be a crisis year. In 2000 GDP growth accelerated more rapidly still, reaching 4.4 per cent for the year as a whole. While currency devaluation and the effects of the Argentinean crisis have adversely impacted on the economy in 2001, positive growth of between 0.5 per cent and one per cent is still expected.

Public Finances

As has already been made clear, the adoption of the Real Plan in 1993 initially did little to hasten the process of fiscal adjustment. That this process needed to be accelerated became increasingly clear over the next four years as the primary surplus was transformed into a deficit and the operational deficit moved alarmingly further into the red.

23 Brazilian Central Bank (2001).

**Figure 5.6: Evolution of the Operational and Primary Deficits
1994–2000 (per cent GDP)**

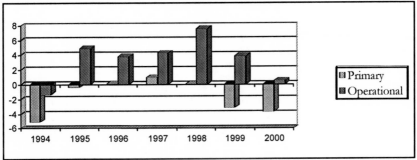

Note: Negative figure indicates surplus.
Source: Brazilian Central Bank (BCB) (2001); Fundação Getúlio Vargas (FGV) (2000).

The increasingly precarious state of Brazilian public finances after the
launch of the Real Plan derived in part from two key problems. First, as
Table 5.7 below indicates, the federal authorities were obliged to transfer
increasing resources to sub-national governments and retired civil servants
as part of their constitutionally mandated spending commitments. In some
part this difficulty resulted from the nature of the 1988 Constitution which
obliged the federal government to transfer substantial sums to the states
and municipalities (the sub-national governments — SNGs) without there
being any duty on the part of the latter to restrain spending.

**Table 5.7: Selected Federal Government Budget Items (per
cent of GDP)**

	1994	1995	1996	1997	1998
Transfer to states and municipalities	2.55	2.83	2.74	2.78	3.02
Active public servants	2.82	2.95	2.66	2.36	2.40
Inactive public servants	1.99	2.32	2.33	2.20	2.46
Retirement benefits	4.85	5.04	5.30	5.43	5.96
Nominal interest payments	13.41	2.90	2.93	2.31	6.03

Source: Gambiagi et al (1999), p. 97.

Second, the tax take, although increasing in absolute terms, failed to keep pace with the overall increase in expenditures. Between 1994 and 1999, total public sector tax revenues as a proportion of GDP deviated little from 30 per cent.[24] The relatively muted expansion of tax revenues resulted from a number of factors, not least the substantial size of the informal sector and the inefficient nature of much of the indirect tax collection system. In addition, the authorities faced two further problems.

On one hand, the high interest rates applied to support the external value of the *real* acted to increase the burden of debt servicing costs, a development with direct and unfavourable implications for the level and pattern of public spending.[25] Against this background and with the tax system both porous and in need of urgent reform it is hardly surprising that the non-debt related activities of the public sector increasingly gave rise to deficits.

Following the Asian crisis of 1997 and the Russian crisis of 1998, however, the authorities were forced to address the increasingly parlous state of public finances. In November 1998 the authorities announced the adoption of an IMF-approved programme of rapid fiscal reform which had at its core the objective of reining in the operational deficit through the generation of progressively larger surpluses on the primary account. In order to achieve this objective the Federal government placed before Congress a fiscal reform package whose fundamental aim was to change irrevocably the financial relationship between national and local levels of government. The package also sought to effect a fundamental reform of the taxation system with the objective of increasing the efficiency with which revenues were collected and reducing the scope for evasion.[26] In addition, the measures also sought to exercise a greater degree of control over the social security system, itself an increasing source of fiscal disequilibrium. Contrary to the expectations of many, by the end of 2000 the government had succeeded in securing the passage of most of its reform measures, the two most important of which were:

a) The Law of Fiscal Responsibility (approved April 2000). The law limits the obligation of the federal government to transfer resources to the SNGs. Specifically the federal government is now prohibited by law from taking on new debts accumulated by state and municipal governments. In addi-

---

24   Gambiagi et al. (1999).
25   Between 1995 and 1998 nominal debt interest payments by the federal government rose from 2.9 per cent to 6.03 per cent of GDP (Gambiagi, 1999).
26   So far, the measures that have been approved increase access of the tax authorities to private bank accounts, making evasion more difficult. However, a systemic reform of the indirect taxation system has still to be initiated despite considerable pressure being placed by President Cardoso on Congress.

tion the law places stringent limits on payroll costs at all levels of government. For the federal government, expenditures in this area are limited to 50 per cent of revenues while for the SNGs the figure is 60 per cent. Under the terms of complementary legislation known as the Fiscal Crimes Act (approved in October 2000) jail terms and other criminal penalties have been established for breaches of the Law of Fiscal Responsibility. In addition, the Fiscal Crimes act obliges public officials and politicians at all levels of government to comply with agreed targets for public debt accumulation. At the same time the Fiscal Crimes Act prohibits the undertaking of new expenditure programmes where it cannot be proved that adequate sources of public revenues exist to cover the costs.

b) Social Security Reform (approved November 1998 and November 1999). Under the terms of legislation approved in November 1998 a number of new rules have been adopted whose effect has been to improve the flow of social security contributions while restricting the scope of social security spending. These rules include the adoption of a minimum retirement age for public sector workers and, for the same employees, the introduction of a direct link between contributions and benefit entitlements where none had previously existed. Follow-up legislation approved a year later and known as the *Fator Previdenciário* extended the concept of a contributions-benefits link to the private sector social security system known as the INSS (National Social Security Institute).[27]

Despite the success of the authorities in securing passage of the legislation described above, the process of fiscal reform remains far from complete. In the first place, the social security system remains beleaguered by substantial deficits (just over R$10 billion in 2000),[28] the tackling of which will require more radical reform initiatives. As a first step, the government is attempting to reintroduce to Congress measures that would oblige retired public sector employees to make limited social security contributions where they were able. However, this proposal is unlikely to meet with a welcome reception in Congress given its highly politically contentious nature. In other areas, too, much remains to be done.

In particular, despite intense effort from Mr Cardoso, the reform of the taxation system has still to get off the ground. The government's current proposals, if approved would simplify and increase the effectiveness of the indirect tax system through the introduction of a more homogenised sales tax. At present, the main sales tax — the ICMS — is levied at different rates and on different products between individual states, causing confusion and

---

27   The INSS social security system provides defined benefits for those who become unemployed or retire. Contributions are made to the system on the basis of a payroll levy whose scale varies with income size.

28   Brazilian Central Bank (2001).

generating high compliance costs for business. Another effect of the present, complex regime is to discourage small businesses from departing Brazil's extensive informal sector. In two further developments, the government is seeking to effect a reform of the corporation taxation system, again with the objective of simplifying the tax code, boosting corporation tax registration and reducing business compliance costs.

Although the process of fiscal reform is far from complete, there is no doubt but that it has already started to exercise a profound effect upon the state of public finances. As the data below make clear, the Brazilian public sector has recently been accumulating a series of increasingly substantial primary surpluses. In generating these surpluses, the authorities initially relied upon emergency spending cuts and one-off increases in indirect taxation rates. However, with the Law of Fiscal Responsibility and social security reform starting to take effect, the generation of surpluses has moved on to a much more sustainable footing. As a consequence of this the government has experienced no difficulty in meeting its stringent IMF-set targets for the primary surplus. With healthy primary surpluses being generated and interest rates in decline, it is of little surprise that the operational public sector deficit fell between 1999 and 2000. However, interest rate rises over the course of 2001 have begun to exert an upward influence on the operational deficit.

Table 5.8: The Evolution of the Public Sector Borrowing Requirement (PSBR), 1990–2000 (per cent of GDP), 12 months to the end of December

Year	Nominal Balance	Operational Balance	Primary Balance
1990	29.60	-1.30	-4.60
1991	23.30	-1.35	-2.85
1992	43.10	2.16	-2.26
1993	59.05	-0.25	-2.67
1994	43.74	-1.32	-5.09
1995	7.18	4.88	-0.36
1996	5.87	3.75	0.09
1997	5.03	4.30	0.94
1998	8.11	7.57	-0.01
1999	10.34	3.85	-3.23
2000	4.00	0.52	-3.67

*12 months to November (a negative figure indicates a surplus).
Source: Brazilian Central Bank (2001); Fundação Getúlio Vargas (2000).

Despite these achievements, however, risks remain. In particular, as has been already hinted, the state of the Brazilian public sector accounts remains vulnerable to an increase in interest rates. Leaving aside the experience of 2001, the effects of such a rate rise have already been made clear by the events of the late 1990s where, between 1994 and 1999, total internal public sector debt rose from 20.3 per cent of GDP to 38.6 per cent.[29]

Financial Markets

In common with other sectors of the Brazilian economy the financial services sector has been the focus of substantial liberalisation efforts over the past decade. Among the most important developments has been the privatisation of the state banking sector. Since 1995 most of these institutions — which were formally owned by the state governments — have been transferred to the private sector. Significantly, foreign financial institutions have been allowed to bid for these banks and have encountered considerable success in doing so. For example, on 20 November 2000, Brazil's largest state bank, the São Paulo based Banespa was auctioned off to Banco Santander of Spain for R$7.05 billion (US$3.5 billion). The liberalisation of the financial sector and its opening to foreign competition has also progressed in other directions. With the non-state banking sector's profitability and solvency threatened by the end of hyper-inflation, over the past six years or so the authorities have proven very keen to grant admission to foreign institutions seeking to purchase Brazilian commercial and investment banks. As a result of this policy several major domestic banks have been taken over by foreign institutions. In tandem with the opening up of the banking sector, the authorities have also proven enthusiastic in welcoming new foreign participants in the insurance industry, a sector that has expanded rapidly over the past decade. As in other sectors the new regulations allow for 100 per cent ownership of Brazilian subsidiaries.

At present, the authorities show no sign of reversing their open-door policy to foreign investors seeking to increase their presence in the Brazilian financial sector. However, it is important to note that, unlike other sectors, foreign investors possess no absolute right to participate in the financial sector. Instead, they require the prior approval of the Brazilian Central Bank, which, while usually a formality, is not necessarily automatic.

With the ongoing liberalisation of the Brazilian financial sector, the authorities have sought to increase the prudential standards applying to institutions. In particular, the Central Bank has played an increasingly strong role in monitoring reserve levels among banks which average 25 per cent of deposits.[30] In the case of a number of troubled institutions, espe-

29 Amann and Baer (2000).
30 Banco Central do Brasil (2000).

cially the state banks, the Central Bank has acted to swiftly inject capital. Partly as a result, the Brazilian banking sector remains generally well capitalised, an attribute which has also resulted from the substantial entry of foreign direct investment in recent years.

As part of their strategy to increase the attractiveness of Brazilian financial markets to both direct and portfolio investors, the Central Bank and the Stock Exchange Commission (CVM) have been seeking to bring national accounting standards into greater alignment with US and European norms. For example, many major Brazilian corporations have now adopted US accounting standards on the treatment of depreciation and off balance sheet liabilities. However, progress in this area has proved to be slower than originally anticipated. This is due to the fact that some enterprises feel it unnecessary to gain access to international capital markets and thus feel expenditure on adopting new procedures to be wasteful. Nevertheless, an increasing number of Brazilian enterprises in both the financial and non-financial sectors have been adopting foreign accounting standards in an attempt to gain access to international financial markets. A good example in this regard is Ambev, the world's third largest brewer whose shares have begun trading on the New York Stock Exchange.

Figure 5.7: The Evolution of the Bovespa Stock Exchange Index, 1992–2000

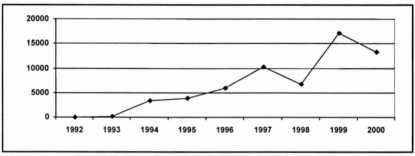

Note: Data refer to closing levels for year. 2000 data refer to October.
Source: Brazilian Central Bank (BCB) (2001).

Thanks to growing volumes of foreign investment, the banking and insurance sectors have embarked upon a much-needed phase of modernisation and development. New management techniques are being employed, information technology systems are being upgraded and aggressive marketing campaigns launched. However, elements of the financial sector remain plagued with difficulties. Over the past five years, the stock market, despite a generalised upward movement in share values (see Figure 5.5) has experienced a troubling wave of de-listings.

The thinning out of the Brazilian stock market has mainly resulted from the effects of the privatisation programme. Prior to privatisation, the shares of majority state owned enterprises had formed the bulk of those listed on both the Rio de Janeiro and São Paulo stock markets. With the foreign take-over of many of these enterprises following privatisation, the new owners have in many cases decided to de-list their subsidiaries from the local stock exchange, seeking instead to consolidate their equity listings in the USA or Europe. As a result of this trend trading volumes have declined, liquidity has decreased and, given the absence of an active local bond market, effective corporate access to domestic non-bank finance has become increasingly limited. In an attempt to reverse this trend the authorities have announced a package of measures that are currently under review by congressional committees.

Central to the proposed measures is the introduction of a new piece of legislation termed the Law of S.A.s. The law, approved in mid 2001, aims to increase the representative rights of minority shareholders, giving them a greater say on board level decisions concerning the disbursement of dividends and the launch of rights issues. According to its proponents, the Law should have the effect of luring back foreign and small domestic investors to the stock market, deepening the pool of available capital and increasing access to equity finance. Among other proposals currently under consideration is a measure that would stimulate the private pension provision sector through the use of more favourable tax treatment. Such favourable tax treatment would centre on reduced taxation of dividends on shares held by pension funds. In addition, incentives might also include more generous tax deductions for individual pension contributors. If effective, this development would also act to increase the flow of funds into the equity market.

The External Sector

Since the adoption of the Real Plan in late 1993, one of the most disappointing aspects of Brazil's macroeconomic performance has been that of the current account balance. As the table below indicates, following the achievement of a large surplus on current account in 1992, by 1993 the balance had swung into deficit, a trend that continued for the rest of the decade.

Table 5.9: The Evolution of Brazil's External Accounts, 1990–2000 (US$ million, current prices)

Year	Imports	(Per cent GDP)	Exports	(Per cent GDP)	Trade Balance	Services Balance	Int. Pay*	Current A/C Balance	(Per cent GDP)
1990	20661	7	31414	8.2	10753	-15639	-9748	-3782	-0.8
1991	21041	7.9	31620	8.7	10579	-13542	-8621	-1407	0.3
1992	20554	8.4	35862	10.9	15308	-11339	-7253	6144	1.6
1993	25659	9.1	38597	10.5	12938	-15585	-8280	-592	-0.1
1994	33105	9.2	43545	9.5	10440	-14743	-6338	-1689	-0.3
1995	49664	9.5	46506	7.7	-3158	-18594	-8158	-17972	-2.5
1996	53346	8.9	47747	7	-5599	-20443	-9173	-23142	-3
1997	59742	10.2	52994	7.6	-6748	-26278	-10388	-30811	-3.8
1998	57743	10.1	51140	7.4	-6603	-28800	-11947	-33625	-4.3
1999	49272	8.7	48011	8.5	-1261	-25829	-15237	-25062	-4.7
2000	55783	8.6	55086	8.4	-697	-25706	-15088	-24608	-4.1

*Interest Payments Overseas.
Source: Brazilian Central Bank (BCB)(2001); Fundação Getúlio Vargas (FGV) (2000).

Underlying the growing difficulties Brazil has faced in maintaining external equilibrium are two key factors. First, despite considerable improvements in competitiveness, Brazil's export sector was not able for most of the period to expand sales sufficiently to counterbalance the upsurge in imports. Moreover, following the introduction of the Real Plan, the currency's relatively high external value allied to robust expansion in demand acted as a magnet for imports. With the abandonment of the currency peg at the beginning of 1999, however, the entire context for the external balance has changed. From being approximately 20 per cent overvalued against the US dollar, the *real* has achieved a new and sustainable competitiveness.[31] With this, the deficit on both the trade and hence current accounts of the balance of payments has shrunk noticeably.

The second key factor underlying the performance of the current account balance lies in a consideration of Brazil's debt repayment burden. Between 1997 and 1999 this expanded considerably as investors applied much higher interest rates to Brazil's external borrowings. Between 1999 and 2000, however, with investor sentiment generally more favourable, international interest rates faced by Brazilian borrowers fell with spreads above the US federal funds rate for Brazilian public debt narrowing from over ten per cent to six per cent. This acted to reduce interest remittances

31 Amann and Baer (2000).

with favourable consequences for the current account balance. One unfortunate consequence of Brazil's poor performance on current account has been a considerable accumulation of debt. As Table 5.10 below makes clear, the level of long-term debt has practically doubled since the mid-1990s.

Table 5.10: The Evolution of Brazilian External Debt
Total External Debt by Category (US$ million end year)

Year	Short Term Debt	(% GDP)	Long Term Debt	(% GDP)
1990	26893	5.7	96546	20.6
1991	30914	7.6	92996	22.9
1992	25114	6.5	110835	28.6
1993	31456	5.8	114270	21
1994	28627	5.3	119668	22
1995	29943	4.2	129313	18.3
1996	37787	4.9	142148	18.3
1997	36715	4.6	163283	20.4
1998	26643	3.4	215134	27.7
1999	28460	5	212596	37.5
2000	27426	4.1	205014	31.5

N.B Data for 2000 refer to debt outstanding at the end of August.
Source: Brazilian Central Bank (BCB) (2001).

In financing the current account deficit, foreign investors have been drawn into the Brazilian market by several attractive investment opportunities that have been presented by Brazil's privatisation and market liberalisation programmes. In particular, the privatisation programme has involved the transfer of large tracts of the public utilities sector into the hands of foreign corporations.

The surge of FDI witnessed in the past few years is also partly explained by the fact that Brazil's rules on capital movements are relatively liberal. In general, direct and indirect investments do not require the prior approval of the Central Bank or any other official authority. However, such investments need to be registered with the Central Bank, as do records of the foreign exchange transactions with which they were facilitated. Equally liberally, both foreign direct and portfolio investors are at liberty to withdraw capital from Brazil without hindrance or penalty. On occasion, this provision has permitted episodes of capital flight, as for example, in the immediate run up to January 1999's floatation of the *real*. More generally though, the adoption of a laissez-faire approach to the management of capital flows has acted as a more general encouragement to foreign investor participation in Brazilian financial instruments and production facilities.

Conclusions

The transformation of the Brazilian economy over the past decade has been impressive in its intensity and shows little sign of slowing. Having pursued an inward orientated industrialisation strategy for much of the post-war period, since the late 1980s Brazil has embarked on a path of progressive integration into the global economy. At the same time, thanks to a well planned, carefully implemented stabilisation programme, the hyperinflation of the past has become a fading memory.

As the Brazilian economy progresses into the new decade it is only appropriate to reflect on these achievements and acknowledge their considerable magnitude. However, such reflection should not be devoid of critical aspect. In particular, despite successive years of positive economic growth and low inflation, the Brazilian economy remains characterised by serious structural failings, not least the persistence of poverty and inequality and excessive vulnerability to alterations in international financial conditions. These difficulties have deep roots, most especially a highly skewed distribution of assets and a perennially low savings rate. Given the political difficulties attached to implementing meaningful reform in these areas it is hardly surprising that, thus far, policy-makers have proved reluctant to institute real change. In the future, however, such change may become unavoidable if only because the financing of growth through FDI inflows and the accumulation of external debt may become less feasible or cost effective. Under these circumstances (which are likely to occur during periods of diminished international financial market liquidity), robust growth could only be assured provided an adequate pool of domestic savings existed.

Of course, boosting domestic savings and tackling inequality are not the only challenges that remain to be faced by policy-makers. As this chapter has reiterated, despite a favourable *real* devaluation and improvements in competitiveness, growth in Brazilian exports has remained surprisingly muted over recent years. With import absorption still relatively high, considerable efforts will need to be made to boost exports further if any significant reductions in the current account deficit are to be realised. In this regard, Brazilian policy-makers are acutely aware of the experience of neighbouring Argentina, where a legacy of disappointing export performance is at least in part responsible for the current crisis. Another serious lingering difficulty yet to be fully addressed concerns the public accounts, a field in which, it has been argued, progress has been generally favourable. However, in one area of this field — social security reform — the speed of change has been extremely limited with the result that the authorities face the prospect of a spiralling social security deficit over the next few years. In these areas, among others, policy-makers will need to act decisively — and swiftly — in order that the achievements of the past decade can be preserved into the future.

CHAPTER 6

The External Constraints on Economic Policy and Performance in Brazil

Celso L. Martone

This chapter analyses the limitations imposed on Brazil's future economic growth by the current balance of payments structure, in the light of the experience of the last 15 years of democratic government. Section one presents the basic facts on the balance of payments; next the developments of the last 15 years are reviewed, further sections analyse the responses of economic policy to external constraints and the country's growth performance. A simple model is then put forward in which the role of foreign saving in domestic capital accumulation is emphasised along with long-term stability conditions, in the light of which Brazil's current external disequilibrium is evaluated. It is shown that the prevailing structural parameters of the economy are inconsistent with long-term stability. The final section discusses some policy alternatives aimed at inducing a more competitive integration of Brazil into the world economy so as to create long-term stability and to achieve a satisfactory growth rate.

Dependency on Foreign Saving

Domestic saving in Latin America is low by world standards, reaching no more than 20 per cent of GDP. Foreign saving, when available, plays an important complementary role in capital formation and growth. Thus, it is not surprising that growth cycles in the region have been closely associated with the international credit cycles. In the last 30 years we have seen a complete credit cycle in the world economy: expansion in the 1970s with the development of international banking, followed by contraction in the 1980s, when most developing countries went through payments crises and had to restructure their foreign debt; and a new expansion phase in the 1990s, known as the 'emerging markets boom'. The recent boost has reversed since the Asian crisis of 1997, but this does not compare to the complete halt of foreign lending in the 1980s. Contrary to the credit expansion of the 1970s, when capital flows to the region took the form of bank loans, the expansion of the 1990s took the form of capital market instruments and foreign direct investment.[1]

---

1   Two interesting appraisals of the debt crisis, its consequences and lessons from a Latin American perspective are Banco Mundial (1993) and Comission Economica para America Latina y el Caribe (1995). For an international perspective, see Cline (1995).

Despite the clear dependency of Latin America on foreign capital, however, the role of domestic factors in economic growth has been dominant, at least in the case of Brazil. As the economic crisis of the 1980s developed, fundamental changes in the institutional environment took place in rapid succession in most countries of the region. The first of these was the return to democracy: Argentina, Brazil, Chile and Uruguay, just to mention the Southern Cone countries, adopted democratic governments almost simultaneously in the mid-1980s. The second was a radical change in the way most countries relate to the world economy, namely, the transition from protectionism to a more open trade system. The third was the move from mega-inflation regimes toward fiscal responsibility and relative monetary stability.

Developments in Brazil have mirrored the general pattern of Latin America, although the country has been a latecomer in some important aspects. Democracy was re-established in 1985, in a situation of no access to foreign lending, high inflation, serious fiscal problems and, perhaps more significantly, pressing demands on the new government. The political frustration long repressed under the military regime materialised in the 1988 Constitution, an essay in forced income redistribution, extension of entitlements of all kinds and fiscal decentralisation, which have created severe constraints to the management of economic policy to this day. The opening of the economy started in 1989, with the partial unification of the foreign exchange markets and the beginning of trade liberalisation through a modest tariff reform. Monetary stabilisation came in 1994 with the Real Plan, and fiscal responsibility as late as 1999 in the wake of a foreign exchange crisis and an adjustment programme with the IMF. Brazil was the last large debtor to conclude a Brady Plan in April 1994. Only in 1992 the country started to be seen as an 'emerging market' and to attract foreign capital.[2]

Figures 6.1 and 6.2 show the Brazilian current account deficit and net external financing since 1980, where the cyclical pattern described above is clearly seen. If we adopt the concept of 'real resource transfer', defined here by the deficit of goods and non-factor services, it can be seen that Brazil received a positive transfer until 1982, then effected a transfer from 1983 to 1994, and again has received a large positive transfer since 1995. Net external financing became negative from 1985 to 1992 through the contraction of bank credit, while foreign direct investment remained almost zero. Brazil's access to the world capital markets started in 1992, allowing a large current account deficit since 1995. However, it should be noted that, after the Asian crisis of 1997 and the exchange rate devaluation of January 1999, the composition of external financing has changed radically: net borrowing became negative, while FDI became increasingly positive.

2   For surveys of the reforms since the late 1980s, see Zini (1993); Baumann (ed.) (2000); and Coes (1995).

Figure 6.1: Brazil: Current Account Balance 1980–2000 (US$ billion)

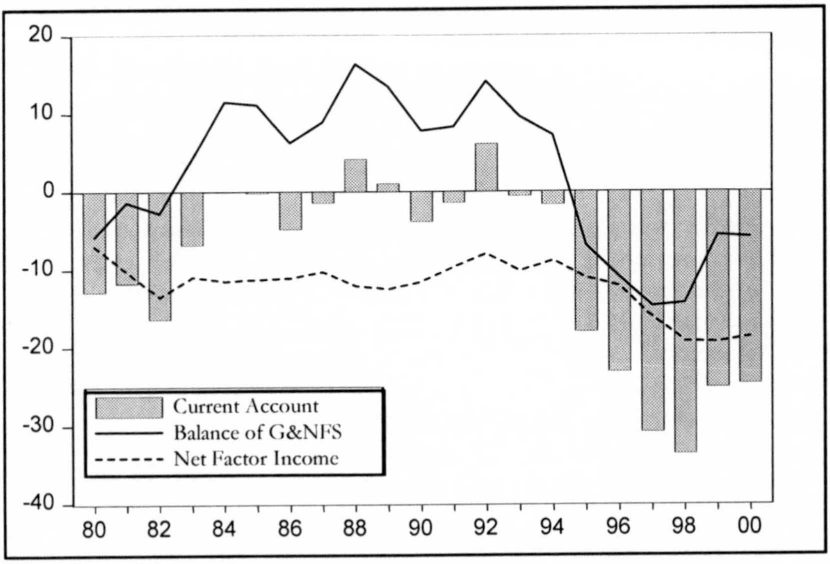

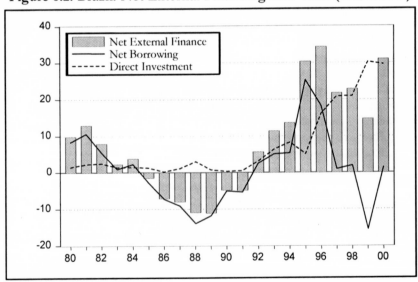

Figure 6.2: Brazil: Net External Financing 1980–2000 (US$ billion)

Economic Policy in a Democratic Environment: 1985–92

The economic situation faced by the democratic government installed in March 1985 and the policy response to it is relevant for the analysis of the more recent period. The balance of payments adjustment, as Figure 1 shows, had been successfully carried out in 1983–84, generating the required resource transfer abroad. The effort of external adjustment, however, implied a severe recession, together with accelerating inflation and serious fiscal problems. Between 1981 and 1984, GDP fell cumulatively 1.2 per cent, while inflation jumped from 94 per cent to 210 per cent per year. The net public sector debt increased from 35.5 per cent of GDP in 1982, the year of the debt crisis, to 50.3 per cent in 1985, as a result of a double process: the financing of the current public sector deficit and the massive transfer of foreign debt from the private to the public sector (see Figure 6.3).[3]

Figure 6.3: Public Debt as a Proportion of GDP (per cent)

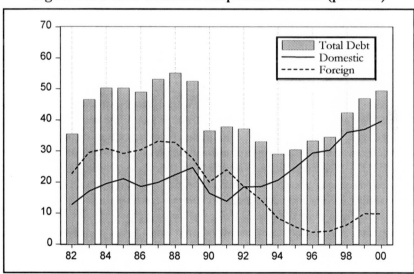

The reduction of domestic absorption relative to income necessary to effect the transfer (eliminate the current account deficit) was produced by a combination of aggressive exchange rate devaluation and strict control of imports and capital flows. As the public sector deficit remained high

3   The assumption of the private foreign debt by the government (in fact, the Central Bank) was a conscious policy instrument, created in the 1970s to reduce the exchange rate risk of the private sector, inducing banks and firms to borrow abroad. Later, during the several debt renegotiations with the creditor banks, it was the consequence of the transformation of foreign debt into sovereign debt.

and no net external financing was available, the inflation tax and the expansion of the domestic public debt were the means of transferring resources from the private to the public sector. Given the widespread indexation of wages and prices and the passive monetary policy, the adjustment implied an accelerating rate of inflation.

The response of the new democratic government to that situation privileged the recovery of the economy, through monetary and fiscal expansion, which further aggravated the fiscal imbalance and inflation and, consequently, reopened the deficit in the current account and depleted the country's international reserves. In February 1986, one year after its inauguration, with inflation running at more than 400 per cent per year (see Figure 6.4), the government launched the first of a series of 'heterodox' stabilisation plans, the Cruzado Plan, based on a general price freeze and a currency reform. The failure of the plan and the aggravation of the macroeconomic imbalances led, in February 1987, to a unilateral moratorium on the foreign debt, which marked the turning point of the Sarney administration. From that point until 1990, when Collor (1990–92) took office, the government limited its action to avoiding hyperinflation and political collapse. At the end of the Sarney government the public debt had increased to 52.5 per cent of GDP and inflation had jumped to over 50 per cent per month.

The relationship between the Brazilian government and the world financial community went through various phases after the debt crisis of the end of 1982. In 1983 and 1984, under the military regime, Brazil maintained an active adjustment programme with the International Monetary Fund (IMF), which was seen as a necessary condition to renegotiate the foreign debt with the private banks and the Paris Club. The fact that Brazil systematically failed to meet the targets of the programme did not preclude the yearly agreements of 1983 and 1984, corresponding to the so-called phases one and two of the debt renegotiations. The Sarney government had a confused policy regarding the foreign debt and the IMF. Between 1985 and the moratorium of February 1987 a standstill prevailed in the debt negotiations and no programme with the IMF existed, which was feasible because Brazil was effecting the required resource transfer abroad. The rapid deterioration in the balance of payments, consequent of the Cruzado Plan and the moratorium, led the Sarney government to a new adjustment programme with the IMF in 1988 and to a multi-year rescheduling of the foreign debt with private creditors, known as phase three of the renegotiations, which paved the way to the conclusion of the Brady Plan four years later. In the ten-year period from the end of the Sarney government in March 1989 to November 1998, when a new foreign exchange crisis occurred, Brazil lived without the formal supervision of the Fund.

Figure 6.4: Monthly Rate of Inflation in Brazil (per cent Change of Consumer Price Index)

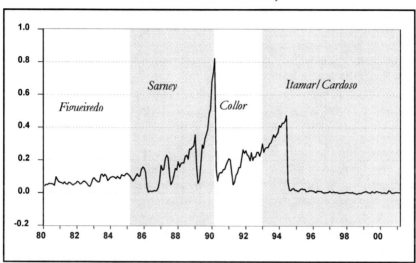

The frustrating experience of the final years of the Sarney administration intensified the criticism of the protectionist and interventionist 'model' prevailing since the 1950s. A new consensus emerged, inspired by developments in other countries, based on two main points. First, Brazil should seek a 'competitive integration' to the world economy, to use the jargon of the time, meaning the liberalisation of the trading system. Second, a deep reform of the public sector should be made, implying the privatisation of state enterprises and the deregulation of the economy. The Collor administration took important steps in implementing the new consensus, and Brazil started to be seen as an emerging market and to attract foreign capital in 1992. Although Collor failed disastrously on the inflation front, the opening of the economy and the privatisation programme paved the way for the successful Real Plan two years later.

The failure of the successive stabilisation plans of the period 1986–92 was due mainly to the political incapacity of the democratic governments to implement a sustainable fiscal adjustment. The public sector needed the inflation tax as a residual source of revenue, which in turn resulted in accelerating inflation. Nevertheless, it can also be argued that the lack of external financing, obliging the country to effect an annual real resource transfer abroad of around four per cent of GDP, left no degree of freedom for a successful stabilisation programme. In fact, the lack of external financing precluded an exchange rate-based stabilisation plan (an exchange rate anchor), and the chronic public sector deficit impeded an independent monetary policy directed at price stability (a monetary anchor). Given the fiscal and the external constraints, the government either decreed general price freezes, like the Cruzado Plan of 1986, and/or the partial confiscation of the private sector's financial wealth, like the Collor Plan of 1990. As both types of expedient were necessarily short-lived, price stability did not last more than a few months and inflation returned more virulent than before, as Figure 6.4 shows.

Economic Policy with Abundant Reserves: 1993–2000

The opening of the economy and the beginning of the privatisation programme, in the context of rapidly expanding world capital markets, began to attract foreign capital to Brazil in 1992. The relaxation of the external constraints, after more than ten years without access to the world financial markets, created the conditions for an exchange rate-based stabilisation plan in July 1994 (the Real Plan). Between 1991 and 1994 Brazil's hard currency reserves went up from US$9.4 billion to US$38.8 billion, equivalent to more than one quarter of the total foreign debt (Figure 6.5). Stabilisation was possible despite the fact that, from 1994 to 1999, the ratio of the net public debt to GDP increased continuously, meaning that a loose fiscal policy was practised until the foreign exchange crisis of the end of 1998. The loss of the inflation tax was replaced by the expansion of the public debt (both domestic and foreign) and by privatisation revenues.

Figure 6.5: The Ratio of Reserves to the Foreign Debt (per cent)

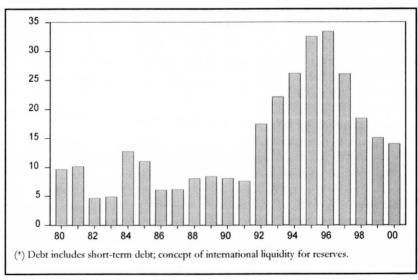

(*) Debt includes short-term debt; concept of international liquidity for reserves.

Concerning the role of the external restriction on economic policy, three distinct phases of the Franco (1993–94) and Cardoso (1995–2002) governments can be distinguished.[4] The first phase, from the Real Plan of July 1994 to the Asian crisis of the second half of 1997, was characterised by an elastic supply of foreign capital and an increasing deficit in the current account. The overvaluation of the exchange rate, resulting from the residual inflation after the launching of the Plan, acted as a subsidy both to foreign borrowing and to imports. The domestic real interest rate was maintained very high — 20 per cent per year on the average of 1994–98 — to sustain the overvalued exchange rate, inducing the capital inflow necessary to finance the increasing current account deficit. The high real cost of the public debt and the monetary sterilisation of the reserve accumulation conducted by the Central Bank were important factors in the snowball increase of the public debt of this period.

The survival of this policy framework depended on the continuous inflow of foreign capital. The regime entered a stressed second phase with the reversal of the capital flows to emerging markets caused by the Asian crisis. It survived another year, until the end of 1998, when the continuous drain of reserves following the Russian crisis forced the government to negotiate a rescue package with the international community and a fiscal adjustment programme with the IMF.

The third phase of the Cardoso administration starting in 1999 represented a radical change from the previous policies. The lax fiscal regime was replaced by a more responsible fiscal policy aimed at stabilising the ratio of the public debt to GDP, requiring the generation of a 'primary' surplus of around three per cent of GDP. A free-floating exchange rate succeeded the pegged exchange rate regime, implying a real devaluation of around 50 per cent (see Figure 6.6).

However, despite the change of the policy regime, the distortions accumulated in the 1994–98 period have generated serious long-term problems for the economy. On the one hand they created a typical stock problem similar to the 1980s. The net external liabilities of the country rose from 43 per cent to 68 per cent of GDP and from 5.4 times to 7.1 times the value of exports between 1994 and 2000, imposing a heavy burden on the balance of payments for the future. On the other hand the reallocation of resources away from the export and import competing sectors, resulting from the overvaluation of the exchange rate, created a chronic deficit in the balance of goods and non-factor services. Between 1994 and 2000 imports grew at an annual average of 9.1 per cent, while exports increased only four per cent.

---

4   It should be said that Cardoso, as the minister of finance, played a decisive role in the Franco administration, including the Real Plan, which effectively won him the presidency.

Figure 6.6: The Brazilian Real Exchange Rate* (R$ per US$ at 2000 prices)

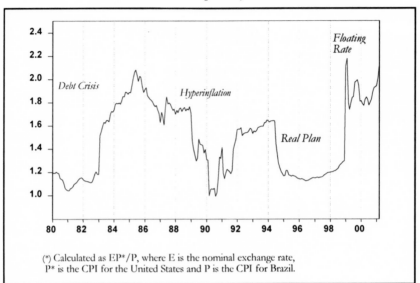

(*) Calculated as EP^*/P, where E is the nominal exchange rate, P^* is the CPI for the United States and P is the CPI for Brazil.

Low Growth and High Instability

The growth of the Brazilian economy under the democratic governments since 1985 has been low and inconstant, as can be seen in Figure 6.7. The rate of investment fell from 25–30 per cent of GDP to 15–20 per cent between the 1970s and the 1990s, while GDP growth fell from 5–10 per cent to 0–5 per cent. In the 16 years of democracy, the average growth rate of the economy was 2.6 per cent per year. Considering the growth of population, per capita income grew a little under one per cent per year on the average of that period.

Lower growth rates have coexisted with high volatility of GDP, as shown in Figure 6.8, where some critical periods have been indicated: the impact of the debt crisis in 1982–83, the short-lived boom of the cruzado in 1986, the hyperinflationary period that followed until 1993, and the Real Plan of 1994. The instability of the economy in that period can be partially attributed to the foreign debt crisis of the 1980s and the hyperinflationary regime up to the mid-1990s. The near monetary stability achieved since 1994 seems to have reduced the fluctuations of income and employment. However, an old source of vulnerability was reintroduced in recent years: the chronic current account deficit in the balance of payments and the high dependency on external finance.

Figure 6.7: GDP Growth and Rate of Investment: 1970–99*

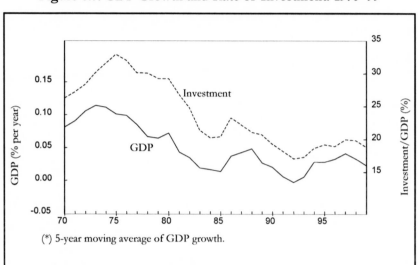

(*) 5-year moving average of GDP growth.

Figure 6.8: The Output Gap in Brazil: 1970–2000*

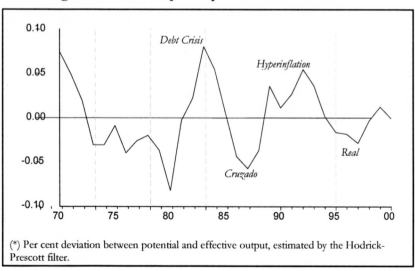

(*) Per cent deviation between potential and effective output, estimated by the Hodrick-Prescott filter.

It is not surprising that the instability of the institutional and economic environment substantially reduced the rate of growth of total factor productivity (the growth of output not explained by the growth of the labour force and the accumulation of physical capital). Figure 6.9 shows that, in the first half of the 1980s and the 1990s, productivity even fell.[5]

Figure 6.9: Brazil: Growth of Total Factor Productivity (Solow Residual)

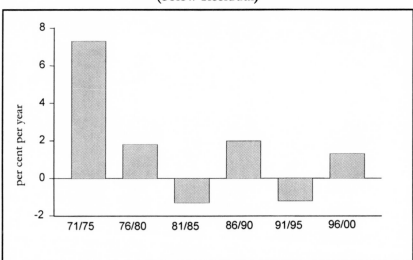

The problem of the low saving rate of the private sector has been aggravated by chronic dissaving of the public sector (Table 6.1). Indirect estimation suggests that the annual depreciation of the capital stock is about 15 per cent of GDP, which implies that the gross investment rate allowed by domestic resources alone would be barely sufficient to keep the capital stock constant, were it not for the availability of foreign savings in the post-stabilisation period.

5   Total factor productivity was estimated by the usual procedure of estimating the 'residual' of a production function in labour and capital. It was assumed that the share of capital in output is 45 per cent and the rate of depreciation is three per cent per year. The estimation of the capital stock was started in 1952 to obtain the largest possible sample.

Table 6.1: The Composition of Saving — percentage of GDP

Years	Gross Investment	Private Saving (1)	Public Saving	Foreign Saving
1994	19.6	21.9	-2.6	0.3
1995	19.2	19.7	-3.0	2.5
1996	18.9	17.2	-1.5	3.3
1997	20.0	18.0	-2.2	4.2
1998	19.8	20.5	-5.0	4.3
1999	20.4	18.1	-1.9	4.2
2000*	20.5	15.3	0.9	4.3

(1) Obtained as a residual. (*) Estimate.
Source: IBGE, National Accounts Statistics (elaboration by author).

Evaluating the External Constraints to Growth

In order to evaluate the external constraints to economic growth, a simple model is developed below, emphasising the dynamic behaviour of the country's net foreign liabilities, on the one hand, and of the public debt, on the other hand.

Per capita output Y is determined by the level of technology A and the per capita capital stock K:

(1) $$Y_t = A_t K_t^q$$

implying that the rate of growth of output is $g_y(t) = g_A(t) + q\, g_K(t)$.

The capital stock increases by gross investment expenditures I minus depreciation at a fixed rate d:

(2) $$K_t = I_t + (1-d) K_{t-1}$$

Taking the increase of total productivity as exogenous, the evolution of per capita output depends on the rate of gross investment, which is equal to total savings, according to the national accounting identity:

(3) $$I_t = s(Y_t - Z_t) + (Z_t - G_t) + e_t (B^*_t + V^*_t)$$

In the above equation, it is assumed that private saving is a fixed proportion s of disposable income (Y-Z), public sector saving is given by tax revenue Z minus current public expenditure G, and foreign saving is given by the deficit of goods and non-factor services (g&nfs) B*, plus net factor payments on foreign capital V*. Foreign currency variables are indicated by a star (*) and the real exchange rate is defined as $e=Ep^*/p$, where E is the nominal exchange rate and p^* and p are the world and the domestic price levels.

The balance of payments identity implies that the country's net foreign liabilities (NFL) F* increase by the current account deficit:

$$(4) \qquad F_t^* = F_{t-1}^* + B_t^* + V_t^*$$

Foreign investors require a rate of return on F* equal to the international interest rate r^* plus a sovereign risk premium s:

$$(5) \qquad V_t^* = (r^*+s)\, F_{t-1}^*$$

In view of (5), we can rewrite (4) as:

$$(4^1) \qquad F_t^* = (1+r^*+s)\, F_{t-1}^* + B_t^*$$

In the small country case, we can assume that the deficit of g&nfs is an increasing function of domestic output Y and a decreasing function of world output Y* and the real exchange rate e:

$$(6) \qquad B_t^* = f(Y_t,\, Y_t^*,\, e_t)$$

In equilibrium, capital mobility implies that the domestic real interest rate (r-p) is equal to the international real rate (r^*-p^*), plus the risk premium s, where p and p^* are the corresponding rates of inflation.

On the other hand, the budget constraint of the public sector is:

$$D_t = (1+ r^*-p^*+s)\, D_{t-1} + (G_t^0 - Z_t)$$

where D is the real public debt and public expenditures were split into primary expenditure (except interest) G^0 and debt service, or $G = G^0 + (r^*-p^*+s)\, D_{t-1}$.

Since we are not interested in determining nominal variables like the rate of inflation and the nominal exchange rate, it is not necessary to add a monetary bloc to the model. Equations (1), (2), (3), (4^1), (6) and (7) can be used to simulate the time paths of the variables Y, K, I, F and D, given assumptions about the parameters q and d, total productivity A, the fiscal policy variables Z and G^0, the international variables r^*, p^*, s, Y*, and the real exchange rate e.

The basic question to be answered is: given the present structure of the economy, is there a reasonable rate of growth of output consistent with stable time paths for F and D? In the long run, there is an upper limit to the ratio of the public debt to GDP, beyond which a hyperinflation or debt confiscation occurs. By the same argument, there is an upper limit to the ratio of a country's net foreign liabilities to GDP, beyond which a payments crisis and/or some kind of foreign debt restructuring occurs. In both cases, long-run economic stability requires that D and F remain within sustainable limits.

For the purpose of this chapter, a quite simple exercise was done. After the change in the policy regime in 1999, it is believed — and the Cardoso administration has systematically emphasised it — that Brazil can sustain a rate of growth of at least four per cent per year in the coming years, while advancing down the path of fiscal and external adjustment. In 2000, in fact, the economy grew four per cent and both the ratio of the public debt to GDP and of NFL to GDP have remained stable. To evaluate this argument, the present structure of the economy, defined by its macroeconomic parameters, is taken as given, assumptions are made on the course of the international variables and it is required that output grow four per cent per year, which is consistent with an investment rate of 20 per cent of GDP and growth of overall productivity of about 1.4 per cent per year, the average of the last five years.

On the international level, we assume that the world real rate of interest is 2.5 per cent per year, the historical average, and that Brazil's sovereign risk premium stays at 450 basis points in the projection period (2005), the same level that prevailed before the Asian crisis of 1997, allowing the domestic real interest rate to remain around seven per cent per year. World inflation if assumed to be two per cent per year and the growth of world trade is seven per cent per year, the average of the last five years.

On the domestic side the real exchange rate remains constant at a level 50 per cent above the one immediately before the adoption of the floating regime in January 1999. The elasticity of imports of g&nfs relative to domestic output is 1.5, and the elasticity of exports relative to world trade is unity.[6] The fiscal adjustment made under the IMF agreement of 1999 is maintained, meaning that public sector saving is around zero.[7]

With these assumptions the model generates net foreign liabilities corresponding to 81 per cent of GDP in 2005 (68 per cent today) and a current account deficit in the balance of payments of 7.4 per cent of GDP (4.3 per cent today), suggesting that the present structure of the economy

---

6   In fact, the elasticity of exports estimated considering the last 20 years is 0.75, consistent with the secular decline of the Brazilian share in world exports from a peak of 1.5 per cent in the mid-1980s to under one per cent today.

7   Public investment has been around two per cent of GDP in recent years. Considering tax collections of 30 per cent of GDP, government expenditure (except interest) of 28 per cent, and debt service of four per cent, we arrive at zero government saving.

is not consistent with long-term stability (see Tables 6.2 and 6.3).[8] The dynamics of F* are dominated by the autonomous growth of the flow of factor income. With the elasticities assumed for B*, the economy is not able to generate a surplus in g&nfs to compensate for the increase in V*, so that F* grows without bound. In other words, if the economy grows four per cent per year, it is not able to effect a real transfer abroad to stabilise its NFL relative to GDP. In fact, it turns out that, given the current structure, there is no positive growth rate that can stabilise this ratio in this decade.[9]

Table 6.2: Recent Performance and Hypotheses Adopted in the Simulation

	1994	1995	1996	1997	1998	1999	2000	2001/05*
Growth of World Trade Volume (1)	10.0	9.8	5.8	10.0	4.1	5.2	10.0	7.0
Brazil's Sovereign Risk (2)	n.a.	n.a.	n.a.	4.9	8.0	11.0	7.5	4.5
Dollar Interest Rate (3)	4.2	5.8	5.3	5.5	5.4	5.0	6.3	4.5
Dollar Inflation (4)	2.7	3.0	2.6	2.2	2.4	1.9	2.6	2.0
Domestic Real Interest Rate (5)	23.3	25.1	16.2	18.6	26.5	15.3	10.8	7.1
Public Sector Primary Surplus/GDP (6)	0.4	0.1	1.0	0	3.2	3.6	3.0	2.0
Brazil's GDP Growth (7)	6.0	4.3	2.7	3.6	0	0.8	3.8	4.0

(1) IMF, World Economic Outlook, per cent annual rate.
(2) EMBI for Brazil, published by Morgan Guarantee. Per cent over the US Treasury bond yield.
(3) Federal Funds Rate in the USA, per cent per year.
(4) CPI in the USA, per cent per year.
(5) SELIC rate corrected for inflation, per cent per year.
(6) Central Bank of Brazil.
(7) Per cent per year.
(*) Assumptions.

8   The current account deficit for 2005 includes reinvestment of foreign capital, so it does not measure the net effect of factor income on the balance of payments. In Brazil, there is justified suspicion that the balance of payments statistics underestimate foreign reinvestment, and of course profits and dividends.
9   If the ratio of F* to GDP grows continuously, the risk premium s will rise, not stay constant as assumed in the simulation, aggravating the problem.

On the other hand the ratio of the public debt to GDP stabilises at 58 per cent, suggesting that the binding constraint on growth is the balance of payments and not the fiscal deficit. The reason for this is the low real interest rate on the public debt (7.1 per cent), contrasting with an average of 20 per cent in the period of the Real Plan (1994–98).

Table 6.3: Projection of the Endogenous Variables (US$ billion unless indicated)

	1994	1995	1996	1997	1998	1999	2000	2005*
Current Account Deficit (1)	1.7	18.0	23.1	30.8	33.6	25.1	24.6	59.1
Net Foreign Liabilities	233.4	251.4	274.5	308.0	341.6	368.8	393.6	642.0
Dollar GDP (2)	543.1	705.4	775.4	803.8	772.7	542.8	578.0	796.4
Public Debt/GDP (per cent)	29.1	30.5	33.3	34.6	42.4	47.0	49.5	58.0

(1) Inclusive of reinvestment.
(2) Evaluated at the market exchange rate.
(*) Assumptions.

Implications and Conclusions

The results of the previous section, even under the favourable set of assumptions made, contradict the argument that the Brazilian economy has entered a 'virtuous circle' of growth and stability after the balance of payments crisis of January 1999 and the consequent change of the government's policy regime. Of course the kind of exercise done above is necessarily simple and can only take into account a limited number of the relevant variables that determine the structure of the balance of payments and its evolution over time. Despite this qualification, the exercise shows that the change of the Brazilian policy regime after 1999 may have been insufficient to produce long-term stability, given the typical stock problem consequent of the rapid accumulation of NFL in the second half of the 1990s.

The argument of the 'virtuous circle' is based on the structural changes that occurred in the 1990s, especially in the last two years of the decade. It is then necessary to examine these changes to evaluate to what extent the relevant parameters of the economy have changed or will change in the future to generate a virtuous circle.

The first argument relates to the change in the fiscal regime under the IMF adjustment programme of 1999–2001, backed by the changes introduced in the social security system and in the civil service, by the increase in the tax burden and, more recently, by the so-called law of fiscal responsibility.[10] These changes have allowed the generation of a primary surplus of three per cent of GDP in 1999–2000 and have probably created reasonable conditions for maintaining it around two per cent in the coming years. Alongside this, the adoption of a floating exchange rate regime has allowed a sharp reduction of the real interest cost of the public debt, from more than 20 per cent per year in 1994–98 to around 12 per cent per year in 1999–2000. If the real interest rate goes down to the assumed 7.1 per cent per year, the overall (inflation-adjusted) public sector deficit may be maintained around a civilised two per cent of GDP.

However, even recognising the importance of the fiscal adjustment, it should be noted that it has not been sufficient to generate significant public savings. A realistic assumption, made in the above simulation, is that public saving will be zero in the near future. If private saving remains around 18 per cent of GDP, the average for the post-stabilisation period, the economy will have to rely heavily on foreign savings to maintain a reasonable growth rate. Therefore, the increase in domestic saving and a reduction of foreign saving is still a challenge for the future.[11]

The second argument is that the floating exchange rate regime (with the resulting large real devaluation) restored the incentive and the confidence to invest in the tradable sector, so that we should expect a high growth rate of exports, as well as a new round of import substitution which, in due time, will generate the required surplus in the balance of g&nfs to stabilise the ratio of NFL to GDP. This argument, although partially correct, has to be qualified by observing that, in the global economy, a 'high' real exchange rate is not the only factor, and perhaps not even the most important, to make a country a competitive place for world production. The institutional and economic environment is also important, as reflected in the availability of modern factors of production and infrastructure, the quality of economic policies and the existence of the correct incentives to production. The so-called 'Brazil cost', represented by large distortions in the tax and social security systems, the archaic labour legislation, the inefficiency of the financial system and of the capital markets and the sluggishness of justice reduce the competitiveness of the country in the world economy.[12]

---

10   This law sets budget and financial guidelines for public administration at all levels, as well as penalties for non-compliance, and may be an important deterrent to irresponsible behaviour as has been so common in the past.

11   It has been argued in Brazil that reforming the tax and the social security systems would increase the private saving rate. In the case of taxes a shift from indirect to direct taxation and the alleviation of the direct tax burden on savings, typical of the income tax regime, could help. As for social security, a move from the 'pay-as-you-go' practice to a true capitalisation regime has been proposed.

12   On the 'Brazil cost', see Fundação Instituto de Pesquisas Econômicas (1997).

Third, it is argued that the composition of NFL today is radically different from what it was in the 1980s. Then, most of NFL was foreign debt owed by the public sector to a limited number of international banks. Today, 43 per cent of NFL represents foreign capital invested in the country, and a large part of the foreign debt is owed by the private sector to institutional investors all over the world. The composition of NFL implies that the country is today less vulnerable to external shocks than it was some years ago, when it depended more on foreign borrowing and short term capital to finance its balance of payments.

However, even assuming that the social rate of return on the domestic investments of foreign firms and on investments of domestic firms borrowing abroad is higher than their social cost to the country, the same 'transformation problem' faced in the 1980s is valid today. In order to transform domestic currency into foreign currency to serve NFL the economy must shift resources from the domestic to the tradable sector, and here again we hit the constraint of the 'Brazil cost'. In fact, the recent inflow of foreign investment has been mainly directed to the non-traded sector of the economy, which seems more attractive than the tradable sector. For instance, under the privatisation programme, important parts of the public utilities have been sold to foreign firms. No matter how profitable these firms may be, they do not generate a single dollar of export revenue. Someone else has to do it to maintain stability in the balance of payments. The fact that economic growth has been low and exports have grown so little, despite the large inflow of capital, are clear signs that the economy is not rapidly and efficiently transforming foreign saving into growth and export performance.

Moreover, in the long run the average cost of serving NFL, from the point of view of the balance of payments, is the risk-free world interest rate plus the sovereign risk premium, no matter the composition of the foreign capital. This premium, in turn, is an increasing function of the country's default risk as perceived by international investors — the higher the dependency on foreign saving, the higher the risk premium, and the lower the probability of long-term stability.

The final argument is that the liberalisation of foreign trade and capital and the privatisation programme improved the quality of investment, producing an upward shift in the production function (here A in equation 1). The same aggregate rate of investment today can generate a higher rate of growth of output than in the past, because the rate of productivity growth is higher. So even if the flow of foreign saving has to be reduced, Brazil can maintain a reasonable rate of growth based on productivity gains. It is difficult to evaluate this argument. The historical experience (Brazil in the 1970s or the USA in the 1990s, for instance) reveals that growth is a simultaneous process, in which output growth is high because capital formation is high and productivity gains are also high. It is not usual to have growth based on productivity gains with low rates of investment.

In conclusion, we may say that the Brazilian economy is at the crossroads. There is no way back, and there are two ways ahead. The positive way is to accelerate the economic and institutional reforms to modernise the structure of the economy, so as to produce the reallocation of resources necessary to achieve long-term stability while keeping a satisfactory rate of growth. The other way is to delay the reforms and increase the risk of a new crisis in the near future, similar to the debt crisis of the 1980s.

From the 1950s to the early 1990s, Brazil adopted compulsively an import substitution strategy aiming at self-sufficiency, which was identified with the creation of a large and articulated industrial sector. This isolationist policy led to serious balance of payments crises in the 1960s and again in the 1980s, which cost many years of recession, high inflation and economic (and political) retardation. The change of regime in the 1990s through the opening of the economy to trade and capital, has not produced the expected gains in terms of economic growth and once more may lead to a new balance of payments crisis in the near future. What went wrong?

The probable answer is that the opening of the economy was partial, in the sense that it was restricted to the lowering of the tariff structure and the elimination of non-tariff barriers on imports, as well as the removal of many exchange restrictions and impediments to trade and capital movements. However, no significant and simultaneous effort has been made to improve the domestic factors that determine competitiveness. On the one hand, there are deficiencies in the economic infrastructure, large distortions in the tax system and the high cost of capital disincentive investment in the Brazilian tradable sector vis-à-vis other countries. On the other hand, the Brazilian government has totally neglected commercial policy, especially an active diplomatic effort to improve the country's access to foreign markets, and export promotion policies were abandoned in the early 1980s. On top of that, to keep prices reasonably stable after 1994, the government maintained a grossly overvalued exchange rate for too long, inducing a transfer of resources away from the tradable sector.

The explanation for the policy mistakes and omissions of the recent period probably lies in the political inability to restructure the public sector, a critical problem that all the democratic governments have failed to solve since 1985. In addition to that, it should be recalled that from 1992 to 1998 Brazil counted on an elastic supply of foreign capital, which made it easier to finance than to correct the imbalances of the economy. After 1998 the supply of foreign exchange has become scarce, but the pressure to fulfil the fiscal targets of the IMF adjustment programme has left little room for risking bold structural changes. Proposals for tax and social security reforms were abandoned by the Cardoso administration, and public investment, being easier to cut or postpone, as the energy crisis of 2001 exemplifies, was sacrificed in the interest of generating the required primary surplus in the public sector.

In the coming years the binding external constraint will again restrict the scope for policies of structural adjustment. Perhaps the main challenge to Brazil is to find a way of moving ahead with the restructuring of the public sector and the creation of a more competitive economy that could guarantee long-term stability in the sense discussed in this chapter.

Appendix
Table A1: Brazil: Foreign Debt and Reserves
(US$ million)

	Registered Debt			Non-Registered Debt	Total Debt	International Reserves
Years	Total	Public	Private			
1980	53847	37270	16577	10397	64244	6193
1981	61411	41788	19623	12552	73963	7507
1982	70198	46858	23340	15166	85364	3994
1983	81319	60292	21027	12237	93556	4553
1984	91091	71752	19339	10948	102039	12995
1985	95856	78679	17177	9269	105125	11608
1986	101759	87116	14623	9286	111045	6760
1987	107514	93075	14439	13660	121174	7458
1988	102555	91038	11517	10914	113469	9140
1989	99285	89476	9809	15811	115096	9679
1990	96546	78839	17707	26893	123439	9973
1991	92996	75420	17576	30914	123910	9406
1992	110835	86673	24162	25114	135949	23754
1993	114270	83520	30750	31390	145660	32211
1994	119668	86867	32801	28627	148295	38806
1995	128732	91421	37311	30524	159256	51840
1996	142148	88431	53517	37787	179935	60110
1997	163283	79967	83316	36715	199998	52173
1998	215215	91984	123231	26429	241644	44556
1999	214076	97363	116713	27392	241468	36342
2000	206190	89780	116410	29961	236151	33011

Source: Central Bank of Brazil.

Table A2: Brazil: Current Account Transactions (US$ billion)

Years	Exports	Imports	Non-Factor Services	Factor Services	Unilateral Transfers	Current Account
1980	20.1	23.0	-3.1	-7.0	0.2	-12.8
1981	23.3	22.1	-2.8	-10.3	0.2	-11.7
1982	20.2	19.4	-3.6	-13.5	0.0	-16.3
1983	21.9	15.4	-2.4	-11.0	0.1	-6.8
1984	27.0	13.9	-1.8	-11.5	0.2	0.0
1985	25.6	13.2	-1.5	-11.3	0.2	-0.2
1986	22.3	14.0	-2.0	-11.1	0.0	-4.8
1987	26.2	15.1	-2.2	-10.3	0.0	-1.4
1988	33.8	14.6	-2.9	-12.1	0.0	4.2
1989	34.4	18.3	-2.8	-12.5	0.2	1.0
1990	31.4	20.7	-3.7	-11.6	0.8	-3.8
1991	31.6	21.0	-3.9	-9.7	1.6	-1.4
1992	35.8	20.6	-3.1	-8.0	2.2	6.1
1993	38.6	25.3	-5.6	-10.2	1.9	-0.6
1994	43.5	33.1	-5.8	-8.9	2.6	-1.7
1995	46.5	49.9	-7.5	-11.1	4.0	-18.0
1996	47.7	53.3	-8.3	-12.1	2.9	-23.1
1997	53.0	59.8	-10.1	-16.1	2.2	-30.8
1998	51.1	57.7	-9.5	-19.3	1.8	-33.6
1999	48.0	49.2	-6.5	-19.4	2.0	-25.1
2000	55.1	55.8	-7.0	-18.7	1.8	-24.6

Source: Central Bank of Brazil.

CHAPTER 7

Internal Constraints on Economic Policy and Performance*

Mauricio C. Coutinho

Introduction

By internal constraints to economic policy we usually mean the political and institutional obstacles that hinder the fulfilment of the economic plans envisaged by the Executive. Although this meaning excessively credits the coherence of the Executive's actions, and oversimplifies the relations between Executive and Legislature, it has been tempting to use it as a framework to the analysis of economic policies in the 1985–2000 Brazilian redemocratisation context, due to a striking contrast: while the absolute discretion of the Executive was one of the features of Brazilian economic policy under the military regime, civil rule has apparently put economic policy under strong institutional restraints.

In fact, redemocratisation implied not only the rebuilding of democratic institutions — free elections at all levels of government, press freedom, an unbound Judiciary, etc. — but added two explicit constraints to the Executive's actions: i) a new federative arrangement, which enhanced the revenues and the autonomy of the states; ii) the expanded prerogatives of the Congress. While the military presidents (until 1982) strictly controlled the choice of governors and issued presidential decrees in economic matters with no restrictions, the political environment of the post-military era includes politically competitive governors and fierce congressional controls.

Two caveats apply to this impressionistic (although standard) account of the political restraints to economic policy. First, the military constitutional order was not altered until the end of 1988. From 1985 to 1988, the constitutional order of the old regime remained as the legal framework to economic policy.

Second, high inflation — the economic ambience of the Brazilian redemocratisation process — put in the hands of the Executive an almost unrestrained licence to try out economic policies. Sarney's 1986–87 period, Collor's first presidential biennial, Cardoso's performance as Itamar's minister, give evidence of the lack of impediments to the deployment of all sorts of anti-inflationary instruments, even in the cases in which they were innovative, hazardous, mired in breach of contracts and highly controversial in legal terms.

* I am grateful to Victor Bulmer-Thomas and Lizia Figueiredo for their comments. The usual disclaimers apply.

This second proviso warns us of the importance of the economic scenario of the period, which is basically twofold. From 1985 to 1994, the inflationary pressure and the successive attempts to bring inflation to a halt shaped both economic policy and its restraints. In this setting, the severe macroeconomic disturbances, typical of the inflationary setting, harmed the opportunities to guarantee a stable growth. When the Real Plan finally succeeded in putting an end to inflation, not only the economic policies, but the internal restraints themselves, changed drastically. Significantly, the end of inflation did not reverse the growth trend.

It is worth mentioning that the 1985–2000 period is marked by major changes in the international scenario, which affected the economy, redefined the limits to growth and added/subtracted degrees of liberty to economic policy. On one hand, the reestablishment of the international financial flows and the attenuation of the debt crisis of the 1980s finally allowed an efficacious anti-inflationary strategy. The Real Plan combined an exchange rate anchor with the overvaluation of the national currency and represented, in this sense, an able answer to a renewed international environment. The Real Plan depended on the relaxing of immediate external constraints. On the other hand, the *real* strategy eventually led to deficits in the current account, which constrained the economic growth. Whereas the balance of payment conditions are not the issue, their ultimate bearing on the economic growth possibilities and on the economic policy practices must be acknowledged.

Economic Growth: An Overview

In sharp contrast to the post-war experience, the growth spells have been brief and uncertain since the beginning of the 1980s. In fact, within the 1985–2000 interval, the ephemeral growth bubbles associated with the stabilisation plans — especially the cruzado and the *real* — and their immediate aftermath, are outlying points within a recessive trend.

The overall performance over the period is very poor. Within the 1985–2000 interval, the GDP underwent a 2.4 per cent annual growth, while the average growth of the per capita GDP amounted to 0.8 per cent. If one includes the last year of the military period in the series (1984–2000), the average GDP growth rate per capita rose to 1.1 per cent, still a very modest performance. It is easy to conclude that the effects of this limited growth on social mobility and on the general improvement of social conditions represent a significant hindrance to Brazilian redemocratisation. However, there is no agreement on the reasons for the slow pace of growth.

Table 7.1: Brazil — GDP — Index and Rates of Growth

Year	Real GDP index 1999=100	Real GDP rate of growth per cent	Per capita GDP index 1999=100	Per capita GDP rate of growth per cent
1985	73.1	7.8	90.9	5.7
1986	78.6	7.5	95.8	5.4
1987	81.4	3.5	97.2	1.6
1988	81.4	-0.1	95.4	-1.9
1989	83.9	3.2	96.7	1.4
1990	80.3	-4.3	91.4	-5.5
1991	81.1	1.0	90.8	-0.6
1992	80.7	-0.5	89.0	-2.1
1993	84.6	4.9	91.9	3.4
1994	89.6	5.9	95.9	4.3
1995	93.4	4.2	98.6	2.8
1996	95.9	2.7	99.8	1.2
1997	99.0	3.3	101.7	1.9
1998	99.2	0.2	100.5	-1.1
1999	100.0	0.8	100.0	-0.5
2000*	104.0	4.0	102.6	2.6

* 2000 = estimates.
Source: Central Bank of Brazil.

Instead of drawing on broad theories of economic development, related to factors that might have a long-term bearing on economic growth — inequality, protectionism, the structure of rights, education — this study will focus on the immediate causes, for several reasons. Firstly, the same broad factors already obtained in the 1930–80 period, a *very* successful phase in Brazilian economic development. Secondly, the full effects of these factors, better suited to the explanation of the long-term development, are hardly felt in the short term. Finally, evident and acceptable reasons can be found for the slow growth rate of the redemocratisation period. These are the macroeconomic disturbances of the inflationary period, especially of the 1982–95 period, and the deterioration of the current account position in the post-*real* period.

In fact, the 1982–95 interval was characterised by a succession of macroeconomic disequilibria and by the economic disturbances provoked by a succession of heroic and failed stabilisation efforts. These disturbances harmed the public sector accounts, destroyed the usual finance instruments and enhanced the economic uncertainty. Economic growth is not likely to prevail in the context of high-level uncertainty and high-grade macroeconomic imbalances.

In the post-*real* period, analysts agree that the limits to economic growth were first of all set by the external conditions. In a sense, the low rate of growth became a natural by-product of a successful anti-inflationary strategy relying upon the overvaluation of the national currency and the liberalisation of imports, and thus on a monetary policy based on high rates of interest. If one adds to these targeted policies an almost suicidal lack of attention to export conditions (infrastructure, diplomatic action, credit conditions), all the factors leading to a recession were in place. At least until the 1999 exchange rate crisis, the economic growth possibilities were absolutely determined by the anti-inflationary strategy of the Real Plan.

A Legacy from the Indexation System

Apart from its immediate social effects, the lack of sustained growth has added a special and rarely acknowledged constraint to economic policy. The end of the military rule brought to the surface repressed hopes and accelerated the demand for rights. The increase in social rights, changes in demographic patterns and the continuity of the urbanisation process generated a new list of social demands, stressing the role to be played by compensatory social policies. Part of these new rights, especially in the social security area, became inscribed in the 1988 Constitution and in its complementary laws, which means they have led to additional and permanent budgetary responsibilities.

Additionally, the passage from a hyperinflation-cum-indexation regime to a stabilised economy was accompanied by a substantial amount of potential public spending. These potential costs are a result of the legal haggling over the indexation clauses, spread over a large array of contracts in the preceding decades. In response to the legal questioning, the Judiciary converted a good amount of indexation demands into effective governmental obligations. The consequences were the undermining of the public banks assets,[1] the inflation of the public sector payrolls and soaring social security expenditures.[2]

The escalation of the legal controversies, both in the pre-*real* and in the post-*real* periods, is just a consequence of the failure of the prior indexation system. This complex system had long been challenged by inflation and was finally dismantled by the succession of stabilisation plans.

---

1   Especially in the case of non-performable agricultural and mortgage loans.
2   The successive stabilisation plans contained controversial indexation clauses, applied to salaries and to social security benefits. A large number of these clauses were eventually argued in the Judiciary, becoming real budgetary expenditures.

Ironically, one of the most important legacies of two decades of economic disorder has been an endless legal haggling over indexation rules, partially converted to effective budgetary expenditure. If one adds these judicially established liabilities to the budgetary demanding new rights, one might reach the conclusion that stabilisation and democratisation are burdensome processes. New budgetary commitments, in the form of social security outlays, genuine social demands and all manner of judicially argued obligations were the inescapable legacy of the inflationary period and of the large array of anti-inflationary shocks, representing an inescapable liability of the redemocratisation process.

It might be said that the assurance of an orderly economic transition in democratic conditions requires a sort of special budgetary buffer. Since the public budgets immediately suffer from excess demand, the poor economic performance highlights the troublesome process of economic and institutional change associated with the end of inflation in a non-authoritarian context. Needless to say, the high rates of interest associated with the Brazilian stabilisation policies, which led to the assignment of an increasing share of public revenue to debt servicing, are an additional reason to bear in mind the additional strains brought about by the low rates of growth.

Real Internal Constraints

Before we concentrate on the effective constraints, it might be useful to reduce to their real proportions the two most frequently mentioned obstacles to economic policy, namely the congressional impediments and the federative arrangement.

Most analysts have stressed a supposed congressional blockage to economic reform. In fact, and apparently against all common sense, since 1985 there has hardly been a single example of executive bills failing to be enacted by Congress. As mentioned above, high inflation gives way to a sense of urgency that prompts the representatives to accept all the Executive's initiatives. But not even politically sensitive issues, highly controversial and unspoken anti-inflationary measures — minimum wage policies, privatisation, social security reform — prompted the representatives to restrict the implementation of the will of the Executive.

In their authoritative research of congressional activities, Figueiredo and Limongi[3] give evidence of the expressive records of the Executive in Congress. Party discipline and a constraining mix of constitutional artefacts and congressional procedural rules, not to mention the existence of a solid parliamentary majority, were sufficient to assure the fulfilment of the objectives of the Executive.[4]

3   Figueiredo and Limongi (1999).
4   Only Collor did not benefit from a solidly established majority in Congress. But Collor's dramatic anti-inflationary policies, although entirely illegal, were supported by the representatives and by the Supreme Court.

The federative arrangement is another explanatory factor. The 1988 Constitution has effectively stressed the states' and local governments' power to tax, especially by keeping the main Brazilian value-added tax (ICMS) at state level. However, in the 1989–94 period the union succeeded in keeping its position in the overall balance of revenues, because inflation eroded ICMS much more than federal revenues, and also because the federal government has chosen to pursue the social security taxes and on other non-shared taxes, such as FINSOCIAL/COFINS and IOF.[5] From 1994 onwards the union has had no trouble in raising federal tax rates and in reducing the states' discretion to levy revenues, especially through the Fiscal Stabilisation Fund (FEF).

In fact, one of the most impressive feats of Cardoso's presidential periods has been the stringent discipline imposed on the states, culminating in the enactment of three powerful budgetary (and political) instruments: a) the case by case agreements concerning the state debts and the rescue of the insolvent state banks, which forced the assignment of an increasing share of the states' revenues to the payment of their debts to the union; b) the Camata law (Complementary Law 96, enacted in May 1999), which fixes a ceiling on wage expenditures at all levels of government; c) and last, the Fiscal Responsibility Law (Complementary Law 101, enacted in May 2000), which fixes a limit to the contracting of new debts, keeps under surveillance the approval of budgetary expenses at the state and municipal level and establishes a set of constraints (including penalties) envisaging the assurance of budgetary discipline.

That Cardoso has brought the governors to their knees is beyond question. Occasional fightbacks — attempts to challenge the so-called Kandir law,[6] some pork barrel politics in Congress — do not conceal the subordination of the states to the union, an outstanding development in face of Brazilian federative traditions.

It should be noted that the strict discipline imposed on states has not applied to inter-state relations, as proved by the 'fiscal wars' the states have sustained throughout the redemocratisation period.[7] Only a constitutional reform aimed at altering the states' value-added tax — for instance, by establishing a full credit to the buyer states in inter-state transactions — would definitely extinguish the 'fiscal wars', but the Federal Executive has fiercely opposed such a reform. As a matter of fact,

5   For an analysis of tax revenue on the pre-*real* period, Coutinho (1996).
6   The Kandir law (Complementary Law 87, enacted in September 1996) exempted exports and capital goods production from the state value-added tax (ICMS). The states had their losses compensated by federal transfers.
7   It seems that the 'fiscal wars' tend to be softened, since the Fiscal Responsibility Law affects their core, the ICMS exemptions. Besides, a much more reactive attitude of São Paulo, since 1999, has threatened the practice of ICMS exemptions by other states.

the Federal Executive has blocked all initiatives to give the fiscal structure a sounder economic basis, since (as we shall see), federal tax revenues have soared under the prevailing arrangement.

In the end, even though 'fiscal wars' have put federal relations under stress, this is a horizontal, rather than a vertical, stress. From the union's point of view, the inter-states stress has no relevance, provided it does not affect states-union relations and provided it does not imperil the targeted budget surpluses. The 'fiscal wars' are a sign of a dysfunctional federalism, but they have not represented a barrier to the fulfilment of the most cherished targets of macroeconomic policy so far.

Insofar as price stabilisation has been the most important Brazilian economic policy issue, both in the pre-*real* and in the post-*real* periods, one might be tempted to evaluate the constraints in view of how decisively they have compromised consistent anti-inflationary policies. Accordingly, the success of the post-*real* policies in avoiding the return of inflation might be taken as a sign of their ability to bypass the constraints, especially by assuring a consistent budgetary performance.

This analysis will follow another approach. Taking into consideration the fact that the election of constraints is contingent upon the ultimate goals to be pursued by economic policy — a statement that does not conceal its normative stance — I shall take a steady and sustainable rate of growth, as well as the reduction of social inequality, as the fundamental goals of Brazilian economic policy. These goals speak for themselves and dispense with further justification. Moreover, they do not exclude macroeconomic stability, to the extent instability has proved harmful to the achievement of economic growth and to the reduction of social inequality.

Under these circumstances the focus will be on issues that are directly related to economic growth or to inequality, namely: a) the quality of the fiscal system; b) the inability to pursue anti-poverty and/or income inequality reduction policies; c) the institutional environment to contracting and to competition. An overview of these topics will make it possible both to set some internal constraints and to shed light on less analysed issues of the Brazilian economic growth and policies.

Fiscal System

Leaving aside the negative impact of inflation on tax revenue, in action until 1994, two factors have impacted on the Brazilian fiscal system: the low rate of growth, and, since 1989, the union's reactions to the new constitutional dispositions. In fact, the 1988 Constitution raised the states', and municipalities', share in the proceeds of the main federal taxes, and established new and burdensome rights, especially in the social security area. From 1989 to 1994 this move was ably counterbalanced by the depression of the public expenditures in real terms, provoked by inflation. Once the end of inflation deprived the federal budget of this natural protective mechanism, and transformed a part of the new constitutional rights into effective public expenditure, the government reacted, setting into effect a set of tax-gathering measures. Successful in terms of tax collecting, these measures proved harmful to efficiency and to equity.

The main measures were: [8]

- A new permanent levy on bank account movements (IPMF/CPMF).

- A new tax on companies' net profits (CSLL).

- A substantial increase — from 0.5 per cent to 2.0 per cent in 1990, and to 3.0 per cent in 1999 — in the social security turnover tax (COFINS), which was converted from a residual into an indispensable source of revenue.[9]

- A substantial and disguised increase in the personal income tax (IRPF) burden, by freezing both the deduction allowances and the tables that determine the percentages of incidence, in spite of the residual inflation and of the nominal earnings increase.

These measures, combined with the sharp decrease in inflation, produced an outstanding result, particularly if one takes into consideration the poor GDP performance. The federal government revenue effort succeeded on its three main fronts: federal taxes proper, social security taxes and FGTS (the main compulsory fund). States were also benefited by the halt of inflation, but their revenues reached the highest level in 1996, whereas the federal taxes maintained their upward trend longer.

The efficacy of the tax gathering strategy of the federal government under Cardoso is not in question. Briefly, in a recessive period, the government has succeeded in imposing on society a strong push in the tax burden. Taking the tax revenue (union plus states)/GDP ratio as an indicator of the overall tax burden, its evolution from 1994 to 2000 is significant: 25.86 per cent in 1994; 27.56 per cent in 1995; 27.2 per cent in 1996; 26.63 per cent in 1997; 27.05 per cent in 1998; 27.91 per cent in 1999; 28.36 per cent in 2000.[10] By way of comparison, by the same criteria the tax burden was 20.55 per cent in 1989. The overall tax burden, which includes municipal taxes, soared from 26.97 per cent in 1994 to 30.71 per

8   For further details see Afonso, Araújo, Rezende and Varsano (2000).
9   The COFINS adds to — and does not replace — the traditional social security payroll tax.
10 Tax revenues including social security and excluding municipalities. See Afonso et al. (2000).

cent in 2000. In short, Cardoso pushed the overall tax burden to a new level, around 30 per cent. Within a decade, the overall tax burden jumped from approximately 22 per cent to 30 per cent.

Table 7.2: Revenues — Federal And State Taxes
Rs 1000 (Dec/99)

Year	Federal Taxes	Social Security	FGTS	State Taxes
1988	89,295,991	43,957,483	8,848,896	50,296,898
1989	87,026,243	45,047,441	12,322,447	64,417,740
1990	111,922,877	47,716,479	13,141,567	68,920,308
1991	87,029,306	50,138,896	12,079,301	65,612,457
1992	85,545,445	43,814,253	11,308,655	60,030,550
1993	96,541,755	47,129,590	11,340,509	56,570,113
1994	113,170,393	44,626,212	11,999,758	63,476,935
1995	121,773,836	52,590,927	14,718,954	75,449,496
1996	124,098,432	58,924,462	15,794,834	80,703,020
1997	134,213,550	60,071,982	16,215,764	79,565,593
1998	142,177,751	60,503,988	20,252,793	78,912,394
1999	154,320,306	55,378,323	18,938,785	77,978,489

Source: BNDES.

Of course, the federal government concentrated its tax gathering efforts in non-shared taxes. In the 1995–99 period, whereas the IPI (the federal industry value-added tax, shared with states and municipalities) revenue declined in real terms, non-shared taxes exhibited a positive performance: the COFINS increased 54.5 per cent, the CPMF became an important component of the tax structure, and the import tax achieved high levels. The problem is, this strategy is overtly harmful to exports and to economic efficiency in general. As far as it leaves aside the value-added taxes, favouring the use of 'bad taxes', such as payroll taxes (social security tax, FGTS), turnover taxes (COFINS, CSLL, PIS) and taxes that burden all kinds of financial yields and transfers (CPMF, IOF), the federal government strategy has severely deteriorated the Brazilian fiscal structure.

It is worth mentioning that the high level of the payroll taxes is, in the long run, a self-defeating strategy. These taxes favour informal employment relations, thus undermining the proceeds from social security. As a matter of fact, less than 40 per cent of the active workers are presently registered in the Social Security records. The majority of the active workers (including employers, self-employed workers, non-registered and registered salaried workers) don't count as social security taxpayers. This disproportion points to a future increase in the social security deficits, since the Brazilian scheme of benefits is universal and applies to the whole population, and not only to the contingent once officially listed in the social security records as contributors.

The turnover taxes and the taxes that burden financial yields and transfers are especially harmful to exports, since they are cumulative and cannot be further compensated by tax credits. A successful export-driven policy depends on a full revision of these taxes, which are, additionally, incompatible with the international trade agreements and with the ongoing continental free trade negotiations. Sooner or later, Brazil will have to consider the substitution of a consolidated value-added tax for the whole bundle of ad hoc and economically harmful taxes, such as COFINS, CSLL, PIS, ISS, FGTS, established in the 1988 Constitution or in its several revisions, and pushed much further by Collor and Cardoso. In all likelihood, as far as the rational consolidation of these taxes in a sort of mega-VAT would bring to the surface the astonishing percentages already concealed in the prevailing system, the necessity of a full revision in the income tax structure would then become manifest.

Income tax is quite illustrative of the deficiencies of the Brazilian tax policies. Although proceeds from income tax are shared with states and municipalities, a fact that does not stimulate revenue efforts in this area, these underwent a 27.9 per cent increase in the 1995–99 interval. However, the proceeds of one of its main components — the 'deducted at source' income tax — experienced a substantial 42.3 per cent rise in the same interval. This result reflects the heavy burden imposed on the confined contingent of medium salaried workers, upon whom the 'deducted at source' income tax falls. A 42.3 per cent revenue increase out of a nearly stagnant basis of personal earnings means a sharp upswing of the percentages of liability, and reveals the appreciable reduction of net earnings that salaried workers have suffered under Cardoso.

The real Brazilian tax system conundrum is that the federal government cannot seek policies based on value added taxes, because one of them (ICMS) is a state tax, the proceeds of the other (IPI) being shared with states and municipalities; it cannot remove ill-conceived taxes, because they were once residual but have achieved a great importance; it cannot design a fair income tax, due to fierce political impediments. Because the improvement of the two basic instruments of modern tax systems — value-added taxes and income tax — has remained entirely blocked, the tax structure has progressively relied on taxes that are detrimental to economic efficiency, export adverse and deeply unfair.[11]

Paradoxically, endless patches and 'democratic' legal amendments transformed the Brazilian fiscal system into a wreckage of the very modern system the military pioneered in 1965–66. Faulty in both aspects — efficiency and equity — the fiscal system has been a major internal constraint to exports, to economic growth and to social justice, despite its brilliant tax gathering performance thus far.

Income Inequality and Anti-Poverty Policies

Although stabilisation in itself is a valuable social asset, since high inflation furthers inequality, the very slight decrease in income inequality after 1994 does not enable us to trust the real policies as a turning point in this matter. Taking this further, if the reduction of poverty and of economic inequality is an obligatory goal to any government action, it is arguable that redemocratisation has been a social failure in this respect.

Let us concentrate on the post-*real* period. Table III shows that there has been a consistent — although very gradual — decrease in the concentration indexes over the 1996–99 interval. One might take this decrease as a positive aspect of the post-*real* period, although it is not possible to project a trend out of this small series. At least, the Gini has stayed consistently far from the yearly high inflation record (in 1989, the Gini reached 0.617!). But in order to avoid the overrating of this slight reduction in income inequality, it suffices to recall that the 1998 and 1999 values mean just the return to the non-laudable levels of the beginning of the 1980s, that is, to the 'normal' standards prior to inflationary disruption.

Table 7.3: Income Distribution

Year	Gini*
1993	0.588
1995	0.589
1996	0.595
1997	0.593
1998	0.588
1999	0.583

* Family income.
Source: Hoffmann (2000).

---

11 The Brazilian tax system as a whole is extremely regressive and equity averse. For a recent appraisal, see Vianna, and Silveira (2000).

An equally cautious approach applies to poverty analysis. In this case, different methodologies can lead to slightly different conclusions. According to Rocha,[12] the percentage of the population below the poverty line has been significantly reduced since the 1970s. However, despite the fact that the *real* has been highly beneficial to the reduction of poverty, progress seems to have been on hold since 1996. After the first effects of the halt of inflation and of the 1995 minimum wage push, the proportion above the poverty line has not consistently decreased.

Hoffmann's much more comprehensive set of indicators — percentage of the population below the poverty line and proper poverty indexes[13] — point to a less dramatic improvement since 1980. According to Hoffmann's results, although it is unquestionable that high inflation increased poverty — the *real*, accordingly, must be credited with the reduction of poverty — its effects seem to have dried up.

The fact is, so ingrained is income inequality in the Brazilian social structure, it is very difficult to think of economic policies rapidly conducive to its reduction, and the new economic developments are not reassuring. To the traditionally asymmetric distribution of assets, should be added inequality-inducing new trends in the labour markets, such as the reduction in the number of public servants, the reduction in industrial occupations, and the expansion of the stratum of high-earning workers in the financial market. Poverty is a much more tractable subject, in the sense that it can be dealt with by a set of widely known measures. As a matter of fact, while nobody denies that high rates of inflation are conducive to the growth of inequality and to the spread of poverty, out of such an ample proposition just a small set of non-conclusive statements seems arguable. These statements are quite generic, but give an idea of the complexity of the inequality problem:

- The inequality indexes are much more affected by the income conditions of the very top income groups than by the performance of the ten to 20 per cent bottom group. That is, benefits to the lowest income groups, however meritorious, will impact little on the inequality indexes.[14] Besides, the top ten per cent group includes the totality of what is usually considered the Brazilian middle class. That is, a Gini impacting redistribution of income would necessarily affect middle class earnings.

- The reduction of the number of people below the poverty line is very responsive to the end of inflation and to changes in the mini-

12   Rocha (2000).
13   Hoffmann uses the Sen index and the Foster, Greer and Thorbecke index.
14   According to Rocha, the Gini (individual income) undergoes a substantial drop — from 0.5646 to 0.5225, in 1998 — when the one per cent highest income group are excluded from the population.

mum wage and in the social security policies. The reform of rural
social security prompted by the 1988 Constitution contributed significantly to the reduction of rural poverty, even though this institutional change was not conceived as a policy targeted at the reduction of poverty.[15] Given the social security legislation, policies in
this area may have an impacting and immediate anti-poverty effect.

- The reduction of income inequality depends neither on intentions nor
  on discourse. Irrespective of Collor's purposes, at least in the short
  range, his policies proved much more efficacious in reducing inequality than those of Cardoso (the Gini dropped from 0.617 in 1989 to
  0.603 in 1990 and to 0.567 in 1992). Besides the brief halting of inflation, in 1990, Collor's policies contributed to shattering the upper
  group income via recession and via losses imposed to financial assets.

This rather loose picture makes it possible to conjecture that governmental measures can hardly reduce income inequality in a progressive and consistent way. Fortunately, economic policy might be used to combat poverty. Most probably, through a well-designed effort, including minimum
wage policies, social security, money and transfers in kind, investment in
urban infrastructure, the governmental action is able to increase the welfare of the low-income groups. Needless to say, as far as the minimum
wage policies directly impact on social security expenditures, they face
severe budgetary restrictions.[16]

Finally, in so far as it is almost impossible to induce a reduction of the
top group's gross earnings, an income tax approach to inequality seems quite
recommendable. The fact is, apart from a decreasing minority of top-level
salaried workers, which includes top rank public servants, the upper middle
class remains undertaxed. There is ample space to expand the income tax
base, through a well-designed inspection of assets and of bank account
movements. The Judiciary has consistently opposed the disclosure of bank
accounts, in the name of the right to privacy, but the possibility of getting
fruitful results by means of a continuous intelligence effort in the income tax
sphere are widely admitted by the specialists. This effort probably offers the
only escape route to the pursuit of effective, but budget heavy, policies
focused on the reduction of poverty and on the promotion of equality.

---

15   The reform of rural social security has been the most significant poverty reduction
     policy in Brazil. For a careful (and impressive) assessment of this policy, see Delgado
     and Cardoso (2000).
16   The minimum wage level affects more than 70 per cent of the social security bene-
     fits. A minimum wage boost would reduce poverty and widen the social security
     deficit.

Institutional Constraints

After the first round of economic reforms — privatisation, the dropping of tariff barriers, social security reform — it became usual to insist on the need for a second round of reforms, aiming at microeconomic efficiency. The content of these 'second generation reforms' is not clear, but current discussion points to issues such as corporate governance, labour market flexibility and the protection of property rights.

The nature and structure of these institutional reforms is not obvious. It is difficult to assess to what extent their absence has been detrimental to economic growth. Besides, this sort of institutional reform generally lacks the historical perspective that should back the reform: Why are institutions as they are? Why did the same institutional setting not block economic growth and entrepreneurial effectiveness in other times? Which social forces lay behind the existing arrangements?

In view of the non-existence of a solid analytical and historical research background on economic institutions, a descriptive, and far from all-encompassing, approach, might be helpful. The intention is to shed light on some well-known characteristics of the Brazilian economic fabric that interfere with competition and resource allocation, and not to point out a comprehensive list of supposed 'imperfections' within Brazilian economic institutions, claiming for reform.

The Tax System — Law Enforcement

Here, the concern is not the structure of the fiscal system, but the ability to enforce law and rules. In terms of its enforcement ability, and of its punitive capacity, the Brazilian tax system puts taxpayers under unequal and lax constraints. Tax evasion has become a rewarding strategy to firms, as a result of several factors: the widespread legal questioning aroused by the succession of anti-inflationary plans and by the continuous changes in the fiscal system,[17] the deficiencies of the fiscal control apparatus and the lethargy of the Judiciary proceedings.

Besides its immediate effects on public revenue, one of the most important consequences of unpunished misbehaviour is the difference in opportunities it promotes. Since the propensity to cheat is unevenly distributed, tax evasion strongly affects inter-firm relations and competition. In allowing the survival of firms that would otherwise be banished from the markets, tax evasion sanctions inefficiency and supports an unusual market structure heterogeneity.

On the other hand, the low levels of law enforcement help to explain one of the main features of business organisation in Brazil, namely, the mixing up

---

17   The fiscal system depended on the indexation practices, and became severely affected by their crisis.

of business incomes and personal earnings. The loose controls on earnings, expenditure, bank accounts and assets allow a large number of owners to under-declare their personal earnings, and stimulate the imputation of all sorts of personal expenditures under the heading of business costs.

It is said that the prevailing Brazilian business strategy has always been to maximise non-taxable personal earnings, instead of intra-firm profits. To their proprietors, firms are a source of non-taxable personal earnings rather than a source of profits to be internally accumulated. This is one of the reasons for the permanent under-capitalisation of firms, as well as for the aversion to strategic inter-firm cooperation. To manage the firms as closed entities, far from partners and from the governmental controls, is part of a strategic behaviour devised to promote tax evasion. 'Poor firm, rich owner', a popular Brazilian business dictum, is very much a consequence of the absence of restraints to evasion.

Risk Bearing

One of the main characteristics of contracting in Brazil is the low level of protection assured to contractors. Bank loans are particularly unprotected because the legally required collaterals are frail and non-executable, and because Judiciary proceedings are slow and costly.[18] According to the analysts, the striking difference between the rates of interest applied to lenders and to debtors is partly explained by the considerable risk associated with frail collaterals.

In a broad perspective, the lack of solid guarantees and the high levels of risk might be taken as a general contracting, and not only a financial market, restraint. Indeed, many trivial commercial transactions are poorly protected against default or business misbehaviour. Non-executable guarantees, the extreme facility in opening and closing firms and bank accounts and lenient tax controls are all factors that stimulate all sorts of misbehaviour, leading to high transaction costs.

If one acknowledges that high rates of interest reflect the risk-premium demanded by lenders, one should also acknowledge the existence of pervasive over-pricing, reflecting the risks of contracting in general. The insecure system of guarantees enhances protective attitudes and raises transaction costs, thus affecting the competition processes to a considerable extent (although one impossible to assess).

The Credit System

The Brazilian economy has traditionally operated under credit constraints. High rates of interest and credit rationing, not to mention the uncertainty

---

18   A preliminary and valuable overview of bank credit, considering guarantees, protection, legal proceedings etc, is in Pinheiro and Cabral (1998).

associated with high inflation and institutional instability, ruled out the access of small and medium-size firms to credit. Personal indebtedness has also been very low, due to credit shortages and to high interest rates, not to mention the sharp contraction of the mortgage loans system, provoked by hyperinflation and by the wrecking of the indexation system.

That is, the Brazilian economy has been very little leveraged by credit, and has been almost deprived of the benefits of long-term loans. It is worth mentioning that long-term credit has been historically provided by the public banks and institutions, having compulsory funds and/or purely inflationary credit issuing as its base. Although some compulsory funds are still in action, their importance as a decisive funding alternative to long-term loans is falling into a decline.[19] Even more important, the possibilities of using public funds as sources of implicit subsidies have been almost eliminated, due to the end of inflation. One of the positive consequences of the demise of the public credit system is the diminution of the pervasive corruption it entailed, especially among the funds and agencies that specialised in regional development.[20]

In short, the public sector is losing its long-term lender role, but no relevant private alternative has been built as yet. The construction of a credit system in a non-inflationary setting, less dependent on public funds, has proved to be a problematic and lengthy task. The Brazilian credit system is in a hiatus between the old inflationary and public funding and a new, and not entirely defined, one. In the meanwhile, the credit shortage has been a strong restriction to long-term investment and growth. Except for the firms that have a direct access to the international credit market, Brazilian firms don't count on financial markets as a regular and considerable fundraising alternative.

Conclusions

In a lecture delivered in London in 1965, Celso Furtado referred to the conservative and anti-reformist stand of Brazilian Congress.[21] How might one carry out a major modernisation programme when Congress blocks the Executive's initiatives? *Mutatis mutandis*, most of the analysts of the present day Brazilian economic reform process support Furtado's 1965 stance in the sense that they attribute the postponement of 'general interest' reforms to the successful blocking strategy of segmented groups, located in the Parliament and in the Judiciary.

---

19 The FGTS is still an important parafiscal fund. It seems doomed to extinction, since it heavily burdens the payrolls. Indexation shocks have also led the FGTS to dramatic balance inconsistencies, that in the end will burden the federal budget.

20 The FINOR and FINAM (northern region and north-east region regional funds), and the state public banks, were and are classical loci of corruption.

21 Furtado (1965).

As we have seen, this naïve view cannot withstand a thorough assessment of congressional activities. The list of highly controversial and politically divisive measures approved by Congress is enormous, and goes beyond standard topics, such as privatisation and social security reform. The Legislative and the Judiciary backed a set of drastic policies, involving such abrasive issues as the salaries of public servants, the rescuing of endangered public and private banks, the step-by-step imposition of budgetary discipline to states and municipalities, and the enactment of taxation bills (new taxes, higher rates).

The fact is, the Executive has had no difficulties in approving what may be termed the 'easy reforms', which have been enthusiastically supported by the press and have faced politically non-decisive opponents, or those unable to attract public sympathy. Privatisation and social security reform are part of the 'easy reform' agenda. The new tax levies might be considered part of the same agenda, since they rely on 'hidden taxes' and the widespread opportunities for evasion leave a convenient escape route to rich citizens and firms.

Much more difficult to cope with is the 'difficult reform' agenda, whose issues either involve inequalities and practices that are ingrained in the Brazilian social fabric, or lead to collisions with really significant economic interests, or scratch at externally determined constraints. This account of the relevant constraints to economic policy and growth was devised to shed light on this agenda, permanently renewed by the contingencies of the world economy.

However, to insist on a sort of reformist stance that builds on the supposed inconsistencies of the institutional and economic setting, thus proposing a recommendable schedule of reforms, is just missing the point. On the contrary, this chapter tries to build on 'institutions as they are', and to acknowledge different institutional and economic constraints to economic policy and growth. In the end, many of these constraints are simply insurmountable in the sense that they are not removable by reform.

PART III
DEMOCRACY AND SOCIETY

CHAPTER 8

The Changing Role of the State:
New Patterns of State–Society Relations in Brazil at the End of the Twentieth Century*

Brasilio Sallum Jr

This chapter addresses some of the huge political changes that transformed the Brazilian state over the last two decades of the twentieth century. I will focus on two processes that altered not only the state but also its relations with the world order and with Brazilian society: political democratisation and economic liberalisation.

I consider these two processes to be part of the broader political transition that transformed the fundamental form of the Brazilian state, which had prevailed since the 1930s. This was a developmentalist state oriented by an import substitution economic strategy, tending to mould society and giving little room for the autonomous organisation and mobilisation of social groups, mainly those connected to the popular classes.[1] I shall call it the 'Vargas State'.

The Brazilian political transition began with the 1983–84 state crisis and ended in the course of the first Fernando Henrique Cardoso government, when the State became stabilised under a new hegemonic pattern, moderately liberal on economic issues and completely identified with representative democracy. In this transition from one state form to another, it must be stressed that the most important process in the 1980s was political democratisation, while economic liberalisation prevailed in the 1990s.

This process of political transition as a whole can only be fully understood if it is considered both as part of the transnationalisation of capitalism (set off by financial globalisation) and of the democratisation of Brazilian society.

This chapter will first outline some features of the Vargas State's crisis that underpin the processes considered here. The following sections study the way the political democratisation and economic liberalisation processes occurred. The chapter ends by outlining the recent shifts in Brazilian politics that point to a renewed developmentalism and to a deeper democracy.

*   I am grateful to Laurence Whitehead, Maria D'Alva Kinzo and Eduardo Kugelmas for helpful comments on this chapter.

1   On the Brazilian developmental State see Draibe (1986). Marçal Brandão (1997) analyses the difficulties that people had participating in politics even before 1964, when the military dictatorship started.

State Crisis and Political Transition

From an economic point of view the distinguishing feature of the Brazilian developmental state crisis was not its fiscal unbalance, but rather the State's inability to face external debt payments in the early 1980s.[2] This crisis jeopardised the standard relationship with foreign capitalists that had underpinned the Brazilian pattern of development up to that point. Therefore, the crisis could only be bypassed or overcome through a new arrangement of Brazil's external links. Depending on the path chosen for dealing with this matter, fractures could be caused either in the relations with important world economic and political centres, or in the state's domestic political support base.

In fact, the changes that were occurring in both spheres increased the possibilities of such fractures. Externally, the Mexican moratorium caused the suspension of the voluntary flow of bank loans to Brazil from 1982 until the early 1990s. In addition to this huge financial blow the dominant economic trends in the central countries and in the multilateral agencies jettisoned Keynesianism and increasingly began to adhere to a new monetarist orthodoxy, bound to public expenditure contention policies and to strict monetary control. All these changes constrained national economic policies to a great extent.[3]

Internally, political changes posed difficulties for an external rearrangement. Indeed, in the 1982 elections, the government party lost its absolute majority in the Chamber of Deputies, while ten important state governments went to the opposition.[4] These electoral results appeared to strip the military regime of its control over the political liberalising process, started by General Geisel in 1973–74.[5]

These political setbacks followed a pattern in which societal changes were pushing the military regime's political liberalisation project beyond its own limits. In fact, from the 1970s onwards a vigorous political process of democratisation shook the foundations of the old developmental state, based on political exclusion. This meant that the lower classes became

2   This is not to say that there was no fiscal imbalance. Bresser Pereira has frequently underlined this imbalance (Bresser Pereira, 1993). However, at that time the crisis was caused mainly by the external debt and it had special and huge consequences for Brazilian state policy. See Whitehead (1993, pp. 1380–2) for a critical analysis of Bresser Pereira's interpretation.

3   These changes in the economic conceptions and policies were studied in Helleiner (1997, chapters 6 and 7)

4   In 1979 an electoral law split the authoritarian regime's two-party system. The PDS (Social Democratic Party) took the ARENA's place as the regime's party and PMDB, PDT, PTB and PT took MDB (Brazilian Democratic Movement)'s place as political opposition. In 1982's election the PMDB elected nine state governors and the PDT just one.

5   For the political liberalisation process see Lamounier (1985) and Velasco e Cruz and Martins (1983).

politically much more autonomous and tried to share material and non-material values that had been exclusively the preserve of the upper and middle classes. By means of elections, activities of new civil associations, or through the renewed performance of old associations, the popular classes, part of the intermediate classes and even some entrepreneurial sectors shook the state's capacity to control society as it had done before.[6]

At this point, the government found itself in a minefield. While external constraints pushed the country towards an orthodox strategy to face the crisis, the new domestic conditions exerted pressure in an opposite direction. And although it chose the path of external adjustment to face the crisis instead of the much more drastic fiscal option, the government seriously damaged its socio-political support, producing a very complex political crisis.[7]

It began as a legitimacy crisis. The 'external adjustment' carried out by the government went against the developmental socio-political coalition prescription, which was to transform national economic growth into the basic value to be pursued by the state. Instead, the government's response was considered recessive, inflationary and a betrayal of confidence, as it heaped all the adjustment costs on domestic debtors.

As a result, part of the elite of the old developmental coalition broke away from the government and gathered around various 'projects' to combat the economic crisis. Most of the entrepreneurial elite was mesmerised by national-developmentalism, and a small minority by a kind of neoliberal project.

These political fractures among the elite lent support to the opposition's actions in Congress and its efforts to mobilise the intermediate and lower classes to fight against the regime's perpetuation. Between January and March 1984 this mass mobilisation produced the most extraordinary demonstration in favour of democratisation — the 'Diretas-Já' campaign. This campaign completely undermined any support for the policy of gradual and limited democratisation led by the regime.

The crisis transferred the government's lack of legitimacy to the authoritarian regime itself. Moreover, a substantial innovation in Brazilian political life emerged at this critical juncture. The idea that there is no democracy without popular participation and that there is no popular participation without the liberty to voice collective demands and to form associations freely was strengthened socially and politically by the active presence of the middle and lower classes.[8] Therefore, bolstered by mass mobilisation, the opposition

---

6   This study follows the line taken by Touraine (1995) regarding the democratisation of political process. This process was sustained by a wider process of democratisation of Brazilian society, which will not be addressed here.

7   There is a detailed account of this crisis in Sallum Jr. (1996, chapter 2).

8   The 'Diretas' campaign challenged the values at the heart of the legitimacy of state power. From then on any hegemony founded on the exclusion of the popular classes would be unsustainable.

produced a crisis in hegemony: from then on, a state predicated upon restrictions to popular political expression and organisation would no longer be acceptable, unless imposed by force. So, the 'Diretas Já' campaign announced a new project for the state, oriented by the new democratic values that emerged from the society's plea for democratisation.

Nevertheless, the military regime defeated the proposal of direct elections for the presidency in the Congress, thus thwarting the deepest effects of the hegemony crisis set off by mass mobilisation. The government simply bypassed the crisis by allowing the election of a civilian government led by the opposition. Indeed, the denial of broad popular participation in choosing a new president generated important conservative effects: the opposition would be able to win only if it made a political pact with dissidents from within the authoritarian regime.[9] Furthermore, the candidates stood within the framework built around proposals made by the government itself as well as by dissident entrepreneurs. Tancredo Neves assimilated some developmentalist proposals, which were supported mainly by industrial entrepreneurs. The rightist candidate, Paulo Maluf, did something similar with the neoliberal project, backed mainly by business associations from the commercial and agro-industrial sectors. Even within these limitations, the proposals were presented in a language in tune with popular aspirations for a true democracy.

Tancredo's overwhelming victory in the electoral college showed the dominant political aspirations of the Brazilian political elite and implicitly expressed the hegemonic project that would prevail over the next presidential period: to build a New Republic — a democracy that would not restrict popular movements and organisations and that held up a renewed national-developmentalism as its economic orientation, willing to combine growth with income redistribution.

The New Republic: Democratisation and Developmentalism

During the Sarney government the authoritarian legacy became adjusted to society's demand for democratisation, turning this societal process into a democratic regime.[10] This process involved breaking down the institutional limits to the popular classes' political participation and organisation, and entailed the expansion of citizens' basic rights. So, it was par-

9   Tancredo Neves was launched as candidate for the presidency by the 'Democratic Alliance', between the oppositionist Brazilian Democratic Movement Party (PMDB) and the regime's dissident Liberal Front Party (PFL). On the other hand, the military regime launched Paulo Maluf's candidacy through its Social Democratic Party (PDS).

10   The elected president, Tancredo Neves, did not take office on 15 March 1985 because he fell ill and died a few weeks after the day he should have assumed office. Instead Vice-President Sarney took over and led the government until 15 March 1990.

tially eliminated one of the Vargas State's central features in any of its political organisation forms.

Indeed, at the outset of the José Sarney government a whole set of rules that blocked political popular participation was altered. The first half of 1985 saw the introduction of the following: a) direct elections over two rounds for the presidency; b) direct elections for the state capitals, safety areas and hydro-mineral stations mayors; c) the Federal District would be represented in the House of Deputies and in the Federal Senate; d) voting rights for the illiterate; e) freedom of party organisation, even for communists; and a slew of other minor alterations in the same direction. Moreover, some changes in union legislation had a great political impact, greatly extending worker participation rights and freeing them from government control: a) union leaders removed from office for 'bad behaviour' were reinstated; b) the Labour Ministry's control over union elections was rescinded; c) the ban, in place since 1978, on intersyndical associations was eliminated, so legalising the central unions that, until then, had only been tolerated.

These and other changes, along with governmental tolerance regarding collective demonstrations, characterised the New Republic as a political arrangement in which the various social groups, including the popular masses, could fight for their interests and ideas with great freedom of organisation and action.

The increased popular participation affected the hierarchy among the state power centres, the governmental management and the scope of citizenship rights. In fact, the hegemonic crisis weakened the hierarchy behind the previous authoritarian regime. In the New Republic the upward popular pressures from below strengthened the autonomy of previously subaltern power centres. So, the National Congress, the Judiciary, the state governments and the political parties gained a wider margin for manoeuvre with regard to the presidency.

These changes to the political institutions and to the range of power of different actors culminated in the 1988 Constitution. This extended the power of the Legislative, the Judiciary and the prosecuting counsel in the governmental decision process. Part of the material basis to exercise power — taxes and financial autonomy — was transferred from the union to the states and municipalities, going so far as to transform the latter into federate units (not subordinate to the states). With regard to citizenship rights the new constitution established a democratic political regime and enlarged the social coverage for all, workers or otherwise, defining the fulfilment of many social rights as a state duty — including some diffuse ones, such as those related to environment — which could be demanded from the public authority by citizens and collectives. Besides, constituents drastically amplified the scope of the public prosecutors' activities, turning the prosecuting counsel into a special branch of state, independent of the three classical powers. The prosecuting counsel could, in its new format, protect the rights of citizens in the face of the state by demanding government obedience to the law.

At the same time, the new Constitution lent a rigid, legal framework to democratised developmentalism: restrictions on foreign capital grew, state companies got more space for their activities, the state gained more control over the market, while public servants, retired people and other workers saw an increase in job stability and benefits. So the 1988 Constitution assured more permanence to the old articulation between the state and the market just when the transnationalisation process and the liberal ideology were about to gain a world dimension on account of the collapse of state socialism.

So, from an institutional point of view, the Brazilian political elite fully accomplished the New Republic project during José Sarney's presidential administration.

Despite these accomplishments, the political elite could not turn the New Republic into a stable system of power, failing to establish a new socio-political coalition to support the project of a democratised developmentalism and so could not overcome the state crisis. In fact, the growing economic instability in Sarney's government was a sign of the state's political fragility. Nevertheless, for the elite it was not only a question of having the right ideas or of making the proper alliances. In reality, the circumstances were too harsh to succeed.

On the one hand, the political elite tried to renew the developmentalist strategy, combining income distribution with economic growth, in an adverse external context which, instead of being a source of capital (foreign loans or investments), continuously took capital out of the country (as international obligations).

On the other hand, they faced those external circumstances while dealing, at the same time, with a society in which social movements and organisations continued to flourish. Perhaps we can say that the scarcity of resources did not give much room for political negotiation in such an optimistic context.

In fact, the elite tried to solve the problems emerging from the crisis of the Vargas State as if the state had not lost most of its political authority and material force. Due to these losses, both the orthodox and heterodox attempts to face economic instability, confronted at times with external threats which resulted from deferring (or the threat to defer) debt payments, at other times with the veto and/or the reticence of members of the old developmentalist alliance which, although loosely bound and largely aimless, continued to bolster the state. It was mainly this political fragility and sluggish progress that gave rise to the popular and middle class movements and organisations of the New Republic.

Indeed, the activities of the new or renewed collectives had a marked impact on state policies, sometimes stimulating sometimes restraining its actions. Several socio-economic sectors organised themselves and shaped public policies in a marked manner, in both conservative and reformist directions. The landowners, for instance, restricted the agrarian reform programme to a minimum and granted land ownership rights widely in the 1988 Constitution. At the other extreme the CUT (Workers Central Union) and other unions made impossible the approval by the National Congress of the so-called Plano Verão (Summer Plan) in its original form, because it tried to stabilise currency through reducing the workers' real salaries in 1989, the year Sarney's successor was to be elected.

In sum, the New Republic became an unstable system of power, where the institutional level, the socio-political sphere and the economic conditions were not well balanced. This instability resulted, from a material viewpoint, in a downward development trajectory. The state went on protecting the internal market but the previous economic dynamism, which had given Brazil one of the highest economic growth rates in the world, had gone. Investment rates had fallen drastically: external savings were not coming in and the state had lost its investment capacity. The state enterprise system, which was at the vanguard of the previous developmentalist model, lost its own dynamism and clung to the adjustment aims, supposed to produce inputs at low prices as a means to fight inflation and/or help the private sector to produce increasing external commercial surpluses The mismanagement of both economics and public finance generated sudden fluctuations in GDP growth, a reduction in average growth and crescent inflationary strains. In the short run, the fight against inflation and the search for alternatives to face it replaced development as the main political issue of that period. All these were powerful obstacles to the generation of an economic counterpart to the political democratisation process in the New Republic. So, in spite of the expansion of the welfare public services, the poor did not increase their share of national income in the 1980s.

Moreover, the difficulties in stabilising a state structure stimulated the growth among the Brazilian elite of a new political project to organise the country. Indeed, in spite of predominating only in the 1990s the liberal hegemony was constructed in Brazil only in the second half of the 1980s. Before that, liberal ideas had a minor impact. They became relevant among the economic elite when businessmen became frightened by the government's reformist actions and, above all, by heterodox stabilisation policies introduced by the Cruzado Plan (prices were frozen between February and November 1986). These policies were interpreted by the economic elite as threats to private property, besides being inefficient in stabilising the currency and in resuming economic growth. From then on, the elite started organising and mobilising in an effort to discipline state structures and actions,[11] broadly along the liberalising lines promoted by the principal lending countries since the 1970s.[12]

So, increasingly from 1987–88 the economic elite started to confront state interventionism, demanding deregulation, better reception for foreign capital, privatisation, and so on. These ideas became predominant in the media and spread out into the middle classes, but not among the political elite, organised workers and public servants, who continued to defend the ideals of 'national property' and 'state regulation'.

That is why the 1988 Constitution, which embodied the New Republic project, became a target for attacks from the entrepreneurial elite and its political and intellectual advocates, and inversely a shield for the workers organisations, public servants, state companies employees and the salaried middle class connected to public service.

The 1989 direct election for the presidency summed up the political results of the previous period. Firstly, the less than five per cent of votes won by the PMDB and PFL candidates ratified the ruling political elite's failure in building a New Republic, as they hoped it would. Secondly, the election was carried out after 30 years of interruption of direct elections for the presidency and with complete freedom of speech and assembly signifying the apogee of the popular and middle classes' participation in the Brazilian politics. It was their growing presence in the public sphere that made way for the leftist candidate's electoral performance. Indeed, Luiz Inacio da Silva (Lula), a former blue-collar worker who stood for the presidency was defeated by a very narrow margin, despite representing such a small political party as the PT (Workers Party).[13] It is important to highlight that this result was obtained without disguising the PT's intentions. Lula promised a real rupture with the autocratic pattern of social domination: the masses would be led to power, the government would carry out income redistribution displacing resources from the top to the bottom of society, a 'true' agrarian reform would be accomplished and, despite intending to democratise the administration of state enterprises, these would be preserved. In sum, this leftist reformism pledged to eliminate social exclusion — at least partially — and was in fact a promise to radicalise the process of social democratisation by giving it a more material basis.

Besides, the electoral process was a turning point in the ideological positions that polarised the party system. From the 1989 campaign onwards the confrontation between democracy and authoritarianism

---

11   For a detailed account of entrepreneurial activities in this period consult Dreifuss (1989) and Diniz (1993).

12   Biersteker (1995) gives an account of this diffusion process.

13   In the second electoral round 37 per cent voted for him, only four per cent fewer than the winning candidate, Fernando Collor de Mello.

which had characterised the party system since the military regime's political liberalisation became less relevant. Party forces reorganised themselves according to new polarisations underpinned by state/market relations. The parties became enamoured of liberal economic ideas on one hand, and by democratised developmentalism on the other. The PSDB (Brazilian Social Democracy Party), an offshoot of the PMDB set up in 1988, shifted decisively to liberalisation, as its candidate Mario Covas highlighted in demanding a 'capitalist shock' for the country. Moreover, the PDC (Christian Democrat Party) and the PL (Liberal Party) also followed a liberal programme. The PDS, the military regime's former party, had conformed since the 1983–84 crisis to market ideas even though these were suffocated by the conservative populism of its candidate, Paulo Maluf, in the electoral dispute. And despite the national-developmentist rhetoric of the Liberal Front Party (PFL) candidate, Aureliano Chaves, his party had shown increasing liberal tendencies since the Constituent Assembly and gave him weak support. At the other extreme, the PMDB, the PDT and the PT opted for radicalised distributive developmentalism. Another ideological polarisation came to light in the 1989 electoral campaign: the opposition between two kinds of democratic ideal. Although all parties were pro democracy those who considered economic liberalisation to be the principal issue accepted representative democracy, even if they questioned the form of government, leaving no place for popular participation other than in elections. On the Left the prevailing idea was to move further towards more participative forms of democracy

Ultimately, the election of Collor de Mello meant that the main political office in the country was occupied by a politician who rejected national-developmentalist economic ideas and was identified with neoliberalism.

In sum, the 1989 election for the presidency was a watershed between two periods in the Brazilian political transition: one in which political democratisation had precedence, and another in which the most important political change was economic liberalisation.

The New Liberal Hegemony and its Consequences

The Collor government partly confirmed the liberal tenor of the 1989 electoral process. It further undermined the national-developmentalist institutional framework and redirected Brazilian society in an anti-state and an internationalising direction. However, in spite of giving the initial push to build a new state development strategy, the Collor government did not succeed in overcoming the state crisis experienced by society since the early 1980s.

During the Collor period import barriers, with the exception of custom duties, were suspended and a four-year programme was implemented by degrees to reduce even those duties.[14] At the same time, a programme of deregulation of economic activities and privatisation of state companies not protected by the Constitution was implemented in order to aid the recovery of public finances and gradually to reduce the latter's role in domestic industry. Finally, the regional integration policy, embodied in Mercosul (1991), aimed at increasing the market for the domestic products of its members.

These measures meant that the former development strategy, which aimed to build an integrated and complete industrial structure using the state as a shield to face external competition and as a lever both for the industrial development and the national private enterprise, had been discarded.

Viewed positively, the intention was to put in place a competitive strategy to integrate the domestic economy into the world economic system. The intention was to preserve only those industrial sectors that, after an adaptation period, showed enough vitality to keep up with foreign industry. So, domestic industry tended to become a specialised sector within a transnationalised industrial system.

This strategic reorientation — although ideologically in tune with domestic entrepreneurs' new liberal inclinations and with international tendencies — was not enough to ratify a new pact that could overcome the hegemonic crisis started in 1983. Although Collor seemed to be an auspicious Caesar emerging from the fissures of a political order in crisis with the intention of overcoming it, his government, instead, contributed to a drastic increase in uncertainty, hugely disappointing the expectations of the competing political forces.

In order to stabilise the currency the Collor Plan jeopardised the juridical safety of private property: besides freezing prices he confiscated and reduced part of the financial wealth of the entrepreneurial and middle classes. Moreover, the government subjected the entrepreneurs' traditional organisations to systematic verbal attacks and enabled some groups of entrepreneurs, at the same time, to give him support in the implementation of his development policy. He tried to exercise power dissociated from the political class and its traditional survival mechanisms, reducing state expenses by arbitrary and massive dismissals of public servants, thus disorganising the public administration, and he also tried to weaken the worker organisations which opposed him through stimulating alternative organisations linked to the government. On the international side the Collor government had further difficulties. Despite its liberal and international orientation, the government's first economic team tried to postpone the end of the moratorium inherited from the Sarney administration and to

---

14   The tariff averages were 31.6 per cent in 1989. These fell to 30 per cent in 1990, 23.3 per cent in 1991, 19.2 per cent in January 1992 and 15 per cent in October 1992, before rising again to 19.2 per cent in July 1993.

weaken the foreign private banks' position in the external debt negotiation. This strategy contributed to the further dissipation of the support he previously had from the Brazilian economic elite, and stimulated the US government's opposition and its reaction in order to protect the US banking system. These external difficulties lessened when a more liberal economic team took office in 1991.[15] It was in such a disturbed political context that Collor was accused of being the secret leader of a corruption network, getting money from opportunities opened by the tenure of political power and that a congressional investigation into this scheme led him to resign the presidency in order to avoid impeachment.[16]

To sum up, in his government Collor failed as a Caesar.[17] His actions stirred up political crisis. Instead of giving the warring factions the means to solve their own impasses he tried to impose an alternative solution from above. He also tried to restore autocratically the currency stability that was the basis of the state's exchange relations and its authority over the market in a society that, although still politically undernourished, had progressed greatly on its way to democracy. Collor de Mello's impeachment would hardly have happened if society had not advanced so much in the belief/conception that government and state should cleave to narrower moral and political limits than previously. Nor would it have happened if various social groups and state power centres had not advanced so much in terms of their capacity for autonomous action. The demonstrations by thousands of young people clamouring in the streets for the president's impeachment; the brave testimonies of subaltern workers against their head of state; the press, the radio and TV, Congress and the Judiciary expressed, each in its own way, that society and the relationship between state and society were more democratic.

In spite of the Collor government's failure to overcome the Brazilian crisis, since the end of the 1980s international economic conditions had become more positive for countries from the periphery. Reinforcing factors and decisions facilitated this change: the huge financial investment growth in the central countries and towards foreign and 'emergent' markets; the external debt 'relief' under the 1989 Brady Plan of negotiation; the economic liberalisation policies improved in the periphery countries.[18] All in all, 'after almost ten years of negative net resources transfers, Latin

---

15   Collor's first economic team was replaced in May 1991. The external debt negotiation during Collor's government is well studied in Candia Veiga (1993).

16   Collor resigned in October 1992.

17   I use the term Caesarism as a metaphor . For a short but rich account of the concept consult Bobbio (1994).

18   On the Brady Plan see Cline (1989). Naím (1995) provides a synthesis of the new capital flows and reforms which characterised the passage from the 1980s to the 1990s.

America experienced positive transfers from the rest of the world. The magnitude of net capital inflows into the country increased drastically in 1992 and 1993, surpassing US$20 billion.'[19]

The huge influx of capital to Brazil,[20] the liberal legacy from the Collor period, social rejection of his autocratic solutions for the crisis, the exacerbation of political-economical instability during the Itamar Franco period and the overwhelming growth of the popular prestige of the leftist candidate for the presidency were some of the conditions and, at the same time powerful levers, for the next attempt, accomplished in 1994, to overcome the hegemonic crisis that undermined Brazilian society from the early 1980s.[21]

These conditions specify the *fortuna* met by some political leaderships who, well-placed within the state, had *virtu* enough to negotiate the association between the centrist and rightist parties as regards the continuity of liberal reforms, the stabilisation of the economy and the taking over of political central power. They achieved all that in launching the successful Plano Real (Real Plan) and also the victorious bid for the presidency of its articulator, the treasury minister Fernando Henrique Cardoso.

The reference to *fortuna* and *virtu* captures, in broad terms, Pocock's idea of a 'Machiavellian moment', which emphasises the role of leadership in state reconstruction.[22] In fact, at this critical conjuncture the leadership was able to take advantage of breathing space (as the new international capital flowed) thanks to the creative management of some of the institutional characteristics of the Brazilian economic and political system so that both the community and the general interest in public order could prevail, in a situation menaced by the confrontation of particularistic interests.

According to this reasoning, the creative utilisation of rules inherent to the constitutional revision generated minimal fiscal conditions to achieve some stabilisation (the Emergence Social Fund, voted by Congress in February 1994),[23] the institution of a parallel currency, the URV (Variable Reference Unit) which generalised the indexation for a few months, creating a sort of 'laboratory hyperinflation' which synchronised prices and salaries; and the creation, on 1 July 1994, of a new currency — the *real* —

---

19   Edwards (1995, p. 82).
20   The external money supply began to return to Brazil in 1991. Its exchange reserves reached US$42 billion in mid 1994, when the Real Plan was launched.
21   There is a good account of the political and economic conditions of the Real Plan in Sola and Kugelmas (1996). Sallum Jr. (1999) gives an account of the first Cardoso government.
22   Malloy and Connaghan (1996) and Mettenhein and Malloy (1998) analysed some Latin American political experiences in the light of what Pocock understands as the 'Machiavellian moment'. Sola and Kugelmas (1996) studied Cardoso's Real Plan and election through the same conceptual lens.
23   During the constitutional revision period reforms were able to be approved by simple majority.

to substitute the URV, anchored to the dollar but not its equal. In sum, all that, besides dozens of specific regulations, would have produced stability. By this means there would have been assured 'an universality principle — incorporated in institutions and practices — superposed to the particularity and contingence inherent to the uncontrolled behaviour of the rival forces' as Malloy and Connaghan describe for the 'Machiavellian moment'.

Nevertheless, the sharp antagonism between 'universal' and 'particular' and the subjectivity of the *virtu* must be restricted in this analysis. In fact this 'universality principle', which was the basis of state reconstruction, was only a step, if an essential one, in the construction of a new hegemonic system of power in Brazilian society. The leadership role, the *virtu*, consisted only in a final political binding to foundations which were being socially constructed from the second half of the 1980s. Besides, although the Real Plan was an intelligent technical form and an essential device to stabilise the currency, it was a secondary element in the 'Machiavellian moment'. Its essence was the political composition between the centre and rightist parties around a project of conquering and reconstructing the state according to a predominantly liberal view.[24] As a matter of fact the parties' leaderships were aware of the link between monetary stabilisation and the electoral chances of victory of the Real Plan supporters.

The extraordinary success of the Real Plan, the election of Fernando Henrique Cardoso for the presidency in the first round, the election of a National Congress in which the winning party alliance had a majority, the victory of the president's political allies in the elections of nearly all the states — all that foretold that on 1 January 1995 representatives of a new hegemonic power system would take the helm in a state which was anchored to a currency that might remain stable: they were ready to complete the task of moulding society.

Since 1995 the rulers have been removing the residue of the Vargas State and building new forms of regulation, following a multifaceted system of ideas whose central feature is a moderate economic liberalism. Its core may be summed up thus: the state should transfer almost all its entrepreneurial functions to private initiative; it should expand its regulatory functions and its social policies; public finance should be balanced and the direct incentives to private companies should remain modest; the privileges of certain public servants should be restrained; and the country should increase its integration into the world economy, although maintaining the priority of strengthening Mercosul integration and other South American relations.

---

24   It is true that in that period the economic and political agents demanded a stabilisation plan. The Real Plan was a carefully prepared response to this demand, in that it was adjusted to produce the greatest possible political effect.

This basic liberal set of ideas was implemented through initiatives that drastically changed the previous state/market relations and the state's order of priorities for economic areas and social groups, in patrimonial and institutional terms. The central target of these policies was to break some of the legal foundations of the national-developmentist state, in part assured by the 1988 Constitution and to diminish state participation in economic activities. The Cardoso government succeeded in that: the constitutional and infra-constitutional reform projects submitted to Congress were approved almost in their entirety. The most relevant are: a) the end of the constitutional discrimination regarding foreign capital companies; b) the transference to the union of the oil and gas exploration, refinement and transportation, held by the Petrobras company, which became a state grantee (although having some advantages as regards other private concessionaries); c) the state was authorised to concede the exploration rights of all telecommunication services (fixed and cellular phones, satellite exploration, etc.) to private companies (previously the public enterprises had a monopoly on these concessions).

Besides embarking on these constitutional reforms, the Cardoso government strongly pressed Congress to approve the complementary law which passed public service concessions to private initiative, authorised by the constitution (electricity, roads, railways etc); got the approval of a law conceived to protect industrial property rights and copyrights, as recommended by the World Trade Organisation (WTO), and preserved the commercial liberalisation programme which had previously been implemented. Additionally, the Cardoso government carried out a huge programme of privatisation and selling-off of concessions. The individual state governments carried out similar programmes on a smaller scale.

Another important area covered by disciplinary measures was public finance: there were fixed maximum limits to all staff payments; the debts of the most important subnational units started to be renegotiated and new loans and renegotiations with the federal government were forbidden for a long time.

This set of initiatives seems to have represented the common code of the new hegemonic bloc. It was carried out by the great majority of deputies, bureaucrats and executive rulers, all kinds of entrepreneurs, media, etc and gradually penetrated the middle class, part of urban syndicalism and the popular masses.

In effect, the legislative measures were easily approved by Congress in spite of the leftist minority opposition hidden behind banners such as 'the public patrimony' and the 'national economy'. The privatisations and the concessions sell-off were successfully achieved, with popular support despite the forensic disputes promoted by the leftist organisations and their followers.

However, strong internal divisions arose in the new hegemonic political bloc, minimally unified in its beliefs and purposes by a moderate liberal code, which produced endless conflicts over economic policy and lent a certain hybrid character to state actions.

At one extreme there is a fundamentalist liberal current, adhering mainly to quick and straight monetary stability and committed to a free market economy, while the other extreme is occupied by a liberal-developmentalist tendency, more inclined towards state intervention and whose central concern has been to balance the objectives of currency stabilisation and the growth of competitive domestic production. During the first Cardoso government the fundamentalist version of liberalism was predominant, consistently guiding the hard core of government economic policy.[25] The fundamentalists tried to get monetary stabilisation with high exchange/high interest policies and without placing the same emphasis on cutting fiscal expenses.[26] The second version of liberalism lacked the consistency of the first: it had neither a programmatic text nor did it systematically orient governmental action.[27] Nevertheless, the liberal-developmentalism inspired some policies designed to counterbalance the negative consequences of liberal orthodoxy to specific economic sectors, or even to promote the growth of some productive activities in the country. It is worth stressing that this kind of developmentalism, instead of aspiring to an integrated industrial system, calls for a meaningful participation of local production in the world economic system. It accepts only well-defined forms of state intervention in the productive system, such as the support of industrial policies, since these were limited in time and in the size of subsidies. Such policies do not aim for import substitution at any cost. The objective has been to increase the competitiveness of some economic sectors and, at most, the 'densification of productive chains' in order to develop domestic economic activities to keep up with international productivity patterns.[28]

---

25 The main representatives of this ideological current in the government were the former president of the Central Bank, Gustavo Franco, and the treasury minister, Pedro Malan. Outside the government its main intellectual advocates are the PUC-Rio economists.

26 In spite of the political rhetoric the exchange overvaluation is not related to the neoliberal ideas, which recommends a 'market exchange'. The Brazilian radical version of liberalism, referred to as neoliberal, adopted the overvaluation to conform Brazilian enterprises to market patterns, that is the international levels of prices and productivity. That is why this kind of liberalism may be called fundamentalist.

27 The representatives of this point of view inside the first FHC government were Jose Serra, planning minister, Luiz Carlos Mendonça de Barros, BNDES president, and José Roberto Mendonça de Barros, political economy secretary. Outside the government the most important name was the federal representative Delfim Neto, who was the minister of planning (among other posts) during the authoritarian regime.

28 Elsewhere I gave an account of these compensatory measures. See Sallum Jr (2000).

During the first Cardoso government, the overvalued exchange rate and high interest rate produced monetary stability, but at the same time led the Brazilian economy toward a serious external imbalance. In order to reduce this imbalance the government kept a policy of high interest rates which had two complementary aims: a) to rein in the domestic economy and consequently imports and the commercial deficit; b) to attract external capital to finance the country's external imbalance, maintaining therefore a high level of reserves to sustain and anchor the *real*.

Beneath this stabilisation programme there was an optimistic view of global financial markets: not only would liquidity remain high but, if the country did well, there would be no lack of loans and investments to balance occasional deficits in the current external transactions account.

The Mexican financial crisis, in December 1994, showed for the first time the risks of conforming macroeconomic policy to the liberal fundamentalist position. In fact, the Mexican crisis made clear that, depending on the international context, a pronounced imbalance in the trading and services accounts could create difficulties in getting external savings.

Despite this warning, and although the government adopted some compensatory policies, inspired in liberal-developmentism, to protect the domestic economy, its basic macroeconomic orientation was retained until the exchange crisis of January 1999. This obstinacy substantially increased national economy fragility regarding the international system and State debility regarding domestic creditors. Indebtedness grew rapidly in order to cover the imbalances that were generated. As a result of this increasing financial need the changes of the international market conditions increasingly affected the capital flows into the country, exposing the national currency to speculative attacks which tended to devalue it.

So, after the Mexican crisis, the 1997 Asian crisis and the August 1998 Russian moratorium paved the way for attacks from speculators. The country lost huge international reserves and the government acted in a similar way: sustaining the currency stability by drastically raising interest rates to maintain reserves and to restrain both internal economic activity and the external imbalance. The result was that, although inflation reached very low levels, the gross domestic product (GDP) was drastically reduced or even negative and the unemployment rates increased substantially.[29]

Despite the fact that, from November 1998, it had monetary support from the US government along with loans from and an agreement with the IMF to prevent instability, the Brazilian exchange policy had to be altered at the start of the second Cardoso term to face capital flight and international reserve losses.

29 The unemployment rates escalated as follows: 4.85 per cent (7 January 1994–7 January 1995); 5.75 per cent (1995–96); 5.77 per cent (1996–97); 7.37 per cent (1997–98); and 8.32 per cent (1998–99).

The implementation of a liberal instead of a national-developmentalist economic strategy redirected the state in several socioeconomic sectors. In this respect, the most obvious and important is that the state enterprises are not the sustainers of government policy. Not only are they being privatised but sectors formerly overseen by direct administration services are also now in the care of private companies. This lessening of the state's entrepreneurial functions did not eliminate state interventionism. Instead it was deeply transformed. The state has been expanding its normative and controlling functions through regulating sector agencies (for the telecom, electricity, oil and gas sectors for instance) and retains much of its capacity to mould economic activity through the buying of goods and services.

Additionally, national private companies ceased to be the privileged focus of state policies. On the contrary, foreign companies have not only been given equal constitutional status to national companies, but also the basic state orientation has been to maximise foreign investments at the expense of its association with national enterprises.[30] Besides this general state orientation (concerning both the union and the states) the government has tried systematically to attract multinational companies to some key branches of industry such as the automotive sector and telecommunications, modulating the tributary laws and the financing system and taking initiatives to 'sell' Brazil's image as an excellent destination for foreign capital. In fact, Brazil became one of the world's biggest destinations for direct foreign investment, second only to China.[31] Furthermore, the liberal strategy privileged the financial sphere over production/commercialisation activities from the launch of the Real Plan until January 1999, through its overvalued exchange/high interest rate policies. The monetary and exchange policies siphoned income over to the financial sector, both foreign and local. Concerning the non-financial sphere, the BNDES (the main Brazilian bank for development) diversified enormously the activities financed by it. Besides manufacture, commercial (shopping centres), tourist (resorts), agricultural activities and the like have also been financed. Commercial agriculture, particularly, not only reaped the benefits of several government measures but also its interests became an important concern for Brazilian government at the international level. Since 1996 — while discussions about free trade agreements with the USA and the other American countries, on one side, and with the European Union (EU), on the other, took centre stage — agricultural issues and the fight against US and European protectionism also turned into a key issue for Brazilian diplomacy.

30 The stabilisation policy itself in the first FHC government contributed to giving advantages to foreign enterprises vis-à-vis national ones.
31 In 1996 the FDI reached only US$9.6 billion, in 1997 it rose up to US$17.9 billion, and then to US$26.8 billion in 1998, to US$31.2 billion in 1999.

The changes in state strategy were sufficiently drastic to break a basic tenet of the old national-developmentist alliance: leaving agrarian property untouched. Monetary stabilisation itself somewhat reduced land property prices, devaluing land by about 45 per cent (on average). Moreover, on government's own initiative, and also under pressure from the MST (Landless Labourers Movement), CONTAG (National Confederation of Agricultural Workers) and the Catholic Church, a large agrarian reform programme has been developed in recent years. This programme includes not only a great number of dispossessions and the consequent settlement of landless agricultural labourers, but also the promotion of a set of institutional reforms and specific measures which saw a rise in the level of taxation on unproductive fields, increased public control over the agrarian structure and the appropriation of immense areas legally occupied by land dealers.

Liberalism, Developmentalism and Democracy

Despite Cardoso's re-election in 1998 and the almost complete maintenance of political support (in the Congress and among state governors) having corroborated that the liberal programme had the acquiescence of the majority, government lost political strength as it had to seek IMF and US support, had to allow monetary devaluation in January 1999 and was afterwards constrained by enormous economic difficulties.

It is true that the replacement of the semi-pegged regime and its overvalued exchange rate by a floating exchange rate system and a brilliant interest policy management succeeded in keeping monetary stability and, after the 1999 stagnation, allowed a GDP growth of four per cent in 2000. Nevertheless, the IMF support was given and renewed in exchange for Brazil's commitment to a severe fiscal adjustment, aiming at a huge yearly surplus in the public accounts (interest owed was not included), large enough to be able to reduce the proportion of public debt in GDP. Moreover, the 2001 and 2002 international downturn, the Argentine crisis and the political risk connected to the 2002 presidential election produced additional economic constraints to the Cardoso government's policies. There was an important reduction of FDI flows to Brazil[32] and it became difficult to rollover the external and internal debts. So once again, Brazil's external dependency and economic fragility were revealed, despite the new floating exchange policy. It could not completely protect the economy from the negative international conjuncture and from the political uncertainties given the enormous external and internal debt produced by the first Cardoso government's stabilisation policy and the chronic deficit of the Brazilian external current account. The Central Bank countervailing measures — to deepen

32   The FDI was US$33.3 billion in 2000, it fell to US$20 billion in 2001 and to US$16.6 billion in 2002.

fiscal adjustment, to raise interest rates and to sign new agreements with the IMF — though protective of Brazilian financial solvency reduced the 2001 and 2002 GDP growth to less than two per cent per year.[33]

The new macroeconomic management emerging after the January 1999 exchange regime crisis implied some changes in State/economic branch relations: non-financial activities tended to gain greater prominence and government stimulated in different ways those economic branches which could help to produce a surplus in external trade. During the second FHC government even a touch of concern for domestic business can be detected, and some assistance has been given to those that looked likely to be able to compete internationally as multinational companies.

These changes can be seen as signs of a political transformation within the hegemonic bloc, which leaned sporadically, from then on, towards the liberal-developmentalist model. In fact, since the beginning of 2000 the Development Ministry, the Science and Technology Ministry, the Planning Secretary and even the presidency showed this kind of transformation and it was stressed during the 2002 electoral process. Even so, the standard-bearers of liberal fundamentalism kept the main levers of power — the Treasury and the Central Bank — whereby they maintained the priority of stabilisation, although fiscal policy had been selected, rather than exchange mechanisms, as the fundamental tool to sustain it. In sum, the hegemonic bloc kept its divisions but the conflicts among them were mainly displaced from the exchange question to fiscal issues. Moreover, despite the strengthening of the developmentalist tendency, this was not systematic, depending as it did on the issues. As a consequence, governmental decisions tended to be slow and unsystematic.

The economic difficulties mentioned above also contributed to weakening the political coalition running the State during Cardoso's second term. In his first term President Cardoso had a high popularity rating mainly based on the sudden monetary stabilisation. This prestige amplified the usual presidential powers and greatly helped him to manage the coalition of governmental parties in order to execute the liberal reformist programme. In addition, the monetary stability achieved by the Real Plan and the policy of economic restraint which predominated in the first Fernando Henrique Cardoso government restricted the popular mass movements and organisations. The end of high inflation undermined worker demands. The liberal hegemony also restricted the mobilisation of state and/or social-democratically oriented unions. Moreover, the widespread popular

33   Despite its considerable fiscal adjustment Brazil couldn't reduce the ratio of debt to GDP. However, the 2002 huge exchange devaluation related to electoral uncertainty helped Brazil to generate a US$13.1 billion external trade superavit which reduced its current external deficit to 1.7 % of GDP (From 1998 to 2001 it had been more than 4.0 % of GDP).

support for the government made it easier to adopt a technocratic style in the exercise of power and also reinforced the difficulties of political participation except in electoral periods. In spite of these difficulties, the mobilisation of the agricultural labourers in favour of the agrarian reform greatly increased and pushed the government to develop the large agrarian reform programme mentioned above.

In the second Cardoso term, however, the president lost much of his prestige, mainly because the government broke its word and devalued the currency in January 1999 — stimulating the fear of inflation. At the same time it could not promptly fulfil his promise of renewing economic growth. High inflation did not return and economic activity started to grow after a little more than one year, but even so the president did not recover the leadership of his first term. So the governmental political coalition lost discipline. This political weakening made the government less effective in getting laws approved in Congress and in defining specific policies, in turn allowing the opposition parties to get stronger. Additionally, these opposition parties have changed significantly in recent years and are increasingly amenable to liberal ideas.

The 2002 electoral fight for presidency expressed very well the changes occurring in the hegemonic bloc, the debility of its political coalition and the ideological shift of the main opposition parties. No presidential candidate stood for liberal fundamentalism. Despite advocating liberal developmentalist ideas, the governmental candidate couldn't get the support of the whole political coalition that backed Cardoso. The coalition's right wing was not able to launch its own candidate for presidency but still showed some regional political strength. On the other hand, the opposition runners were in tune with liberal developmental ideas, despite the exacerbated nationalist rhetoric of some of them. In particular, the Workers' Party (PT), and its candidate Lula, made great efforts to adjust themselves to the establishment. They allied not only with some leftist parties but also with the Liberal Party, inviting an entrepreneur from the PL to be the candidate for the vice-presidency and promising to preserve the axis of Cardoso's macroeconomic policy.

Summing up, in the 2002 elections the whole set of political tendencies tried to represent the establishment left wing. This meant that all of them advocated more state control over the market, more state incentives to productive activities and more state protection to the poorest without breaking the liberal framework, which moulded the sociopolitical coalition in power.

So the electoral victory of the Workers' Party candidate for the presidency did not mean any break with the liberal hegemony established years before. Indeed, the new government agenda is a liberal developmentalist one: its aim is not to rebuild the entrepreneurial national State but to reform the State so that it might push private development and social equality.[34] It is noteworthy that in the new government orthodox policies are implemented only as 'an inevitable but transitional medicine' while external and internal debt and the international downturn continue to constrain state power. Contrary to Cardoso's technocratic style of decision-making the new government advocates more political participation and has established many advisory groups of invited social organisation representatives to help in the definition of government policies. It is still too soon to know if Lula's government will succeed in materialising those intentions.

In any case, the amazing set of institutional reforms accomplished in the 1990s defined the basic institutions framework that will regulate state/market and national economic system/world capitalism relations at the beginning of the new century. This picture will hardly be altered in the medium term, as it is the expression of the institutional consolidation of a new hegemonic perspective in society. The changes in macroeconomic policy increasingly bent towards liberal developmentalism and the new leftist government do not alter the central features of the new hegemonic perspective. External dependency and Mercosul were the most fragile links in the new form of integration between the country and world capitalism. On one hand, the chronic incapacity of internal savings to push investments threatens continuous economic development in Brazil. On the other hand, the economic and political weakness of Mercosul members and lack of harmony between them may complicate its consolidation into a regional bloc. In addition, the USA is pushing hard to subordinate Mercosul to an integration that comprises the whole American continent under its leadership.

In a wider context, Brazilian progress towards a more democratic society has been remarkable. There is a clear expression of increasing intolerance on the part of the popular and middle classes towards the political elite's predatory behaviour and also a growing demand for fairness in income distribution. These demands for accountability tend to consolidate the democratic political institutions and, as the inflationary valve is reasonably blocked — the typical escape mechanism of that elite in the face of the distributive pressures — it seems more likely that together with economic growth there will be some reduction in the Brazilian indices of material and cultural inequality.

In the last decades of the twentieth century, however big the changes might have been, Brazil still did not escape the peripheral condition. The return of accelerated growth and Mercosul consolidation will not be enough to allow this. To emerge from this condition will require the social and economic inclusion of the poorest, who remain marginal to the material gains of the modern civilisation. This is the biggest and hardest task confronting Brazilian society in the twenty-first century.

---

34   It is important to stress that in Brazil and in most Latin American countries economic liberalism was not against the Welfare State but opposed to the Entrepreneur State and in favour of social policies.

CHAPTER 9

Class Mobility in Brazil from a Comparative Perspective[*]

Carlos Antonio Costa Ribeiro and Maria Celi Scalon

T his chapter describes changes in the class structure and social mobility patterns in Brazil from 1973 to 1996. These changes are related more to macro-structural processes than to the country's re-democratisation in the 1980s. The chapter should thus be viewed as a description of the structural context during re-democratisation, considering that there are no causal relations between the political regime (democracy or military dictatorship) and the type of inequalities we describe. The inequalities examined here are actually the product of long-lasting historical processes and not specific conditions in the political conjuncture.

It is a well-known fact that the economic growth and industrialisation in Brazil were rapid and virtually uninterrupted from 1945 until the early 1980s. It was over the course of this period that the country made the definitive transition from a rural and agrarian society into a predominantly urban and industrial one. In contrast, contrary to trends in previous decades, during the 1980s and 1990s the Brazilian economy remained close to stagnation.[1] Despite some indication that the Brazilian class structure changed during this period,[2] we still lack precise answers to the following questions: How did the Brazilian class structure change during these periods of growth and crisis? What were the impacts of rapid industrialisation on social mobility patterns? Did the class structure become more open, more closed, or did it remain with the same degree of rigidity? In other words, did relative mobility rates change? Are changes in the class structure and mobility patterns in Brazil atypical when observed in comparison to other countries? Our purpose in this chapter is to provide plausible answers to these four questions.

The first step is to define a scheme of social classes that can be used to make historical and international comparisons. Fortunately the Brazilian

[*] Previous versions of this chapter were presented at the 50th Meeting of the Research Committee on Stratification and Mobility (RC28) of the International Sociological Association (held in May 2000 in Libourne, France) and in the conference 'Fifteen Years of Democracy in Brazil,' organised by the Institute of Latin American Studies at the University of London (in February 2001 in London). We wish to thank John Goldthorpe, Hiroshi Ishida and Elisa Reis for their valuable comments.

1   For a history of economic policy in Brazil, see Abreu (1990).
2   For a literature review, see Guimarães (1999).

data can be classified according to a class scheme that has been widely used in comparative research. This class scheme was initially proposed by Erickson, Goldthorpe and Portocarrero (1979) and by Goldthorpe, Llewellyn and Payne (1987) to study social mobility from a class structure perspective. In the international comparative research circles this scheme is known as EGP (the initials of Erickson, Goldthorpe and Portocarrero). According to English sociologist John Goldthorpe, who has developed the most consistent work in defining the theoretical contours of class mobility, the study of social mobility using the EGP class scheme and log-linear statistical models is especially suited to describe empirically the formation of social classes and social fluidity patterns, or inversely, rigidity patterns in the class structure. Before we describe why the study of social mobility is central to understanding class formation and social fluidity, we will briefly describe the theoretical foundations guiding the elaboration of the seven classes in the EGP scheme that are used in this analysis.

Considering that the debate on social classes is fundamental to contemporary sociological theory, any attempt to present it in the few pages of the present chapter would be doomed to incompleteness. In this sense, we will limit ourselves to presenting briefly the main characteristics of the theoretical perspective we are adopting.[3] The EGP class scheme was designed to describe social classes according to their typical employment relations. The first distinction that should be observed is that between employers and employees. According to the scheme, employers are differentiated according to the size of their establishments and the number of persons they employ, while autonomous workers can be defined as 'self-employed' and/or small owners with no employees. In contrast, Goldthorpe defines two distinct types of work contracts with employees: a restricted labour contract or labour relationship, characterising labour relations with blue-collar workers or members of the working class, and another, referred to as a service relationship, involving autonomy for employees and characterising labour relations with professionals, administrators and managers, i.e., upper level white-collar workers. Under the labour contract or labour relationship, wages are defined directly according to the employees' level of effort or production. This type of labour contract gives the employer not only great freedom to replace employees, but also the possibility of supervising employees' work either directly or through supervisors or foremen. The second type, i.e., the service relationship, is characterised by the fact that employers must establish relationships of trust and commitment with employees, who by virtue of their expert knowledge or delegated authority, cannot be supervised. In addition to characteristics pertaining to employment relations, the EGP scheme

---

3   For a fuller discussion of class theory and social mobility, see Scalon (1999).

also incorporates distinctions as to the sector of activity, i.e., rural or urban. The class scheme derived from these theoretical considerations groups in each class individuals having comparable occupational positions in terms of income levels, degree of economic security, possibilities for career advancement and degree of autonomy to perform work activities.

Following these theoretical principles, data on the occupation of respondents and their fathers contained in the National Sample Surveys of Households (PNADs) from 1973, 1988 and 1996 were re-coded so as to construct the seven social classes in the EGP scheme. Precisely these classes were used to classify the data from the various other countries studied in the CASMIN[4] Project (Comparative Analysis of Social Mobility in Industrial Nations).[5] The social classes are the following:[6]

I+II – Professionals, administrators and managers (with a service relationship involving broad delegation of authority to such employees).

III – Non-manual routine workers (with a mixed contract, i.e., a labour contract generally involving a low degree of delegation of authority to employees, while allowing the employer to exercise some degree of direct supervision of work)

IVa+b – Petty bourgeoisie or small owners with or without employees (employers or self-employed).[7]

IVc1 – Rural employers and landowners.

V+VI – Technicians and supervisors of manual labour, and skilled manual workers (a labour contract or relationship, but involving a minimum degree of delegation of authority in the case of supervisors).

VIIa – Unskilled manual labourers (labour contract).

VIIb – Unskilled rural workers (labour contract).

---

4   Project led by Goldthorpe in the mid-1980s, with the help of Swedish and German collaborators.
5   The main publication for this project is Erickson and Goldthorpe (1992).
6   We adopted the roman numbers that were used by the formulators of the EGP class schema.
7   Since the number of large proprietors and employers is always small in any *survey* of the total population of a country (which is the case of all the *surveys* we are analysing here), large proprietors and employers are included in class I+II. If we could distinguish the class of large proprietors, we would have a class with too small number of cases that would not allow any statistical analysis to be significant. Moreover, in the modern capitalist world most large enterprises do not have a unique owner. In fact, many professionals, administrators and managers are simultaneously employers and partners of the enterprises in which they work, see Goldthorpe (1982).

Over the course of this chapter we use these seven social classes to describe and perform a comparative analysis of class formation and the degree of social fluidity in the Brazilian class structure. In the analyses of relative mobility rates in which we compare various countries, we group these seven classes into five: 1) white-collar workers (I+II/III); 2) petite bourgeoisie (IVa+b); 3) rural workers (IVc1+VIIb); 4) skilled manual workers (V+VI), and 5) unskilled manual workers (VIIa). While class formation is analysed based on the description of absolute social mobility rates, social fluidity is analysed using log-linear models that describe the relative mobility rates.

Absolute mobility rates are obtained by simple percentage calculation of inflow and outflow patterns (derived from the mobility tables cross-classifying class origin in rows with class destination in columns), and of total mobility indices. These rates and indices describe the evolution of the class structure of a given country over time. They can also be used to compare class formation patterns in different countries. For example, using these absolute rates, it is possible to determine which classes are expanding and which are shrinking over time, the class origin of members in each social class, and the amount of mobility due to changes in the size of each class of origin (the father's class) and class of destination (son's class). Since the class origin and class destination distributions are always different in any mobility table, there is always a certain amount of social mobility that results from differences between the marginals (origin and destination) of the tables. What one observes in comparative research is that the degree of social mobility as measured by absolute rates varies considerably from country to country and over time in the same country according to the different trajectories leading from agrarian and rural economies to industrial and urban ones. In other words, class formation depends to a major extent on the rhythm and speed of industrialisation. In the social mobility literature there is a certain consensus regarding the relationship between absolute rates and economic transformations. Different authors agree that absolute mobility rates vary from country to country and over time according to the specific characteristics and fluctuations in the pace of industrialisation in each historical period and in each country.[8]

In contrast, there is great controversy as to the relationship between industrialisation and fluctuations in the relative mobility rates. While liberal theories predict that with the industrialisation process there will be an increase in social fluidity,[9] partisans of class analysis contend that the latter is independent of the industrialisation process and rarely changes over time or

---

8   See, for example, Duncan (1966); Blau and Duncan (1967); Bendix and Lipset (1959); Hout and Hauser (1992); Erickson and Goldthorpe (1992); Hout (1989).

9   See, for example, Ganzenboom, Luijkx and Treiman (1989); Kerr et al. (1960); Hout (1988).

from country to country.[10] According to the latter perspective, social fluidity decreases only as a consequence of specific policies aimed at greater socio-economic equality and not as a direct consequence of the economic development process. But how is social fluidity empirically defined and analysed?

The degree of social fluidity in the class structure is analysed according to relative mobility rates, which are nothing more than odds ratios obtained from log-linear models describing the degree of statistical association between class origin and class destination. For example, relative social mobility rates compare the odds of people with origins in different social classes reaching the same class destination. If these mobility chances are well distributed, we could say that class of origin is weakly associated with class of destination (if the odds ratio is equal to one, there is no association between the variables), but when mobility chances are poorly distributed we can say that class of destination is highly associated with class of origin (and the odds ratio will be greater than one). In other words, when the association between class of origin and class of destination is weak, one can say that there is a high level of social fluidity and when the association is strong there is a low level of social fluidity, or inversely, the class structure is considered to be rigid. Researchers frequently refer to relative mobility rates to measure inequality of opportunities in a given stratification system.

As stated above, our goal in this chapter is to answer the questions we posed in the introductory section. However, for our answers to be clear it was necessary to explain not only the theoretical framework defining the class scheme we adopted but also what we understand as class formation and social fluidity. Before analysing the absolute and relative social mobility rates in Brazil and other industrialised countries, we will describe the main characteristics of industrialisation and urbanisation in Brazil. The Brazilian case is interesting for a comparative study of class mobility precisely because the transformation of a predominantly agrarian and rural social structure into a markedly industrial and urban one was very recent. Among the countries to which we compare Brazil in this chapter, only Ireland, Northern Ireland, Poland and Hungary have undergone similar transformations since World War II. Even so, the transformations in these countries have certainly been quite distinct from that of Brazil. Such differences in the pace and characteristics of industrialisation are predicted by the social mobility theory and are readily perceivable in the absolute rates presented in this study. In contrast, as we indicate above, there are competing theories on the relationship between social fluidity and economic growth. Hence, our analyses will bring new evidence from the Brazilian case to enrich the theoretical debate on social mobility and socioeconomic transformations.

---

10 For example, Goldthorpe (1985); Featherman, Hauser and Jones (1975); Goldthorpe and Marshall (1992); Erickson and Goldthorpe (1992 and 1993).

Brazilian Structural Changes

The studies on industrialisation in Brazil claim that the transition to an industrialised society is still on course. The idea that 'traditional' societal characteristics parallel 'modern' ones is not only prevalent, but also leads to a critique of the very idea that industrialisation per se brings wellbeing.[11] Brazil has a rich economy — according to some indices the eighth richest in the world — and at the same time it has one of the highest indices of income and wealth inequality ever measured.[12] The former government economist and scholar Edmar Bacha coined the sensationalistic expression 'Bel-India' in order to describe the socioeconomic structure of the country as a mixture of rich and 'modern' Belgium with poor and 'traditional' India. With a GNP per capita of US$5,000 in 1998, Brazil cannot be seen as a poor country and the poverty of a significant part of the population can only be a consequence of unequal distribution of wealth and income. In this section of the chapter we will present some information indicating not only the paradoxical situation of 'Bel-India', but also some data showing the characteristics of the structural changes that have been taking place in the country since mid-century.

Brazil had the fastest economic growth among Latin America countries. From 1950 to 1980 the GNP index grew constantly at a rate of 4.3 per cent per year. The state-supported development of the modern sector of the economy changed the labour market structure, mainly through the transference of labour force from rural to industrial and service sectors. Although industrialisation in Brazil began in the 1930s, it was only after the Second World War that it reached fast and constant rhythms of growth.

We can point to two major changes in class structure. The first is the increase in capitalist work relations during the 1960s and 1970s. The proportion of employees was less then half of the economically active population (EAP) in 1960, but it rose to 59 per cent in 1980 and more than two-thirds in 1997. The second is the expansion of the intermediate occupational stratum and the process of bureaucratisation of work. For example, the number of people employed in routine non-manual jobs jumped from 2.5 million in 1960 to 8.2 million in 1980. These 8.2 million constitute a new urban middle class.[13]

These processes were linked to the evolution of an industrialised and urbanised labour market. The industrial sector grew remarkably during the 1960s and the 1970s; but this tendency declined during the 1980s. In fact,

---

11   This kind of idea is very common in the Brazilian sociology at least since Fernandes' (1964) works. A more contemporary version of this idea is present, for example, in the works of Bacha (1978 and 1985).

12   Bacha and Klein (1989).

13   Hasenbalg and Silva (1988), chapter 1.

in the 1980s and 1990s, the tertiary sector was the one with fastest rates of growth. From 1979 to 1989, for example, the number of people employed in this sector grew from 4.5 million to 8.1 million.

The table below shows the temporal distribution of the EAP for the three sectors of the economy.

Table 9.1: Proportion of People 10 Years Old and Over in the Economically Active Population according to Economic Sector, 1940–1996

Year	EAP Per Industry Sector (%)			
	Primary	Secondary	Tertiary	Total
1940	67	13	20	100
1950	61	17	22	100
1960	55	17	27	100
1970	46	22	32	100
1980	31	29	40	100
1996	26	21	56	100

Source: Census and PNAD. IBGE.

The process of urbanisation was even more dramatic. In the 1960s Brazil became an urban society. The evolution of the urban population can be seen in the figure below:

Figure 9.1: Urban and Rural Population

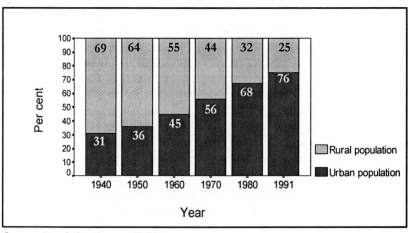

Source: Population Census, IBGE.

In 1996 the urbanisation rate was around 80 per cent. These data show much more than a mere population change, because they indicate major transformations in the economy, the employment structure and the access to goods and services.

However, the secondary (industrial) sector of the economy is concentrated in the south-east (São Paulo and Rio de Janeiro) and the new classes — linked to the modern labour market — are mixed with more traditional forms of production. This is a common situation in Latin America, as Shanin (1978) explains: 'In Latin America the mode of capitalist production is combined, in various forms, with other modes of production, generating a degree of complexity difficult to understand.' In addition, the urban population in Brazil grew at a faster rate than the industrial development, which means that it was difficult to incorporate workers into the formal labour market, provoking unemployment and under-employment.

Moreover, the 1990s were marked by the introduction of a new economic model based on the commercial and financial opening of the market, the privatisation of public services and national companies and many other policies designed to attract international private capital. In this context, the state no longer plays a major role. The increase in imports added to the restricted capacity of national companies to compete in the international market and led to 'de-industrialisation'. That is, the labour force moved to job positions in the commerce of goods and other sectors in which there is almost no legal protection and regulation of work. According to the latest estimation of the IBGE (Brazilian Geographic and Statistic Institute), the level of industrial employment dropped 48 per cent between 1990 and 1999.

As a consequence, at the beginning of the 1990s four million people living in urban areas were looking for a job and 23 million were working in the informal labour market — which is the same number as workers occupied in the formal sector. This trend had been reinforced during the decade; and the informal sector had shown a fast rate of increase — as is displayed in the figure overleaf.

Although the figure shows the expansion of the informal sectors over the last decade, structural changes presented earlier indicate that in general people's quality of life improved considerably. The transference of the labour force from rural to urban sectors led to a deep transformation in the social structure and had as a major consequence the upward mobility of a great amount of workers and their families. However, diverse forms of inequality — and particularly income inequality — kept growing, and a huge gap opened among the different social groups. For example, it can be shown that in 1997 the ten per cent of people with the highest salaries received around 47 per cent of the total income obtained through work, while the ten per cent with the lowest salaries received only one per cent of this total.[14]

14   Barros, Henriques and Mendonça (2000).

Figure 9.2: Non Agricultural Informal Sector

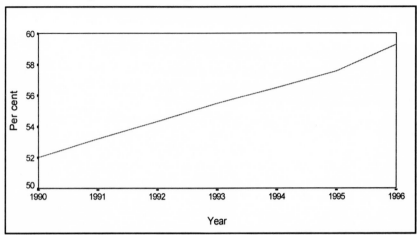

Source: PNAD.

In 1998 the 40 per cent of workers with the lowest income received an average monthly salary of US$90 — a sum that was below the legal minimum salary — while the ten per cent with highest income earned an average monthly salary of US$1,800.[15] Of the poorest 40 per cent, 32.1 per cent were not formally employed and 30.5 per cent were self-employed; these figures dropped to 6.8 per cent and 20.8 per cent, respectively, when the richest ten per cent were considered. However, we find that only 8.8 per cent of the 40 per cent in lower income work are in industrial jobs, while 14.6 per cent in the ten per cent with highest income are employed in this sector. The Gini index had been increasing in the last 30 years, indicating that income inequality has continued to grow over time. Table 9.2 shows Gini index trends:

Table 9.2: Gini Index per Year in Brazil.

Year	Gini Index
1960	0.50
1970	0.56
1980	0.59
1991	0.61

Source: Census. IBGE.

15   *O Globo*, 29 March 2000, p. 22.

As we have seen in this section, the social changes through which Brazilian society has gone since the 1940s are of great magnitude. However, the levels of inequality also continue to grow. How did social mobility patterns behave in such a context of structural changes and increasing income inequality? That is the question explored in the next section using absolute and relative mobility rates.

Cross-Temporal Comparison of Social Mobility in Brazil

In this section we use data from the National Household Survey (Pesquisa Nacional por Amostragem Domiciliar — hereafter PNAD) of 1973, 1988 and 1996 to analyse absolute and relative mobility rates. The PNAD has been collected every year by the Brazilian Census Bureau (Instituto Brasileiro de Geografia e Estatística — IBGE) since 1967 and includes basic information about population characteristics, work, income, education and habitation. Each year a supplementary section including special themes is added to the basic sample. In 1973, 1988 and 1996 these supplementary sections included questions on social background and social mobility.

The sample design of the PNAD is a three stage probabilistic selection of households. The primary units selected are the counties, the secondary units are the sectors of the census and the tertiary units are the households. For each selected household information is collected for every habitant over 10 years of age and weights are assigned to make those habitants representative of the population as a whole. Social mobility information was collected only for the head of the household and his or her partner — wife or husband.[16]

The questions concerning social mobility are virtually the same in the three data sets and allow the construction of comparable class schemas. Therefore, these surveys allow cross-temporal comparison using the same variables.

In the following analysis we use Erickson, Goldthorpe and Portocarrero's (1979) seven classes schema and Erickson and Goldthorpe's (1993) five-class schema. The tables used in the international comparisons are from the CASMIN project.

In the two next sections of the chapter we present some temporal and cross-national comparative analyses of mobility rates. Although the international comparisons undertaken here do not apply a structured model to analyse the data — that is, we do not model the comparisons — the analyses are interesting because they put Brazil in an international perspective. In contrast, the temporal comparisons follow a structured approach because they use models to analyse the changes in fluidity over time.

Absolute Mobility Rates

In order to present some temporal and cross-national comparative analyses of absolute mobility rates, we describe the historical trends in these

---

16   Details of sample design can be found in PNAD96.

rates in Brazil comparing data for three surveys — 1973, 1988 and 1996 — and undertake international comparisons contrasting the Brazilian data with data from other countries. As we have shown, the Brazilian social structure had changed dramatically in the preceding forty years. As a consequence, the distribution of occupational positions was rearranged to fit in a new labour market. In this sense, the analyses of absolute mobility rates can help to describe the impact of those changes on social mobility.

We begin by presenting total mobility rates. The proportion of respondents whose class destination is different to their father's class (the total mobility rate) in Brazil increased from 1973 to 1996. In 1973 it was 61.1 per cent, rising to 66.9 per cent in 1988, and 66.4 per cent in 1996. These figures are not atypical if compared to other countries in the 1970s; the findings contradict what other Brazilian studies had claimed using a different occupational scale.[17] It is important to note that the total mobility index varies according to the number of class categories used. Mobility tables using more class categories lead to more accurate measures of total mobility. Since we used seven categories in our analysis, rather than only the three used by Pastore and Silva (2000), we shall conclude that our figures are more accurate than theirs.

The following table displays total mobility rates for some industrialised countries:

Table 9.3: Comparative Total Mobility Rates for Seven Class EGP in the 1970s

	Total Mobility
Brazil	61
England	65
France	65
FRG	62
Hungary	76
Ireland	58
Northern Ireland	63
Poland	60
Scotland	64
Sweden	73
United States	73
Australia	70
Japan	73

Source: Erickson and Goldthorpe (1993) and PNAD (1973).

17   Pastore and Silva (2000), p. 49.

Before presenting comparisons of outflows and inflows we will examine the trends in the distribution of class origin and class destination in Brazil. Table 9.4 presents these distributions for 1973, 1988 and 1996 according to the EGP seven class schema. The distribution of class destination reflects the (male) class structure of Brazilian society in each year. In contrast, the distribution of class origins does not represent the class structure of any given period because the ages of the fathers vary substantially and men who never had a son do not appear in the distributions.[18] Instead, it shows that the origins of the respondents in a particular survey year have changed over time.

Table 9.4: Distribution of Destination and Origin Classes, Total Mobility and Immobility Rates in Brazil: 1973, 1988 and 1996

Classes		Destination			Origin		
		1982	1988	1996	1982	1988	1996
Prof., Admin. and Managers	I + II	8.0	11.4	10.4	3.1	4.6	4.7
Non-manual Routine Workers	III	9.5	11.5	12.3	3.0	4.5	5.9
Petite Bourgeoisie	IVa + b	6.8	10.3	10.6	6.6	7.7	7.6
Rural Employers	IVc	4.5	1.5	1.2	6.3	2.5	2.7
Skilled Manual Workers	V + VI	18.7	20.7	21.1	9.3	12.6	14.6
Non-skilled Manual Workers	VIIa	22.4	22.8	24.2	7.7	11.2	12.4
Rural Workers	VIIb	30.0	21.8	20.2	64.0	56.9	51.9
Total		100.0	100.0	100.0	100.0	100.0	100.0
Total Mobility		61.1	66.9	66.4			
Total Immobility		38.9	33.1	33.6			

Examining Table 9.4, the first things one notes are the changes in the class distribution from the 1970s to the 1980s and 1990s. In fact, these two last decades presented a very similar pattern of distribution in class positions. Note that the only class to follow a different pattern is that made up of unskilled manual workers (VIIa), which grew from 1988 to 1996, probably as a result of the increasing number of people working in the informal sector, a trend shown in Figure 9.2.

The next most obvious trend in class destination is the contraction of the farm working class or class VIIb. In 1973 30 per cent of the male working population was in the farm workers class, while in 1996 only about 20 per cent fell within this class. This contraction in rural society can also be observed if one examines the trend of class IVc1 (the class of rural employers). While in 1973 around 4.5 per cent of the workers were rural

18   Blau and Duncan (1967).

employers, in 1996 only 1.2 per cent were in this class. In contrast to these decreases, all other classes increased in size from 1973 to 1996.

This is not surprising, given the rapid process of urbanisation experienced by Brazilian society since the 1960s. Moreover, after the 1970s this society has been increasingly based on industrial and especially on service sector work.

The urban working classes (classes V+VI and VIIa) increased from 41.1 per cent in 1973 to 45.3 per cent in 1996. This is not a remarkable increase. However, it is interesting to compare the size of the urban manual working classes with the size of the other classes. In 1996 45.3 per cent of the men were in urban working class positions (classes V+VI and VIIa), while only 33.3 per cent were in urban non-manual classes (classes I+II, III and IVa+b). In 1973 these figures are 41.1 per cent and 24.3 per cent, respectively. Comparing 1973 and 1996 we must conclude that the whole urban sector expanded, with the non-manual classes increasing as well as the manual. Nevertheless, considering the total proportion of these five classes, we find that manual workers represented 37.2 per cent of all workers in 1973 and 42.4 per cent in 1996. This means that the increment in the urban labour force was mainly characterised by the growth in the manual sector. In other words, in the urban sector the manual positions grew faster than the non-manual.

Another interesting comparison is between the sizes of the class of professionals, administrators and managers (class I+II) — which includes the most specialised workers in the labour market — and the size of the unskilled urban and rural workers (classes VIIa and VIIb). The percentage of unskilled workers diminished from 52.4 in 1973 to 44.4 in 1996 (most of this decrease was due to shrinking of the rural working class). In contrast, the percentage of professional, managerial and administrative workers (class I+II) increased from 8.0 in 1973 to 11.4 in 1988, and decreased just a little to 10.4 in 1996. Although these changes indicate an increase in highly specialised work and a decrease in unskilled work, it is noteworthy that the percentage of specialised work is still small if compared with the level of unskilled work.

The petty bourgeoisie was the class that experienced the highest level of growth from 1973 to 1996. An increment of almost 56 per cent can be seen as a result of some of the structural processes pointed out in the previous discussion on Brazilian social structure, mainly the urbanisation and the expansion of the service sector.

Using the concept of 'structural mobility'[19] we can obtain a descriptive measure showing the amount of mobility that is due to transformations in the distribution of social position. The structural mobility indexes for the three years were 35.8 per cent in 1973, 36.1 per cent in 1988 and 33.2 in 1996. We can see that this index is stable over time.[20]

19   Pastore (1981) and Scalon (1999).
20   This conclusion about 'structural mobility' must be considered provisional because the measurement we used is not totally reliable (see Sobel, 1983).

The structural mobility index is calculated by subtracting the proportion of the destination class from the proportion of the origin class, but only for the classes in which the results from the operation have a positive sign. If we examine the distribution of classes we find that the only positions that have a higher proportion in the origin than in the destination are classes IVc1 and VIIb — the two rural classes. So, we can argue that structural mobility in Brazil was characterised predominantly, or even solely, by the movement from the rural to the urban sector. Moreover, we can argue that this pattern of transference of labour force from rural to urban jobs continued over time.

In sum, the data confirms that the inequality of position continues to be high in Brazil. Although the rural working class diminished rapidly after 1973, it seems that the workers were simply transferred from rural to urban manual positions.

Table 9.5: Comparative Inflow Rates: Percentage in Selected Classes from Different Class Origins (European Countries in the 1970s and Brazil)

Per cent of the Professional, Administrative and Managerial Class (I + II) originating in				Per cent of Industrial Working Class (V/VI + VIIa) originating in			
Industrial Working Class (V/VI + VIIa)		Agricultural Classes (IVc1 + VIIb)		Industrial Working Class (V/VI + VIIa)		Agricultural Classes (IVc1 + VIIb)	
England	45	Poland	34	England	74	Brazil (1973)	66
FRG	41	Brazil (1973)	27	FRG	5	Brazil (1988)	59
Sweden	40	Brazil (1988)	27	Ireland (1987)	63	Brazil (1996)	52
Poland	35	Brazil (1996)	26	Ireland (1973)	57	Hungary	46
Hungary	32	Hungary	25	Sweden	51	Poland	46
Ireland (1987)	32	Ireland (1973)	23	France	47	Sweden	32
Ireland (1973)	28	Ireland (1987)	18	Poland	42	France	29
France	28	Sweden	17	Hungary	39	Ireland (1973)	27
Brazil (1996)	29	France	10	Brazil (1996)	35	Ireland (1987)	24
Brazil (1988)	27	FRG	8	Brazil (1988)	31	FRG	16
Brazil (1973)	24	England	4	Brazil (1973)	25	England	7

Source: Breen and Whelan (1996).

The increase in professionals, administrators and managers (class I+II) was not dramatic and shows that these positions are still held by only a small portion of the (male) working population when compared to the lower positions in the class structure. The data on class destination in 1973, 1988 and 1996 confirms that in Brazil people occupy highly unequal positions in the class structure and that the majority of the population works in non-qualified manual jobs.

Nevertheless, the distributions of class destination and class of origin do not tell us if the class structure is closed, nor if there is a high level of elite recruitment. In order to address such concerns, we have to examine inflows. We will begin by comparing selected inflows in Brazil to some European countries using the CASMIN seven class schema. The table above displays some inflow comparisons.

Table 9.5 shows that in relation to the professional and managerial class in Brazil, the most striking feature is not the extent of social closure but the degree of heterogeneity of the origins from which the groups are drawn. In 1996 29 per cent of the service class in Brazil had origins in the industrial working class. This figure is slightly higher than the figure for Brazil in 1973, and is similar to some European countries in the 1970s (France, Ireland, Hungary and Poland) and to Ireland in 1987. When compared with European countries in the 1970s, Brazil is distinctive in having a high inflow to the service class of men from the agricultural classes. In 1973 27 per cent of the service class had origins in the agricultural classes. This figure remains almost the same in 1988 and 1996 (27 and 26 per cent, respectively) and continued to be higher than any other European society in the 1970s. Self-recruitment in the service class continued around 17 per cent from 1973 to 1996. In other words, more than 80 per cent of the service class is recruited from outside. Given the class schema we have used, the idea of elite social closure does not apply to the Brazilian case. However, this massive recruitment from other classes could be seen as a consequence of a later industrialisation in Brazil compared to the European countries.

These results confirm the findings of Pastore and Silva (2000) who used a different class schema. However, it is important to notice that we and Pastore and Silva (2000) are using a highly aggregated class for defining 'elite'. In other words, what is not closed is broadly defined as 'elite', if we were to analyse 'elite' closure in a more precise way — that is, defining elite more specifically — our results would probably have been different.

If it is remarkable that around one third of the service class is recruited from the agricultural classes, it is no surprise that more than half of the industrial working class in Brazil comes from the agricultural classes. In fact, 66 per cent of the industrial working class in 1973 came from the agricultural classes. Although this percentage falls to 59 in 1988 and 52 in 1996, it continued to be higher than any European country in the 1970s. In addition, self-recruitment in the industrial working class in Brazil is lower than in any European country, although it has increased from 25 per cent in 1973 to 35 per cent in 1996.

In contrast to the heterogeneity of urban working class origins, it can be claimed that the rural manual class (VIIb) is quite closed and homogeneous. Self-recruitment in class VIIb is responsible for around 90 per cent of its composition over the three years considered here (see Table B in Appendix 1).

In sum, the data indicate that rural migrants in Brazil were absorbed in both the service and the industrial working class. However, most of the rural workers went to urban manual positions (66 per cent in 1973). The fact that the structural change from a rural to an urban society in Brazil was very recent can easily be observed in the comparisons above. Although some other interesting inflow trends can be observed in the inflow Table B in Appendix 1, we will now present some data on outflows.

Outflow rates provide useful information on the chances of men from given class origins of being found in particular class destinations. Table 9.6 compares selected Brazilian outflow rates with those of some European countries in the 1970s and Ireland in 1987.

Table 9.6: Comparative Outflow Rates: Percentage of Individuals of Selected Class Origins Found in Different Classes (European Countries in the 1970s, and Brazil)

Per cent of those of Professional, Administrative and Managerial Class Origins (I + II) Found in				Per cent of those of Industrial Working Class Origin (V/VI + VIIa) Found in			
Professional, Administrative and Managerial (I + II)		Industrial Working Class (V/VI + VIIa)		Professional, Administrative and Managerial (I + II)		Industrial Working Class (V/VI + VIIa)	
Poland	67	Hungary	34	FRG	22	Hungary	73
FRG	61	FRG	26	Sweden	22	Poland	71
France	60	Poland	25	Poland	21	FRG	69
England	59	Sweden	25	England	18	Ireland (1987)	69
Sweden	56	England	22	France	17	Ireland (1973)	68
Ireland (1987)	56	Ireland (1987)	22	Hungary	16	England	66
Ireland (1973)	55	Ireland (1973)	21	Ireland (1987)	11	Sweden	63
Hungary	52	France	21	Ireland (1973)	11	France	61
Brazil (1973)	*46*	*Brazil (1973)*	*21*	*Brazil (1973)*	*11*	*Brazil (1973)*	*61*
Brazil (1988)	44	Brazil (1988)	20	Brazil (1988)	13	Brazil (1988)	56
Brazil (1996)	37	Brazil (1996)	24	Brazil (1996)	11	Brazil (1996)	59

Source: Breen and Whelan (1996).

Table 9.6 gives us some insight into class inheritance, and mobility to higher and lower class positions. In Brazil the percentage of men with origins in the service class who remained in this class was 46 in 1973 and declined to 37 in 1996. This figure is lower than the figures for the European countries in the 1970s and indicates that service class inheritance is not high in Brazil. In contrast, downward mobility from the service class to industrial

working class in Brazil in 1973 was around 21 per cent, similar to the figures for England, France and Ireland in the 1970s. In 1996 one in four men
from the service class went down to industrial working class (24 per cent).

Upward mobility from the working class to service class has been very low
in Brazil. In 1973, 1988 and 1996 only one in five men experienced upward
mobility from the working class to service class. In this respect the Brazilian
figures are similar to the Irish figures for 1973 and 1987. Inheritance in the
working class has been around 60 per cent in Brazil from 1973 to 1996.

It is also remarkable that downward mobility is seldom found among the
upper classes. As can be seen in Table 9.6, Brazil, France and Ireland are the
countries with the lowest proportion of downward mobility from class I+II
to the manual sector. From this observation it can be concluded that upward
mobility was not a result of the exchange of positions among workers of different origins, but rather a result of structural transformations that opened
new positions in the upper occupational groups in the labour market.

The outflow rates of the petty bourgeoisie show that the flux from this
class to the professional, administrative and managerial class (I+II), non-
manual routine class (IIIa+b); and rural classes (VIIb and IVc1) had
decreased over time. On the other hand, the inheritance, or immobility,
had increased and also the flux to the industrial working class. The inflow
rates indicated that petty bourgeoisie (IVa+b), as the other classes, is mainly composed of men with an origin in the rural sector. But the most striking result is that from 1973 to 1996 the proportion of men in the petty
bourgeoisie with origins in the non-manual classes had doubled. The proportion of men coming from industrial backgrounds also increased. These
results indicate that petty bourgeoisie — which we observed had expanded over time — has been recruiting people from urban strata and, particularly, from the non-manual sectors. Self-recruitment was maintained
almost constant from 1973 to 1996 (see Appendix 1 for precise figures).

What conclusions can be drawn from the examination of origin and
destination distributions, outflows and inflows in the Brazilian data?

Bendix and Lipset (1959) formulated the 'threshold hypothesis' affirming
that the transition from a pre-industrial to an industrial social structure promotes high levels of intergenerational mobility. In other words, this transition
would mark a momentum leading to high levels of absolute mobility, but not
to an increase in social fluidity. The Brazilian experience does not show any
specific historical point where there was a dramatic shift from agriculture to
industry and service. Although the 1950s and the 1970s represent two historical spurts of industrial development, the data seem to indicate that the
shift from rural to urban work occurred gradually over the years rather than
drastically in a specific period. This is probably a consequence of the fact that
urbanisation in Brazil took place before real industrial development.[21]

21   Lopes (1971).

Sorokin's ([1927] 1959) idea that old barriers are often substituted for new barriers and that the fluctuations in absolute mobility rates do not result in diminishing inequality seems applicable to the Brazilian case. As we have learned from our analyses, elite positions have been protected from experiencing downward mobility, guaranteeing reproduction and inheritance, and the decrease in the agricultural working class was paralleled by an increase in the urban manual working class.

Moreover, we could verify that Brazilian total mobility rates, when subjected to a cross-national comparison, had not displayed a different pattern. Thus, in opposition to Pastore (1981) and Pastore and Silva (2000), we cannot sustain the idea that mobility in Brazil is remarkably high. It is just within the range of other industrialised countries. However, it is true that social mobility in Brazil — at least as captured by the 1973 data — is marked by structural changes and shifts from rural to urban work and this change certainly had a profound impact on the mobility regime and life chances of Brazilians.

In fact, from the distribution of class origins and destinations we learned that the most striking phenomenon is the transference of labour force from rural to urban sectors. This is not a surprise, considering the data we presented before indicating the fast process of urbanisation and industrialisation that took place after the 1960s. The expansion of the petty bourgeoisie resulting from the growth of the service sector should also be noted.

The inflow rates indicated that the recruitment of men of agricultural origin is noteworthy in all destination classes considered. Nevertheless, the rural sector is quite isolated since self-recruitment from the agricultural class is responsible for 90 per cent of its composition.

The openness of urban classes and the endogenous nature of the rural sector can only mean that the movements towards upper classes do not represent a process of exchange, but rather the need to fill the increasing number of positions created during the process of industrialisation and urbanisation. Moreover, it is the manual urban working classes that incorporated the greatest proportion of workers with rural origins. So, it can also be argued that Brazil is characterised by short distance mobility.

We also verified that immobility is lower in Brazil than in European countries, and the same can be said of downward mobility. And this just confirms that upward mobility had no equivalent in downward mobility, which means there was no exchange.

The previous analyses indicate that mobility in Brazil was due to structural change rather than to exchange among class positions. If this is true, we have to ask ourselves the extent to which mobility was translated into more equality. This is one of the reasons why we have to analyse relative mobility rates in order to verify if the structural transformations created more social fluidity and opportunities in the class structure.

Relative Rates

In this section we will present an initial analysis of the relative mobility rate. That is, we will not be modelling — in the full sense of the term — the Brazilian mobility regime, rather we will be making some very general tests regarding the nature of this regime. In fact, we adopt the Independence Model, the Constant Social Fluidity Model, and the Uniform Difference Model (UNIDIFF) — the equations for these models are given in Appendix 2. These models are used to analyse two sets of mobility tables. First, we analyse the 7 by 7 mobility tables for people between 20 and 64 years of age in 1973, 1988 and 1996. Second, we examine the 5 by 5 Brazilian mobility tables for four birth cohorts aged 25–34; 35–44; 45–54; and 55–64 in 1973 and compare this table with similar tables from many other countries analysed within the CASMIN project. The idea behind these comparisons is simply to verify if social fluidity decreased, remained the same, or increased over the last few decades in Brazil, and to make comparisons between the Brazilian trends and trends in other countries using data from the 1970s.

The Independence Model tests the hypothesis that there is no association between origin and destination. That is, the hypothesis that origin and destination not only differ by cohort or survey year, but also that origin and destination are independent (there is no association between origin and destination). In contrast, the Constant Social Fluidity Model (CnSF) tests the hypothesis that there are associations between class origin and class destination, between cohort or survey year and class destination, and cohort or survey year and origin. Moreover, since there is no three-way interaction (origin, destination and cohort or survey) the CnSF implies that the level of association between class of origin and of destination is constant over time. The odds-ratios are similar over time — over cohorts or survey years.

The aim of the comparison of the CnSF model with the baseline conditional Independence Model is to indicate how much of the association in the tables can be explained by the CnSF model when contrasted with the baseline Independence Model. Finally, we apply the Uniform Difference Model (UNIDIFF) to the data. This model is used to observe the direction in which, and the extent to which, the overall strength of the association between origin and destination classes differs across cohorts or surveys. A UNIDIFF estimated parameter (or coefficient) of less than one reduces the size of the origin–destination association relative to the baseline model — which in our cases are either 1973 or the oldest cohort — while a coefficient greater than one increases the origin–destination association relative to the baseline value. The use of the UNIDIFF model ensures an improvement to the analysis on temporal changes in 'social fluidity' or relative mobility rates in Brazil, because until now Brazilian data was analysed using only the Common Social Fluidity model or the non-three way interaction model.[22] In fact, the UNIDIFF model is a more efficient model to test the association between origin and destination increases or decreases over time, instead of measuring only if there is constant or non-constant association over time (which is the test made by the CnSF model).

The fit of the Independence model, the Constant Social Fluidity model and the UNIDIFF model to the three-way table (7 by 7 by 3) comparing class origin and class destination (in seven categories) with the three survey years (1973, 1988 and 1996) is in Table 9.7.

Table 9.7: Results of Fitting the CnSF Model to Intergenerational 7 by 7 EGP Class Schema Mobility Tables for 1973, 1988 and 1996. (N = 115,018)

Model*	L^2	df	p	rL^{2**}	diss.	BIC
(OS)(DS)	36,733.0	108	0.000		20.5	35,474.5
(OS)(DS)(OD)	388.3	72	0.000	98.9	1.6	-446.9
(OC)(DC)(OD)diag	379.0	70	0.000	99.1	1.5	-436.7
UNIDIFF	260.2	69***	0.000	99.3	1.4	-540.2

* O = origin; D = destination; S = survey year.
** rL^2 represents the reduction in L^2 for the baseline independence model that is achieved by a more complex model.
*** We assume that UNIDIFF takes up an additional 3 Df over CnSF.

Although the models do not fit the data according to the respective p-values, the CnSF model accounts for 98.9 per cent and the UNIDIFF for 99.3 per cent of the association under the baseline Independence Model. Moreover, the BIC statistic indicates that the UNIDIFF model explains the data well, and represents a significant (at .05 level) improvement over the CnSF model — according to hierarchical comparison DL^2 = 128.1 with 3 degrees of freedom.

The UNIDIFF model indicates that relative mobility rates change over time (the parameters for 1988 and 1996 are respectively -.12 and -.17). More precisely, social fluidity patterns seem to be increasing from 1973 to 1996, that is, origins and destinations are less associated in 1988 and 1996 than they were in 1973. This result contradicts not only Silva's (1988 and 2000) findings for Brazil — using the CnSF model and a different class schema — but also the FJH hypothesis about constant social fluidity over time. Our general test implies that the relative chances of mobility

22   Silva and Roditti (1988); Silva and Pastore (2000).

increased from 1973 to 1996.[23] The chances of a person from a lower class achieving a position in an upper class in relation to a person from an upper class staying in this class increased from 1973 to 1996. This does not mean that a person with origins in a lower class has the same chances as a person with origins in an upper class of achieving a higher position, but it means that these chances were less unequal in 1996 than they were in 1973.

How does the Brazilian trend in relative mobility rates stand in relation to other countries' trends? In order to answer this question we needed similar data from other countries. These data were not available for use. However, we have mobility tables partitioned into four birth cohorts — 25–34, 35–44, 45–54 and 55–64 — for many countries. These tables are all from surveys undertaken during the 1970s and were previously analysed by Erickson and Goldthorpe (1992). Applying the Independence, Constant Social Fluidity and UNIDIFF models to these tables we can observe and roughly compare trends in relative mobility rates before the 1970s in these countries.

Table 9.8 shows the results of fitting these models to the mobility tables cross-classifying origins (measured by fathers' class), destinations (measured by first job) and birth cohorts (25–34, 35–44, 45–54 and 55–64) for each one of the following countries: Brazil, England, France, West Germany, Hungary, Ireland, Northern Ireland, Poland, Scotland, Sweden, Australia, United States and Japan. The analyses presented below do not make a structured comparison between these countries' trends in relative mobility rates, instead they simply apply the above-mentioned models for each country table at a given time. The purpose of these analyses is to see in which countries it is possible to detect changes in relative mobility rates. Our analyses are useful for the observation of changes that happened in the association between origins and destinations before the 1970s in each one of these countries. The fact that some countries presented a decrease in the association between origins and destinations — becoming thus more fluid over time — does not mean that they have a more open mobility regime than the other countries. Instead, it just indicates that origins and destinations are becoming less associated over time in one particular country. For example, the fact that the model predicting an increase in fluidity fits the Hungarian case and does not fit the Japanese case does not mean that the mobility regime is more open in Hungary than in Japan. In fact, we are not directly comparing these countries. We are only comparing the changes over time in each country. As a consequence, the results for Hungary and Japan, for example, indicate only that the Hungarian mobility regime is becoming more open over time, but the Japanese is not. In Table 9.8 below we present the fit of the models to each country's table and in Table 9.9 we present the estimates of UNIDIFF and the Diagonal Changes model.

---

23 Featherman, Hauser and Jones (1975).

Table 9.8: Results of Fitting the Independence, the CnSF and the UNIDIFF models to Intergenerational Class mobility for Four Birth Cohorts (55–64, 45–54, 35–44 and 25–34)

Model	G2	df	p	rG2	diss	G2 S −1,746
Brazil (N = 38,234)						
OC DC	22,372.00	64	0.00		31.2	1,083
OC DC OD	214.6	48	0.00	99	2	55.6
UNIDIFF	124.2	45	0.00	99.4	1.2	62.9
England (N = 8,343)						
OC DC	1,695.00	64	0.00		16.1	405.3
OC DC OD	53.1	48	0.28	96.9	2.6	49
UNIDIFF	51.8	45	0.23	96.9	2.5	58.3
France (N = 16,431)						
OC DC	6,370.60	64	0.00		24.7	734
OC DC OD	96.7	48	0.00	98.5	2	53
UNIDIFF	82.7	45	0.00	98.7	1.9	62.4
West Germany (N = 3,570)						
OC DC	1,092.00	64	0.00		21.1	567
OC DC OD	81.9	48	0.00	92.5	4.4	65
UNIDIFF	69	45	0.01	93.7	3.8	64.4
Hungary (N = 10,319)						
OC DC	2,386.00	64	0.00		19.2	457
OC DC OD	69.9	48	0.02	97.1	2.4	52
UNIDIFF	61.5	45	0.05	97.4	2.2	60.2

Table 9.8 continued

	Ireland (N = 1,746)					
OC DC	902.3	64	0.00		29.2	902
OC DC OD	60.2	48	0.11	93.3	5.2	60
UNIDIFF	55.9	45	0.13	93.8	4.8	55.9
	Northern Ireland (N = 1,808)					
OC DC	780.6	64	0.00		25.5	756
OC DC OD	44.5	48	0.62	94.3	5	45
UNIDIFF	42.6	45	0.57	94.5	4.8	43.2
	Poland (N =27,993)					
OC DC	7,357.70	64	0.00		19.6	519
OC DC OD	66.7	48	0.04	99.1	1.4	49
UNIDIFF	65.6	45	0.02	99.1	1.3	60.3
	Scotland (N = 3,985)					
OC DC	1,146.60	64	0.00		18.1	538
OC DC OD	66.3	48	0.04	94.2	4.4	56
UNIDIFF	65	45	0.02	94.3	4.3	62.2
	Sweden (N = 1,882)					
OC DC	403.9	64	0.00		17.3	379
OC DC OD	45.2	48	0.58	88.8	5.1	45
UNIDIFF	36.5	45	0.81	90.9	4.2	38.2
	Australia (N = 2,348)					
OC DC	536.2	64	0.00		17.7	415.2
OC DC OD	40.1	48	0.79	92.5	4.7	42.1
UNIDIFF	37.4	45	0.78	93	4.2	43.2

Table 9.8 continued

	USA (N = 17,782)					
OC DC	2,930.00	64	0.00		15.9	345.5
OC DC OD	48.2	48	0.47	98.3	1.9	48
UNIDIFF	44.2	45	0.51	98.5	1.7	58.4

	Japan (N =1,871)					
OC DC	434.6	64	0.00		19.2	410
OC DC OD	48.5	48	0.45	88.8	3.8	48.4
UNIDIFF	45.8	45	0.44	89.4	3.6	46.7

Table 9.8 above shows that the Constant Social Fluidity Model (OC, DC, OD) improves over the independence model in all the countries, that is, origin and destination are not independent in these countries and the patterns of association are constant over cohorts. However, in Brazil, France, West Germany, Hungary and Sweden the UNIDIFF model improves over the Constant Social Fluidity. This means that in these countries association between origins and destinations changed over the cohorts. Table 9.9 presented the parameter estimates for the UNIDIFF model and another model (not presented in the table above), the Diagonal Changes model. The UNIDIFF model tests the hypothesis that the association between origin and destination is changing over time. If the UNIDIFF fits the data and the estimates are decreasing from the oldest to the youngest cohorts in a particular country then we can say that the relative chances of mobility are becoming less unequal over time. In addition, if the estimates from the Diagonal Changes model follow a similar pattern then there is some evidence that immobility is decreasing, that is, origins and destinations in the diagonal of the mobility table are becoming less associated over time.

Table 9.9: Improvement in Fit (deltaG2) over CnSF Model and Parameters for UNIDIFF Model and Diagonal Change Model (data for cohorts from the 1970s)

Nation	(a) Uniform Difference				(b) Diagonal Change			
	Parameters for cohorts				Parameters for cohorts			
	deltaG2	2	3	4	deltaG2	2	3	4
Brazil	90.4*	0.06	0.02	-0.13	81.1*	0.06	-0.11	-0.33
England	1.3	0.01	0.07	0.05	1.6	0.06	0.08	0.07
France	14.0*	0.10	0.13	0.15	7.4	0.08	0.13	0.15
West Germany	12.8*	-0.13	0.18	-0.05	4.6	-0.11	0.09	-0.06
Hungary	8.4*	-0.08	-0.19	-0.16	8.1*	-0.05	-0.23	-0.15
Ireland	4.3	-0.15	0.07	-0.09	3.5	-0.29	-0.03	-0.20
Northern Ireland	1.8	0.02	-0.12	-0.10	3.8	0.08	-0.04	-0.20
Poland	1.0	0.03	0.04	0.04	2.0	0.06	0.00	-0.01
Scotland	1.3	0.04	0.05	0.11	7.5	0.03	0.02	0.23
Sweden	8.6*	0.35	0.14	-0.15	5.1	0.17	-0.08	-0.19
Australia	2.7	-0.18	0.00	-0.11	2.2	-0.15	0.02	-0.05
USA	4.0	-0.07	-0.04	-0.12	1.7	-0.04	0.002	-0.06
Japan	2.7	0.23	0.21	0.28	1.5	0.12	0.22	0.24

* Significance at five per cent level

According to the table above it is only in Brazil and Hungary that both UNIDIFF and Diagonal Change Models improve fit over the CnSF model. In Brazil and Hungary the parameters estimated indicate an increase in fluidity and a general decline in the propensity for class immobility. The UNIDIFF model also fits better than CnSF for the French, German and Swedish data. In France there seems to be a decrease in fluidity, while in Germany and especially in Sweden there is probably an increase in fluidity.[24] In the Brazilian case one reasonable hypothesis for the increase in social fluidity is that the massive change from rural to urban work that occurred from the 1960s is somehow related to the increase in social fluidity that our models indicate.

The analysis we present herein about social fluidity trends in Brazil is the first to analyse data on a Latin American country using the UNIDIFF model. Our findings indicate that the general claim that trends in relative mobility rates tend to be constant over time[25] is not observed in Brazil.

24 See Erickson and Goldthorpe (1992, pp. 94–95) for a discussion of these cases.
25 Featherman, Jones and Hauser (1975); and Erickson and Goldthorpe (1993).

These findings are important because they bring new evidence from a nation that has been passing through major structural changes. That is, Brazil has not only passed through a period of economic development, but has rapidly changed from a rural to an urban and industrial society since the 1940s. Apparently, in cases passing through big structural changes — like Brazil and maybe Ireland, Hungary, Poland, South Korea and others — the hypothesis of constant relative mobility rates does not apply. It would be interesting to improve the comparative analysis for such countries that passed through rapid economic and structural changes in recent decades. There are data available for carrying out such analysis, and the methods are much better today, but the literature on comparative social mobility has not been sufficiently developed in this respect.[26]

Conclusions

The analyses we develop over the course of this chapter allow us to provide answers to the questions we posed at the beginning. In these conclusions we briefly present our answers, indicate some weak points and propose new directions for future research.

1.   How did the class structure in Brazil change from 1973 to 1996?

We answer this question by simply inspecting Table 9.4. According to this table, from 1973 to 1988 there was a significant decrease in the size of social classes (in the class destination distribution) of rural landowners and rural workers. In addition, we observed that from 1988 to 1996, the class structure (the class destination distribution) remained practically the same. The main change appears to have occurred from 1973 to 1988, a period marked by major structural transformations in Brazilian society, during which rapid industrialisation and urbanisation helped reshape the Brazilian class structure.

However, we note that the percentage of men in unskilled manual occupations (urban or rural) remained quite high throughout the period. There was merely a transfer of rural labour to urban labour without significant alterations in terms of the difference between skilled and unskilled labour.

Having accepted the classificatory principles we utilise to define the social classes described in this chapter, the main limitation to our response relates to the limited number of classes (seven) we used. An analysis using more than seven social classes would allow us to observe changes and continuities in the shape of the class structure with greater precision. In addition, if we had data on the class distribution at more than three points in time, we would be able to verify at which precise moments the changes occurred (such an analysis using only the occupational distribution of respondents would be possible, since there are surveys available for practically all years from 1973 to the present).

26   One of the few studies is Simkus, Jackson, Yip and Treiman (1990).

2. What impact did rapid industrialisation have on social mobility patterns?

The impacts were certainly quite significant. Their main indication can be observed in the great disparity between the distributions of class origin and class destination in the three years studied (Table 9.4). The fact that the class origin and class destination distributions are very different means that a large number of men had to seek class positions different from their class origin. According to our observations, the total mobility index in Brazil is not very different from that in other countries. This observation contradicts previous studies on social mobility in Brazil which, through less accurate comparisons, tended to claim that the Brazilian rate was one of the highest in the world.[27] Nevertheless, detailed analyses of inflow and outflow rates indicate that Brazil's rapid and relatively recent industrialisation had highly significant impacts on both the gross mobility patterns and the composition of social classes.

Gross mobility patterns or outflows (as observed in Table 9.6 and Table A in Appendix 1) indicate a major transfer of rural labour to the other classes. Even in the professional and administrative class there is a large percentage of individuals with their origins in the rural and urban working classes. In other words, the degree of reproduction or immobility in the elite is low, especially if observed in comparative terms. Considering that this pattern is also found in other countries that underwent rapid industrialisation in the post-war period (like Hungary and Ireland), we should conclude that this high mobility index is due principally to structural changes.

As for social class composition, Table 9.5 and Table B in Appendix 1 demonstrate that both in the urban working classes and the professional and administrative classes there is a significantly high percentage of individuals with their origins in the rural classes. For example, in the urban manual labour class, two out of three individuals have their origins in the rural sector, while only one is from the urban manual labour class itself.

The high rural-to-urban social mobility rate and the low reproduction of the urban classes (among both the elite and manual labourers) is characteristic of countries with late industrialisation, like Brazil, Poland, Ireland and Hungary. One notes that the elites in traditionally industrialised countries like England, Germany and Sweden consist of a larger proportion of urban manual labourers than in recently industrialised countries.

We can thus conclude that the high mobility patterns and low reproduction of social classes in Brazil are a consequence of the historical moment in focus, marked by the transformation of an agrarian and rural society into an urban and industrial one.

---

27 Pastore and Silva (2000); Hasenbalg and Silva (1988).

3.　Did the class structure become more open, more closed, or did it maintain the same degree of rigidity? In other words: did relative mobility rates change?

According to the log-linear models used to analyse Brazilian data, we observed that there was an increase in the degree of social fluidity in the Brazilian class structure, i.e., this structure became less rigid over the years. This conclusion contradicts the results proposed previously by Silva and Roditi (1988), who use the constant social fluidity model (CnSF) to defend the hypothesis of a constant degree of fluidity over time.[28] The UNIDIFF model we use fits better than the CnSF model to the Brazilian data. The estimators derived from fitting the UNIDIFF model indicate that social fluidity in Brazil increases over time. However, it is important to highlight that the degree of rigidity in the social structure was still quite high in 1996, i.e., other countries that do not display changes in the levels of social fluidity have always had (according to available data) lower degrees of rigidity than those observed in Brazil, even in 1996.

The main problem with the analysis of relative rates presented in this chapter relates to the fact that the tests that were implemented are of a global nature. In other words, although the UNIDIFF model is the most sophisticated used thus far to analyse variation in social fluidity over time in Brazil, it does not allow a detailed analysis of the variation in fluidity in specific cells in the mobility table. Utilisation of more sophisticated models could indicate, for example, that fluidity increases in given classes, decreases in others and remains unaltered in the rest. As we mentioned, the UNIDIFF model only implements a global test. At any rate, the analyses presented here are the most accurate that have been developed to date to explain the Brazilian data.

4.　Are the changes in class structure and mobility patterns in Brazil atypical when observed in comparative perspective with other countries?

As we noted in answering question number 2, absolute mobility patterns in Brazil are typical of recently industrialised countries, like Ireland, Hungary and Poland.

As for relative mobility rates, Brazil differs from the other countries analysed in that it displays an increase in the degree of social fluidity. However, we should emphasise that this result does not demonstrate that the Brazilian social structure is more open than other countries' structures. In fact, within the international context Brazil is still a country characterised by extreme inequality of opportunity.

28　The so-called FHJ hypothesis, for Featherman, Hauser, and Jones (1975).

Appendix 1

Table A: Cross-Temporal Comparison of Outflow Rates in Brazil From Class Destination:

III	Outflow Rates to Class Origin:							
	I+II	III	IVa+b	IVc1	V+VI	VIIa	VIIb	
1973	30.9	30.9	7.6	0.4	15.1	13.8	1.3	100.0
1988	26.5	29.3	10.7	0.3	16.3	15.0	1.9	100.0
1996	22.9	29.3	11.3	0.4	16.8	17.1	2.2	100.0

IVa+b	Outflow Rates to Class Origin:							
	I+II	III	IVa+b	IVc1	V+VI	VIIa	VIIb	
1973	23.5	21.0	20.4	2.1	13.0	15.8	4.2	100.0
1988	25.5	16.5	25.9	1.3	13.9	13.4	3.4	100.0
1996	20.2	17.9	27.2	1.2	13.7	16.2	3.6	100.0

IVc1	Outflow Rates to Class Origin:							
	I+II	III	IVa+b	IVc1	V+VI	VIIa	VIIb	
1973	10.3	9.3		23.5	11.7	16.2	20.1	100.0
1988	17.6	9.7		13.9	13.7	15.6	15.5	100.0
1996	9.9	10.4	14.8	7.9	16.8	21.8	18.3	100.0

V+VI	Outflow Rates to Class Origin:							
	I+II	III	IVa+b	IVc1	V+VI	VIIa	VIIb	
1973	13.1	17.5	5.5	0.7	38.0	20.8	4.4	100.0
1988	14.1	17.1	9.0	0.3	34.9	21.1	3.5	100.0
1996	11.2	16.4	9.2	0.1	36.3	23.3	3.4	100.0

VIIa	Outflow Rates to Class Origin:							
	I+II	III	IVa+b	IVc1	V+VI	VIIa	VIIb	
1973	9.4	16.3	5.8	0.6	27.9	34.9	5.1	100.0
1988	12.2	18.0	8.4	0.3	24.0	33.0	4.1	100.0
1996	11.0	17.1	8.5	0.2	24.0	35.5	3.9	100.0

VIIb	Outflow Rates to Class Origin:							
	I+II	III	IVa+b	IVc1	V+VI	VIIa	VIIb	
1973	2.4	4.7	5.5	4.3	16.6	23.4	43.0	100.0
1988	4.6	6.4	8.4	1.7	19.4	24.4	35.1	100.0
1996	4.7	6.7	8.4	1.6	18.8	24.8	34.9	100.0

To Class Destination:

I+II			Inflow Rates from Class Origin:				
	I+II	III	IVa+b	IVc1	V+VI	VIIa	VIIb
1973	17.8	11.6	19.2	8.1	15.1	9.0	19.2	100.0
1988	17.7	10.5	17.3	3.8	15.5	12.0	23.2	100.0
1996	17.0	13.1	14.9	2.6	15.8	13.1	23.5	100.0

III			Inflow Rates from Class Origin:				
	I+II	III	IVa+b	IVc1	V+VI	VIIa	VIIb
1973	7.3	9.9	14.5	6.2	17.1	13.3	31.9	100.0
1988	7.8	11.4	11.0	2.1	18.6	17.4	31.6	100.0
1996	7.3	14.2	11.1	2.3	19.5	17.3	28.2	100.0

IVa+b			Inflow Rates from Class Origin:				
	I+II	III	IVa+b	IVc1	V+VI	VIIa	VIIb
1973	2.8	3.4	19.7	8.4	7.4	6.6	51.7	100.0
1988	5.7	4.7	19.4	3.4	11.0	9.2	46.6	100.0
1996	6.7	6.3	19.5	3.8	12.7	9.9	41.1	100.0

IVc1			Inflow Rates from Class Origin:				
	I+II	III	IVa+b	IVc1	V+VI	VIIa	VIIb
1973	0.5	0.3	3.0	32.8	1.4	1.0	61.1	100.0
1988	3.6	0.9	6.6	22.8	2.1	1.9	62.0	100.0
1996	2.9	1.8	7.2	17.4	1.6	2.0	67.1	100.0

V+VI			Inflow Rates from Class Origin:				
	I+II	III	IVa+b	IVc1	V+VI	VIIa	VIIb
1973	2.0	2.4	4.6	4.0	18.8	11.6	56.6	100.0
1988	2.3	3.5	5.2	1.6	21.1	12.9	53.3	100.0
1996	2.6	4.7	4.9	2.2	25.1	14.1	46.3	100.0

VIIa			Inflow Rates from Class Origin:				
	I+II	III	IVa+b	IVc1	V+VI	VIIa	VIIb
1973	1.3	1.9	4.6	4.6	8.6	12.1	66.9	100.0
1988	2.0	3.0	4.5	1.7	11.6	16.2	61.0	100.0
1996	2.5	4.2	5.1	2.5	14.1	18.3	53.4	100.0

VIIb			Inflow Rates from Class Origin:				
	I+II	III	IVa+b	IVc1	V+VI	VIIa	VIIb
1973	0.4	0.1	0.9	4.2	1.4	1.3	91.7	100.0
1988	0.7	0.4	1.2	1.8	2.0	2.1	91.8	100.0
1996	0.9	0.7	1.3	2.5	2.5	2.4	89.8	100.0

Appendix 2

This appendix describes the four log-linear models used to analyse relative mobility rates presented in this chapter.

The first one used was the Independence Model that tests the hypothesis that there is no association between class of origin (O) and class of destination (D) in each cohort (C) or survey (S) analysed. In the following equations we define the models for the cohorts (C) (in the cases where we analysed the PNADs of 1973, 1988, and 1996, all terms defined by C must be substituted by S [designing survey]). The expression for the Independence Model in the additive form is:

$$\log F_{ijk} = m + l_i^O + l_j^D + l_k^C + l_{ik}^{OC} + l_{jk}^{DC}.$$

In this equation, F_{ijk} represents the expected frequency in cell ijk of the table crossing origin (O) on the lines (i), destination (D) on the columns (j), and having cohort (C) as a third variable (k). At the right-hand side of the equation are the following terms: m, representing the mean; l_i^O, l_j^D and l_k^C representing respectively the effects of the marginal distributions of origin, destination and cohort; and the two terms defining the interactions between origin and cohort (l_{ik}^{OC}) and destination and cohort (l_{jk}^{DC}). Since the term defining the interaction between origin and destination (l_{ik}^{OD}) is not present in the equation, the fitting of this model to the data would mean that there is no association between origin and destination. However, the probability of fitting this model to any mobility table is extremely low. Thus, the Independence Model is used only as a baseline model to access the fitting of other models to the data.

The second model used in this chapter is the Constant Social Fluidity Model (CnSF) that is simply the model excluding the interaction among the three variables analysed (origin, destination, and cohort). The equation is the following:

$$\log F_{ijk} = m + l_i^O + l_j^D + l_k^C + l_{ik}^{OC} + l_{jk}^{DC} + l_{ij}^{OD}$$

Since this model includes the term for the association between origin and destination (l_{ij}^{OD}) and, what is even more important, does not include the term for the interaction among origin, destination and cohort (l_{ijk}^{ODC}), its fitting to the data means that origin and destination are associated and this association is constant across all cohorts. In other words, all relative mobility rates, represented by odds ratio, are identical for each one of the cohorts.

The third model is the so-called 'Uniform Differences' (UNIDIFF).[29] The model includes one term that describes the association between origin and destination (X_{ij}) multiplied by another term describing the strength of

---

29 For a general description of this model see Xie (1992).

this association in each cohort (b_k). It is this last term that defines in which direction the association between origin and destination is changing, that is, it defines if social fluidity is increasing, decreasing or remaining constant in each birth cohort. The equation for the UNIDIFF model is the following:

$$\log F_{ijk} = m + l_i^O + l_j^D + l_k^C + l_{ik}^{OC} + l_{jk}^{DC} + b_k X_{ij}$$

Finally, we used the Diagonal Changes Model that includes an estimator for the cells in the main diagonal of the mobility table for each cohort (a $_k$ d_{ij}). This estimator is used to observe if immobility is changing, that is, if immobility is increasing or decreasing from cohort to cohort. The equation for this last model is the following:

$$\log F_{ijk} = m + l_i^O + l_j^D + l_k^C + l_{ik}^{OC} + l_{jk}^{DC} + l_{ij}^{OD} + a_k \, d_{ij} \, .^{30}$$

---

30   For an introduction to log-linear models see Powers e Xie (2000).

CHAPTER 10

Democratic Consolidation and Civil Rights: Brazil in Comparative Perspective

Leandro Piquet Carneiro

The Crisis of Civil Rights in Latin American Democracies

In the past two decades 12 of 17 Latin American and Caribbean countries went through a process of political transition from authoritarian to democratic regimes (Colombia, Costa Rica and Venezuela were excluded from the denominator). During the phase of political transition and the establishment of new democratic regimes in Latin America, the political agenda had as its main focus the issue of *institutional design*: when the basic agreements that defined plebiscitary democracy as the ultimate objective of the new regimes had been guaranteed a huge number of decisions still had to be made with regard to the regulation of the political, electoral and institutional processes that would give substance to the new regional democracies. Should new constitutions be written or old ones be amended? Should the previous electoral and party legislation prevailing during the military rule be reinstated or should entirely new laws be created? Would those same parties and institutions whose activities were interrupted for decades be able to re-establish their representational ties with voters and promote the extension of civil rights adequately?

Among those countries that went through the transitional process the answers to these questions varied greatly. It should also be emphasised that these questions had, and still have, an impact on the stabilisation and on the performance of the new democratic regimes. When the lengthy and important process of legal and institutional definition that characterised the transition came to an end, the focus of comparative studies was directed towards other issues.

In the present Latin American context, social and political tensions are not primarily the product of expectations of authoritarian regressions that could happen as a result of ideological clashes capable of producing radical divisions of the *polis*. This, however, is not the same as to affirm that, from the ordinary citizens' point of view, the quality of these democratic regimes is satisfactory. Seen from the optic of public opinion, the situation of the region's democracies is relatively homogeneous: low legitimacy and difficulties in the management of public policies in the economic and social areas. This process has been described by O'Donnell as the *second transition*, extending from the installation of the first democratic government until the effective establishment of a democratic regime. This second transition has not only a political dimension, it also has a socioeconomic and cultural one.[1] In this process there is a risk of two possible types of political regression: the 'quick' type, resulting from a civil self-coup or from a military coup, or the 'slow' type, resulting from the gradual reduction of civil power and of the validity of the rights and guarantees ensured by liberal constitutions.[2] Schematically, we could in fact say that the model proposed by O'Donnell for the analysis of democratic consolidation in Latin America leaves the way open for the possibility that the new democratic regimes may be corrupted by the split between democracy in the political sphere and authoritarianism in the social, economic and cultural spheres.[3]

A dimension less frequently analysed in the literature about political transition relates to the crisis that affects not only the institutions of political representation and those designed to supply services of a social nature, but also those designed for the provision of justice and security. The distinction between political, civil and social rights,[4] widely accepted in contemporary political theory, allows us to establish political and ontological differences between those types of rights that can be useful for the study of the present phase of democratic consolidation in countries subjected to political transitions.

Whereas social rights can be seen as subjected to a particularistic logic, and even to pervasive forms of clientelist control,[5] civil and political rights constitute a type of power that can be used to generate movements of various sorts. This happens in so far as these rights, because they are based on freedom of thought, expression, assembly, demonstration and association, allow individuals to organise themselves in the defence of their own interests and identities.[6] That is to say, civil and political rights 'define freedoms that the State cannot encroach on'.[7]

---

1   O'Donnell (1988), p. 43.
2   *Ibid.*, p. 44.
3   O'Donnell (1994; 1996). This question is also analysed by Pinheiro et al. (1991) and Adorno (1995) who make use of the concept 'socially implanted authoritarianism' to describe a wide range of political phenomena that, in the authors' view, would be characteristic of the Brazilian political culture. '[The Brazilian state apparatus] seems to be inscribed in a large authoritarian continuity that marks Brazilian society (and its 'political culture') (and makes it) directly dependent on the hierarchical systems implanted by the dominant classes and reproduced regularly with the help of the instruments of oppression, the criminalisation of the political opposition and the ideological control over the majority of the population' (p. 55). In my view, however, the generality and exaggerated historical amplitude of the formulation hinders its usage in empirical studies focusing on democratic consolidation in Brazil or in other Latin American countries.
4   Marshall (1965).
5   Santos (1988; p. 115; 1994 [1979]; p. 13 and *passim*).
6   Marshall (1964).
7   Barbalet (1988), p. 21; Foweraker and Landman (1997), p. 15.

Several formulations have been put forward to represent the development of civil rights in Western societies.[8] The institution of stable polyarchies[9] is obtained by the institutionalisation of rules of political competition (liberalisation) in the ambit of the elite or of limited social groups, followed by a process of gradual expansion of voting rights (participation). However, the 'Latin American political process was characterised by the incorporation of the masses into the dynamics of political competition before we succeeded in making the institutionalisation of those very rules of competition stable'; a process that 'identifies the source of the recurring instability in the Latin American systems'.[10]

Finally, I shall look at how these distinctions between the forms of rights and the historical processes that led to their universalisation may be useful for the debate on the consolidation of democracy in those countries that went through transitions from authoritarian regimes, such as Brazil.

In the first stage of the transition, generally successful in the seven countries listed above, political rights were strongly demanded, negotiated and achieved. Three out of these seven countries went through political transitions between 1977 and 1987, and one in 1992 (El Salvador, with the end of the civil war) and three went through transitions in the 1950s, and remained under democratic regimes thereafter. At present, the enjoyment of basic political rights exists in all these countries. In some cases, as in Brazil, the extension of voting rights to those below the age of 18 and to illiterates stretched the dimension of the *polis* to a maximum. That is to say, what can be noted is a convergence of political systems with regard to accepting the electoral-plebiscitary principle, although those systems may show some differences in terms of the range of political participation, the degree of genuine representativeness of government institutions and of the distribution of institutionalised political power.[11]

In the second stage of the transition, the main problems affecting the new Latin American democracies cannot be attributed primarily to the institutions of political representation. After all, these institutions have, with various degrees of efficiency, demonstrated their capacity to produce stable democratic governments for Latin American standards. It can even be affirmed that, at the moment, we are going through the longest and most extensive cycle — in terms of the countries it reached — of democratic stability in the region since those countries' independence. Nevertheless, the building of democratic regimes capable of being regarded as fully legitimate in the population's eyes still remains a goal to be achieved.

8   Essential references in contemporary political theory are the works of Bendix (1964), on the European case and Carvalho (1996), on the Brazilian case.

9   This issue is discussed by W.G. dos Santos, in his interpretation of Dahl's model (1997 [1972]) on the formation of polyarchies (Santos, 1988, 1992).

10   Santos (1988) p. 112.

11   Lima Jr. (1997), p. 31.

A new arena appears in this process: that of the institutions designed to ensure the enforcement of civil rights. In this area, the deficiencies of many of the 'new' and 'old' democracies pile up. The crisis that affected Latin American democracies leading to nine coups d'état (Argentina, Brazil, Bolivia, Chile, Ecuador, El Salvador, Guatemala, Honduras and Peru) between 1958 and 1975, was, above all, between states and between elites. It reflected a background of strong ideological polarisation, low adherence to democratic values and principles on the part of the local elites and also a high polarity between economic and political models in the international sphere. The relevance of these factors for the production of a possible *authoritarian wave* tends to be fairly low. However, if in fact there exists a threat to the survival of democratic regimes in Latin America, where does it come from? Two suspects are mentioned in a good part of the literature:[12] (i) the fragility of democratic values among the major elite groups and the population in general; and (ii) the governments' inefficiency in the provision of law and order. The second factor is particularly important for the purpose of this chapter. It is possible to demonstrate that it is also associated with the risk of a reduction in the civil control over police and military actions necessary to quash the acts that violate the law. In this sense, the source of political instability may be attributed not only to the fact that political participation and the institutionalisation of competition rules are out of step, as suggested in the institutionalist models derived from Dahl's interpretation (1972), but also to the incongruous relationship between political participation, democracy in the political field and the absence of guarantees of civil liberties in the wider social field.

This type of problem, that has at its core the enforcement of civil rights, may be detected in almost all of the continent's democratic regimes, be they in the 'new' or in the 'old' democracies. Before carrying on with the description of these problems, I intend to pause and examine the following question: What are the meanings and implications for democracy of the judicial system's (including the police system's) inefficiency? Or further still: What effect does the lack of appropriate civil rights guarantees have on the political system? The answers to these questions must take into account two different levels: the theoretical-normative and the empirical.

In empirical terms, the major sources of information about the situation of human rights in the world (Freedom House, Amnesty International, the UN Commission for Human Rights and the US State Department) point to a significant deterioration of the situation of civil rights in Colombia, Brazil and Venezuela in the second half of the 1990s, and even in countries with a long democratic tradition, such as Costa Rica.[13]

12　Huntington (1994 [1991]), pp. 281–2.
13　The problems observed in this country are partially a result of an increase in the criminality rate (UN Commission for Human Rights, 1994 Report; chapter 2).

Brazil, Chile, El Salvador and Spain went through political transitions from authoritarian to democratic regimes in the last democratisation wave (in the 1980s) and three of them also in the 1940s and 1950s. Therefore, for the first group of countries, there is an agenda that involves not only the problems resulting from adjustment to the new constitutional designs, the objective of which was to guarantee democracy in the political plan, but also the definition of policies in the areas of justice and security, capable of guaranteeing the full enforcement of civil liberties.

In some cases, such as Brazil, these institutions are still strongly structured according to the mentalities, ideologies and operational procedures characteristic of the authoritarian period, and the process of making them compatible with the new democratic order may occur at a slower rate than that taking place in other public institutions.

The difficulty in making political democracy and civil liberties compatible also pervades in the continent's 'old democracies'. Colombia and Venezuela are examples of how this process of adjustment to the institutions of security and justice — key institutions for the guarantee of civil rights — to the principles of democracy may be lengthy and often incomplete. Aggravating factors such as the presence of an armed opposition[14] or an increase in the criminality rate may contribute to make the process even more difficult. The crisis of the security and justice institutions may be detected not only through the population's subjective assessment, but also reflected in the systemic indicators of the civil and political rights situation. The process of the spilling over of this crisis — that we may regard as a crisis of civil rights — towards the political system as a whole is a phenomenon still hardly discussed in the literature, and the construction of scenarios may be useful, particularly with regard to an analysis of the Colombian and Venezuelan cases.[15]

Is there a Civil Rights Crisis in Latin America?

Table 1 below suggests a classification of longitudinal trends of civil and political rights in the countries studied. These trends were estimated on the basis of the index of the violation of civil and political rights published by Freedom House. The available series runs from 1980 to 1994 and the classification of trends was based on the *sign test*.[16] The procedure adopted to classify the rights trend in these countries was based on the analysis of the

14   In the 1960s the armed forces were used to fighting the guerrilla movements, both in Venezuela and in Colombia, where this situation continued until the 1990s. A successful example of adjustment is offered by Costa Rica that, after the 1948 civil war, got rid of its armed forces.
15   Uprimny (1993), Romero (1997).
16   The sign test is a non-parametric procedure that permits the testing of hypotheses about the distribution similarity between two variables originating from two related samples.

relationship between the variables measuring the civil and political rights situation at a time *t* and its temporal lags (t-1). Negative signs in the test indicate that the violation of rights at time *t* was greater than at time *t-1*; positive signs indicated the opposite relationship. The civil and political rights trend was then classified as 'better' whenever the proportion of positive signs in the test was greater than that of the negative ones. The classification 'worse' reflects the opposite situation. Countries where parity in the sign test were observed ($t = t-1$)[17] were classified as 'stable'

Table 10.1: Longitudinal Trends of Political Rights and Civil Liberties (1980–94)

	Civil Liberties		
Political Rights	**Better**	**Stable**	**Worse**
Better	Chile El Salvador		Brazil
Stable		Costa Rica Spain	
Worse			Venezuela Colombia

Source: Freedom House (1994), *The Annual Survey of Political Rights and Civil Liberties,* 1993–94. Statistical Abstract of Latin America (1996), (p.32).

In the comments that follow about the rights situation I also considered the Amnesty International reports and the country profiles prepared by the UN Commission for Human Rights. And in a less systematic fashion, the Country Reports on Human Rights Practices of the US State Department.

Costa Rica and Spain have maintained, throughout the period considered, the lowest levels in the violation of political rights and civil liberties. The analysis of the Amnesty International reports and of those published by the UN Commission for Human Rights (1993 and 1997) on these countries confirms this diagnosis. They are countries where not only are government policies for the defence of rights well assessed by these international organisms, but where there also seems to exist an effective civil con-

---

17   For the years 1993–94 Freedom House has changed its methodology to calculate ratings, causing an increase in the rights violation indexes for Costa Rica and Spain, an increase that was not considered in the computation of the trend.

trol of the actions of the police and the military.[18] Generally speaking, the three sources considered permit us to classify the situation of the political rights and civil liberties in these two countries as better than that in the other countries and with a relative tendency towards stability. With regard to Costa Rica and Spain, an adequate response on the part of judicial institutions in the registered cases of abuse was also noticeable.

Chile and El Salvador present a convergent and better trend in relation to the state of political rights and civil liberties. The situation of these rights has shown a positive development in the 15 years considered. The reasons for this improvement, however, can be attributed to very different factors. In the case of Chile, the rigid discipline and high efficiency of the police institutions led to a situation in which, after 1987, the authoritarian practices of the previous period were monolithically replaced by the logic of submission to civil governments. In spite of the charges of use of torture in police establishments and illegal detention of political activists found in the reports of both Amnesty International and of the UN Commission for Human Rights, it can be concluded that the civil control over police and military actions is greater in Chile than in those countries where the authoritarian regimes were less harsh, as in the case of Brazil, or even than those, such as Colombia and Venezuela, that have maintained democratic regimes over the past 30 years. In Brazil, tensions in the human rights field are more related to the investigation and punishment of crimes perpetrated during the military regime than to the present day-to-day operation of police and military institutions.

No matter how similar the El Salvadoran and the Chilean trends may be, the factors that led to the improvement of the political rights and civil liberties situation in the former country are significantly different. US aid to the Salvadoran army and police during the civil war was conditioned to the adoption of reformulation policies for those institutions. And the peace treaty (Treaty of Chapultepec, signed in Mexico in January 1992) established the need to develop a 'new police' and a 'new army'.[19] The presence of a UN peace force in the country exercised even greater pressure on police institutions and on the armed forces, encouraging them to maintain minimum standards of legality in their actions. However, recent trends of accentuated increase in the rates of violence and criminality and

18   Nevertheless, the Amnesty International 1996 Report points to a police force's involvement in actions of torture, arbitrary detention, and threats to opponents and to activists of separatist (Spain), environmentalist and trade unionist organisations (Costa Rica). Compared with other countries, the abuses registered may be classified as having a minor impact in so far as, in these countries, an adequate response on the part of the Judiciary and in governmental policies on the defence of human rights was observed.

19   Rouquié (1994), p. 323.

the culmination of both the UN Peace Force's presence and the US aid, may lead to a rapid reversal of the positive trends detected in the reports and indices on political rights and civil liberties.[20]

The indicators used point to an increase in the number of violations of civil liberties in the two oldest South American democracies and in Brazil. However, the factors producing this trend are significantly different in the three countries. Colombia presents a long tradition of political violence this century: the thousand day war (1899–1902) and the period known as 'The Violence' (La Violencia) (crudely, 1948–58) were events that strongly influenced the political development of that country. Archer (1995) calls attention to the difference between the type of violence practised before 1960 and that prevailing after the National Front (Frente Nacional) agreements.

The 1930s violence, and the violence prevailing until the early 1960s, were basically *internal* to the state. From the mid-1960s onwards, with the adoption of the political line of 'all forms of struggle' by the main left parties, the political violence adopted the form of violence *against* the state.[21] The bipartisan governments of the period 1958–74 permitted the stabilisation of the political democracy that has lasted so far, but were not able to control the violence of left-wing groups, of the paramilitary and of organised groups devoted to the refinement and exportation of illegal drugs from the 1980s onwards.[22] The historical series indicators of *political violence* and *political repression* used by Duff and McCamant (1976) show that, between 1950 and 1969, Colombia was characterised by low levels of political repression and high political violence. In other words, the response to the internal conflict did not include restrictions to political rights and civil liberties.

The indices summarised in Table 10.1 suggest, however, that this pattern changed slowly in the 1980s and 1990s. Although the new constitution, promulgated in 1991, succeeded in extending the areas of political participation and the guarantees to civil liberties,[23] the huge pressure exercised by the increase in the number of crimes and by the guerrilla groups' actions brought about a reduction of the civil control on the actions of the armed forces and of the police. As a consequence, it has been possible to observe both a deterioration of the civil liberties situation in the 1980s and 1990s, and the occurrence of a similar trend in the case of political rights.

---

20 Cruz (1996).
21 Archer (1995), p. 167.
22 Smith (1993).
23 The Constitution ratified in 1991 makes the post of governor elective, guarantees representational quotas to the Indian minorities, explicitly forbids any form of torture, establishes the right of habeas corpus and the figures of the ombudsman and of the attorney general and restricts the state of emergency to 90 days, among other measures.

Both the Amnesty International report, and those of the UN Commission for Human Rights and of Freedom House, concur in their identification of practices of torture in police establishments and in the registering of extra-judicial executions and extensive violations of political rights and civil liberties during the attempted coups of 1989 and 1992 in Venezuela. The levels of these violations have remained relatively high if one considers the country's democratic tradition. As in the Colombian case, in Venezuela an erosion of civil control over the actions of the armed forces and of the police is also noted.

Twelve years after the demise of the authoritarian regime the situation of the civil liberties in Brazil contrasts with the expansion of political rights achieved in the same period. The new democratic constitution promulgated in 1988 extended the right to political participation practically as far as it could go. It also introduced a series of provisions — previously non-existent in Brazilian Law — to deal with the defence of civil liberties.[24] The latter, however, are rights-on-principle rather than rights-in-use. In terms of violations of civil liberties the country is regarded as a particularly negative example in the continent and this diagnosis is shared by all sources considered in this study: the UN Commission for Human Rights committee in charge of evaluating the situation of human rights in Brazil,[25] Amnesty International (1996), the US State Department (1996) and Freedom House's annual survey. This has been one of the characteristics of the second transition in Brazil: the adaptation of the security and justice institutions — essential for the conversion of civil liberties into rights-in-use — to those legal proceedings characteristic of democracy has taken much longer than that observed at the level of the institutions of political democracy.

If the problem is transposed to a theoretico-normative level, the answer to the question posed at the beginning of this chapter, about the impact on the political system of the lack of adequate guarantees to civil liberties, implies a recognition that a model of democracy without civil liberties is simply not available. The right to hold property, to free movement, to equal treatment before the law, to guarantees against arbitrary arrest are all found among the characteristics that define modern democratic regimes and constitute typical issues dealt with by the systems of security and jus-

---

24 The 1998 Constitution lowers the minimum voting age to 16 (until the age of 18 voting is optional) and extends voting rights to the illiterate. In the civil rights field, the Constitution introduces a series of provisions in defence of civil liberties: considers racism a crime, guarantees ample religious freedom and also freedom to organise politically, and defines torture as a crime, among other rights-on-principle.

25 The Committee, in its September 1996 report, affirms that 'summary and arbitrary executions committed by securities forces and by death squads ... the prevalence of torture, arbitrary and unlawful detention and violence against detainees and other prisoners are seldom properly investigated and very frequently go unpunished' (United Nations Human Rights Brazilian Committee, paragraphs 311–13).

tice.[26] Legal institutions in a democratic society have as a fundamental goal the guarantee of equal opportunities in access to the protection of the law, an element without which no democracy can fulfil itself as a political and social structure capable of ensuring 'the continuous responsiveness on the part of the government to the preferences of its citizens, regarded as politically equal'.[27] In this sense, and in extreme cases, the inefficiency of the police and legal system has as a consequence an increase in political instability.

'Old' and 'new' Latin American democracies face similar crises with regard to the operation of their institutions of security and justice. This can be evaluated with the help of the qualitative and quantitative indicators of the civil rights situation in the countries studied. The new democratic cycle has been laid on a fragile foundation in countries such as Brazil and El Salvador and the continent's old democracies seem to be entering a turbulence zone the consequences of which are still unknown. The extension of political rights was achieved without a corresponding development of the institutions designed to ensure the enforcement of civil liberties. The agenda present in the studies of institutions — predominant in the interpretations about the democratic consolidation in Latin America — gives clear emphasis to the issues of consolidation of institutions of political representation and frequently neglects the relevance of the Judiciary's institutions (that include police) in the transition and institutionalisation of the democratic regimes.[28] The hypotheses on the problems of the second transition formulated throughout this chapter attempt to make clear the importance of these institutions for the democratic consolidation of the countries of the region.

A decade after the political transition in the main countries of the continent has been finalised we are face to face with a paradox that has existed for a long time in Latin American political thought: the achievement of political rights was not sufficient to bring to an end the continuous violations of civil liberties, in which the very public agencies responsible for the maintenance of order, and before which the Judiciary institutions are powerless or inefficient, are involved.

Two research issues may be brought to the fore in this context. First, it is my intention to discuss some of the policies designed for the control of police practices and in force in Brazil today. The control of police violence has been the object of innovative policies in Brazil. Some interesting results are beginning to appear, and this seems to indicate that the cycle leading to the deterioration of the civil rights situation observed in the past two decades is possibly being reversed.

Secondly, an aspect frequently neglected in the literature about the political transitions in Latin America has to do with public opinion's sup-

---

26 Bendix (1964).
27 Dahl (1997 [1972]), p.25.
28 O'Donnell (1996); Munck (1994); Mainwaring and Scully (1995).

port of policies and institutional practices that are not exactly in agreement with the normative principles of a polyarchy. Dahl (1989), in *Democracy and its Critics*, defines democratic regimes as those in which, among other characteristics, there is an effective civil control over police and military violent coercion, a control exercised by civilians who, in turn, must be subjected to a process of democratic selection.[29] This definition applies not only to the institutional plan, but is also useful to describe the values and norms manifested by the public in a democratic system.

In this sense, the probable implications for the functioning of democratic regimes of the presence of a certain level of public preference for policies based on a principle opposed to that of 'civil control over police and military violent coercion' can be explored. That is to say, the presence of a 'seriously asymmetrical disagreement' in society,[30] in which a minority shows a strong preference for police actions of an extra-judicial nature against a majority that prefers, with less intensity, the civil control of police and military actions. Will this asymmetry of preferences, therefore, have any perceptible impact on the performance of police and military institutions, and consequently on the very definition of the democratic character of the regime?

Coping with the Crisis: Improving Police Action in Brazil

The available data indicate that approximately ten per cent of the homicides that take place in Rio de Janeiro and São Paulo are perpetrated by members of the police.[31] Surveys of victims' profiles also show that three per cent of the population and five per cent of the male population were the victims of extortion practised by a member of the police in a period of 12 months.[32] These simple figures intend to show that police practices and the organisational values and culture of these institutions are problems that hinder the formulation and implementation of policies designed to reduce crime in the major Brazilian cities such as Rio de Janeiro and São Paulo.

An issue as yet not widely discussed in the Brazilian literature on crime has to do with the forms of external control of the police and the various types of police-community relationship. On the one hand, there are some examples of policies that are being developed by the Brazilian police in the hope of improving the quality of the services provided by the police and also of establishing rigid legal control over police action. On the other, and in the counter-current of this main tendency, there are examples of policies that intend to respond to the higher crime rates through measures that encourage

---

29   Dahl (1989), p. 245.
30   Dahl (1989 [1956]), p. 101.
31   Cano (1997).
32   Piquet Carneiro (1999).

the use of police violence. The objective in this section is to bring together available data and estimates that can provide the elements for a qualitative discussion about the issues of police action in the Brazilian context.

Whereas the crime issue can be analysed as a problem affecting the economic development of the region, the question of police action is clearly associated with the issue of consolidation of the democratic regimes in Latin America.

The policies aiming at the control of police work are central to this debate. The change towards standards of behaviour compatible with the enforcement of civil rights, the struggle against corruption and the improvement in the relationship with the community have all too frequently been considered goals for police work. However, one must consider the hypothesis that the success of these policies — which, among other things, are intended to reinforce the mechanisms for external control of the police — depend, in a large measure, on the attitudes, norms and values of the system operators — that is, of their organisational culture — and, to a certain extent, also on the values and attitudes of the population in general and of the elites towards police work.

The available assessments of police practices in Brazil have shown, on the one hand, the systematic use of violence in police actions and, on the other, how precarious the instruments of external control of police operations still are. Recent research has attempted to measure the magnitude of the problem of police violence.[33] Cano's study discusses the impact of the implantation, by the Public Security Secretariat of the State of Rio de Janeiro, in November 1995, of the Programme of Promotion of the Police for Acts of Bravery. This programme would have encouraged the use of violence by the police in their routine activities. The period of reference for the research runs from January 1993 to July 1996, covering periods before and after the adoption of the Programme of Promotion of the Police for Acts of Bravery.

With the aid of the civil police records (Register of Occurrences) Cano drew the victims' profiles and the circumstances of death, cross-tabulating the police information with data gathered at the city morgue (IML). The indicators used to measure the degree of police force employed were the proportion of deaths and injured in the conflicts between the police and the population and the percentage of deaths assigned to the police in the total number of homicides that had occurred in the city during the research period. The figures indicated that approximately ten per cent of the homicides in the city of Rio de Janeiro are perpetrated by the police. In the US cities studied this percentage only rarely reaches the five per cent mark (Figure 10.1).

---

33   Mesquita (1998); Pinheiro (1997); Cano (1997).

Police violence can also be evaluated by the *lethality rate*, that is, the ratio number of deaths/number of injured in conflicts involving the police. In these conflicts the indicator shows the number of deaths to be greater than the number of injuries. According to Cano, this would point to a lack of 'honesty' in the police's actions. The implementation of the above-mentioned policy of Promotion for Acts of Bravery doubled the number of deaths resulting from police intervention, that jumped from an average of 16 to 32 per month. The *lethality rate* also nearly doubled, the ratio number of deaths/number of injured having gone from 1.6 to 3.5.

Figure 10.1: Proportion of Homicides Perpetrated by Members of the Police out of Total Homicides (selected cities)

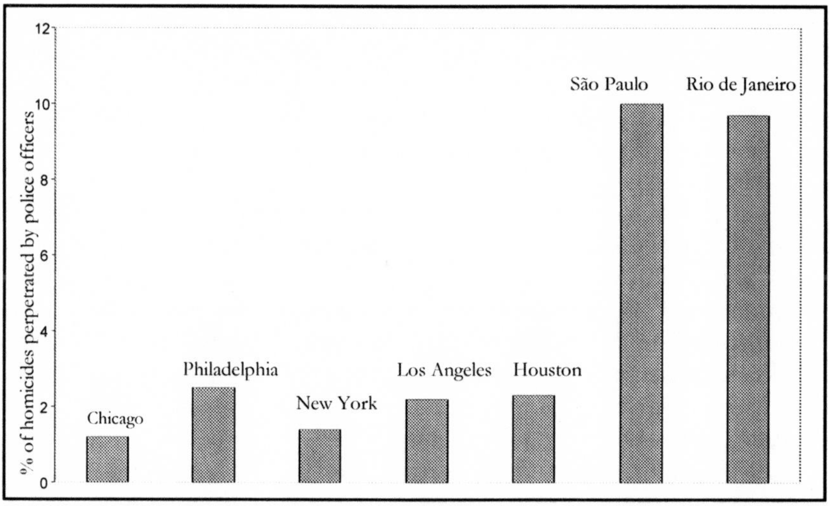

Source: Cano (1997).

The data reveal a fairly singular lethality pattern in the police's actions in Rio de Janeiro and São Paulo: in Rio de Janeiro alone the police kill in one year approximately the same number of people killed by the entire US police force in the same period.[34] The analysis of the data gathered in the City Morgue death registers led Cano to suggest that, in fact, many of the 'suspects' had been summarily put to death. On average, 4.6 bullet holes were found in the bodies of police victims, a large number of which were in the victim's head. There was also clear evidence of shooting at close range, and body injuries not produced by firearms, suggesting that some of the suspects had in fact been subdued prior to the execution.

---

34 Cano (1977).

The problem of police violence in São Paulo was also studied by Pinheiro, Izumo and Fernandes (1997), in their 'Fatal Violence: Police Conflicts in SP (81–89)'. The authors examined the circumstances of fatal violence in conflicts involving police agents in the period between 1981 and 1989. The historical series organised by Pinheiro et al. of the deaths perpetrated by the São Paulo police was recently updated by Mesquita (1998) (Figure 10.2 below).

Figure 10.2: Long-Term Evolution of Homicides Perpetrated by the São Paulo Police

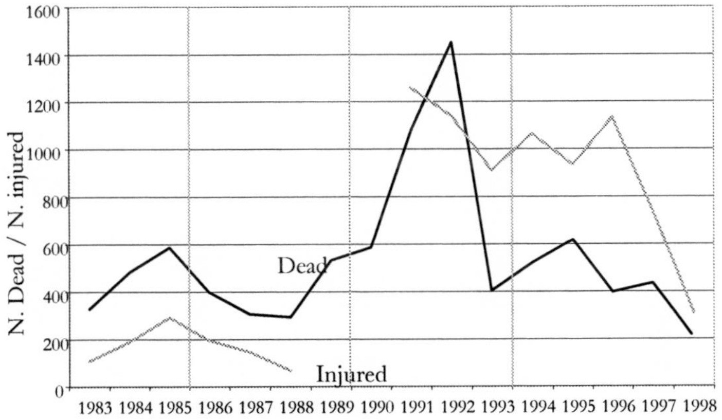

The vertical lines indicate changes in government. The analysis of the data in this series strongly suggests that only from 1994 onwards did the ratio dead/injured (regarded as an indicator of excessive use of force on the part of the police) reach a 'normal' level, that is, one in which the number of people killed through police intervention was lower than the number of those injured. The longitudinal data representing the number of deaths committed by Rio de Janeiro and São Paulo police (Figures 10.3 and 10.4) show that the level of police violence varies according to the type of policies put into practice by the local executive government.

The inflexion of the curve representing homicides commited by the police in the State of São Paulo may be attributed to at least two main factors: police action and the Follow-Up Programme of Military Police Involved in High Risk Occurrences (PROAR) established from September 1995, the aim of which was to develop mechanisms to keep police behaviour in check.

**Figure 10.3: Number of Suspects Killed by Police: Rio de
Janeiro and São Paulo**

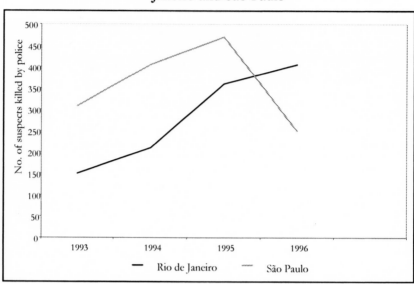

Source: Cano (1997).

Here we must make a detour to examine the structure of the PROAR in
greater detail. One of the programme objectives is the possible recovery,
in psychological and emotional terms, of police officers involved in hazardous occurrences, i.e. those occurrences the military police call 'critical
events or tragic circumstances that were the cause of serious stress for the
military police members involved, with direct physical and emotional consequences'. According to the information supplied by the programme
leaders, this means any situation where police action has resulted in injuries
or death (whether or not caused by the police).

The assumptions behind the programme are that: 1) causing deaths or
bodily injuries, even when in self-defence, leads to psychological and emotional imbalances of varying degrees in the members of the military police;
2) due to the authoritarian culture crystallised in the military police, there are
those in the corporation who value confrontation; with this, police officers
involved in hazardous situations are highly valued by peers and society alike,
and this appreciation gives rise to further confrontations with victims; 3) the
police member taking part in an occurrence of high risk usually becomes
part of a deviant group, that pressurises all its members into conformity with
group rules, continuously reinforcing these members' behaviour and becoming more and more resistant to external influence. It is also assumed that the

deviant group's resistance leads to a situation in which the police hierarchy begins to wear thin, opening the way for the appearance of informal leaders. All this hinders any change of attitude on the part of those members of the police who were involved in a hazardous situation.

Thus, the programme in question was designed to seek the development of new attitudes among police officers previously involved in serious occurrences, reinforcing the hierarchy principle within the Police Corporation and the need to avoid further occurrences which may result in injuries or death. To achieve such objectives the PROAR has, among other things, concentrated on improving the police's work environment.

To date, 2,884 military police have been through this programme — the great majority of whom were non-graduated officers (privates and sergeants) as these would be the ones most likely to be involved in a hazardous situation, given the fact that street patrolling is almost restricted to non-graduated officers.

Table 10.2: Total Number of Police Participating in the PROAR per Year

Year	Number of Police Officers
1995	123
1996	245
1997	828
1998	966
1999	1083
Total	3245

Source: State Secretariat for Public Security, São Paulo.

1999 totals were the result of a projection based on the first 8 months of that year.

Table 10.2 above displays the longitudinal evolution of the number of police that have been through the programme. From January 1997 the programme also started to consider cases of insubordination and participation in occurrences that resulted in injuries. From April 1998 the programme began to include participation in occurrences in which the police officer used his/her gun (even if this did not lead to deaths or injuries). Presumably this explains the significant increase in the number of police taking part in the programme from that year onwards.

Among the policemen/women participating in the PROAR, 60.1 per cent of the total number of cases were members of the police that had been involved in 'resistance followed by opponent's death'. The second most frequent cases were those resulting in body injuries: 890 people, representing 30.6 per cent of the total; next were firearm shots with 256 cases, or 8.9 per cent of the cases and finally, emotional disturbances with only four cases or 0.1 per cent of the crimes as can be seen in Table 10.3 below.

Table 10.3: Nature of Incident (until September 1999)

	N	Per cent
Emotional disturbances	4	0.1
Firearm shots	256	8.9
Body injuries	890	30.9
Resistance to arrest followed by death	1,734	60.1
Total	**2,884**	**100.0**

Source: State Secretariat for Public Security, São Paulo.

Evaluations carried out by the military police themselves (no other assessments were available) indicate that the programme has been successful in its attempts to reduce instances of violent behaviour by police members; in the breaking down of those organisational structures that lead to the formation of 'deviant groups' linked to violent practices and even in the control of transgressors within the police.

I hope to demonstrate, through the data presented here, that some of the public security policies developed in the 1990s in Brazil do not seem to have as their main focus the control of police violence, as shown by recent experiences in Rio de Janeiro. On the other hand, the analysis of the São Paulo government's programme indicates that a significant reduction in the number of homicides committed by the police can be achieved with the help of public policies.

Conclusion

The reported experiences illustrate some of the innovative public security policies focusing on policing methods and police violence control that exist in Brazil today. The issues raised in the introduction suggest that the problem of public security institutions is inserted into the much broader theme of institutional consolidation in a new democratic Brazil. The aim in bringing this broader discussion to the fore is to give emphasis to the notion that the adapting of public security and legal institutions to democracy involves a long period of transition; that we are still very much at an initial stage in this process; and that, therefore, we are still far from achieving the type of control standards that prevail in a democratic system. Nevertheless, the very fact that initiatives such as those discussed in this chapter exist seems to show that the perspectives on this front are fairly promising.

It is still too early to make affirmations about the degree of 'internalisation' or the level of success of the policies mentioned. The debate has been very much at a normative level and the small number of evaluation papers are of a purely qualitative nature, nearly always ethnographies. The present list of evaluations suggests that there is an urgent need for studies that will assess the experiences in progress, making use of standard procedures for evaluation studies such as, for instance, control cases and the combination of quantitative and qualitative methodologies. This lack of methodologically adequate studies to aid the discussion on the impact of those public security policies adopted in Brazil is today the greatest obstacle to a systematic discussion on the need to increase civil control over police and military action.

The cases reported in this study indicate that there are innovative public security policies centred on the control of police violence. The available data indicate that approximately ten per cent of the homicides taking place in Rio de Janeiro and São Paulo are perpetrated by members of the police.[35] Surveys of victims' profiles also show that three per cent of the population and five per cent of the male population were victims of extortion practised by a member of the police in the period of 12 months. These data suggest that police practices, and the organisational culture of public security agencies are problems that hinder the formulation and implementation of crime control policies in Brazilian cities such as Rio de Janeiro and São Paulo.

It is important to remember that the adjustment of security and justice institutions to those legal procedures characteristic of a democracy have taken longer in political institutions, not only in Brazil, but in nearly all countries that have gone through the transition from authoritarian regimes in the past decade. The initiatives mentioned above show, however, that there are also good perspectives on this front.

In the mainstream of the institutionalist literature, references to the problems referred to in this chapter, such as, for instance, the crisis of civil rights and the cultural aspects associated with democratic consolidation, are still scarce. The evidence gathered in this study suggests that civil rights have become an important field of action for social and political agents

35   Cano (1997).

during the democratic consolidation phase. A weak performance on the part of security and justice institutions may even compromise the operation of the political institutions.[36] The introduction of the analysis of specific public policies aimed at the security and justice institutions, in the ambit of the studies on democratic consolidation, may contribute towards the identification of new factors that at present affect the legitimacy and the performance of the region's democratic regimes.

---

36   For a discussion of the causality relations between civic culture and administrative
     efficiency of public institutions see Putnam (1993).

CHAPTER 11

The Race Issue in Brazilian Politics*

Antonio Sérgio Alfredo Guimarães

The issue of race and politics in Brazil can be approached from different angles. One of these might be the way in which politicians and public policies deal with matters relating to racial differences within the Brazilian population. Alternatively, one could look at the way in which some racial minorities organise politically, either in terms of developing a specific ethnic feeling or by means of institutions and political parties. One could also refer to the particular way in which different racial contingents have been absorbed into a unique Brazilian national identity.

Over the years, however, Brazilian political science has constructed its own distinctive method of approaching the race issue. Bolívar Lamounier (1968) and Amaury de Souza (1971) list three substantive questions for studying the relationship between race and politics in Brazil. The first is whether blacks and whites display different political behaviour; the second is whether there is a collective political behaviour on the part of blacks that expresses racial solidarity; and the last is 'how the political system operates to demobilise the potential for collective political behaviour'. Souza and the majority of those who have written about the relationship between race and politics in Brazil have restricted their studies to the first of these questions,[1] while Lamounier has dedicated his energy to examining the third. This chapter will try to deal briefly with all three questions.

The discussion on race and politics, as sketched out above, must face a preliminary challenge in Brazil — the task of establishing the existence of a race issue. Like the rest of Latin America, Brazil was formed from the American colonial matrix, that is, the transplantation of European peoples to the Americas in a position of dominance over both the indigenous populations and the large population of enslaved Africans. Nevertheless, it will be maintained here that there is a general belief in a certain Brazilian exceptionalism that has supposedly overcome the original racial differences. This is because the Brazilian solution to the problem of integrating formerly enslaved black people and the descendants of indigenous peoples into the national society occurred in two stages. First, it denied the existence of biological differences (innate abilities), political differences

---

*   Translated from the Portuguese by Elisa Larkin Nascimento and Jenny Ann Trinitapoli.
1   Silva and Soares (1985); Castro (1993); Berquó and Alencastro (1992); Prandi (1996).

(rights), cultural differences (ethnicity) and social differences (segregation or prejudice) between these peoples and the European descendants, with or without race mixture. Secondly, it is because the Brazilian solution incorporated all these original differences into a unique syncretic and hybrid matrix, in biological terms as well as in cultural, social and political terms. This is what we conventionally call racial democracy.

In order to develop the theme of this chapter, I find myself obliged to demonstrate that this idea of Brazilian exceptionalism is part of the problem, meaning that it is an historically dated political solution, which is now in headlong decline.

This chapter will begin by briefly putting into historical context the process of building a Brazilian national identity in which the first 'solution' to the race issue was settled. Secondly, the results of studies on the voting behaviour of Brazilian blacks will be presented. This will be followed by an examination of the emergence of black social movements. In addressing these issues special emphasis will be devoted to the changes recorded since 1985.

Brazilian Racial Democracy

Brazilian modernity is a product of the last 70 years. Sociologists and political scientists have generally delimited that modernity with reference to the 1930 Revolution, which put an end to the First Republic (1889–1929). In comparison with the Empire (1823–89), the First Republic sought to modernise Brazil by adopting new institutions, Europeanising customs[2] and encouraging European emigration.[3] It also maintained continuity with the Empire in the form of a conspicuously polarised nationality marked by enormous distance between whites and blacks — the civilised and the provincial. It was only after 1930, particularly with the New State regime (1937–45) and the Second Republic (1945–64), that Brazil definitively acquired a 'people', meaning that the nation invented for itself a tradition and an origin.

The fundamental idea of the new nation was that different races do not possess innately different civilising qualities but rather different cultures. Brazil began to think of itself as a hybrid, mestizo civilisation — not only European but also the product of miscegenation among whites, blacks and Indians. The Brazilian 'ethnic melting pot' was capable of absorbing and *Brazilianising* the cultural traditions and manifestations of the various peoples that immigrated during their respective eras, rejecting only those considered incompatible with modernity (superstition, animism, etc.). This idea allowed for the cultivation of a uniquely Brazilian 'high culture' that was also compatible with 'popular culture', a phenomenon that emerged in the 1922 Modern Art Week. But in a way it was the social sciences, not only

2   Freyre (1936).
3   Seyferth (1990); Schwarcz (1993).

the arts and literature, that invented this modern Brazil, through seminal works like those of Gilberto Freyre (1933 and 1936), Sérgio Buarque de Holanda (1936) and Caio Prado Júnior (1937).

The material and economic foundations for this modernity were laid by the 1930 Revolution. They consisted, basically, of incentivising industry and substituting the foreign labour force with a Brazilian one, leading to the constitution of a true proletariat with recognised and regulated political status.

The importation of about five million Africans supplied the labour market of the colony (1560–1823) and the young independent state during its first decades of existence (1823–52). However after the abolition of the slave trade, Europe became the main source of labour for Brazil's export agriculture and emerging industry. An estimated four million Europeans emigrated to Brazil between 1850 and 1932, mainly Portuguese, Italians and Spaniards. This foreign labour force, concentrated almost entirely in São Paulo, the states of the southern region and Rio de Janeiro, dominated the industrial and artisan labour supply, completely excluding the black and mestizo populations from the market.

The end of foreign immigration in the 1930s and the constitution of a market reserve for Brazilian workers made the incorporation of an enormous mass of mestizo and black workers possible. They migrated to São Paulo and to the states of the Brazilian south and south-east from various parts of Brazil, primarily Minas Gerais, rural São Paulo, Rio de Janeiro and the states of the north-east — the most heavily populated regions.

Until the 1930s it had been recognised that Brazil had a race issue with biological and demographic foundations. Thus, as long as the importation of African slaves continued or as long as the volume of European immigration was negligible, we were seen by our elites as a nation without a people and without a national culture.[4]

With European immigration came the perceived threat of cultural division of the country. As Nina Rodrigues expressed in exemplary terms at the end of the nineteenth century:

> Even the most careless and imprudent Brazilian cannot fail to be impressed by the possibility of the future opposition, which can already be glimpsed, between a white nation, strong and powerful, probably of Teutonic origin, which is being constituted in the states of the South, where the climate and civilisation will eliminate the black race, or subjugate it, on the one hand; and, on the other, the states of the North, where lives a mixed race, vegetating in the sterile turbulence of a live and ready intelligence, but one associated with the most decided inertia and indolence, with laziness and sometimes subservience, and thus

4   Skidmore (1976).

in danger of being converted into the submissive pastures of all the exploitation wrought by petty dictators.[5]

In other words, this period was characterised by fear for the quality of the Brazilian demographic stock, for the absence of cultural uniformity, and for national unity — all these fears nourished by beliefs about race.

Vargas in politics, Freyre in the social sciences and the Modernist and regionalist artists and writers in the arts were the personalities primarily responsible for providing the 'solution' to the race issue. During centuries of colonisation and biological and cultural miscegenation diluted in the Luso-Brazilian and mestizo matrix, European demographic and civilising predominance had never been complete enough to impose segregation upon blacks and mestizos. On the contrary, the dominant strategy was always that of 'transformation' and 'whitening', meaning the incorporation of socially successful mestizos into the 'white' ruling group.

While the First Republic was responsible for Europeanising Brazilian customs and bringing millions of Europeans into the south and south-east regions of Brazil, to the detriment of the mestizo population emerging from the colonial legacy, the 1930 Revolution and the Second Republic had the foresight to defuse the ethnic bomb that was forming just as Nina Rodrigues had feared.

Racial democracy as a 'solution' to the black issue did not signify, however, an effort to combat inequalities in income and social opportunities between blacks and whites. Only partially, in the areas of culture and ideology, did it involve curbing discrimination and prejudice. In legal terms, for example, only one law, the Afonso Arinos Law of 1952, recognised racial prejudice as a problem in Brazil and began punishing it as a misdemeanour. Nevertheless, its practice continued, widespread and unrestrained. Still, one must recognise that, in ideological terms, belief in racial democracy and in the Brazilian people's mixed origin served to solidify the formal pretence of equality for blacks, mulattos and mestizos in Brazilian society.

As we will see, not even racial democracy was enough to diffuse black social protest. First, however, some words about dismantling racial democracy during the last 15 years are in order.

While internal migrations and the creation of a solid national culture with mixed and popular foundations, originating mainly in the north-east, Bahia, Rio de Janeiro and Minas Gerais, managed to defuse the ethnic bomb that was forming in São Paulo before the 1930s, they were nonetheless incapable of preventing the emergence and continuation of new problems like race and regional prejudice and growing racial inequalities. In the same way, the belief in racial democracy which has been woven into the legend of Brazilian exceptionality was no longer a plausible solution once

---

5   Rodrigues (1933), p. 19.

other post-colonial societies, like the United States and Canada, began overcoming racial segregation through solutions like multiracial and multicultural coexistence in a democratic context that was more egalitarian in terms of opportunities.

Furthermore, racial democracy ended up becoming excessively associated with nationalist sentiments, the official ideology of the military regime and the process of economic expansion in the 1950s, 1960s and 1970s. The exhaustion of Import Substitution Industrialisation and the downfall of authoritarianism, which led to the crisis of the 1980s, eroded the very foundations of nationalism and its myths. Feelings of national demoralisation and disintegration corresponded with the economic crisis and the crisis of governability. Brazil began to experience phenomena previously unknown or already erased from national memory, all of them opposing their founding myths: a) the demand for attribution and recognition of their indigenous ethnicity by populations long integrated into the national life as '*caboclos*';[6] b) the emigration of large numbers of Brazilians, mainly to the United States, in search of a new life; c) the appearance of separatist movements in the country's south, as well as racist attacks on blacks and immigrants from the north-east in São Paulo; d) the desire for a double nationality (a second passport) among the white middle-class of European descent.

In other words, Brazil, for Brazilians, was no longer the best country, nor the only country, at least not in terms of social organisation. The significant increase in formal education and growth of the labour market in the previous decades now translated into enormous feelings of frustration. Differences among Brazilians also became increasingly visible.

The Black Vote and Political Science

Focusing specifically on São Paulo between 1888 and 1988, George Andrews (1991) offers an interpretative synthesis of the political tendencies of black Brazilians. His argument is that, historically, the political sympathies of the black population had always been with the monarchy, for it was known that the emperor leaned toward the abolition of slavery much more than the large landowners. Similarly, the First Republic, which closely followed Abolition, was a republic of large landowners that used political means to promote cultural policies of Europeanising customs and was never looked upon with favour or loved by blacks. Only Getúlio Vargas's New State, with its policies for protecting Brazilian workers and instituting state tutelage of trade unions (and later the labour politics of Vargas, Jango and Brizola) regained the political sympathies of the black masses on the same scale as the imperial family. In his synthesis, Andrews reproduces the consensus of a great part of the literature available on the subject.

6   Generally, this term refers to persons of mixed-race but with prominent indigenous phenotype in rural areas.

Gilberto Freyre made the first attempt to explain the differentiated political behaviour of blacks in modern Brazil. The two excerpts cited below effectively synthesise his opinion about black people's preference for populist politicians, mainly for the labour tendency represented by Vargas, Goulart and Brizola:

> The ironic side of the simultaneous disappearance of two institutions — slavery and the monarchy — was that former slaves found themselves in the position of men and women who had no Emperor or autocrat of the Big House to protect them, consequently becoming the victims of deep feelings of insecurity (...) Years were needed for political leaders to understand the true psychological and sociological situation of these former slaves, disguised as free workers and deprived of the patriarchal social assistance they were given in old age or in sickness by the Big House or, when that house did not do them justice, by the Emperor, the Empress, or the Imperial Princess.[7]

> This explains — coming to modern Brazil — the great popularity of Getúlio Vargas when, as president, for some time with dictatorial powers, he decided to establish the social legislation that gave the great majority of Brazil's working population protection against old age, sickness and exploitation by commercial or industrial corporations. This also explains why Vargas came to be known as the 'Father of the Poor' and won a degree of popularity with the people that surpassed that obtained by D. Pedro II [the Emperor] in 48 years of good, honest and paternalist government.[8]

In 1968 Bolívar Lamounier initiated a new scientific tradition in the study of the relationship between race and politics in Brazil by setting forth a research agenda that addressed three broad issues: a) differential voting behaviour between whites and blacks; b) autonomous political organisation of blacks; c) methods of integrating black people into the political system. For Lamounier the Brazilian case offers an apparent paradox: deep and growing social inequalities between whites and blacks coexist with the relative absence of violent conflicts and with the near non-existence of race issues in the political sphere. Without treating in detail the first of these issues, but accepting Freyre's observation that blacks, more than whites, support populist and labour leaders, Lamounier concentrates his attention on the last of the themes and offers an explanation for the paradox he has pointed out. In his view, first of all, the Brazilian state has been capable of generating symbols of black integration and incorporation that suffice to counterbalance

7　　Freyre (1956), p. 46.
8　　*Ibid.*

tensions arising from racial prejudice and discrimination. Second, the state has been perceptive enough to anticipate racial tensions or abort them at the source. Third, Brazilian social institutions have been successful in co-opting emergent and aggressive black leadership.

Amaury de Souza (1971) was the first to use voting records and multi-varied analysis, controlling social class, educational levels and other vari-ables of social position, to demonstrate that blacks really do display polit-ical behaviour different from those of whites. Souza validates the theory that had already been promoted by Freyre in theoretical terms.

From that point forward the interpretation that the black vote was con-centrated on populist politicians, at least with regard to the period of the Republic, became anchored in empirical research on voting intentions. De Souza (1971) concluded that in the 1960 presidential elections, blacks, independent of their socioeconomic status, voted more consistently for Jango than whites, revealing a certain pattern in the black vote, which sys-tematically leaned toward the populist and labour candidates. In analysing Brizola's victory in the Rio de Janeiro State gubernatorial elections a decade later, Gláucio Soares and Nelson do Valle Silva (1985) amply demonstrate a voting preference for the Vargas heir's candidacy among '*pardos*', meaning mulattos, even when controlling other explanatory vari-ables like socioeconomic status, degree of urbanisation, etc.

Using voting intention data from four medium-sized Brazilian municipal-ities in the 1989 elections, Mônica Castro (1992) also documented the exis-tence of a specifically black vote. A vote that operates in complex tandem with socioeconomic status: while the poorest blacks tend to be politically apa-thetic (abstaining from the polls or invalidating their vote), more economi-cally well off blacks tend to favour the Left. Castro did not, however, find sig-nificant differences between the behaviour of *pardos* and *pretos*.[9] Gilberto Freyre (1956) interpreted blacks' preference for the emperor and for Vargas-style populism as a product of their feelings of insecurity and as a search for social protection by strong and dominant figures. Souza (1971) and Andrews (1991), however, suggest that such a preference had solid material founda-tions and returns. In the case of populism, for example, Souza argues that the Vargas-era labour laws gave black Brazilians guarantees regarding their inclu-sion in class society.[10] His data also shows that there was greater upward mobility among young blacks than whites in 1960, although this greater mobility was insufficient in eroding the identification of blacks with the

9   *Pardos* are lighter-skinned, *pretos* dark-skinned blacks. This is a 'native' distinction as well as one made by the official Brazilian Census Bureau, IBGE. There is a widely accepted convention now both among intellectuals and black activists of classing *pre-tos* and *pardos* together, the sum of the two categories being referred to as the 'black' (*negro*) or Afro-Brazilian population.

10   Souza (1971), p. 64.

working class and the poor. Ideologically, 'at least during the first years of liberal democracy, from 1945 to 1964, the political categories of blacks and the people were almost interchangeable'.

Reginaldo Prandi, interpreting the same period, asserts:

> It is the populist strain of Vargas labour politics that explains black people's adherence to this party and its candidates. Populism denies the class struggle and dilutes the races into a homogeneous unit, the people, which is ideologically the source of all legitimacy. Racial differences make no sense, nor does any racial identity movement; populism, then, is an ideology of blacks' integration as equals.[11]

After the promulgation of the 1988 Constitution, which extended suffrage to the illiterate, incorporating millions of blacks into the Brazilian electorate, and in the face of a growing black movement preaching the vote for black candidates, the relationship between race and politics once again began to concern political scientists. Benedita da Silva's candidacy for governor of Rio de Janeiro state in 1989, with the racial and class polarisation that followed, frightened Brazilian political, economic and intellectual elites. Could we be moving towards the *racialisation* of Brazilian politics? Could blacks in Brazil be developing communitarian political sentiments and behaviour?

Through their analysis of data from sample surveys carried out in São Paulo and in Vitoria (Espírito Santo state), Berquó and Alencastro (1992) see the possibility, given the end of the disenfranchisement of illiterates, for a black ethnic vote to arise in Brazil. By this they mean a tendency of African descendants to vote for candidates that represent the Brazilian black community, even though only 14 per cent of those who consider themselves black actually state such an intention. Until then the ethnic vote had been restricted to ethnic communities in São Paulo (Italians, Syrians and Lebanese, Portuguese, Japanese, etc.) and Rio de Janeiro (Portuguese).

Analysing voting intention data for the 1994 elections, Prandi (1996) also noted blacks' electoral preference for certain candidates (Lula, Brizola, Quércia) to the detriment of others (FHC, Amin, Enéas), even when variables like geographical region, age, sex, income and educational levels are controlled. In Prandi's view, colour was the main factor for predicting voting intention, surpassing education and age. However Prandi rejects the interpretations of Souza, Castro, Berquó and Alencastro, Soares and Silva, who interpret this vote as being motivated by ideology or ethnicity. He prefers to return to an explanation akin to that of Freyre: the idea that deep feelings of insecurity and impotence would supposedly lead blacks to identify with the programmes of a few charismatic candidates.

---

11   Prandi (1996), pp. 63–4.

An attempt will now be made to explain the political position of the blacks through another perspective — their incorporation into national politics through black protest.

Black Movements

Black protest in modern Brazil, that is from 1930 to the present, has grown during the moments of greatest tension in the national fabric. In the 1930s, for example, different ethnic groups such as Italians, Syrians and Lebanese, as well as Portuguese, were so well organised that black and mestizo Brazilians felt threatened by exclusion. At the same time, São Paulo regionalism began to take on separatist tones.

The Brazilian Black Front (Frente Negra Brasileira — FNB), which arose during this period, was an ethnic organisation in the sense that it cultivated specific community values; however, it based its criteria for recruitment and identification on 'colour' or 'race', not on 'culture' or 'traditions'. In fact, the FNB sought precisely to assert that blacks were 'Brazilians' by renouncing the Afro-Brazilian cultural traditions considered responsible for the stereotypes attributed to black people and denouncing the colour prejudice that excluded Brazilian blacks from the labour market in favour of foreigners.[12] The FNB was also a political organisation that actually became a political party before being abolished by the New State regime. While it contained some socialist dissidents, the majority of the FNB was politically rightist with fascist overtones and even included a paramilitary group. Thus, in 1932 blacks were reluctant to join the São Paulo Constitutionalist Revolution, which was regionalist and separatist in nature, and in 1937 they supported the Vargas coup, which in a certain way implemented some policies meeting their demands. We were dealing, then, with black protest against a social order (that of the First Republic) that had materially and culturally cornered the black and mestizo populations into secondary and marginal spaces. Although its policies enjoyed mass support, the Vargas dictatorship dispensed with free political organisations. Black protest could only re-emerge with the restoration of civil liberties seven years later.

As we have seen, the re-democratisation process of 1945 was marked by a strongly nationalist political project, both in economic and cultural terms. This represented, on one hand, the rejection of European and US economic liberalism and cultural imperialism, and on the other the construction of state-regulated capitalism and an indigenous national culture with a popular foundation. This plan of nationhood offered blacks more effective economic participation and began to consider different cultural traditions of African or Luso-Afro-Brazilian origin as Brazilian: the baroque colonial art of Pernambuco, Bahia and Minas, Catholic proces-

12   Bastide (1955, 1983); Fernandes (1955, 1964).

sions, public square festivals, samba, Carnival, *capoeira*, *Candomblé*, *Congadas*, regional culinary traditions, etc. In other words, political federalism was, in some ways, fortified by the nationalisation of the different cultural region-alisms, all of these racial in nature. The national matrix became seasoned with the increasing mobility of the population and by the 'integration of blacks into class society', referring to their integration as *workers* and as *black Brazilians*. While Brazil was not in fact a racial democracy, the idea that it would come to be one in the future was good enough for the national social imagination.

Black protest, however, did not disappear. On the contrary, it broadened and matured politically during this period. First, because racial discrimination, to the extent that markets and competition were expanding, became more problematic. Second, because prejudice and stereotypes continued to oppress black people. Third, because the great majority of the black population was still marginalised in shantytowns (*favelas*, *mucambos*, *alagados*) and in subsistence agriculture. It was precisely the blacks climbing the social ladder, those recent-ly incorporated into class society, who would most forcefully verbalise the problems of discrimination, prejudice and inequality.

The main black organisation in Brazil at this time was the Black Experimental Theatre (Teatro Experimental do Negro — TEN) of Rio de Janeiro. Clearly cultural at the outset, its goal of opening the field of national scenic arts to black actors grew into one of professional training, of collective psychodrama for the black population and of recovering the image and self-esteem of black Brazilians. Its main intellectuals, Abdias do Nascimento (1950, 1968) and Alberto Guerreiro Ramos (1957), especially the latter, went further in their critique of European and North American cultural imperialism, preaching that social science should commit itself to a plan of nation-building. Because for Guerreiro Ramos the Brazilian peo-ple were indeed black, there was no sense in speaking of a 'black issue' or cultivating as exotic certain forms of cultural expression that were innate to the situation of poverty and ignorance in which the majority of Brazil's poor population was found (he was referring mainly to Afro-Brazilian reli-gions). TEN's intellectuals and their ideology were consistent with the nationalist and populist politics of the period, and their greatest expression was manifested in the Vargas labour tradition. From an ideological per-spective, Guerreiro Ramos radicalised Gilberto Freyre's exaltation of racial mixture and the mulatto, according to which all Brazilians carry in their soul the mark of miscegenation. In this sense, he made negritude the assumption of a Brazilian national identity free of the inferiority com-plexes left over from Portuguese colonisation.[13]

---

13   See Bastide (1961).

While civil society was basically anaesthetised during this repressive period between 1964 and 1978, in contemporary times black protest has been recovered in all its vehemence by the Unified Black Movement (MNU).

The profile of the MNU, founded in 1979, is radically different from that of its predecessors.[14] Politically, it is aligned with the revolutionary Left; ideologically, it assumes, for the first time in the country, a radical racialism. Its most evident and recognised influences are: first, Florestan Fernandes's critique of the racial order originating in the slave system, which the Brazilian bourgeoisie had kept intact and which had made racial democracy a myth; second, the civil rights and black nationalist movements of black Americans in the United States; third, the freedom struggle of the peoples of southern Africa (Mozambique, Angola, Rhodesia, South Africa). In addition to these one must recognise at least three more influences: the international feminist movement, which made possible the emergence of black female activism; the new Brazilian trade unionism, which took its protest to the factory floors and removed its leadership from the orbit of traditional political parties; and the new urban social movements, which kept civil society mobilised throughout the 1980s.

Black Protest Ideology during the 1980s: *Quilombismo*[15]

During the 1980s the MNU was a divided movement — split between a leftist leadership, generally young university students, some of whom were involved with the fight for democracy organised by the socialist organisations protected by the PMDB, and another leadership committed to cultural resistance, which spontaneously spread throughout the poorest black population, influenced by the culture of mass consumption. The presence of a historical leadership with an international character, like that of Abdias do Nascimento, closely related to Brizola's labour politics, was also a decisive component of the movement's ideological development. Because of length and time constraints, allow me to examine only *quilombismo*, the doctrine created by Abdias, an ideology that permeated the black movement of the 1980s, allying cultural radicalism with political radicalism.

Abdias do Nascimento's doctrine on *quilombismo* exhibits two central influences. The most obvious is Afro-centrism, a doctrine created in postwar France and the French Caribbean but that was very influential for blacks (in Britain and the Commonwealth as well as North America) during the 1970s voiced by African intellectuals from Nigeria and Ghana living in the United States and Britain. Afro-centrism inspired the task of connecting black Brazilians to a transnational black 'nation', which would

---

14   Gonzalez (1982) Santos (1985).
15   *Quilombo* refers to the community established by runaway slaves in Brazil, *quilombismo*
      to the culture and characteristics these communities took on.

evolve in occidental culture, but had its strongest roots in the Ancient Egyptian Empire and in the African presence of the pre-Columbian Americas. At the same time, this movement evidently dealt with inventing traditions and reclaiming the black civilising process. The second influence was clearly Marxism, primarily through its connection to the Brazilian nationalism of the 1960s. From this Marxist nationalism Abdias extracted not only formal analogies and revolutionary vocabulary, but also the fundamental idea that the emancipation of black Brazilians signified the emancipation of the entire Brazilian population from capitalist exploitation. The universal character of black emancipation in Brazil was intimately connected to an idea of an exploited majority and not of an oppressed minority, as in the United States. The broad definition of *black* as *African descendant* (not only as people of black colour or phenotype) was essential to this struggle. As a matter of fact, this amplified definition of black had already been made by Guerreiro Ramos and by Abdias[16] himself when, in the 1950s, they took possession of the ideas of negritude coming from the Francophone world, mainly Senegal and the Antilles, that had a strong impact in Paris. As Roger Bastide (1961) argued, at this point black Brazilians gave a rather distinctive meaning to the negritude movement, denying its cultural aspects (seen in Brazil as a barbaric anachronism) and emphasising its libertarian and nationalistic character. The novelty in the 1980s was adopting both a nationalist and cultural position at the same time.

The adoption of a bipolar racial classification (*black* and *white*, abolishing the intermediary categories *pardo* or *moreno*) seems to be politically motivated. Far from being the product of minds 'colonised' by US cultural imperialism or imprisoned by archaic radicalism,[17] it was the conscious decision of a movement that opted for a struggle in which blacks could be assimilated to an exploited working class instead of being relegated to the position of an oppressed minority.

Like all political movements the black movement was nourished by tradition and by its connection to other contemporary movements occurring both within and outside Brazil. The black movement extracted much of its ideological efficacy and its current manifestation from such movements. These were the contributions of the principal intellectual and political leaders like Abdias do Nascimento and Lélia Gonzalez.

Take, for example, Abdias do Nascimento's *quilombismo*. In his internal reference Abdias sought to integrate the programme of *quilombismo* with

16 Now that I have established a certain continuity between Abdias's thoughts from the 1950s to the 1980s it is necessary to clarify that between 1960 and 1980 his thought shifted from an axis of negritude to one of Afro-centrism.

17 The distance the black movement kept from the biological notion of 'race' is reiterated innumerable times. See Nascimento (1980), p.163: ('I advise the backbiters, intriguers, malicious and quick to judge: the word race, in the sense used here, is defined in terms of history and culture and not of biological purity.')

the movement to re-democratise Brazil, through a radical Marxist-inspired struggle for emancipation (Table 11.1, item A).

Similarly, Abdias defined the black Brazilian not only as the most exploited member of Brazilian society, but also as the majority, mobilising ancient traditions of the mulatto identity of the bush captains, persecutors of the *quilombolas* (Table 11.1, item B). Abdias also drew an analogy between the struggle of black Brazilians and the struggle against apartheid in South Africa, defining Blacks as workers par excellence, the most Brazilian of all Brazilians, a majority oppressed by a racist minority composed primarily of foreigners (Table 11.1, item C).

Emphasising aspects of residential segregation, exclusion from the formal sector and police brutality, Abdias used analogies to connect Brazilian and South African racism (Table 11.1, item D). At the same time, the reference to police brutality was indivisibly linked to the human rights movement, that in this era was already mobilising the political forces fighting for Brazil's re-democratisation. More clearly, Abdias argued that the situation of authoritarianism and the absence of rights has been permanent for blacks (Table 11.1, item E). For Abdias the answer was an anti-imperialist nationalist struggle, connected to the national liberation movement and class struggle, but that protected Brazilian blacks' cultural peculiarities and specific needs vis-à-vis other blacks in the diaspora or the Brazilian proletariat (Table 11.1, item F).

An analysis of Lélia Gonzalez's classic text and of the MNU documents shows the same elements, although not very explicitly. The black Brazilian movement was nourished ideologically by the struggles for emancipation being simultaneously waged by other black peoples (in the United States, South Africa, Lusophone Africa) and by the traditions of popular resistance in Brazil — of abolition and of Black Experimental Theatre.

The Limits of Co-optation

As in the two previous periods (1930–37 and 1945–64), contemporary black protest was also formed in an atmosphere of intense intellectual effervescence and political mobilisation in Brazilian society. However, unlike the FNB and the TEN, which quickly found responses to their demands within the framework of traditional politics, whether in the New State coup or by way of Vargas' labour politics and nationalism, the MNU's radicalism has made current black protest longer lasting. Moreover, the MNU is only one among the many black organisations created in the last 15 years. Other organisations of varying ideological and political orientation and goals have emerged with the common objective of combating racism; among these, cultural, political and legal action NGOs stand out.

The recent black movement has brought an agenda that allies the politics of recognition (of racial and cultural differences), identity politics (racialism and the ethnic vote), citizenship politics (the fight against race discrimination and the assertion of black people's civil rights) and re-distributive politics (affirmative or compensatory actions) to the Brazilian scene.

A small list of the black movement's demands in the last 15 years gives an idea of their breadth and radicalism. First, the MNU rejected the official date that celebrates the incorporation of blacks into Brazilian society (13 May, the date of the abolition of slavery) and instituted the festivities of 20 November, which marks the death of Zumbi, who led the Palmares Quilombo resistance in 1695. Second, the MNU began to demand a total change in education, through eliminating stereotypes and prejudices against blacks from schoolbooks, curricula and teaching techniques and instilling, on the contrary, black self-esteem and pride. Third, it demanded a special campaign by the Brazilian government to make it clear to the black population (*pretos* and *pardos*) that they should declare their colour as '*preta*' in the demographic census of 1991 and 2000. Fourth, it sued for and won the case that promulgated the modification of the constitution to make racism a crime without bail or statute of limitations and was later successful in passing legislation to regulate the constitutional provision, thereby making it enforceable. Fifth, it articulated a national campaign to denounce racial discrimination in Brazil, preaching and obtaining, in some places, the creation of special police stations to combat crimes of racism. Finally, it is now concentrating on demanding affirmative action policies to combat racial inequalities in the federal government.

Some of its demands have found quick responses from the Brazilian state, particularly those that could more easily fit into the contemporary matrix of nationality, whose nature is one of syncretism among the three founding races. Indeed, it was out of the very peculiar understanding of multiracialism and multiculturalism as synthesis (in the Freyrean tradition), and not as coexistence among equals (in the North American manner), that Brazilians began to accept some of the black movement's ideas, such as respect for cultural traditions and expressions of African origin and for the black aesthetic. The fact is that the Brazilian state was also agile in responding to the calls in this vein, whether by creating cultural foundations (the Palmares Foundation, for example) and state-level black community councils; incorporating black symbols (like the official recognition of Zumbi as a national hero and of 20 November as the Day of Blacks); developing more appropriate legislation to combat racism (the 1988 Constitution and Laws 7.716 and 9.459, which regulate the crime of racism); or changing school curricula in some municipalities where the pressure and presence of blacks is more intense, to allow for multiculturalism.

Other demands, however, like those that deal with fighting racial inequalities in income distribution and access to public services and demand affirmative and innovative policies, still face considerable resistance. This is true even though new institutions are slowly being created to deal with demands including: college entrance examination preparatory courses for blacks and the poor, exemption from college entrance examination fees for those coming out of such courses, bills of law that reserve places in public (non-tuition-paying) universities for students coming out of the public school system, the introduction of colour identification questions in higher education institution entrance forms and records, etc.

The broad range of demands has guaranteed the continuous nourishment of black political activism in greater measure than that of its co-option. In the same way, slogans like the ethnic vote (blacks should vote for blacks) and the cultivation of black consciousness (of a racial nature) are unlikely to be well absorbed. The reaction has been for the ideological and party profile of black activists to diversify rapidly due to the efforts of all political parties deliberately to court the black vote. In some instances, black leaders with great charisma, such as Benedita da Silva in Rio de Janeiro (1989), have appeared, and may reappear, on the political scene to compete for elected office in leftist parties (for example the PT[18] and PDT[19]). Through various radical proposals to modify racial inequalities, their presence may threaten to destabilise the system.

Finally, this chapter will examine a few other reasons why contemporary black protest has been more lasting and more difficult for the state to absorb. Beyond the reasons I have already suggested (national identity crisis, radicalism and the wide range of black demands), there is now a new international scenario from which the Brazilian state is no longer able partially to isolate itself, whether in economic terms or in cultural and political terms.

With regard to the effort to absorb protest and co-opt activists, state action has had to limit itself to the creation of foundations and some state-level councils, while political parties have sought to bring some black demands and politicians into their programmes.[20] But governmental parties and institutions incorporate only part of the black leadership, that is, those who are affiliated with or sympathetic to the political parties in power. This excludes both opposition leaders and activists independent of political parties. The latter, grouped in non-governmental organisations and funded by international donations, have been very active. Both the scope of these organisations, which make activism a profession, and the sources of their funding guarantee them greater autonomy and radicalism in their actions and proposals. Moreover, these organisations not only cooperate, they also compete with each other for ethnic representation.

18 Workers' Party (Partido dos Trabalhadores).
19 Democratic Labour Party (Partido Democrático Trabalhista).
20 Pereira (1982).

Secondly, consumer society and the internationalisation of cultural industry have made possible the appearance of black cultural movements, influenced not only by Brazilian folk culture of African origin, but also by the culture of the Black Atlantic. Movements that congregate the urban youth, such as Rio de Janeiro's funk,[21] Afro-Bahian carnival blocs,[22] the reggae of Maranhão State,[23] and São Paulo's rap,[24] are independent of any political or ethnic organisation. Some are very radical in their protest, a fact that is forcing black political leaders to keep abreast of these movements.

Conclusions

In this chapter I have sought to develop an original understanding of the state of the relationship between blacks and whites in Brazil, starting with a reinterpretation of what is called Brazilian 'racial democracy'. Fernandes treated racial democracy as an ideology of domination, as a myth, no more than a cynical and cruel way of maintaining the socioeconomic inequalities between blacks and whites, covering and silencing the permanence of colour prejudice and racial discrimination. This is the way in which most black Brazilian intellectuals understand 'racial democracy'. Denouncing its cruelty (such an ideology anaesthetises and alienates its victims) has been the main instrument for political mobilisation and the formation of a combative racial identity.

Countering this interpretation are some anthropologists who argue that 'racial democracy' is properly a founding myth of the Brazilian nation, in other words, a fundamental part of its civilising process.[25] Although this myth has not completely eradicated discrimination and prejudice, it permits greater intimacy and interaction between blacks and whites, solidifying a foundation for overcoming racism.

My understanding is that we should see in 'racial democracy' a political commitment from the modern state of the Republic of Brazil that was in force from Vargas's New State until the end of the dictatorship. Such a commitment has resulted in the incorporation of the Brazilian black population into the workforce, in the amplification of formal education and, finally, in the creation of infrastructures of a class society that challenge the stigmas created by slavery. The image of blacks as 'ordinary Brazilian people' and the banishment of the concept of 'race' from Brazilian social thought, substituted by concepts of 'culture' and 'social class,' are the greatest expressions of this commitment.

Since the 1980s Brazilian democratisation has sought to actualise this commitment but has encountered growing difficulties. First of all, racial

21   Vianna (1988).
22   Risério (1981).
23   Silva (1995).
24   Félix (2000).
25   Fry (1995).

inequalities, not only prejudice and discrimination, have become subjects of denouncement and are providing motivation for political demands. Second, the formation of a black identity has demanded the adoption of multiracial and multicultural policies that surpass the state's concept of society as being divided into classes (which marked the pact of racial democracy). Third, black mobilisation in Brazil has not followed the pattern of minority politics, but is based exactly on the idea that the Brazilian people are black, aspiring to the emancipation of an exploited majority.

Table 11.1 Some Ideological Elements of *Quilombismo*

Anti-capitalism (A)	'Black people have a collective project: the erection of a society founded on justice, equality and respect for all human beings on freedom; a society whose intrinsic nature makes economic or racial exploitation impossible. An authentic democracy, founded by the destitute and disinherited of the country. We have no interest in the simple restoration of obsolete types and forms of political, social and economic institutions; this would serve only to procrastinate the advent of our total and definitive emancipation, which can come only with radical transformation of existing socioeconomic and political structures. We have no interest in proposing an adaptation or reformation of the models of capitalist class society.'[26]
Bi-racialism (B)	'Citation of the bush captains is important. As a rule they were mulattoes, that is, light-skinned Blacks assimilated by the white ruling class and pitted against their African brothers and sisters. We must not allow ourselves today to be divided into a categories of "Black" and "mulattoes", weakening our fundamental identity as Afro-Brazilians, Afro-Americans of all the continent, that is, Africans in the Diaspora.'[27]
Oppressed majority (C)	'Along with the briefly enslaved and then progressively exterminated Indians, the African was the first and only worker, throughout three and a half centuries, who built the structures of this country called Brazil. I think it dispensable to evoke once more the vast lands Africans sowed with their sweat, or to remember again the cane fields, cotton fields, coffee fields, gold, diamond and silver mines, and the many other phases or elements in the formation of Brazil, nourished with the martyred blood of slaves. The Black, far from being an upstart or a stranger, is the very body and soul of this country. Yet despite this undeniable historical fact, Africans and their descendants were never treated as equals by the minority white segments that complement the national demographic tableau, nor are they today. This minority has maintained an exclusive grip on all power, welfare, health, education and national income.'[28]

26 Nascimento (1980), p. 160.
27 *Ibid.*, p. 156.
28 *Ibid.*, p. 149.

Table 11.1 continued

Exclusion, terror (D)	'The contemporary condition of Black people has not changed since then, except for the worse. At the margins of employment or left in situations of semi-employment and underemployment, Black people remain largely excluded from the economy. Residential segregation is imposed on the Black community by the double factor of race and poverty, marking off, as Black living areas, ghettoes of various denominations: *favelas, alagados, porões, mocambos, invasões, conjuntos populares or "residenciais"*. Permanent police brutality and arbitrary arrests motivated by race contribute to the reign of terror under which Blacks live daily, In such conditions, one comprehends why no conscious Black person has the slightest hope that a progressive change can occur spontaneously in white society to the benefit of the Afro-Brazilian community.'[29]
Black civil rights (E)	'Almost 500 years of *Authoritarianism* is enough. We cannot, must not and will not tolerate it anymore. One of the basic practices of this authoritarianism is the brutal contempt of the police for the Black family. Every kind of arbitrariness is fixed indelibly in the routine police raids conducted to keep the Afro-Brazilian community terrorised and demoralised. With these raids, beatings, murders and torture the impotence and "inferiority" of Black people is confirmed to them daily, since they are incapable of defending themselves or of protecting their family and members of the community. This constitutes a situation of perpetual humiliation.'[30]
Anti-imperialism (F)	'In this passage the authors [of a Manifesto] touch upon an important point in the Quilombist tradition — the nationalist character of the movement. Nationalism here must not be translated as xenophobia. Quilombismo being an anti-imperialist struggle, it articulates itself with Pan-Africanism and sustains a radical solidarity with all peoples of the world who struggle against exploitation, oppression and poverty, as well as inequalities motivated by race, colour, religion or ideology. Black nationalism is universalist and internationalist in itself, in that it sees the national liberation of all peoples respecting their unique culture and political integrity, as an imperative for world liberation. Faceless uniformity in the name of a 'unity' or 'solidarity' conditioned upon conformity to the dictates of any Western social model is not in the interests of oppressed non-Western peoples. Quilombismo, as a nationalist movement, teaches us that every people's struggle for liberation must be rooted in their own cultural identity and historical experience.'[31]

29   *Ibid.*, pp. 149–50
30   *Ibid.*, p. 162.
31   *Ibid.*, p. 155.

CHAPTER 12

Education Reform in Brazil under Democracy

Anthony Hall

Introduction

Education has long been viewed as a key factor in the pursuit of both democracy and development. A century ago, US philosopher John Dewey (1953) argued that progressive education is a vital component of successful democracy, promoting independent thinking and cooperation. Based on analyses of the assumed historical links between education and industrialisation in the West, post-war economists prescribed formal education expansion in the developing world to supply the missing human capital necessary for sustained growth.[1] Sociologists of the functionalist school also supported educational expansion as a vehicle for transmitting values considered essential for a modern society such as competition, personal achievement and consensus, while reinforcing the system of social stratification as a role allocator.[2] In addition to these economic, political and sociological arguments in support of formal education provision, demand has also been fuelled by demographic growth, rapid urbanisation in the developing world and by social pressures. The high financial returns to schooling, especially at higher levels, have heightened personal aspirations and portrayed the acquisition of formal instruction as the prime means of escaping poverty and gaining modern sector employment.[3]

The post-war period has thus seen various intellectual and more pragmatic forces combining to pressure policy-makers and planners to expand formal education provision in the South. Indeed, the system in Brazil did expand rapidly during this period. From 1950–60, primary education enrolments in Brazil grew by 71 per cent, and by a further 66 per cent from 1960–70.[4] In 1965, compared to most developing countries, Brazil's primary schooling system was considered superior due to its relatively high enrolment rates, especially for girls. Yet, by 1970 just 67 per cent of children aged 7–14 entered primary school in Brazil (Figure 12.1). During the same period, expansion of higher education was proportionately far greater, although secondary schooling lagged behind, with a 16 per cent

1   Schultz (1961); Becker (1964).
2   Parsons (1951); Davis and Moore (1967).
3   Psacharopoulos and Woodhall (1985); Todaro (2000).
4   Graham (1972), p. 281.

enrolment rate in 1965, rising to 39 per cent by 1987. Driven by human capital theory and rising middle-class expectations, university enrolments in Brazil grew by 230 per cent from 1958–68, and by 80 per cent in just three years from 1965–68 in the immediate aftermath of the military coup.[5] Government spending on education rose from 2.4 per cent of GDP in 1960 to 3.8 per cent by 1970. At the same time, an increasing flow of overseas funding for education was directed at supporting university expansion.[6]

Figure 12.1: Primary Education in Brazil: Gross and Net Enrolment Levels, 1970–2000

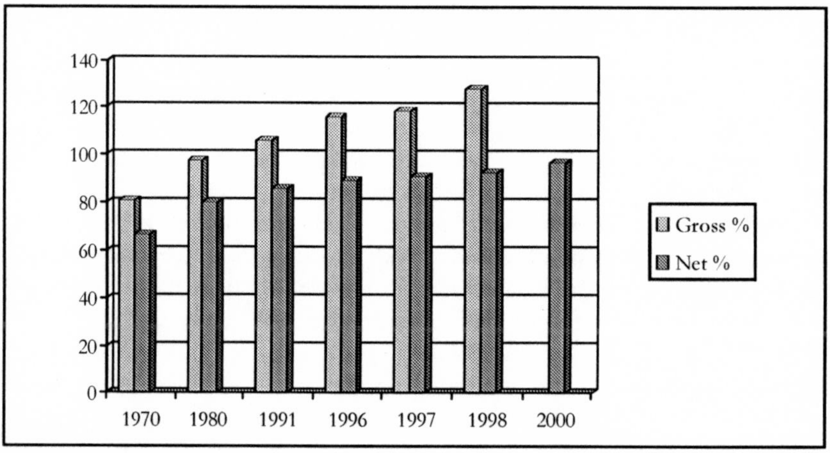

Source: Brazil (2000a), p. 53.

By the 1980s, linear growth of enrolments had continued and seemed impressive enough on the surface (Figure 12.2). However, such indicators hid a number of serious problems in terms of education quality and performance. Two education reform laws had been passed (Law 5540–1968 and Law 5692–1971) under the military regime, but these failed to improve the education system, which continued to be starved of resources and heavily biased in favour of the tertiary sector, driven largely by urban, middle-class demand. Reforms under the post-military 'New Republic' to improve access to, and quality of, basic education fared little better. Funding was distributed spasmodically and unsystematically and often bore little relation to educational need. The funding system based on ICMS tax and revenue sharing with municipalities and states was unequal

5   *Ibid.*, pp. 281–6.
6   *Ibid.*, p. 289.

and biased against primary education. Clientelism and party politics predominated in funding allocations, leaving unmet those constitutional obligations that had been set in 1988.[7]

Figure 12.2: Expansion of Enrolments in Brazil, 1960–98 (000s)

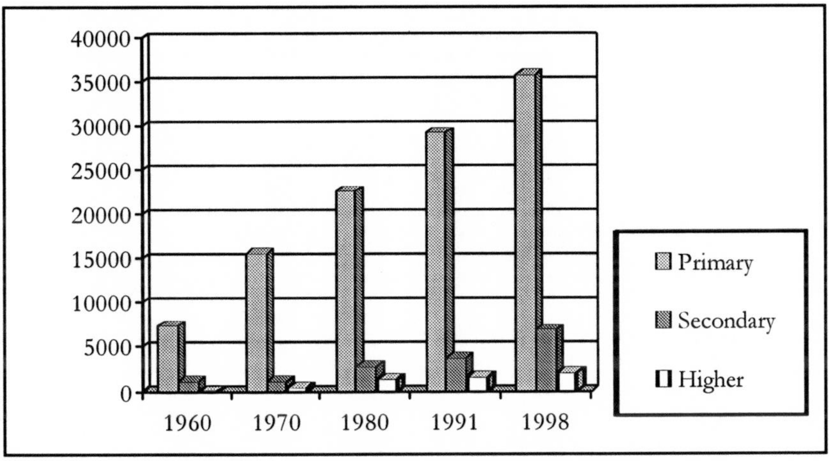

Source: Graham (1972), p. 281; Velloso and Albuquerque (1999, p. 50.

Over the period covering the end of military rule and the first decade or so of democratic Brazil to the mid-1990s, education indicators improved somewhat, but very slowly, while fundamental shortcomings continued to be apparent. By 1992, only 26 per cent of adults had completed their primary education, while just 14 per cent had been through secondary school, rising by 1996 to 30 per cent and 17 per cent, respectively. In 1992, 17 per cent of the population over 15 years of age was classed as illiterate and 37 per cent as functionally illiterate (that is, with less than four years of schooling). Poorer regions had notably higher indices, reaching levels of 50 per cent illiteracy and 78 per cent functional illiteracy in the rural north-east.[8] Not unsurprisingly, the north and north-east have also experienced the lowest average period of schooling per capita, standing at 5.8 and 4.4 years respectively in 1996, compared with 6.3 and 6.6 years in the south and south-east of the country.[9]

7   Jaguaribe et al. (1989); Araujo e Oliveira (1999).
8   IBGE (2001).
9   Guimarães de Castro (1998).

Figure 12.3: Completion, Repetition and Absentee Rates at Primary Level (per cent), 1981–2010

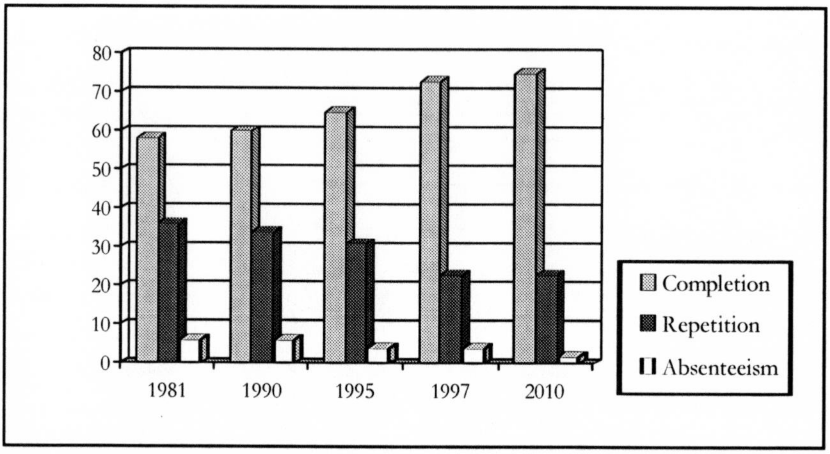

Source: Guimarães de Castro (1998).

In 1981 (see Figure 12.3), grade repetition rates stood at 36 per cent for primary school, dropping by only five points over the following fifteen years. Consequently, the average age-grade gap at primary level was high in 1982 at 76 per cent, falling to 47 per cent by 1996, although it remains significantly higher in the final years of the seven-year primary cycle. The latest census figures show that in 1999, at the end of the primary cycle at 14 years of age, some 73 per cent of pupils were behind in their studies and had to repeat years, the figure having fallen from 82 per cent in 1992.[10] Once again, strong regional disparities have been evident, with much higher mean grade-gap indices in 1996 in the north (62 per cent) and north-east (66 per cent) compared with the relatively prosperous south (27 per cent). The gap at age 14 for some north-eastern states is well over 90 per cent.[11] Not only does grade repetition slow down children's school progress and undermine their self-esteem, but it also increases costs by an estimated 30 per cent.[12] Standing at 30 per cent, Brazil's level of functional illiteracy remains one of the highest in Latin America. Once again, the north-east has more than double the proportion of functionally illiterate at 46 per cent compared with the south and south-east at around 22 per cent.[13]

10   IBGE (2001).
11   *Ibid.*
12   Guimarães de Castro (1998); Gomes Neto and Hanushek (1996).
13   IBGE (2001).

In 1997 over half (54 per cent) of primary school teachers in Brazil had no further education qualification beyond secondary level. Some 17 per cent progressed no further than primary level (one-half of this number failing to complete), with one-third of rural teachers falling into this category. Once more, regional differences are apparent, with higher proportions of such poorly qualified teachers in the north (28 per cent) and north-east (21 per cent) compared with just four per cent in the south.[14] By the early 1990s, Brazil had one of the worst education performances in Latin America. Only Haiti had a lower primary school completion rate, while Brazil was last in terms of the proportion of children completing primary school without repetition.[15]

The education picture in Brazil by the early 1990s was therefore mixed but still rather bleak. In the early 1960s Brazil's system of basic education matched or surpassed that of countries in a similar income bracket, yet by 1990 quality was poor and uneven. In the early 1960s Brazil's primary school completion rate stood at 60 per cent but by 1980 it had fallen to 19 per cent. These figures improved during the 1980s, but by 1992 the average period of formal education for the economically active population remained embarrassingly low at 4.9 years, the poorest performance among the larger and more powerful nations in Latin America.[16] At that time, Brazil was ranked as the most inefficient at the primary level, taking an average of eight years to put children through five years of basic education. Brazil's poor education performance under democracy until the early 1990s was attributed to several major factors.[17] These included: (i) concentration of wealth amongst an elite reluctant to pay the taxes that would be used to finance education for the poor; (ii) an inward-looking development strategy that generated little demand for educated labour; (iii) the clientelistic nature of education administration which discouraged managerial efficiency; and (iv) a decline in education spending per child as the population grew. Pressures thus mounted both within Brazil and within the wider global policy-making scenario for fundamental changes in education policy, coinciding with the new reform-minded administration of President Fernando Henrique Cardoso from 1995.

Education Reform in the 1990s

Given the continuing poor education indicators in Brazil, there was a growing perception amongst specialists and policy-makers that major changes in the system were urgently needed. A group of prominent intel-

14　Guimarães de Castro (1998); Brazil (2000a).
15　Brazil (1997).
16　IBGE (2001).
17　Birdsall and Sabot (1996).

lectuals had dramatically expressed this sentiment in a major publication entitled, 'Brazil: Reform or Chaos'.[18] Significantly, this was given as a categorical statement or challenge rather than as a question. A major international symposium held in 1991 in Rio de Janeiro, drawing together national and international experts, highlighted Brazil's education crisis and lamented the 'Opportunity Foregone' in terms of the lost potential for harnessing education to stimulate development.[19]

In addition to domestic concerns, there was a mounting global consensus that universal improvements were necessary in both the quantity and quality of educational provision. Since the 1960s, UNESCO had been advocating universal primary education (UPE) as a goal for developing countries by 1980, and by 1970 in Latin America. Disappointing progress in achieving these targets led to the landmark *World Conference on Education for All*, staged in Jomtien, Thailand, in 1990, which called for universal access to basic education as a fundamental human right in the battle against poverty. At a follow-up conference in 1996, the aim of reaching UPE by 2015 was set, one of several current international development targets.

This principle was underlined at the follow-up to Jomtien, the *World Education Forum*, held in Dakar, Senegal in April 2000. The Dakar 'Framework for Action' defined education not just as a fundamental human right but also as 'the key to sustainable development and peace'.[20] The 1990 *Convention on the Rights of the Child* (Articles 28 and 29), ratified by almost all nations, declared the obligation of governments to provide free and compulsory primary education. This emerging, rights-based view was reinforced in 1995 at the *World Summit for Social Development* in Copenhagen and the *Fourth World Conference on Women* in Beijing. In its annual report, UNICEF re-emphasised these principles, declaring that 'ensuring the right of education is a matter of morality, justice and economic sense'.[21]

Underpinning these declarations was a wealth of research that demonstrated the undisputed economic and social value of investing in education, especially at the basic and primary levels and for girls in particular. Human capital theory has demonstrated that investment in education brings about productivity gains, whether in industry or in agriculture, inducing higher financial returns to individuals and improved rates of economic growth.[22] Social rates of return, on the other hand, are greatest at the primary level, where educational expenditure may, especially when combined with other interventions, help to reduce poverty and

---

18   Jaguaribe et al. (1989).
19   Birdsall and Sabot (1996).
20   UNESCO (2000).
21   UNICEF (1999), p. 7.
22   Becker (1964); Schultz (1961); Haddad et al. (1990).

improve human development indicators. These include strengthened liveli-hoods, greater control over fertility, better nutrition, and lower rates of maternal and child mortality.[23]

As well as drawing attention to the potential development benefits that may accrue from educational investment, a growing body of literature sup-ports the view that many of the problems affecting education performance can be mitigated through reforms of existing funding and management sys-tems. Based on careful evaluations of education administration in a range of developing countries, it has been concluded that such systems are frequent-ly over-centralised, undemocratic and wasteful of valuable resources, both human and financial. Policies of decentralised management, local participa-tion and demand-side funding were advocated in response.[24] Education is now portrayed not just as inherently good for development and the strength-ening of basic human rights, but education reforms would allow policy-mak-ers to radically improve performance in this sector.

In Brazil, this message did not fall on deaf ears. Committed and powerful individuals pushed hard for change. President Fernando Henrique Cardoso, who took office in 1995, has undoubtedly been a strong advocate of educa-tion reform as a top government priority, especially at the primary level. Senator Darcy Ribeiro, the renowned anthropologist, was instrumental in pushing Brazil's landmark 1996 legislation through Congress, just a year before his death. Minister of Education Paulo Renato Souza and his advisers have been heavily engaged in leading the process of education reforms. As in other Latin American countries during the 1990s, social reforms have thus been engineered from the top in the pursuit of greater efficiency, accounta-bility and quality, rather than through popular pressures.[25]

In order to raise primary education standards in Brazil, the government introduced a package of measures in December 1996 through the new National Education Law 9349 (Lei de Diretrizes e Bases da Educação Nacional -LDB), also known as the *Lei Darcy Ribeiro*. This consolidated in a single piece of legislation a broad range of reforms at all levels of the educa-tion system. At the same time, a Constitutional Amendment (14/96), regulat-ed by Law 9424, established the Fund for the Maintenance and Development of Primary Education and Valorisation of Teachers (Fundo de Manutenção e Desenvolvimento do Ensino Fundamental e de Valorização do Magistério–FUNDEF). Under these laws, both municipal and state Secretariats of Education have been obliged to reorganise and streamline their education systems with a view to promoting greater efficiency and efficacy.

23   World Bank (1990); Bown (1990); Summers (1994); Todaro (2000); DFID (2000).
24   World Bank (1986); Fuller and Habte (1992); Patrinos and Araisingam (1997).
25   Grindle (2001).

The municipalisation of primary education was one of the main accomplishments of these reforms. The FUNDEF earmarks 60 per cent of selected state and local tax revenues allocated to education (which themselves comprise 25 per cent of the total) specifically for primary education. In other words, 15 per cent of total tax receipts would be allocated to the primary sector. Of this money, 60 per cent is earmarked for paying teachers and 40 per cent to cover other costs such as school infrastructure. Crucially, these funds are distributed in proportion to enrolments (the 'money follows the pupil' principle). The Ministry of Education provides supplementary funding where necessary to guarantee a minimum level of spending per pupil, which is adjusted annually by the federal government. Severe criminal penalties are laid down for abuse of the FUNDEF.

Under the new decentralised system, municipal secretaries of education have acquired much a much wider role than ever before and (in theory at least) exercise greater control over, and responsibility for, primary education development. The secretaries' new responsibilities start with the task of maximising primary enrolments, perhaps the easiest job given the new and direct financial incentive to recruit pupils. However, their role extends far beyond maximising educational expansion in terms of the quantity of primary school pupils catered for. It also embraces the whole issue of improving the quality of provision and management of the system. This involves taking charge of overall planning and policy-making as well as providing pedagogical and administrative-financial support. Secretaries are now expected to have technical skills in these areas rather than being merely political appointments with little or no regard for professional capacity.

Thus, municipal secretaries of education are now responsible for overall educational planning at local level. Under the LDB law, the municipality is responsible for the authorisation, licensing and supervision of both public and private primary schools. A Municipal Education System (Sistema Municipal de Educação — SME) and a Municipal Education Plan (Plano Municipal de Educação — PME) have eventually to be put in place. The latter must be consistent and integrated with state and national education plans. A Municipal Education Council (Conselho Municipal de Educação — CME) must also be established to allow the participation of local stakeholders, including municipal officials, school directors and the community. Municipal and state education systems would be integrated through the proposed Regional Education Councils (Conselhos Regionais de Educação).

Under the LDB, municipalities are also responsible for pedagogical development as a means of enhancing the quality and management of primary education. Support must be provided to the newly established School Councils (Conselhos Escolares), for the preparation by each school of a School Development Plan (Plano de Desenvolvimento da Escola — PDE) and for the incorporation of primary education within the national school evaluation system. The PDE should be consistent with the municipal plan (PME) and with local as well as national curriculum guidelines. These arrangements should take into account the need to adapt school organisation and curriculum content to local circumstances. School councils, comprising representatives of teachers, parents and municipal officials, are responsible for developing and implementing the PDE.

Another aspect of pedagogical development concerns teacher training. In view of the poor levels of primary school teacher education, the LDB establishes goals and guidelines for the acquisition of minimum standards and qualifications. Under their local education plans (PME), municipalities are required to establish career development plans (*planos de carreira*) for all teachers and to provide access to tertiary level, in-service teacher training courses. Training is to be provided for both professional teachers and lay teachers (*professores leigos*), the latter forming the majority in many instances. Teachers' salaries would be significantly increased in line with their new qualifications. Teachers and school directors are to be recruited through a competitive process (*concurso público*) involving public exams and selection boards, rather than being the mere political appointees of mayors.

In addition to planning the primary education network and pedagogical development, under the LDB municipal secretaries are responsible for administering educational funding allocated through the FUNDEF. As noted above, this comprises municipal and state revenues as well as supplementary federal funding (four per cent of the overall total) where such revenues are inadequate to meet the per capita minimum funding level per pupil stipulated under Law 9.424/96. This is a significant new role for municipal secretaries since the new funding mechanism has resulted in a substantial increase in funding for primary schools overall. The municipal education network, which has the major responsibility for primary schooling, has seen its share of the FUNDEF increase overall from 38 per cent in 1998 to 43 per cent in 1999 and 44 per cent in 2000. During the year 2000, funding per pupil in the north-east reached R$350 (about £110), more than double what it would have been without FUNDEF. In the north, it rose by 47 per cent. The poorest areas of the country have therefore benefited most from the restructuring of primary education funding. Increases in the wealthier south (8.5 per cent) and south-east (8.7 per cent) were significant but far more modest.[26]

Under the Constitutional Amendment (14/96) which set up FUNDEF, municipal secretaries of education have a legal responsibility to make sure that the primary education budget is properly spent, with 60 per cent going to pay for teachers' salaries and 40 per cent to cover other approved educational costs. Within the municipal system of financial planning, the sec-

26   Brazil (2000c, 2000d).

retary is responsible for managing primary education spending and accounting for expenditures under a range of budget headings, calling for new managerial and accounting skills. Each municipality is also obliged by law to set up a FUNDEF council (Conselho de Acompanhamento e Controle Social do FUNDEF). This comprises representatives of teachers, local citizens and municipal officials whose duty it is to monitor and control primary education spending and report regularly to the local municipal elected body. According to a recent MEC/FIPE study, 98 per cent of Brazil's municipalities have now set up such a council, although how many are actually operational is unspecified.[27] FUNDEF accounts are subject to scrutiny by municipal, state and federal finance authorities (*tribunais de contas*). Municipal Secretaries of Education and FUNDEF councillors have thus acquired onerous responsibilities and are subject to strict penalties under the law if found guilty of failing to perform their duties. They can be barred from public office or suffer criminal prosecution.

One of the problems with FUNDEF funding has been that it was designed to cover just the two cycles of primary or 'fundamental' education (years 1-4 and 5-8), excluding preschool, adult and secondary education. Under the new administration of President Luis Ignácio Lula da Silva, there are plans to replace this mechanism with a new 'Fund for the Development of Basic Education' (Fundo de Desenvolvimento da Educaçao Básica (FUNDEB). The proposed FUNDEB would increase government funding for education from 18 to 20 per cent of total (not just selected) tax revenues. It would also establish mechanisms for ensuring a fairer distribution of local and federal revenues for all sectors of basic education. Not only would this stimulate enrolments more evenly across all sub-sectors; teachers' salaries could be more evenly and fairly set. Underlining this commitment, the Ministry of Education announced in January 2003 that funding per primary pupil under the existing FUNDEF would be increased by 6.7 per cent (to R$446 for years 1–4 and R$468 in years 5–8). Yet the Ministry admitted that this was inadequate and that further increases would be considered.[28]

During the reform process of the 1990s, the north-east has been a special focus of government and international attention in an attempt to improve its poor education performance. In 1993–94, the Ministry of Education took out loans with the World Bank totalling US$418 million to finance rural primary education in the nine states. With counterpart funding, the North-east Basic Education Project (NEBE) was budgeted at $747 million. However, inertia in the education system during the early 1990s meant that by 1995, just ten per cent had been spent, requiring special measures via the UNDP to accelerate the implementation process and

27   ESP (2000c).
28   ESP (2003).

coincide with the 1996 LDB reforms. These extra measures focused on monitoring school construction and refurbishment, training of municipal education officials, computerisation of education management information and implementation of a new model of child-friendly, rural primary school, the *escola ativa*, based on the Colombian *escuela nueva*.

Other education reforms include the introduction of a unified curriculum for the primary sector for children aged 7–14. Guideline parameters have been drawn up for basic subjects with adaptations to cater for rural and urban environments as well as for Brazil's Amerindian population.[29] An evaluation department for elementary education has also been set up within the Ministry of Education's research department (INEP). The 'Evaluation System for Basic Education' (Sistema de Avaliação do Ensino Básico — SAEB) was set up in 1990. Funded by the World Bank, it is assisted by UNDP and has implemented a national programme of educational performance assessment through bi-annual sample surveys across the country. SAEB is judged to have been reasonably successful in achieving this goal.[30] Another innovation at the primary level is the *bolsa-escola*, in which female heads of household are paid a fixed sum per month as long as their children attend school regularly. Pioneered in Brasilia by then governor Cristovam Buarque, the system is being adopted in Belo Horizonte, Rio de Janeiro and São Paulo and it is anticipated by the Ministry of Education that R$1.7 billion would be distributed in such grants during 2001.[31]

Education Reform Impacts: Initial Evidence

Given the long lead-in time for education reforms to have an impact, it is perhaps early days to make definitive judgements about the consequences of changes started in 1996 under the LDB reforms. However, one area that has seen marked progress is that of net primary school enrolments. This figure leapt from 91 per cent in 1996 to 95 per cent in 1999.[32] From 1995 to 1999, an extra 3.4 million pupils entered primary school (an increase of ten per cent), while two million new pupils joined secondary school (a 45 per cent increase). Increases at primary level were especially significant in the north (20 per cent) and north-east (23 per cent), the poorest regions of the country where many children had previously been excluded from the education system.[33]

Other statistics bear out the improving trends in Brazil's formal education provision.[34] Functional illiteracy fell from 37 per cent in 1992 to 29 per cent

29   Brazil (2000b).
30   Mello e Souza et al. (1998).
31   ESP (2001a).
32   Brazil (2000c).
33   Brazil (2000d).
34   IBGE (2001).

in 1999. Average length of schooling over the same period increased from 4.9 to 5.8 years, with females enjoying an extra year of formal education overall compared to their male counterparts. Average grade repetition by the end of the primary cycle had fallen by nine points from 82 per cent in 1992 to 73 per cent in 1999. However, even in the best-performing southern region of the country, over 56 per cent of primary school pupils are still behind in their studies (compared with 88 per cent in the north-east).

The marked expansion in primary enrolments was undoubtedly due to the direct financial incentive given to municipalities after 1996 to increase school intake. The FUNDEF set primary level funding proportionate to enrolments for the first time, with the federal government supplementing municipal income to ensure a basic minimum level of finance per pupil. Many poorer municipalities and regions with a low tax base that fared badly under the old system now benefited from this change in policy. Government resources allocated to primary education increased overall by 21 per cent from 1996–97.[35] With a primary enrolment rate (years 1–4) of 97 per cent in 2001, Brazil is fast approaching the attainment of UPE, a goal set in 1981.[36]

However, if quantitative targets have been reached, it is generally acknowledged that the quality of educational performance still leaves much to be desired, not just in Brazil but all over the developing world.[37] There has been a notable increase in school and class sizes since 1997, as well as the adoption of hot-seating practices, suggesting that teaching and management capacity are being stretched to the full.[38] There have also been widespread allegations of fraud in relation to the use of the FUNDEF which, in 2001 alone, distributed around R$19.5 billion (almost US$10 billion at the time) to states and municipalities. It has been alleged that some Brazilian municipalities have employed dubious tactics, including the use of 'ghost' pupils, in order to artificially inflate enrolment figures and maximise federal funding. The Ministry of Education has no legal duty to directly monitor expenditure under FUNDEF, which is the responsibility of the financial authorities (*tribunais de contas*) at federal, state and municipal levels as well as local FUNDEF Councils

There have been calls for a parliamentary enquiry into these allegations, on the grounds that up to 20 per cent of FUNDEF resources could be compromised, to the value of over R$3 billion.[39] The Education Sub-Commission of the Federal Chamber of Deputies detected FUNDEF-related fraud in 359 municipalities, including the purchase of luxury vehicles and non-existent books.[40] Other legal challenges have been mounted by munic-

35 Brazil (2000c).
36 *Correio Brasilense* (2001).
37 World Bank (1995).
38 Brazil (2000d).
39 ESP (2000a).
40 ESP (2000b).

ipalities that have lost out financially since 1998 with the introduction of pupil-based funding through FUNDEF and have seen their federal support cut due to the small size of their school population.

A note of caution is in order in relation to overall funding levels for basic education in Brazil. Much has been made of the guaranteed funding per pupil under the FUNDEF scheme that, despite the above-mentioned problems, has undoubtedly made more resources available to most municipalities for basic education. A wider question, however, concerns the continued high level of government subsidy for federal (public) universities, which primarily benefits urban middle class students, and the implications for basic education funding. About 13 per cent of Brazil's population aged 20–24 is enrolled in institutions of higher education, comparing unfavourably with its neighbours such as Argentina (39 per cent) and Chile (27 per cent). Furthermore, the level of spending on staffing per student is second only to the USA, and is double that of France, Spain and the UK. At the same time, Brazil spends far less per pupil than any of these countries on basic education. Higher education in Brazil accounts for less than two per cent of total enrolments but absorbs over 25 per cent of the public education budget.[41] Federal universities alone absorb 60 per cent of the federal education budget.

Public institutions of higher education in Brazil (federal, state and municipal) are highly elitist. Only 2.6 per cent of Brazil's poorest 40 per cent of the population have access to higher education, rising to 21 per cent for the wealthiest decile.[42] Some 40 per cent of tertiary enrolments are in the public sector, where fees are non-existent or very low. Federal universities charge only nominal fees. Yet around 44 per cent of federal university students come from the top ten per cent income bracket.[43] Poorer students, who are either obliged to work during the daytime, when federal institutions function, or cannot get through the public university selection system (*vestibular*) are, paradoxically, driven towards the far more expensive private tertiary system. As has been pointed out, private interests continue to successfully subvert the achievement of education policy goals.[44] One policy implication is that ways need to be found to encourage wealthier students to bear a greater share of the real costs of a public university education, reducing the heavy public subsidy, and thereby releasing funds to assist poorer undergraduates or to finance basic education.

However, some indicators of education progress during the late 1990s are encouraging. Primary school completion rose from 64 per cent in 1995 to almost 73 per cent in 1997, while repetition rates have continued to decline,

41   Guimarães de Castro (1998).
42   IBGE (2001).
43   Paul and Wolff (1996); Guimarães de Castro (1998).
44   Plank et al. (1996).

from 30 per cent to 23 per cent over the same period.[45] This has been due in large measure to the flexibility introduced under the 1996 reforms for schools to adopt automatic grade promotion within two basic elementary 'cycles' (years 1–4 and 5–8 respectively) as an alternative to traditional yearly repetition. This new practice now benefits 23 per cent of primary school children in Brazil, although it is concentrated in São Paulo and Minas Gerais states.[46]

However, in spite of its benefits, the system of automatic grade promotion has been severely criticised by some education specialists in Brazil as being designed to produce superficial improvements in education indicators while disguising continued poor teaching and learning standards. This allegation seems to be borne out by a Ministry of Education/SAEB evaluation of post-reform progress from 1997 to 1999. This concluded that the performance of primary school children in Portuguese and mathematics had fallen by up to eight per cent in many areas.[47]

One vehicle for improving primary education quality has been through the introduction in Brazil of a new model of rural primary school known as the *escola ativa*. In Latin America, this follows 20 years of experience with the Colombian *escuela nueva*.[48] These so-called 'child-friendly' schools have also been set up in Guatemala, the Philippines and Thailand.[49] Introduced into Brazil in 1997, there are presently about 200 such schools operating in 44 municipalities. The *escola ativa* differs from conventional primary schools in several respects. They are carefully located for easy access, have curricula deemed to be more appropriate to the learning needs of rural children and use locally adapted teaching materials. They also have multigrade classes, automatic grade promotion and employ teaching methods that are in theory centred on the learning needs of the individual child. In addition, they encourage interaction with the local community and with parents in school governance and associated activities.

Initial results with the *escola ativa* are encouraging and the new methods have had quite a positive impact, improving pupil participation and continuation rates. In other countries, similar child-friendly programmes have encouraged girls in particular to attend school.[50] In Brazil, several nascent problems have been observed, which is only to be expected in such experiments.[51] Teachers require specialist training in the new ethos and pedagogy, which is not always provided. Inadequate attention has been given to systematically monitoring and evaluating the new system so that it may be

45   Brazil (2000c).
46   Brazil (2000d).
47   *Ibid.*
48   Schiefelbein (1992).
49   UNICEF (2000).
50   *Ibid.*
51   Hall (2001).

adjusted accordingly. Materials, books and equipment are often late in arriving or not provided at all, while state legislatures have been slow to ratify legal support for schools in policies of automatic grade promotion authorised under the LDB.

One of the major impediments to improving school quality is the chronic lack of qualified teachers, especially in poorer regions of Brazil. The new legislation requires municipal authorities to provide training for professional and lay teachers and to establish career development plans with fixed salary scales. In addition, school directors and teachers should be recruited through open public competition rather than being nominated. There are some signs of progress on this front. In 1996, 44 per cent of Brazil's primary teachers had some form of post-secondary qualification, rising to 47 per cent by 1999, a faster rate of increase than that witnessed in the early part of the decade. The number of unqualified teachers fell by a significant 41 per cent overall from 1994–99.[52] Regional differences are still pronounced, however, with the north and north-east still retaining far higher proportions of teachers with minimal or no formal qualifications.

Yet there are efforts underway to tackle this problem through the provision of financial incentives for teachers to undergo training as part of a formal career development plan.[53] The FUNDEF came into operation on 1 January 1998, earmarking 60 per cent of its resources for teachers' salaries in the public sector. Recent studies show that the average pay rise for primary school teachers from 1997–2000 as a direct result of the new policy has been around 33 per cent, from an average of R$620 (US$310 at the time) to R$826 (US$413) per month.[54] Furthermore, teachers' salaries in the north and north-east, traditionally the lowest, grew by 35 per cent and 70 per cent respectively over the same period. Since 1996, national curriculum guidelines have also been introduced for pre-school and primary schooling, for indigenous and adult education.[55] Policy-makers are therefore hopeful that salary increases and provision of teacher training, together with new curriculum guidelines and provision of textbooks, will gradually produce an improvement in the quality of education delivered within the enlarged primary sector of the public education system.

In addition to improving the quantity and quality of educational provision, another major area of concern after the 1996 reforms has been to strengthen management of the newly decentralised primary education system. As already mentioned, municipal secretaries of education (as in other sectors) have traditionally been almost exclusively political appointments.

52   Brazil (2000c).
53   Brazil (2000e).
54   Brazil (2000d).
55   Brazil (2000b).

The possession of technical capacity in education management, where it existed, was a question of fortunate coincidence rather than a precondition for holding office. A nationwide survey supported by UNESCO revealed that in Brazil as a whole in 1999, some 84 per cent of municipal education secretaries and 70 per cent of school heads were political appointees. In the northern and north-east states of Brazil, these figures were higher still, approaching 100 per cent in many cases.[56] Clearly, political criteria in recruitment will continue to dominate for the foreseeable future, but efforts are being made to make appointments procedures more transparent and democratic through the greater use of open job competition.

At the same time, it is recognised that municipal education secretaries must be equipped with essential managerial skills in order to enable them to perform their enhanced roles in a more effective and professional manner. In an effort to bring this about, a training programme for municipal education officials (PRASEM) has been underway since 1998. Funded through the World Bank, with technical support from UNDP and UNICEF, this programme is run by a special unit within the Ministry of Education (Fundescola). It is designed to strengthen education management capacity at municipal level by providing education secretaries, other municipal officials and FUNDEF council members with the knowledge and skills required for performing their post-reform roles more effectively. Under the above-mentioned North-east Basic Education Project during 1997–98, over 3,000 municipal education officials and a further 1800 FUNDEF council members were trained in a series of 36 four-day sessions staged over the region.[57] Participants are also given comprehensive documentation on the new legislation and official duties. PRASEM has since been extended to the centre-west, major urban centres in the north-east and southern Brazil.[58]

Such a high profile and relatively expensive scheme as PRASEM is laudable and to be welcomed as a valuable innovation. However, its success in strengthening municipal education management will only become apparent over time when the longer-term impacts can be gauged. Its effectiveness in transferring managerial skills on a permanent basis to municipal education officials is likely to be compromised by several factors.[59] The quality of training procedures and materials is generally excellent, although the sheer intensity of the process, concentrated into just four days, may reduce its effectiveness. In this sense, expectations may be over-ambitious regarding the ability of poorly educated and often inexperienced municipal staff to absorb large quantities of complex legislative and financial information.

56   Waiselfitz (2000).
57   World Bank (2000).
58   Fundescola (2000).
59   Hall (2001).

Further contextual problems may also seriously reduce the potential benefits from training. First, mayors will in most cases continue to call the shots over local education matters, despite formal appearances to the contrary. Political expediency may thus override educational priorities, such as enhancing school quality, for example. Second, without a cheaper and more sustainable system of follow-up training, many of the initial gains from PRASEM will be either lost altogether or seriously diluted over time. This is especially so given the political instability at municipal level, the regular turnover of technical staff and the deep-seated rivalries that seriously undermine continuity in educational activities. Creating an institutional memory thus remains a major challenge to policy-makers and education practitioners.

Conclusion

Education performance in democratic Brazil has become an increasingly sensitive political issue. Steady improvements have been achieved in basic education indicators, especially in primary enrolments and completion rates through the 1990s. In the run-up to Brazil's 2002 presidential elections, this encouraged a heady optimism in some official quarters about the potential of education to stimulate economic and social development. For example, the minister of education, Paulo Reenato Souza, declared in unequivocal terms that greater access to education would help to reduce income concentration in Brazil. Accordingly, the country was 'constructing a more just society, because we have invested in basic education'.[60] The new administration of President Luis Ignácio Lula da Silva has been even more vociferous in its commitment to investment in education as a key to development and a basic human right. Such a position is conceptually underpinned both by moral obligations and by the assumed link between improved access to formal education, the generation of skilled human capital, the consequent stimulus to economic growth and employment and expected decrease in income inequalities. The question of income distribution is not just a moral or an academic issue. Research shows that poverty levels are especially sensitive to changes in the degree of income inequality, rather than merely to overall economic growth *per se*. It is therefore crucial for policy-makers to consider how educational reform and expansion may best be harnessed to stimulate a more egalitarian pattern of economic growth and poverty reduction.

However, there is no evidence to support the view that wider access to schooling has reduced income disparities in Brazil. There has indeed been an expansion in education access during the 1990s benefiting all social classes to some extent, as detailed above. What is perhaps surprising, how-

60   ESP (2001b).

ever, is how stubbornly social inequities persist in spite of such growth in the education sector. The latest census figures clearly reveal that this rise in enrolments has not been accompanied by a reduction in economic inequality. During the 1990s, real income levels for all classes in Brazil rose by 30–40 per cent. However, differentials have remained constant. In 1999, the poorest 50 per cent earned 14 per cent of total income, while the richest one per cent took home 13 per cent. Neither of these figures has changed since the beginning of the decade.[61]

These statistics are revealing, for they challenge the convenient assumption made by many politicians and policy-makers that there is an automatic link between education expansion and more egalitarian development. Research evidence from Brazil suggests that economic growth does not necessarily generate upward social mobility for the educated.[62] Education provision cannot in itself generate employment or help to reduce inequality without concomitant reforms in economic sectors. Without access to basic factors of production and the creation of paths to wealth generation through industrial and commercial investment, as well as improved access to agricultural land and credit, education will have little direct productive impact.

Members of Brazil's 'Movement of the Landless' (MST) are only too aware of this fact. They have placed strong emphasis on access to basic education as an integral part of their livelihoods strategies and struggle for land. By 2001, there were 1,200 schools in MST settlements with some 150,000 children enrolled, employing 3,800 teachers.[63] The record of some East Asian countries that adopted 'shared growth' strategies also illustrates the principle that education reform must proceed hand-in-hand with economic progress. Land reform and dynamic rural development combined with an export-oriented trade strategy have generated demand for skilled and semi-skilled labour, thus stimulating the demand for education. At the same time, in countries such as South Korea, more public resources have been made available to education while birth rates have fallen rapidly, thus increasing available funding per pupil. In addition, spending on basic education has increased substantially as a conscious policy option, an investment in future growth. At the same time, higher education spending has been held in check in view of the declining social returns and educated unemployment which characterise countries with an inflated tertiary sector.[64]

Yet even if education is no automatic key to development, very poor levels of schooling are bound to act as a barrier to economic growth and social progress. In this sense, stimulating the supply of, and demand for, high quality basic education will surely contribute positively towards productivity

61   IBGE (2001).
62   Adelman et al. (1996).
63   Branford and Rocha (2002), chapter six.
64   Birdsall and Sabot (1996).

and growth, and perhaps even to lower levels of income inequality in the longer-term. Research on the impact of education expansion in Brazil on output suggests that there is a potentially positive link, especially when educational resources are distributed in a more egalitarian fashion.[65]

Since the 1996 reforms, democratic Brazil had taken significant strides to address these fundamental issues by expanding access to primary schooling, improving the quality of learning and teaching, guaranteeing minimum levels of spending per pupil for basic education while streamlining management at municipal and state levels. Only time will tell just how effective these reforms will prove to be in enhancing opportunities for the majority of Brazil's children. Yet, ultimately, the greater democratisation of Brazil's education system itself will depend to a large extent on the willingness and capacity of government to challenge those entrenched elite and middle-class interests that currently benefit unduly from the present set-up, especially at the tertiary level. More resources and continuous political support for basic education will be necessary in the coming decades if hitherto deprived children are to enjoy the benefits of school and employment. If this does not happen, from an educational standpoint at least, democracy in Brazil may well prove to be something of an illusion.

---

65   Lau et al. (1996).

CHAPTER 13

Mass Media and Politics in Democratic Brazil

Mauro P. Porto*

Brazil's current democracy was inaugurated in 1985 when the first civilian president took office after 21 years of military dictatorship. One of the watershed moments was 15 January of that year, when the indirect electoral college that was created by the military to perpetuate their power chose a moderate member of the civil opposition, Tancredo Neves, as the new president. On that historic day, while the people celebrated in the streets at the end of the dictatorship, Tancredo went for lunch to celebrate his victory. For the occasion he did not gather the leaders of the political parties that were part of the Aliança Democrática (Democratic Alliance), the coalition of opposition leaders and dissidents of the military dictatorship that launched his candidacy. Tancredo commemorated his election at the mansion of Globo Organisations, the main media conglomerate of the country, which includes the dominant television network (TV Globo). With him were Roberto Marinho, the owner of this powerful media empire, and Antônio Carlos Magalhães, one of the military 'dissidents' participating in the coalition that elected Tancredo. According to several accounts, Marinho had a decisive influence in the formation of Tancredo's cabinet, especially in the appointment of Magalhães as the minister of communications.[1] The Brazilian media were, therefore, a key presence in the 'founding moments' of Brazilian democracy.

The dynamics of the Brazilian transition, and the struggles to define and consolidate the new democracy, have all been marked by the presence of a powerful cultural industry, particularly TV Globo. In Brazil, as in many other 'new democracies', modern electronic communication technologies were already in place when democracy emerged. This specific historical context raises some important questions that have been neglected by the academic literature on democratic transition and consolidation.[2]

*   I am grateful to Daniel Hallin, Afonso de Albuquerque and the participants of the Conference 'Fifteen Years of Democracy in Brazil' (Institute of Latin American Studies, London, 15–16 February 2001) for their critical comments.

1   Hertz (1987), pp. 13–70; Lima (1988), p. 115; Motter (1994), pp. 126–7; Conti (1999), pp. 162–3.

2   Because of its focus on intra-elite negotiations, research on democratic transitions tends to ignore how the political environment in general, and the media in particular, constrain political choice, influencing the kinds of change that occur (O'Neil, 1998, p. 7). The study of democracy and politics requires attention to social structure, including the media, a fact that has been too often overlooked in recent analysis of democratisation (Power and Roberts, 2000, p. 236).

What role have the mass media, particularly television, played in the establishment and development of the democratic politics and institutions in Brazil? Have they helped to strengthen or to weaken the new regime?

This chapter seeks to offer some answers to these important questions. As a starting point, I propose to scrutinise the media in all its complexity, avoiding simplistic analytical devices. To this end it is necessary to consider different factors when evaluating the influence of the media in political processes. For analytical purposes it is possible to conceive of the media's role according to the following approaches:

1. *Media as instruments*: the media as tools manipulated by different agents (owners, elites, dominant classes, the state, etc.) to promote particular political aims. Studies in this tradition frequently seem to suggest that conscious political decisions or some kind of conspiracy determine media behaviour.

2. *Media as creators of culture*: the media as institutions that contribute to reinforce and/or change particular ways of making sense of the world. Studies in this tradition call attention to the values, representations and interpretative frameworks that originate from, or are promoted by the media, that become part of the political culture.

3. *Media as autonomous organisations*: the media as independent institutions with their own values and norms. This approach tends to focus on media content production processes, stressing the level of professionalism and the active and autonomous role of journalists, scriptwriters and others in the production of media messages.

4. *Media as audience-dependent*: the media as businesses that, at least in commercial systems like Brazil's, depend on attracting the largest possible audience to sell them to advertisers. This would constrain the activities of media institutions, since a partisan attitude in politics could alienate consumers and undermine their credibility as institutions.

5. *Media as mirrors*: the media as institutions that simply reflect political reality, as neutral conductors of information. This approach is frequently presented in arguments about the norm of objectivity in journalism, and in those studies which argue that the media merely reflect the culture of the time.

This list is far from exhaustive. There are many other possible ways to conceive of the role of the media in the political process. The different approaches are also not mutually exclusive. Most studies consider a variety of factors and are not limited to a single framework. Nevertheless, these categories can be very useful in understanding the role of the media in democratic politics and in identifying limitations in research agendas and frameworks. For example, most studies on media and politics in Brazil tend to emphasise instrumental manipulations, even when they consider other aspects of the role of the media. The five categories also point to different assumptions about the ability of the media to shape public opinion and political processes. The views of the media as instruments and as creators of culture tend to emphasise stronger media effects, while the approach that sees the media as a mirror suggests that their effects are limited or non-existent. The other two approaches (media as audience-dependent and as autonomous organisations) tend to occupy an intermediary position.

In the framework outlined in this chapter it is suggested that although instrumental manipulations are important aspects of media's political role, mainly in countries like Brazil with a tradition of partisan and politically active media, we also need to recognise the complex ways in which they affect political processes. Particular emphasis is placed on the following hypothesis: *the more the process of democratisation advances in society, the more important become the approaches that go beyond instrumental views of the media.* According to this perspective, when the organisations of civil society become stronger and more diverse, and the process of democratisation advances, factors such as the role of audiences, media professionals and cultural frameworks originated from the media become more relevant.

On the other hand, it is not enough simply to suggest that the media act in complex ways, combining different functions. The analyst should specify when and how each aspect becomes relevant. This chapter attempts to accomplish this difficult task by linking the media to the different phases of Brazilian democracy. The text is organised as follows. First, I present the main features of the Brazilian media landscape, stressing in particular the central position of TV Globo. I then present the main features of the relationship between media and politics in three periods: the transition period of José Sarney's presidency (1985–89), the crisis period of Collor's ascension and fall (1990–92) and the subsequent era under Fernando Henrique Cardoso (1994–2000). Finally, I present some conclusions about the role that the mass media, especially TV Globo, have played in contemporary Brazilian democracy.

The Brazilian Media Landscape: The Centrality of TV Globo

The following analysis discusses the role of the mass media in general, but focuses on television, particularly on the role of TV Globo. This choice is due to the limited scope of this chapter, but is also a consequence of the centrality of television as a medium — and of TV Globo as a network — in Brazilian society. Television has a dominant position as a source of information and entertainment for Brazilians. National surveys conducted in 1989 and 1990 revealed that between 86 per cent and 89 per cent of those interviewed had television as their main source of information about politics.[3] The media in general, and television in particular, have also much higher levels of credibility among the mass public than do political institutions.[4]

Television is the most important medium in Brazil and TV Globo is the dominant network. It has an absolute majority of the national audience ratings, and its dominance increases during prime time.[5] It also absorbs most of the advertising spending on television, has the highest number of affiliated stations and full coverage of the national territory.[6] Besides dominating the television market, Globo Organisations is characterised by vertical and horizontal integration, with businesses activities in several areas, including newspapers, radio, a publishing house, a recording company, cable and satellite television, telecommunications, internet, among many other sectors.[7]

Outside television the media has a more limited influence. The total penetration of newspapers is only 42 copies sold for each 1,000 inhabitants, putting Brazil among those countries with the lowest newspaper penetration in the world, behind some of its South American neighbours.[8] But since the national elite closely monitors newspapers, they have an important agenda-setting function.[9] On the other hand, the weekly news-magazines, particularly *Veja*, have a broader readership when compared to newspapers and thus a greater potential to influence the formation of public opinion.[10] These specific features lead them to play a different political role in Brazil, when compared to *Time* and *Newsweek*, their counterparts in the United States. Unlike these publications, Brazilian magazines also compete with television and newspapers for 'hard news', frequently providing scoops and leading the political coverage.[11]

3   Lima (1998), p. 213.
4   Figueiredo (1998).
5   TV Globo has 58 per cent of the audience in prime time, between 8:00 p.m. and 9:59 p.m., while SBT comes in second, with 24 per cent (Relatório AIP/IBOPE September 1999). The programmes broadcast by TV *Globo* in prime time, the newscast *Jornal Nacional* and the telenovelas, are the main sources of information and entertainment for Brazilians.
6   TV Globo concentrates 49 per cent of the advertising investment on TV, while SBT comes in second with 20 per cent (Relatório Monitor/IBOPE, January–December 1999). It has 113 affiliated stations and covers 99.96 per cent of the dwellings with television sets, while SBT has 108 stations and covers 94.46 per cent of the dwellings ('SBT já tem 108 afiliadas, 5 a menos que a Globo,' *Folha de São Paulo*, 3 de janeiro de 2001).
7   Amaral and Guimarães (1994); Lima (1998); Brittos (2000).
8   The total circulation of the three main newspapers are: *Folha de São Paulo*, 472,000; *O Estado de São Paulo*, 367,000; and *O Globo*, 335,000 (World Association of Newspapers *World Press Trends*. Paris: FIEJ, 2000).
9   Kucinski (1998), pp. 24–6.
10   The total circulation of the three main weekly news-magazines is the following: *Veja*, 1,152,032; *Época*, 497,506; and *Isto É*, 381,256 (Instituto Verificador de Circulação – IVC).
11   José (1996), pp. 57–8.

I do not include radio in my analysis, since it has not developed a national character in Brazil and it is characterised by a fragmentation of formats and audiences.[12] Research with radio audiences suggests that it is the most important and popular source of musical entertainment, but that television and newspapers are preferred as news sources.[13] Nevertheless, radio does have an important political role in Brazil, mainly among the low-income population, as demonstrated by the increasing number of radio show hosts who become politicians and achieve success in electoral processes.[14]

The Media in the Democratic Transition and in the New Republic (1984–89)

The Media and the End of the Authoritarian Period

The final collapse of the military dictatorship began in 1984 when opposition parties and social movements united in the Diretas Já campaign to demand direct elections for president. The campaign gathered the largest demonstrating crowds in the history of the country, with approximately ten million people participating in rallies in a period of little more than three months.[15] At the beginning of the campaign, TV Globo's prime time newscast, *Jornal Nacional*, either did not provide nationwide coverage of the mass rallies or presented them in a distorted way. Only two weeks before Congress voted and rejected the proposed constitutional amendment that would have restored direct elections for the presidency TV Globo changed tack and provided its audience with broad national coverage.[16] The network was forced to change its coverage due to the pressure of a popular movement and even advertisers threatened to pull back their ads if the network insisted in ignoring the campaign.[17] This episode suggests that there are some limits to the instrumental use of the media by their owners. When society is organised and active, and when partisan coverage may result in loss of audience ratings and advertisers, the media may have no other alternative than to abandon their political alliances.

Despite the pressures, Congress rejected the proposed constitutional amendment that would have restored direct elections. The opposition forces then split themselves among those who still wanted to struggle for direct elections and those who wanted to defeat the regime in the electoral college. This second group, which included the main opposition party (PMDB), decided to form an alliance with the dissidents within the regime

---

12   Straubhaar (1996), pp. 223–4.
13   *Ibid.*, p. 223.
14   Esch (1997); Nunes (1998); Silva (2000).
15   Alves (1988), p. 51.
16   Ramos (1985); Lima (1988); Straubhaar (1989).
17   Conti (1999), p. 37.

(PFL) and launch its own candidate in the electoral college created by the military. This alliance launched the candidacies of Tancredo Neves for president and of José Sarney, one of the 'dissidents' of the dictatorship, for vice-president. TV Globo played a key role in mobilising support for the transfer of power via an indirect election, appropriating the symbols of the *Diretas Já* and linking them to Tancredo's candidacy.[18] Tancredo was elected president in the electoral college, but hours before taking office he fell ill. In a climate of institutional crisis, Sarney was sworn in as president on 15 March 1985, inaugurating the 'New Republic'. The country watched tensely as the health of the elected president deteriorated. After weeks of suspense, during which most of the media hid the seriousness of his illness, Tancredo died on 21 April. During all these traumatic episodes, TV Globo's news coverage was a major factor in legitimating the new regime. The network, which had been a strong ally of the military dictatorship, perceived the growing support for a new coalition and switched to support it, following its own interests and assuring its own legitimacy in the eyes of the public.[19]

Media and Clientelism in Sarney's Presidency

Sarney's presidency started the reforms that would define the institutional framework of the New Republic. One of the most important moments was the decision to give the Congress elected in 1986 the status of Constituent Assembly and the task of drafting a new constitution. Different forces in society, mainly those organised around the National Front for Democratic Communication Policies, hoped that the new constitution would bring democratic changes in communication infrastructure and policies, overcoming decades of authoritarian and monopolistic practices.[20] Nevertheless, the main political actors during Sarney's presidency were linked to the media, particularly to TV Globo, and would oppose all major attempts to democratise the communication system. The New Republic was an era of democratic changes and hopes, but it was also a period in which the legacy of the authoritarian past was not only maintained in some areas, but even strengthened. One example was the expansion of 'electronic colonelism' during Sarney's presidency.

In a classical study of the Brazilian political system, Victor Nunes Leal (1978) used the term *coronelismo* to designate the system of political compromise that characterised the relationship between the state and local bosses, or colonels. But if in the 1940s, when Leal wrote his seminal study, *coronelismo* was a rural phenomenon in a predominantly rural country, the consolidation of urbanisation and of the cultural industry in the 1970s

---

18   Alves (1988), p. 53.
19   Guimarães and Amaral (1988); Straubhaar (1989).
20   Motter (1994a).

originated a new kind of relationship between the state and local oligarchies. Political bosses began controlling the electorate not only through traditional coercive methods, but also by owning and using the local media, creating the new phenomenon of 'electronic coronelismo'.[21]

Since the first regulations on broadcasting in the early 1930s the law has given the prerogative of approving and distributing the concessions of broadcasting licences to the executive power. The result was a total lack of public control over the licensing process and its politically motivated use by federal governments. These clientelistic practices reached a new level during Sarney's presidency. During the Constituent Assembly Sarney pressured its members to approve two key measures. He mobilised resources and allies to keep presidentialism as the country's system of government, against the tendency of the assembly to favour a parliamentary system. He also lobbied Congress actively to approve the five-year limit for his term as president, opposing attempts to limit his presidency to four years. To achieve success in both cases Sarney and his minister of communication, Antônio Carlos Magalhães, extensively used broadcasting licences as political currency to buy support. Over the course of his presidency Sarney distributed 1,028 radio and TV licences, a historical record, 539 of them (52 per cent) in the last nine months of the Constituent Assembly. Of the 91 Congress members who received new licences, 92 per cent of them voted to keep presidentialism as the system of government and 90 per cent voted in favour of a five-year term limit for Sarney.[22]

The New Republic consolidated a new structure of political power, a system of 'electronic clientelism' based on state oligarchies and their local media empires.[23] Several of the major political actors of the Brazilian transition to democracy were active participants in this new power scheme, including Sarney himself. When he became president, Sarney was already in control of the media market of his home state, Maranhão, owning the most important newspaper, three radio stations and one TV station.

---

21   According to Motter (1994a, p. 120), the term was coined by political scientist Antônio Lavareda and first applied to investigate the links between the media and state oligarchies by Stadnik (1991). Motter has provided the most comprehensive analysis of the phenomenon during Sarney's presidency (1994a, 1994b) and new studies have shown that the phenomenon has persisted even in the 'modern' presidency of Cardoso (Costa and Brener, 1997). It should be noted, though, that the system of electronic colonelism is weaker in the main industrial and urban states, including São Paulo and Rio de Janeiro. In these states, newspapers, mainly the national ones, operate more independently, while local political groups do not exert strong control over the ownership of TV and radio stations.

22   Motter (1994a, 1994b).

23   As Hallin and Papathanassopoulos (2002) argue, the concept of clientelism is crucial in order to understand the media systems of Southern Europe (Greece, Italy, Spain and Portugal) and Latin America, including the Brazilian case.

During his term as president, Sarney distributed 16 new licences to his family members.[24] His minister of communication, Antônio Carlos Magalhães, also built a media empire in his home state, Bahia, in close alliance with Globo Organisations. As minister, Magalhães was accused of promoting the bankruptcy of Nec do Brasil, a subsidiary of the powerful Japanese multinational NEC Corporation. Magalhães played an active role in creating the conditions for the purchase of the company by Globo Organisations, which took place in December 1986. Apparently, as a reward for his support, a few weeks later the TV station owned by Magalhães (TV Bahia), received the right to broadcast TV Globo's programming. TV Globo broke an 18-year contract with TV Aratu, owned by an opponent of Magalhães, and sealed a new alliance with the federal government and the local oligarchy.[25]

In the new era of 'electronic clientelism', consolidated by the New Republic, the path to power in most states requires the control of the local media. An analysis of 21 states of the federation has shown that in 19 of them leading newspapers were linked in ownership with radio stations and with a television station. In 12 of them, the TV station was part of the TV Globo network.[26] As several studies have shown, these local media empires are usually controlled by the oligarchy that dominates the local politics.[27] The dominance of the political situation in most states can be achieved through two basic steps. First, it is necessary to obtain licences for radio and TV stations from the federal government, offering political support in exchange. The second step is to win the right to broadcast TV Globo's programming, since it is the dominant network. Although the new constitution included measures that restricted the politically motivated use of TV and radio licences, electronic colonelism continues to be a key feature of the Brazilian political system.[28]

---

24   Motter (1994a), p. 191; (1994b).
25   Hertz (1987), pp. 62–9; Motter (1994a, pp. 193–4; 1994b, pp. 108–9).
26   Amaral and Guimarães (1994), p. 32.
27   Stadnik (1991); Amaral and Guimarães (1994); Motter (1994a, 1994b); Costa and Brener (1997); Lima (1998).
28   The 1988 Constitution established, for example, that licences needed to be approved by Congress. This change was an important step towards restricting the political use of the licences by the executive power. Nevertheless, the constitution also established quorum and voting rules in order for Congress to reject licences authorised by the Executive, making it very difficult for the Parliament to reject them (Motter, 1994a, pp. 296–7). The changes also left out of Congress control the *repetidoras*, the relay stations that retransmit the broadcasting signals of the networks. This 'lapse' allowed presidents to continue using licences as political currency, as did Cardoso in his successful struggle to get Congress approval of his right to run for re-election (Costa and Brener, 1997).

The Media and Collor de Mello: Electing and Overthrowing a President (1989–1992)

Electing the President in the Age of Television

The first direct presidential election of the New Republic took place in 1989. The historical context of this important contest was very different from that of the previous presidential election, 29 years earlier. Besides higher levels of urbanisation and an immense growth of the electorate, a fundamental difference between the two elections was the emergence of a powerful and nationally-integrated cultural industry, dominated by television in general, and TV Globo in particular. These new audiovisual industries constructed a new 'electronic stage', replacing the direct contacts between the electorate and traditional political institutions by a political process mediated by the media.[29] A key aspect of the role of the media in democratic Brazil is the transformation of the ways campaigns are organised and conducted. These communication technologies have replaced several functions of traditional political institutions, such as political parties, strengthening the role of political consultants and marketing specialists.[30]

In a context of widespread dissatisfaction with the government, the front-runners of the presidential race in 1989 were all opponents of president Sarney. Early in the campaign the candidate of the leftist Workers Party (PT), Luis Inácio Lula da Silva (or simply Lula), enjoyed a strong lead in the polls. But an unknown politician, governor of the small state of Alagoas, Fernando Collor de Mello, would finally defeat Lula in the second round of the presidential election. This section considers the role played by the media in this important contest.

Collor's own political roots were linked to the media. Following the traditional pattern of the 'electronic colonelism', his family owned most of the media in the state of Alagoas. The clan was already in control of the main newspaper of the state when the big 'jump' came: the concession by TV Globo of the right to broadcast its programming.[31] After taking office as governor in 1986 Collor started a campaign for the moralisation of the public administration. He became known as the *maharajah hunter*, meaning an administrator who aims to get rid of public servants who are paid huge salaries and do not even go to work. He was also known for his strong opposition to president Sarney's policies.

Collor started to attract unusual levels of attention from the national media for a governor of a small and backward state. For some, these early appearances of the governor revealed an articulated plan or conspiracy of the media to elect Collor.[32] Nevertheless, these instrumental views about

---

29   Lima (1998), pp. 210–4; Rubim (1999), pp. 15–16.
30   Avelar (1992); Carvalho (1999); Figueiredo (2000).
31   Conti (1999), p. 61.
32   See, for example, José (1996), pp. 27, 39.

the 1989 election tend to ignore how this early coverage was often contradictory, raising growing doubts about the effectiveness of Collor's moralising campaign.[33] They also ignore the fact that the political establishment, and not only the media, seemed to be impressed by Collor's anti-Sarney and oppositional rhetoric. In this early phase of the campaign, even Lula, who would be Collor's main opponent in the presidential election, praised the governor in the press.[34] Thus, instead of conceiving the role of the press in purely instrumental terms, it is important to stress how Collor was sensitive to the rules, norms and values that guide the functioning of the media, mainly journalists' notion of 'newsworthiness', using them to gain access to the public sphere. Collor had a sense of the importance of 'spectacle' for journalists' production of the news,[35] exemplifying the importance of approaches that award some level of autonomy to the media.

To understand the central role played by the media in the 1989 presidential election, it is necessary to stress their role as producers of culture, in elaborating particular ways of interpreting or framing the world of politics. In the case of the 1989 election this approach was developed by those who analysed the role of the media in the construction of the 'political scenario' within which the election took place. The reasons for Collor's victory have been interpreted as linked to the scenario that was constructed in and by the media, especially TV Globo, through newscasts, *telenovelas*, polls and marketing.[36] These studies have emphasised, for example, the role of such TV Globo *telenovelas* as *Vale Tudo* (Anything Goes), *O Salvador da Pátria* (The Saviour of the Homeland) and *Que Rei Sou Eu?* (What King Am I?) in the construction of a specific representation of the Brazilian nation in the period that preceded the 1989 election. According to this 'culturalist' analysis of the election, *telenovelas* established specific constraints to the campaign and Collor's marketing strategy identified the main features of the scenario, tailoring the candidate's style and discourse accordingly.[37] Collor became the 'outsider', the only candidate who could rescue the country from the 'moral, political, and ethical crisis' caused by bad politicians and *maharajas*.[38]

The 'culturalist' interpretation of the 1989 electoral process has been contested by some authors, who suggest that TV Globo's *telenovelas* and newscasts basically reflected the audience's values and opinions, thus adopting the view of the media as a mirror. According to this perspective television was not a major force in determining the election results. Collor's victory was credited to his ability to reflect the electorate's aspira-

33   Lattman–Weltman et al. (1994), pp. 29–30; Conti (1999), p. 108.
34   Conti (1999), p. 122.
35   *Ibid.*, p. 14.
36   Weber (1990); Lima (1993); Rubim (1999), pp. 15–36.
37   Lima (1993), pp. 108–11.
38   *Ibid.*, p. 109.

tions and interests, the same aspirations and interests that were simply captured, and not promoted, by the *telenovelas'* scriptwriters.[39] Nevertheless, *telenovelas* have historically played an active role in discussing and interpreting political and social issues in Brazil. Through micro-cosmos that represent the nation, Brazilian *telenovelas* have both reflected and constructed a powerful idea of nationhood among their audience.[40] Thus the usefulness of the culturalist approaches.

Collor's illegal use of the annual TV and radio programmes, by which parties have the right to a party political broadcast once a year, was another major factor in determining his emergence as the front-runner in the polls. In April and May 1989 the candidate appeared in the broadcasts of two small and obscure parties (PTR and PSC), despite this being a clear violation of the electoral laws. Collor's standing in the polls grew after each appearance on TV and he gained the lead in April, just after the PTR's broadcast.[41] The weakness of media regulation in Brazil, as well as the lack of enforcement of the few existing provisions, were some of the factors that allowed Collor to publicise his imagery and rise in the polls.

Besides the programmes that political parties have the right to broadcast every year, all elections in Brazil are preceded by the free political advertising time (*Horário Eleitoral de Propaganda Gratuita* — HEPG). Since 1962 all television and radio stations are obliged by law to give 'free' time for the political parties and their candidates during electoral campaigns. No other democracy in the world gives more free time in the media to the candidates than Brazil.[42] Free political advertising is thus an important democratising element of the Brazilian media, giving to parties and candidates an unmediated access to the public sphere. In the 60 days of the campaigning on TV and radio before the first round,[43] the Workers' Party (PT) presented a dynamic and innovative programme, which was based on a parody of the country's dominant network. The PT launched *Rede Povo* (The People's Network), making reference to the name and appropriating the symbolisms and language of TV Globo to promote the can-

---

39 Lins da Silva (1993); Marques de Melo (1992).
40 See Porto (2000b).
41 Lima (1993), pp. 109–11; Lattman–Weltman et al. (1994), p. 18; Conti (1999), pp. 143–5.
42 Schmitt et al. (1999), p. 291.
43 Since the 1988 Constitution a second round takes place in majoritarian elections (for president, governors and mayors) with the two candidates attracting the greatest vote, when none of them obtains at least 50 per cent of the valid vote (annulled ballots excluded) in the first round. In the first round of the 1989 election, in November, Collor obtained 28.5 per cent of the vote and Lula 16.1 per cent (with only a 0.6 per cent advantage in relation to the candidate in third place, Leonel Brizola). The second round took place in December and Collor defeated Lula 53 per cent to 47 per cent.

didacy of Lula.[44] The programme was a success and had an important impact in the election. During the free electoral campaign on TV and radio, between September and November, Lula saw a 100 per cent growth in his performance in the polls, while Collor lost 36 per cent of his support.[45]

TV Globo's *Jornal Nacional*, the main TV news bulletin in the country, also shaped the outcome of the 1989 presidential election in important ways. One of the most important and controversial aspects of TV Globo's role in the election was the editing of the second of the two debates between Collor and Lula by *Jornal Nacional*. The second debate took place three days before the second round, on 14 December. Since this date was also the last day of the free political advertising of the candidates on radio and TV, they would not be able to present their own evaluations of the debate. Hence, the way that the most popular news programme edited and evaluated the candidates' performances became a central issue. The day after the debate TV Globo's lunchtime news programme, *Jornal Hoje*, presented a balanced evaluation of the event. Nevertheless, the prime time *Jornal Nacional*, which has a much broader audience, broadcast a quite different edited version of the debate. Collor not only appeared more frequently (eight times, one more than Lula), but spoke more (3 minutes and 34 seconds, compared to Lula's 2 minutes and 22 seconds), and Lula was shown in some of his most insecure and hesitant moments.[46] Although it is hard to measure the impact of *Jornal Nacional*'s editing of the debate, polls conducted immediately after it suggest that it had an important effect in a very close election.[47]

A Rupture with the Old Pattern? The Media and Collor's Impeachment

After taking office, Collor established a 'spectacular' and 'media-centred' presidency. Although previous presidents had also relied on events planned for media coverage, Collor took the process to a new level. Two

---

44 See Albuquerque (1999) on the campaign of the candidates on TV during the 1989 election. The decision to imitate Globo in the PT's party political broadcast was marked by intense internal disputes in the campaign command. Some members of the team wanted to distance the programme from and criticise the mainstream media. The group that prevailed insisted that TV Globo's language and 'pattern of quality' was already consolidated in the public's imagery and that the best strategy would be to appropriate its language. The aim would be to subvert the dominant discourse, using it to support the causes of the Brazilian workers (Conti, 1999, pp. 203–20).

45 Conti (1999), p. 204.

46 Conti (1999), p. 269.

47 Straubhaar et al. (1993); Kucinski (1998), p. 113. According to Conti (1999, p. 267), the decision to replace the more balanced edition of the lunchtime newscast with *Jornal Nacional*'s version favouring Collor was taken after the network's owner, Roberto Marinho, intervened. He ordered Alberico Souza Cruz, then director of TV Globo's journalism department, to prepare a report more favourable to Collor for the prime-time newscast. This episode is another example of the instrumental use of the media by their owners.

weekly ceremonies of his presidency revealed this new pattern. In the 'ramp ceremonies', Collor concluded his week of work every Friday by leaving the presidential palace in the company of personalities, athletes, comedians, cabinet members or children. On Sunday mornings he went jogging around his residency, wearing T-shirts with different themes, including anti-drugs, ecological and 'philosophical' messages.[48] The media provided extensive coverage of both events.[49]

In an apparent paradox, the 'spectacular president' did not have good relations with journalists and the press, developing good personal relations instead with television executives, especially with TV Globo's owner Roberto Marinho.[50] The president also attempted to intimidate the media and curb freedom of the press, establishing a major conflict with the main newspaper, *Folha de São Paulo*. Apparently as retaliation for the critical coverage that the newspaper had given to his campaign, the president ordered the federal police to raid its headquarters in March 1990, alleging irregularities in the way *Folha* handled its advertising revenues. The newspaper responded with strong editorials that compared Collor to Mussolini, the Italian dictator.[51] When *Folha* published several news stories in July denouncing corruption in the use of the federal government's advertising budget, including attempts to use it to buy political support from some media outlets, Collor's reaction was again fierce. He decided to sue the publication, becoming the first president to prosecute a newspaper in the courts. The case was later dismissed.[52]

Despite these conflicts, the media provided broad support to the new president and his neoliberal policies. Collor's first economic plan, *Plano Collor*, adopted radical and unprecedented measures, including the freezing of all current and savings accounts containing more than US$1,250 dollars. In a clear contradiction to his neoliberal rhetoric, Collor did what, during the campaign, he had warned Lula would do. He promoted an unprecedented intrusion of the state in the private property of the middle and upper classes. More surprising than the measures was the reaction of the mainstream media. They gave full and unanimous support to the economic plan, despite

---

48   Conti (1999), p. 337.
49   Not all of Collor's media events went according to plan. After the president posed driving a motorcycle in Brasília, the press discovered that it had been smuggled. When visiting Sweden, Collor tried to drive a truck, but it skidded off the road. When Collor set fire to a pile of marijuana confiscated by the federal police, the excess gasoline caused an explosion that scorched some of the members of his delegation (Conti, 1999, p. 337). The press was also frequently very critical of the president's stunts (*ibid.*; José, 1994, p. 42).
50   Conti (1999), pp. 436–7.
51   *Ibid.*, pp. 301–13.
52   *Ibid.*, pp. 349–50, 507–8.

their liberal beliefs and anti-state-intervention positions.[53] Thus, the commitment of the media to the new president and his conservative agenda, established during his campaign against a more radical alternative, proved to be stronger than fears of governmental intervention in the market.

Although the media supported the president's policies, they began reporting a growing number of charges of corruption against Collor. As early as October 1990 the press, mainly the weekly news magazines, started to publish stories about a corruption scandal involving the president's campaign treasurer, Paulo César Farias, known as PC.[54] These early exposés about corruption involving the president and his campaign manager did not cause a political scandal or major difficulties for Collor. The situation changed dramatically when the president's brother, Pedro Collor, gave an interview to the news-magazine *Veja* in May 1992. The interview denounced the corruption in the federal government led by PC, and suggested that the president was also involved. As a result, Congress established a parliamentary investigative committee, or CPI, to investigate the charges. A few months later, in September, after the CPI presented its report accusing Collor of direct involvement in corruption, and after a new mass movement took over the streets demanding the end of Collor's presidency, the Chamber of Deputies voted in favour of his impeachment by 441 votes to 38. The Senate then began the trial of the president and a few hours before it gathered in December for its final deliberation, Collor presented his resignation. However, by a vote of 73 to 8, the senators decided not to accept the resignation and approved the impeachment, stripping Collor of his political rights until 2001.

The media were active participants in the heated struggles over the impeachment of the president they had supported in 1989. The two main weekly news-magazines, *Veja* and *Isto É*, in particular, played a leading role in investigating charges, revealing new details of the corruption scheme and 'anticipating' the impeachment of the president.[55] One specific feature of this coverage was the fact that the press adopted the style of story telling of the Brazilian *telenovelas*, presenting the impeachment process as a family drama, focusing on personalities and ignoring institutional or structural factors that could help understand the dynamics of corruption in Brazilian politics.[56]

Television provided a much more restrained coverage of the impeachment process than the press, particularly in comparison to the weekly news-magazines. As in the 1984 Diretas Já campaign, TV Globo's initial

---

53   *Ibid.*, pp. 324–5; José (1996), p. 40.
54   Kucinski (1998), p. 174.
55   Fausto Neto (1994); Lattman–Weltman et al. (1994); José (1996); Rubim (1999); Conti (1999); Waisbord (1997, 2000); Herscovitz (2000); Lins da Silva (2000).
56   Waisbord (1997); Herscovitz (2000).

coverage of the pro-impeachment movement revealed its alliance with the government. In a first phase, *Jornal Nacional*'s coverage of the charges and of the CPI's work was characterised by a strong presence of government sources, with few references to the links between PC and the president.[57] The programme allocated minimum time to the coverage of the denunciations, focusing on 'facts' and avoiding political commentary.[58] But the mass movement for the impeachment was rapidly growing in strength and TV Globo finally changed its news coverage when the investigative parliamentary committee presented its report in August 1992, considering the president guilty and initiating the impeachment trial.[59]

But if TV Globo's journalism provided a 'cold' and sporadic coverage of the impeachment process, mainly before the CPI report was approved in August, one of its fictional programmes played a very different role. On 14 July 1992 TV Globo launched *Anos Rebeldes* (Rebellious Years), a mini series set in the late 1960s, in a time of growing political repression and of mass mobilisations against the military dictatorship. The mini series portrayed with some sympathy the life and dilemmas of young Brazilians who had chosen to join urban guerrilla movements in order to fight the authoritarian regime, causing the ministry of the armed forces to protest at the way the past was being 're-written'.[60] The fictional programme legitimated the street rally as a form of political expression for a new generation of protesters, who started to appropriate the music, the language and symbols of *Anos Rebeldes* in their pro-impeachment demonstrations.[61] There was a fundamental irony in the role played by TV Globo in the process of impeachment. While the *Jornal Nacional* news programme provided a restrained and 'cold' coverage of the political crisis, *Anos Rebeldes* contributed to strengthen the pro-impeachment demonstrations.[62]

Despite the active role of the media in the impeachment of Collor de Mello, his fall from power was not a simple result of the investigations and exposés presented by an autonomous media performing a watchdog role. In his excellent analysis of the role of investigative journalism in Latin American politics, Waisbord stresses, for example, the importance of the 'politics of sources'.[63] According to this author, the closeness between

---

57   Porto (1994).
58   Waisbord (2000), p. 76; Conti (1999), p. 626.
59   Porto (1994), p. 143–5. According to Conti (1999, p. 660), it was Roberto Marinho who ordered Alberico Souza Cruz to change *Jornal Nacional*'s coverage and start emphasising the links between PC and Collor. This intervention of the network owner is an example of the importance of the view of the media as audience-dependent. Marinho knew that if TV Globo continued to protect the president it could lose audience and credibility.
60   Conti (1999), p. 627.
61   Rubim (1999), pp. 51–56.
62   Conti (1999), p. 650.
63   Waisbord (2000), p. 93.

journalists and official sources is indispensable for the media to be able to delve into wrongdoing. Cooperation of highly placed sources is a precondition for investigative journalism and the media frequently provide the stages for inter-elite battles in which information is leaked by powerful sources with the intention to harm rivals.[64] To understand, for example, why the president's brother, Pedro Collor, decided to give the explosive interview to *Veja*, it is important to consider his conflicts with Paulo Cesar Farias, or PC, Fernando Collor's campaign treasurer and a central figure in the corruption scheme. PC had started investments in the media market of the Collors' home state, Alagoas, threatening to undermine the media outlets managed by Pedro Collor. The president's brother started to consider PC his archenemy and felt betrayed by Collor because of his support to PC's projects.[65] Thus, one of the main reasons for the impeachment of Collor de Mello was the close relationship between the media and the dissatisfied sectors of the hegemonic bloc.[66] The media did not cause the impeachment or determine the outcome of the political process in a simple way. It would be more accurate to interpret their role as providing the central stage in which the intra-elite conflicts took place. In this process, the mass media publicised and supported the charges and interpretations put forward by those sectors of the hegemonic bloc that were unsatisfied with Collor de Mello.

The Media and the New Consensus: Brazil Under Fernando Henrique Cardoso (1994–2000)

The 1994 Presidential Election

After Collor's impeachment in 1992, vice-president Itamar Franco took office and led a new coalition of forces that was set to overcome the crisis. In an attempt to fight increasing inflation rates and a scenario of economic crisis, Franco nominated Senator Fernando Henrique Cardoso, a renowned sociologist, as his new minister of finances in May 1993 and put him in charge of developing a new economic plan. The result was the Real Plan, an ambitious plan aimed at eliminating inflation and bringing the much desired economic stability. The plan was successful in its main objectives and Cardoso emerged as the only candidate from governmental and centrist political forces that appeared to be able to defeat the Workers' Party (PT) candidate, Lula, who enjoyed a comfortable lead in the polls throughout 1993 and the first half of 1994. Cardoso, a member of the

64 *Ibid.*, p. 115.
65 José (1996), p. 53; Conti (1999), pp. 527–8; Herscovitz (2000), pp. 21–2.
66 José (1996), p. 117. Another major reason why highly placed sources started to leak information to the press about PC's corruption scheme was that entrepreneurs were angry with the increase in the value of the bribes they needed to pay to the scheme (Kucinski, 1998, p. 174; Waisbord, 2000, p. 99).

Brazilian Social Democratic Party (PSDB), established a coalition of conservative forces, including the 'dissidents' of the military dictatorship who had founded the Liberal Front Party (PFL), and left the ministry in April to launch his candidacy to the presidency.

The success of the new economic plan in reducing inflation was a major factor in the victory of Cardoso in the 1994 presidential election.[67] Research based on national surveys[68] and on focus groups[69] shows the strong impact of the Real Plan in the voting decisions of the electorate. Nevertheless, the interpretation of Cardoso's victory as a simple and unmediated result of the plan is misleading. The success of both the plan and of Cardoso's candidacy depended on how they would be publicised by the media.[70] They also depended on the capacity of Cardoso to build a sense of 'social order' in a context of high levels of popular frustration with previous and failed attempts to fight economic and social instability.[71]

In the 1994 presidential election TV Globo's prime time newscast favoured the candidacy of Cardoso, first through the usual explicit inequality in the treatment of the candidates and later on in more implicit and subtle ways. Between March and May *Jornal Nacional*'s coverage dedicated more space to Cardoso and also framed the candidates in particular ways.[72] Cardoso was presented in terms of his ability to unify political forces and build consensus, while Lula was linked to interest groups (particularly to trade unions) and to conflict and discord.[73] Later on in the campaign, the news programme presented a more balanced coverage of the candidates in terms of space and time. Nevertheless, Cardoso was favoured in more implicit and indirect terms by an extensive and positive coverage of the Real Plan, which associated the survival of the economic plan with the person of the candidate.[74]

The way that *Jornal Nacional*'s coverage of the Real Plan influenced the 1994 electoral process was revealed by a curious episode. On 1 September, one month before the election, the minister of finance who replaced Cardoso, Rubens Ricúpero, was talking to the journalist Carlos Monforte at TV Globo's studios while waiting to give a live interview. Not aware that the conversation was already being sent to the satellite, Ricúpero started to tell the journalist how he was allowing the media to support the govern-

---

67 Fernando Henrique Cardoso overtook Lula in the polls at the end of July and was elected in the first round in October, since he obtained more than 50 per cent of the valid votes (Cardoso obtained 54 per cent of the valid votes and Lula 27 per cent).
68 Mendes and Venturi (1994).
69 Kinzo (1996).
70 Rubim (1999), p. 81.
71 Pinto (1996).
72 Albuquerque (1994).
73 *Ibid.*, pp. 34–8.
74 Fabricio (1997).

ment candidate in an indirect way. Ricúpero said that he was very useful to TV Globo because the network could give space and special treatment to him as the minister of finance, instead of supporting Cardoso openly, and nobody could complain. Some viewers who owned parabolic antennas recorded the 'informal' conversation and the candidates opposing Cardoso made it public. As a result of the scandal, president Itamar Franco fired Ricúpero, but the episode had no repercussion in the polls. Despite the fact that it did not affect the outcome of the election, the 'parabolic scandal' revealed how Ricúpero and the Real Plan were making it possible for the media, particularly TV Globo, to favour Cardoso in more subtle ways.

Besides the implicit and explicit ways TV Globo's news coverage favoured Cardoso, it also important to stress the role of the *telenovelas* in the electoral contest. As in the 1989 election, the prime time melodramas contributed to build a specific scenario within which the elections took place, representing politics as a dirty activity and establishing parallels between fictional characters and 'real' candidates. The *telenovelas Renascer* (Revival), *Fera Ferida* (Wounded Beast), and *Pátria Minha* (My Homeland) discussed political and social problems explicitly and intensely, generating a climate of optimism and trust that contributed to increase the impact of Real Plan in the electoral process.[75]

There were new and important changes to the free political advertising time of the candidates in the 1994 contest. Law 8.173, which regulated the access of the candidates to radio and television, forbade the use of images generated outside the studios. By restricting the use of images in the programmes, legislators demonstrated a rationalist bias, suggesting that political ideas should be expressed discursively, not by images.[76] In this way the law made the programmes less interesting for the audience, greatly reducing their informative potential, and increasing the power of the news programmes to define the terms of the political debate.[77] Despite these limitations, the audience ratings of the free party political broadcasts on TV were very high and the programmes became a key space in which candidates built their rhetorical strategies and positioned themselves in relation to the new economic plan.[78]

Media and Social Conflict: The Case of the Landless Movement (MST)

During Cardoso's first term as president one of the most organised and active social movements of the country started to gain more visibility, generating intense debates within and outside the media. The Landless

75   Porto (1998b).
76   Rubim (1999), p. 61.
77   Miguel (1997); Rubim (1999), pp. 61–2; Albuquerque (1999), pp. 50–1.
78   Porto and Guazina (1999).

Movement (Movimento dos Trabalhadores Rurais Sem-Terra — MST) has been struggling for agrarian reform since its foundation in 1984 in close alliance with the Workers Party (PT). The basic strategy of the movement has been to move a cluster of families onto government-owned or unproductive private land and stay there until they are granted title to the land.[79] One of the most controversial aspects of the movement is the use of violence in some of these occupations, raising growing concern among elites and the media about MST's methods. Nevertheless, much of the violence is perpetrated against the MST by landowners and the military police, since elite resistance to land reform 'has remained one of the most persistent exclusions of the Brazilian political system'.[80]

The land occupations promoted by MST have received growing media coverage, but this coverage has tended to frame the movement in very negative terms, although there are differences among different media outlets. For example, in 1997 TV Globo's *Jornal Nacional* and SBT's *TJ Brasil* covered the Landless Movement in different terms. *TJ Brasil* stressed the elements of violence, danger, conflict, adopting a 'dramatic frame.' On the other hand, *Jornal Nacional*, besides stressing these elements, added a moral critique of the movement, complaining about its irrationality and irresponsibility, thus applying a 'moral frame'.[81] A content analysis of the newscasts *Jornal Nacional* and *Jornal da Record* conducted in the following year showed that TV *Globo* tended to frame the movement as violent, with a particular emphasis on the pillages of businesses by landless families.[82]

But while TV news, particularly *Jornal Nacional*, has tended to frame the MST in negative terms, a *telenovela* aired by TV Globo in 1996–97 portrayed the movement in very different terms. The *telenovela O Rei do Gado* (The Cattle King), written by Benedito Ruy Barbosa, was a remarkable case of political intervention on the part of television fiction. In the second part of the story, which was set in contemporary times, Bruno Mezenga becomes the main protagonist. He is the 'Cattle King', the owner of several cattle farms around the country. When the MST invaded one of his farms, Mezenga met Luana, a lonely landless worker who immediately falls in love with him.

O Rei do Gado introduced into prime-time television the lives and dilemmas of the landless and their movement, frequently framing them in positive terms. The *telenovela* criticised some aspects of the movement, suggesting, for example, that it should abandon some of its radical attitudes and symbols.[83] Despite these critiques, the leaders of the MST stressed the

---

79 Hochstleter (2000), pp. 176–7.
80 *Ibid.*, p. 177.
81 Aldé and Lattman–Weltman (2000).
82 Lima and Guazina (1998), pp. 16–7.
83 In the *telenovela* the members of the Landless Movement choose green as the colour of their flag, replacing the red flag that represents the socialist orientation of the 'real' MST.

positive contribution the *telenovela* gave to the cause of agrarian reform. João Pedro Stédile, member of MST's National Coordination, wrote in the press that 'the transformation of outlaws into *telenovela* characters … is an important artistic contribution to the construction of a more equitative reality'.[84] The *telenovela* was therefore an important countervailing force to the traditional ways the mainstream media framed an important social movement.

Another important character in *O Rei do Gado* was the senator, Caxias, who distinguished himself from traditional politicians for his honesty and his relentless struggle for an agrarian reform. The fictional senator engaged in a direct dialogue with 'real' senators, in a striking mixing of fiction and reality. First, on November 1996 a progressive senator and well-known intellectual, Darcy Ribeiro, used his opinion column in the newspaper *Folha de São Paulo* to praise the fictional senator for his standpoints and president Cardoso for listening to them and for pushing Congress to increase taxes on non-productive lands. A few weeks later the *telenovela*'s senator paid homage to his 'colleague' and great educator, Darcy Ribeiro.[85] When the fictional character was assassinated in the *telenovela*, Darcy Ribeiro wrote another column lamenting the death of 'his senator'. On 17 January 1997, the *telenovela O Rei do Gado* aired the episode in which the body of Senator Caxias was mourned in the lobby of the building of the National Congress. Two 'real' senators of the Workers' Party (PT), Eduardo Suplicy and Benedita da Silva, appeared in the episode to pay homage to the deceased fictional senator.

It is hard to know what impact the *telenovela* had on the public's views on the issue of agrarian reform and on the MST. Ethnographic research in low-income communities has shown that much of the audience of the *telenovela*, especially women, did not notice the references to 'real' politicians and political problems or found the political content to be boring.[86] Other viewers criticised the appearance of real senators as political opportunism.[87] When discussing the portrayal of the MST by the *telenovela*, inhabitants of a small north-eastern town mentioned news stories from *Jornal Nacional* revealing the contradictions in TV Globo's role. One of the viewers said: 'If these people [the landless] were going to get the land to work that would be OK. The senator left those writings that are beautiful, but the real side of the landless movement we see in the newscast.'[88] Thus, while *O Rei do Gado* helped to portray MST in more sympathetic terms, *Jornal Nacional* was a major source of negative projection that undermined much of the legitimacy of this important social movement.

84   Quoted in Hamburger (1999), p. 311.
85   La Pastina (1999), p. 214; Hamburger (1999), pp. 302–3.
86   La Pastina (1999), pp. 219–22.
87   Hamburger (1999), p. 318.
88   Quoted in La Pastina (1999), p. 233.

Cardoso's 1998 Re-election and the Media

Before ending his first term as president, Fernando Henrique Cardoso started to pressure Congress into approving a constitutional amendment to allow politicians in executive office (president, governors and mayors) to run for re-election. As we have seen, Cardoso used the concessions of relay television stations as political currency to buy support in Congress for the amendment. On 13 May 1997 *Folha de São Paulo* published a series of reports denouncing a money-for-votes gambit in Congress to gain support of the re-election proposal. The investigative reports were based on five taped conversations featuring influential politicians, including the minister of communications, Sergio Mota, a close friend and ally of the president.[89] Despite the charges of corruption on the basis of the president's political basis, Congress approved the constitutional amendment, and in 1998 Cardoso became the first president to run for re-election. As in his first election four years earlier, Cardoso defeated Lula in the first round.[90]

In the 1998 election Cardoso's most important asset continued to be the economy, since inflation remained low, but he had to face several challenges in the campaign. Between April and June there was wide criticism in the media over the way the president confronted urgent problems, including the drought in the north-east, a fire in the Amazon rainforest, the increase in unemployment and MST's land invasions.[91] Another major difficulty for the president's campaign was the growing evidence of problems in the economy after April, when the country started to experience negative growth rates in the Gross National Product, a decline in average income and growing unemployment rates.[92] Cardoso's re-election seemed threatened by this difficult scenario and between April and June he lost eight per cent of his support, establishing a technical tie with his main opponent (33 per cent for Cardoso and 30 per cent for Lula).[93]

But Cardoso had a privileged position and resources as an incumbent, attracting greater media attention than his opponents. A study of the four main newspapers in a seven-day period in August showed that Cardoso got 59 per cent of the campaign coverage, while only 38 per cent was dedicated to Lula.[94] Cardoso also dominated the television news coverage. An analysis of the news programmes of all networks in August showed that he obtained approximately three times more airtime than Lula.[95]

---

89   Waisbord (2000), p. 136.
90   Cardoso obtained 53 per cent of the valid votes, while Lula came second with 32 per cent.
91   Miguel (2000), p. 67; Azevedo (2000), p. 39.
92   Azevedo (2000), pp. 36–8.
93   *Ibid.*, p. 39.
94   Kucinski (1998), p. 146.
95   *Ibid.*, p. 147.

In the case of *Jornal Nacional* there were important changes in the 1998 campaign coverage. Deepening the changes that began in 1994, when the news programme supported Cardoso in more subtle ways, and in a clear contrast to the more explicit support given to Collor in 1989, TV Globo's main news report did not explicitly manipulate the campaign coverage to benefit one of the candidates. There was a reasonable balance in the space given to the candidates in terms of time and in the number of appearances.[96] On 30 September and 2 October, *Jornal Nacional* even gave a free and unmediated space for the candidates to present their proposals. Each candidate had the opportunity to speak for between 33 and 56 seconds, without journalists framing or interpreting their discourses.[97] But the more balanced treatment of candidates does not mean that *Jornal Nacional* did not affect the outcome of the election or that it provided neutral coverage. One of the most consistent and striking research findings regarding the 1998 election is the decline of *Jornal Nacional*'s campaign coverage, which banned the social problems that had embarrassed the government in previous months from the screen. Greater emphasis was given instead to the *fait-divers*, banal news stories about curiosities, including trivial events involving media personalities and bizarre cases with animals.[98] Thus, *Jornal Nacional* helped Cardoso in more indirect terms, by de-politicising and shrinking the campaign coverage. In this way the negative social problems that had dominated the agenda in the previous months tended to disappear.[99]

The 'cold' and de-politicised character of the campaign was reinforced by changes in the regulation of the free advertisement time and by the absence of debates. The government's allies proposed, and were successful in having approved, the reduction of the time devoted to the campaign on radio and television. In 1994 the presidential campaign on TV lasted for 60 days, with four programmes a week. In 1998 the free political broadcast time was reduced to three times a week during a 45-day period, plus 15 or 30 seconds spots, which were aired during regular commercial breaks.[100] Another important change was the unprecedented decision not to hold debates with the candidates. Because of Cardoso's opposition to them, and because of the lack of interest on the part of the media, no debates were conducted in 1998. This

---

96   Miguel (2000), p. 73.
97   Miguel (1999), pp. 273–4.
98   Lima and Guazina (1998); Kucinski (1998), p. 141; Azevedo (2000); Miguel (2000).
99   According to some accounts, the change in the agenda of the media was a result of the intervention of the president. In May 1998, Cardoso gathered members of the national elite, including media owners, and expressed his concern over the negative tone of the media coverage and with the growth of Lula in the polls. The media responded by adopting a more optimistic news coverage (Kucinski, 1998, pp. 149–50; Venturi, 2000, pp. 117–8).
100   Miguel (2000), p. 73.

decision, together with the reduction of the free political broadcast time and the decline of the campaign coverage, made the 1998 election the shortest and most de-politicised electoral contest of the democratic period.[101]

The media constructed a scenario favourable to the re-election of Cardoso not only by presenting a reduced and de-politicised news coverage, but also by framing the economic crisis in particular ways. When by August 1998 the Brazilian economy began facing severe difficulties, a few months before the election, a major issue became how the media would project the causes of the crisis. Cardoso was in a vulnerable position and there was a growing awareness that the exchange rate of the national currency, the *real*, was artificially inflated.[102] Cardoso's campaign interpreted the economic crisis as a result of difficulties in the international sphere, mainly after the Russian crisis, and presented his candidacy as the only one with the necessary experience to overcome the difficulties created by forces that were beyond his control.[103] The media in general, and *Jornal Nacional* in particular, followed this line of interpretation, framing the economic crisis as a consequence of the difficulties facing the world economy.[104] There was a clear resonance between Cardoso's campaign strategy and the scenario constructed by the media.[105]

Conclusions

In the first 15 years of the process of redemocratisation in Brazil the mass media were key actors in the political process. They have transformed the way political and electoral processes are conducted, increasing the role of marketing specialists and replacing several functions of traditional political institutions. Television in particular allowed 'outsiders', such as Collor de Mello, to reach the electorate without the mediation of traditional political institutions, including political parties. They have also altered the way that politicians govern, since the success of new policies and economic plans depends to a great extent on how they will be publicised by the media. Governments know the importance of the interpretations provided by the media on the causes and responsibilities of existing problems, mainly in times of social or economic crisis.

101 Azevedo (2000), p. 41.
102 Knowing that currency devaluation could threaten his victory, Cardoso postponed the measure until after the election. When he finally devalued the *real* in January 1999, the Brazilian currency fell approximately 40 per cent (Miguel, 2000, p. 79). As a result, the popularity levels of the president fell dramatically.
103 Miguel (2000), p. 79.
104 Lima and Guazina (1998); Azevedo (2000); Miguel (2000); Soares (2000).
105 It should be noted, nevertheless, that Lula's campaign was unable to build a credible interpretation of the economic crisis and to identify the responsibility of Cardoso for the difficulties the country was facing (Venturi, 2000, p. 112). This fact became evident in the focus groups conducted by Lula's own campaign team with voters (Almeida, 2000, p. 167).

The Brazilian media have played a contradictory role in the consolidation of the new democracy. The consequences of investigative journalism for the legitimacy of the new regime offer a good example. On one hand, investigations contribute to increasing political accountability, publicising wrongdoing and pushing Congress and the Judiciary to prosecute those involved in corruption.[106] On the other hand, the media exposés, which increased in number with the end of censorship and of the military dictatorship, have established a direct and harmful connection between corruption and democracy in the mass public, contributing to the undermining of the legitimacy of the new regime.[107] The role of the media explains to a great extent why the support for democracy among the population in Brazil is one of the lowest in Latin America.[108]

In democratic Brazil, media owners have used their power to intervene at decisive moments, pursuing particular political goals and supporting specific alternatives and candidates. Nevertheless, the power of the media in general — and of TV Globo in particular — to manipulate the political process should not be overestimated. As the campaigns for direct elections in 1984 and for the impeachment of Collor de Mello in 1992 show, there are limits to the ability of the media to sustain a hegemonic position, mainly in times of crisis. When facing the opposition of a stronger civil society in these historical moments, TV Globo was forced to change its news coverage and to abandon traditional alliances.

There have been also important changes in the role of the media in recent years and these changes cannot be properly understood in terms of the instrumental view. In electoral processes, for example, TV Globo's *Jornal Nacional* has replaced more explicit manipulations in favour of particular candidates, as in 1989, with more subtle forms of constructing favourable scenarios, as in 1994 and 1998. In other words, there are relatively less *quantitative* inequalities in the coverage, in terms of the time devoted to each candidate, and more *qualitative* differences in the way the national problems and the candidates are framed by the newscast. It is no accident that Brazilian researchers have found in the concept of framing a useful analytical tool to understand the political role of the media, partic-

---

106 Waisbord (2000).
107 Campello de Souza (1989); Porto (1996); Lins da Silva (2000).
108 Porto (1996), p. 48; Lins da Silva (2000), p. 191. This is not to suggest that journalists should not expose corruption and wrongdoing, but that journalists and the media organisations have the responsibility of developing news coverage that separates the dishonesty of particular politicians from the essence of democracy and its institutions. As senior advisors of the Inter-American Development Bank put it, the media should complain 'about dishonesty and inefficiency while at the same time acknowledging honest and efficient performance, thereby holding those who commit acts of corruption accountable without undermining the institutions themselves'. Jarquin and Carrillo-Flóres (2000), p. 199.

ularly of TV Globo. Moreover, research involving TV viewers has shown that the way *Jornal Nacional* frames political issues and events has important effects on how audiences make sense of them.[109]

Media framing can be seen as just a more sophisticated or subtle instrumental manipulation. Nevertheless, when researchers explain interpretative frames solely in terms of conscious political decisions they neglect important aspects of the media institutions they analyse. The emphasis on manipulation stresses extra-journalistic factors, ignoring the professional values and routines that characterise the news production process.[110] As we have seen, one of the most important routines is the traditional reliance on official sources, which tends to give a privileged position to the points of view of the government. Social movements like the MST have to rely on land occupation and other forms of protest to gain access to the media, since they are not considered 'authoritative sources' in journalistic terms. Instrumental approaches also ignore the fact that explicit manipulations can alienate viewers and undermine the credibility of the media as institutions.[111] Thus, the media will usually avoid partisan news coverage when it can result in a decline in the number of viewers, readers or listeners. This fact can be illustrated by the changes that took place in *Jornal Nacional* in 1996, when Cid Moreira, who had been the newsreader of the programme during its first 27 years, was retired by TV Globo. Moreira was replaced by journalists who started having a more active and interpretative role as anchors and also to work as editors. One of the aims was to recover the credibility of TV Globo's main newscast, which was facing declining audience ratings.[112]

Instrumental views about the role of TV Globo in Brazilian politics have a particularly hard time explaining the political role of television fiction, mainly the *telenovelas*. As we have seen, fictional programmes have led TV Globo to play a contradictory role in the impeachment of Collor de Mello and in the portrayal of an important social movement, the MST. While *Jornal Nacional* has tended to side with government interpretations in these two cases, the mini series *Anos Rebeldes* and the *telenovela O Rei do Gado* presented points of view that were absent from its news reports or that conflicted with its news coverage. The role of television fiction in Brazil cannot properly be understood if the relatively autonomous role of scriptwriters is ignored. Although they are severely constrained by the media institutions for which they work, their own values and views affect the political content of the programmes.[113]

109   Porto (2000a).
110   Albuquerque (1998)
111   Almeida (1998).
112   Porto (1998a).
113   See Porto (2000b).

Returning to the initial hypothesis of this study, it is now possible to conclude that other variables besides political manipulation are central to a full explanation of the political role of the media. As we have seen, one of the main reasons why these other factors become more relevant is the consolidation of more democratic practices and institutions. When democracy advances in society, oligopolistic media conglomerates like TV Globo have greater difficulty in maintaining their old instrumental interventions. This does not mean that these powerful institutions will not intervene in the political process, particularly at times of crisis. The media institutions that dominate the Brazilian media landscape will continue to sustain hegemonic projects and alliances, frequently undermining the consolidation of more democratic practices and institutions. This will continue to happen mainly because of the lack of democratic regulations for the communications sector and the persistence of clientelistic practices. Nevertheless, it is impossible to understand fully the political role of the media in Brazil if the new conditions brought about by the democratisation of the country are ignored.

BIBLIOGRAPHY

Abranches, Sérgio Henrique (1988) 'Presidencialismo de coalizão: dilema institucional brasileiro,' *Dados: Revista de Ciências Sociais*, vol. 31, no. 1, pp. 5–34.

Abreu, Marcelo Paiva (1990) *A ordem do progresso: 100 anos de politica economica republicana (1889-1989)* (Rio de Janeiro: Campus).

Abrucio, Fernando (1998) *Os barões da federação* (São Paulo: Hucitec).

Adelman, I., Morley, S., Schenzler, C. and Vogel, S. (1996) 'Education, Mobility and Growth,' in N. Birdsall and R.H. Sabot (eds.) (1996) *Opportunity Foregone: Education in Brazil* (Washington, DC: Inter-American Development Bank/Johns Hopkins University Press), pp. 319–36.

Adorno, S. (1993) 'A Criminalidade urbana violenta no Brasil: um recorte temático,' *BIB, Rio de Janeiro*, no. 35. 1° semestre, pp. 3–24.

Adorno, S. (1995) 'A violência na sociedade brasileira: um painel inconcluso em uma democracia não consolidada,' *Sociedade e Estado*, vol. X, no. 2, pp. 299–342.

Afonso, Araújo, Rezende and Varsano (2000) 'A Tributação Brasileira e o Novo Ambiente Econômico: a Reforma Tributária Inevitável e Urgente,' *Revista do BNDES* (Rio de Janeiro), no. 13.

Albuquerque, A. de (1994) 'A campanha presidencial no "Jornal Nacional": Observações preliminaries,' *Comunicação & Política*, vol. 1, no. 1 (1994), pp. 23–40.

Albuquerque, A. de (1998) 'Manipulação editorial e produção da notícia: dois paradigmas da análise da cobertura jornalística da política,' in Antônio Albino Rubim, Ione Maria Bentz and Milton José Pinto (orgs.), *Produção e recepção dos sentidos mediáticos* (Petrópolis: Vozes), pp. 9–27.

Albuquerque, A. de (1999) *'Aqui cocê vê a verdade na tevê': a propaganda política na televisão* (Niterói: MCII).

Alde, A. and Lattman-Weltman, F. (2000) 'O MST na TV: sublimação do político, moralismo e crônica cotidiana do nosso "estado de natureza",' trabalho apresentado ao IX Encontro Anual da Associação Nacional de Programas de Pós-Graduação em Comunicação (COMPÓS), Porto Alegre, Brasil, 30 de maio a 2 de junho.

Almeida, J. (1998) 'Reforma agrária no ar: o povo na TV, de objeto a sujeito,' trabalho apresentado ao IV Congreso Latinoamericano de Ciencias de la Comunicacíon (ALAIC), 12 a 16 de setembro.

Almeida, J. (2000) 'Reflexões sobre o marketing de Lula em 98,' in Antônio Albino Rubim (org.), *Mídia e eleições de 1998* (Salvador: UFBA/Editora Universitária), pp.159–174.

Almond, G. (1988) 'The Return to the State,' *American Political Science Review*, vol. 82, pp. 853–74.

Alves, M.H.M. (1988) 'Dilemmas of the Consolidation of Democracy from the Top in Brazil: A Political Analysis,' *Latin American Perspectives*, vol. 15, no. 3 (1988), pp. 47–63.

Amann, E. (2000) *Economic Liberalisation and Industrial Performance in Brazil* (Oxford University Press).

Amann, E. and Baer, W. (2000) 'The Illusion of Stability: The Brazilian Economy under Cardoso,' *World Development*, vol. 28, no. 10.

Amann, E. and Baer, W. (forthcoming) 'Neo-liberalism and its Consequences in Brazil'.

Amaral, R. and Guimarães, C. (1994) 'Media Monopoly in Brazil,' *Journal of Communication*, vol. 44, no. 4, pp. 26–40.

Amnesty International (1999) *No One Sleeps Here Safely: Human Rights Violations against Detainees* (London: Amnesty International).

Amorim Neto, Octavio (1995) 'Cabinet Formation and Party Politics in Brazil,' paper for delivery at the meeting of the Latin American Studies Association, Atlanta.

Anderson, C. J. and Guillory, C.A. (1997) 'Political Institutions and Satisfaction with Democracy: A Cross-National Analysis of Consensus and Majoritarian Systems,' *American Political Science Review*, vol. 91, no. 1, pp. 66–81.

Andrews, George (1991) 'O protesto político negro em São Paulo – 1888–1988', *Estudos Afro-Asiáticos*, no. 21.

Arantes, Rogério Bast (1997) *Judiciário e política no Brasil* (São Paulo: Educ/FAPESP/IDESP).

Arantes, Rogério Bast (2000a) 'The Judiciary, Democracy and Economic Policy in Latin America,' in Stuart Nagel (ed.), *Handbook of Global Legal Policy* (New York: Marcel Dekker).

Arantes, Rogério Bast and Nunes, Fábio José Kerche (1999) 'Judiciário e democracia no Brasil,' *Novos Estudos*, no. 54, pp. 27–42.

Arantes, Rogério Bastos (2000b) 'Ministério público e política no Brasil,' unpublished doctoral dissertation (São Paulo, University of São Paulo).

Arantes, Rogerio Bastos (2001) 'Jurisdição política constitucional,' in Maria Teresa Sadek (ed.) *Reforma do judiciário* (São Paulo: Fundação Konrad Adenauer).

Arat, Z.F. (1991) *Democracy and Human Rights in Developing Countries* (London: Lynne Rienner Publishers).

Araujo and Oliveira, J.B. (1999) 'O dilema do modelo brasileiro de educação', in J.P. dos Reis Velloso and R. Albuquerque (eds.) (1999), *Um modelo para a educação brasileira no século XXI* (Rio de Janeiro: José Olympio Editora), pp. 63-87.

Archer, R. (1995) 'Party Strength and Weakness in Colombia's Besieged Democracy,' in S. Mainwaring and T. Scully (eds.), *Building Democratic Institutions: Party System in Latin America* (Stanford: Stanford University Press), pp. 164–99.

Avelar, L. (1992) 'As eleições na era da televisão,' *Revista de Administração de Empresas*, vol. 32, no. 4, pp. 42–57.

Azevedo, F. (2000) 'Imprensa, campanha presidencial e a agenda da mídia,' in Antônio Albino Rubim (org.), *Mídia e eleições de 1998* (Salvador: UFBA/Editora Universitária), pp. 31–56.

Azevedo, Rodrigo Ghiringhelli de (2000) *Informalização da justiça e controle social: Implantação dos juizados especiais criminais em Porto Alegre* (São Paulo: Instituto Brasileiro de Ciências Criminais).

Bacha, Edmar Lisboa (1978) *Politica economica e distribuição de Renda* (Rio de Janeiro: Paz e Terra).

Bacha, Edmar Lisboa and Klein, Herbert S. (1989) *Social Change in Brazil, 1945–1985: The Incomplete Transition* (Albuquerque: University of New Mexico Press).

Baer, W. (1995) *The Brazilian Economy* (Praeger)

Ballard, Megan J. (1999) 'The Clash Between Local Courts and Global Economics: The Politics of Judicial Reform in Brazil,' *Berkeley Journal of International Law*, vol. 17 (Fall), pp. 230–76.

Banco Mundial (1993), *América Latina y el Caribe: diez años después de la crisis de la deuda externa* (Washington, DC).

Banks, D. (1992) 'New Patterns of Oppression: An Updated Analysis of Human Rights Data,' in T. Jabine and R. Claude (eds.), *Human Rights and Statistics: Getting the Record Straight* (Philadelphia: University of Pensylvania), pp. 364–91.

Barcellos, Caco (1992) *Rota 66: a historia da polícia que mata* (São Paulo, Editora Globo).

Barros, Ricardo Paes de, Henriques, R. and Mendonça, R. (2000) 'Desigualdade e pobreza no brasil: retrato de uma estabilidade inaceitável,' *Revista Brasileira de Ciencias Sociais*, vol. 15, no. 42, pp. 123–42.

Bartolini, Stefano and Mair, Peter (1990) *Identity, Competition, and Electoral Availability: The Stabilisation of European Electorates* (Cambridge: Cambridge University Press).

Bastide, Roger (1955) 'Efeito do conceito de cor,' in *Relações Raciais entre Brancos e Negros em São Paulo* (Unesco-Anhembi).

Bastide, Roger (1961) 'Variations on Negritude', *Presence Africaine*, vol. 8, no. 36.

Bastide, Roger (1983) 'A imprensa negra do Estado de São Paulo,' *Estudos Afro-brasileiros* (São Paulo).

Baumann, Renato (ed.) (2000) *Brasil: uma década em transição* (Rio de Janeiro: CEPAL/Editora Campus) (English edition forthcoming).

Bayley, D.H. (1992) 'Comparative Organization of the Police in English-Speaking Countries,' in Michael Tonry and Norval Morris (eds.), *Modern Policing* (Chicago: University of Chicago Press), pp. 509–46.

Bayley, D.H. (1992) *Police for Future* (New York/London: Oxford University Press).

Beato F., C.C. (1998) 'Determinantes da criminalidade em Minas Gerais,' *Revista Brasileira de Ciências Sociais* (São Paulo), vol. 13, no. 37, pp. 74–87.

Becker, G.S. (1964) *Human Capital: A Theoretical and Empirical Analysis, with Special Reference to Education* (Princeton: Princeton University Press).

Becker, H. (1966) *Outsiders: Studies in the Sociology of Deviance* (London: Collier Macmillan).

Bendix, R. (1964) *Nation-Building and Citizenship: Studies of our Changing Social Order* (Berkeley: University of California).

Bendix, Reinhart and Lipset, Seymour Martin (1959) *Social Mobility in Industrial Society* (Berkeley: University of California Press).

Benevides, M.V. (1983) *Violência povo e polícia* (São Paulo, Brasiliense).

Berquó, Elza and Alencastro, L.F. (1992) 'A emergência do voto negro,' *Novos Estudos Cebrap*, vol. 33, pp. 77—88.

Bethell, Leslie (1985) 'The Independence of Brazil,' in Leslie Bethell (ed.), *The Cambridge History of Latin America. Vol III From Independence to 1870* (Cambridge: Cambridge University Press), chapter 4.

Bethell, Leslie (1991) 'The Decline and Fall of Slavery in Nineteenth Century Brazil,' *Transactions of the Royal Historical Society*, 6th series, vol. 1.

Bethell, Leslie (1992) 'Brazil,' in Leslie Bethell and Ian Roxborough (eds.), *Latin America between the Second World War and the Cold War, 1944-1948* (Cambridge: Cambridge University Press).

Bethell, Leslie (1994) *On Democracy in Brazil* (London: Institute of Latin American Studies).

Biersteker, Thomas (1995) 'The "Triumph" of Liberal Economic Ideas,' in Barbara Stallings (ed.), *Global Change, Regional Response* (Cambridge: Cambridge University Press), pp. 174–96.

Birdsall, N. and Sabot, R.H. (eds.) (1996) *Opportunity Foregone: Education in Brazil* (Washington, DC: Inter-American Development Bank/Johns Hopkins University Press).

Blau, Peter and Duncan, Otis Dudley (1967) *The American Occupational Structure* (NY: Wiley).

Bobbio, Norberto et al. (1994), *Dicionário de Política*, 6th edition, vol. 1 (Brasilia-DF: Editora UNB).

Booth, J. and Seligson, M.A. (1994) 'Paths to Democracy and the Political Culture of Costa Rica, México and Nicaragua,' in L. Diamond (ed.), *Political Culture and Democracy in Developing Countries* (Lynne Rienner), pp. 59–99.

Bown, L. (1990) *Preparing the Future: Women, Literacy and Development* (London: ActionAid)

Brandão, Gildo M. (1997), 'A ilegalidade mata: o Partido Comunista e o sistema partidário (1945–64),' *Revista Brasileira de Ciências Sociais*, vol. 12, no. 33, pp. 23–34

Branford, S. and J. Rocha (2002) *Cutting the Wire: The Story of the Landless Movement in Brazil* (London: Latin America Bureau).

Brazil (1997) *Brazil — A Call to Action: Combating School Failure in the Northeast of Brazil* (Brasília: Ministry of Education, World Bank, UNICEF).

Brazil (2000a) *EFA 2000 Education for All: Evaluation of the Year 2000* (Brasilia: National Institute for Educational Studies and Research-INEP).

Brazil (2000b) *National Curriculum Parameters* (Brasília: SEF/Ministry of Education).

Brazil (2000c) *Desempenho do sistema educacional brasileiro: 1996-1999* (Brasília: Ministry of Education).

Brazil (2000d) *Informe dos resultados comparativos do SAEB 1995, 1997 e 1999* (Brasília: Ministry of Education).

Brazil (2000e) *Plano de Carreira e Remuneração do Magistério Público* (Brasília: Fundescola/Ministry of Education).

Brazilian Central Bank (BCB) (2001) *Boletim Mensal*, February and March.

Brazilian National Statistical Office (IBGE) (2001) *Pesquisa Mensal de Emprego*, March; *Contas Nacionais*, March; *População*, March.

Breen, Richard and Whelan, Christopher T. (1996) *Social Mobility and Social Class in Ireland* (Dublin: Gill and Macmillan).

Bresser Pereira, Luiz Carlos (1993) 'Economic Reforms and Cycles of State Intervention,' *World Development*, vol. 21, no. 8, pp. 1337–53

Bretas, M. (1985) *Policiar a cidade republicana* (Rio de Janeiro: Revista da OAB).

Briceño-León, R., Piquet Carneiro, L. and Cruz, J.M. (1999) 'O apoio dos cidadãos à ação extrajudicial da polícia no Brasil, em El Salvador e na Venezuela,' in *Cidadania, justiça e violência* (Rio de Janeiro: Fundação Getúlio Vargas).

Britcham (1999) *Doing Business in Brazil* (British Chamber of Commerce publication).

Brittos, V. (2000) 'As Organizações Globo e a reordenação das comunicações', *Revista Brasileira de Ciências da Comunicação*, vol. 23, no. 1, pp. 57-76.

Brum, A. (1997) *Desenvolvimento Econômico Brasileiro* (Editora Vozes).

Bulmer-Thomas, V. (1994) *An Economic History of Latin America since Independence* (Cambridge: Cambridge University Press).

Bulmer-Thomas, Victor (ed.) (2001) *Regional Integration in Latin America and the Caribbean: The Political Economy of Open Regionalism* (London: Institute of Latin American Studies).

Buvinic, M. and Morrison, A. (1999) *Notas técnicas: prevención de la violencia* (Washington, DC: Banco Interamericano de Desenvolvimento).

Cain, M., Claude, R. and Jabine, T. (1992) 'A Guide to Human Rights Data Sources,' in T. Jabine R. Claude (eds.) *Human Rights and Statistics: Getting the Record Straight* (Philadelphia: University of Pennsylvania), pp. 392–443.

Camargo, Aspasia et al. (1989) *O golpe silencioso. As origens da republica corporativa* (Rio de Janeiro).

Campello de Souza, M. do C. (1989) 'The Brazilian "New Republic": Under the "Sword of Damocles",' in Alfred Stepan (ed.), *Democratizing Brazil* (New York: Oxford University Press), pp. 351–94.

Candia Veiga, J.P. (1993) 'Divida externa e o contexto internacional,' Masters Degree Thesis in Political Science, São Paulo University.

Cano, I. (1997) *The Use of Lethal Force by Police in Rio de Janeiro* (Rio de Janeiro: ISER).

Cano, Ignacio (1999) *Letalidade da ação policial no Rio de Janeiro: A atuação da justiça militar* (Rio de Janeiro: ISER).

Cardia, N. (1997) 'O medo da polícia e as graves violações dos direitos humanos,' São Paulo, *Tempo Social. USP*, vol. 9, no. 1, pp. 249–65, May.

Carey, John M. and Shugart, Matthew S. (1995) 'Executive Decree Authority: Calling Out The Tanks, Or Just Filling Out The Forms?' in John M. Carey and Matthew S. Shugart (eds.), *Executive Decree Authority: Calling out the Tanks or Just Filling Out the Forms?* (Cambridge: Cambridge University Press).

Carvalho, José Murilo de (1980) *A construção da ordem: a elite política imperial* (Rio de Janeiro: Editora Campus).

Carvalho, José Murilo de (1987) *Os bestializados: o Rio de Janeiro e a república que nao foi* (São Paulo: Companhia das Letras).

Carvalho, José Murilo de (1988) *Teatro de sombras: a política imperial* (Rio de Janeiro: Instituto Universitário de Pesquisas do Rio de Janeiro).

Carvalho, José Murilo de (1995) *Desenvolvimiento de la ciudadania en Brasil* (Mexico: Fondo de la Cultura).

Carvalho, José Murilo de (1996) 'Cidadania: tipos e percursos,' *Estudos Históricos*, vol. 9, no. 18, pp. 337–60.

Carvalho, José Murilo de (2001) *Cidadania no Brasil – o longo caminho* (Rio de Janeiro: Civilização Brasileira).

Carvalho, R. (1999) *Transição democrática brasileira e padrão mediático publicitário da política* (Campinas: Pontes).

Castro, Marcus Faro de (1997) 'O Supremo Tribunal Federal e a judicialização da política,' *Revista Brasileira de Ciências Sociais*, vol. 12, no. 34 (June), pp. 147–56.

Castro, Mônica M. M. de. (1992) 'Raça e comportamento politico,' *Dados* (Rio de Janeiro), vol. 36, no. 3, pp. 469–91.

Catterberg, E. (1990) 'Attitudes Towards Democracy in Argentina during the Transition Period,' *International Journal of Public Opinion Research*, vol. 2, pp. 155–68.

Cavalcanti, Rosângela Batista (1999) *Cidadania e acesso à justiça* (São Paulo: Editora Sumaré).

Cheibub, Z.B. (1995) 'Valores e opiniões da elite: notas sobre os padrões de apoio a políticas sociais,' *DADOS*, vol. 38, pp. 57–92.

Chevigny, P. (1990) 'Police Deadly Force as Social Control in Jamaica, Brazil and Argentina,' mimeo.

Chilcote, Ronald (1982) *Partido Comunista Brasileiro: Conflito e Integração 1922-1972* (Rio de Janeiro, Edições Graal).

Cicourel, J. (1968) 'Police Practices and Official Records,' in Roy Turner (ed.), *Ethnomethodology* (London: Penguin Books).

Cline, William (1989) 'From the Baker Plan to the Brady Plan,' in Israt Husain and Ishac Diwan (eds.), *Dealing with the Debt Crisis* (Washington, DC: World Bank Symposium)

Cline, William (1995) *International Debt Reexamined* (Washington, DC: Institute of International Economics).

Clutterbuck, R. (1986) *The Future of Political Violence: Destabilization, Disorder and Terrorism* (New York: Royal United Services Institute).

Coelho, E.C. (1988) 'A criminalidade urbana violenta,' *Dados – Revista de Ciências Sociais*, IUPERJ (Rio de Janeiro), vol. 31, no. 2, pp. 145–83.

Coes, Donald V. (1995) *Macroeconomic Crises, Policies and Growth in Brazil: 1964-90* (Washington, DC: World Bank).

Comission Economica para America Latina y el Caribe (1995), *América Latina: políticas para mejorar la inserción en la economía mundial* (Santiago de Chile: Naciones Unidas).

Conti, M. (1999) *Notícias do Planalto: a imprensa e Fernando Collor* (São Paulo: Companhia das Letras).

Correio Brasiliense (2001) 'Leio, mas não compreendo,' 11 March.

Costa, Emilia Viotti da (1975) 'The Political Emancipation of Brazil,' in A.J.R. Russell-Wood (ed.), *From Colony to Nation; Essays on the Independence of Brazil* (Baltimore: Johns Hopkins University Press).

Costa, Emilia Viotti da (1985) 'Independence: The Building of a Nation' in Emilia Viotti da Costa, *The Brazilian Empire: Myths and Histories* (Chicago: University of Chicago Press).

Costa, S. and Brener, J. (1997) 'Coronelismo eletrônico: o governo Fernando Henrique e o novo capítulo de uma velha história,' *Comunicação & Política*, vol. IV, no. 2, pp. 29–53.

Coutinho, M. (1996) *The Brazilian Fiscal System in the 1990s: Equality And Efficiency under Inflationary Conditions* (London: Institute of Latin American Studies).

CPDOC-FGV/ISER (1996) *Lei, justiça e cidadania* (Rio de Janeiro: CPDOC-FGV/ISER).

Cruz, J.M. (1996) 'La violencia en El Salvador,' in L.A. Gonzáles and J.M. Cruz (eds.), *Sociedad y violencia: El Salvador en la post-guerra* (San Salvador: IUDOP – UCA), pp. 89–106.

da Silva, M.F. (2000) 'Rádio e eleições: relação que traz voto,' in Vera Chaia and Miguel Chaia (orgs.), *Mídia e política* (São Paulo: PUC/NEAMP).

Dahl, R. (1956) *A Preface to Democratic Theory* (Chicago, IL: University of Chicago).

Dahl, R. (1971) *Polyarchy: Participation and Opposition* (New Haven: Yale University Press).

Dalton, R.J., McAllister, I. and Wattenberg, M. (2000) 'The Consequences of Partisan Dealignment,' in R.J. Dalton and M. Wattenberg (eds.), *Parties Without Partisans: Political Change in Advanced Industrial Democracies* (Oxford: Oxford University Press), pp. 37–63.

Dalton, Russel, Flanagan, Scott and Beck, Paul (eds.) (1984) *Electoral Change in Advanced Industrial Democracies: Realignment or Dealignment?* (Princeton: Princeton University Press).

Davis, K. and Moore, W.E. (1967) 'Some Principles of Stratification,' in R. Bendix and S.M. Lipset (eds.), *Class, Status and Power* (London: Routledge and Kegan Paul).

Deheza, Grace Ivana (1997) *Gobiernos de coalición en el sistema presidencial: América del Sur*, PhD dissertation, Instituto Universitario Europeo.

Delgado and Cardoso (orgs) (2000) *A Universalização dos Direitos Sociais no Brasil — a previdência rural nos anos 90* (Brasília: IPEA).

Dellasopa, E., Bercovich, A. and Arriaga, E. (1999) 'Violência, direitos civis e demografia no Brasil na década de 80: o caso da área metropolitana do Rio de Janeiro,' *Revista Brasileira de Ciências Sociais, Anpocs*, vol. 14, no. 39, February.

Devellis, R. (1991) *Scale Development: Theory and Applications* (Newbury Park, CA: Sage).

Dewey, J. (1953) *Democracy and Education: An Introduction to the Philosophy of Education* (New York: Macmillan).

DFID (2000) *Education for All: The Challenge of Universal Primary Education* Consultation Document (London: Department for International Development).

Di Tella, T. (1992) 'Latin American Political Models in the Transition to the Twenty-First Century,' in L. Albala-Bertrand (ed.), *Democratic Culture and Governance: Latin America on the Threshold of the Third Millennium* (UNESCO), pp. 51–62.

Diamond, L., Linz, J. and Lipset, S.M. (1990) 'Introduction: Comparing Experiences with Democracy,' in L. Diamond, J. Linz and S.M. Lipset (eds.), *Politics in Developing Countries: Comparing Experiences with Democracy* (Colorado: Lynne Rienner Publishers, Inc.), pp. 1–38.

Diniz, Eli (org.) (1993) *Empresários e modernização econômica: Brasil anos 90* (Florianópolis: Ed. UFSC/IDACON).

Domingo, Pilar (1999) 'Judicial Independence and Judicial Reform in Latin America,' in Andreas Schedler, Larry Diamond and Marc F. Plattner (eds.), *The Self-Restraining State: Power and Accountability in New Democracies* (Boulder: Lynne Rienner).

dos Santos, Wanderley Guilherme (1986) *Sessenta e quatro: Anatomia da crise* (São Paulo: Vértice).

Draibe, Sonia (1985) *Rumos e metamorfoses – estado e industrialização no Brasil: 1930/1960* (Rio de Janeiro-RJ: Paz e Terra).

Dreifuss, René (1989) *O jogo da direita – na Nova República* (Petrópolis-RJ: Vozes).

Duff, E. and Mccamant, J. (1976) *Violence and Repression in Latin America* (New York: The Free Press).

Duncan, Otis Dudley (1966) 'Methodological Issues in the Analysis of Social Mobility,' in Neil S. Smelser and Seymour Martin Lipset (eds.), *Social Structure and Mobility in Economic Development* (Chicago: Aldine).

Edwards, Sebastian (1995) *Crisis and Reform in Latin America – From Despair to Hope* (New York: World Bank/Oxford University Press).

Erickson, Robert and Goldthorpe, John H. (1992) 'The CASMIN Project and the American Dream,' *European Sociological Review*, vol. 8, pp. 283–306.

Erickson, Robert and Goldthorpe, John H. (1993) *The Constant Flux: A Study of Class Mobility in Industrial Societies* (Oxford: Oxford University Press).

Erickson, Robert, Goldthorpe, John and Portocarrero, Luciene (1979) 'Intergenerational Class Mobility in Three Western European Societies,' *British Journal of Sociology*, vol. 30.

Esch, C.E. (1997) 'Do microfone ao plenário: o comunicador radiofônico e seu sucesso eleitoral,' Dissertação de Mestrado, Universidade de Brasília.

ESP (2000a) 'Deputado quer CPI para apurar desvio do Fundef,' *Estado de São Paulo*, 28 March.

ESP (2000b) 'TCU vai investigar desvios do Fundef,' *Estado de São Paulo*, 10 February.

ESP (2000c) 'Cai participação de municípios no ensino,' *Estado de São Paulo*, 17 October.

ESP (2001a) 'Valor do Bolsa-Escola é baixo diz governador,' *Estado de São Paulo*, 20 February.

ESP (2001b) 'Igualdade cresce com escolaridade, diz Paulo Renato,' *Estado de São Paulo*, 6 April.

ESP (2003) 'Ministério define reajuste para o Fundef em 6.7%,' *Estado de São Paulo*, 28 January.

Fabrício, G. (1997) 'O jornal nacional da Rede Globo e a construção do cenário de representação da política,' Dissertação de Mestrado, Universidade de Brasília.

Fausto, Boris (1997), *A revolução de 1930. História e historiografia* (16th, rev. ed., São Paulo: Editora Schwarcz).

Fausto Neto, A. (1994) 'Vozes do Impeachment,' in Heloiza Matos (org.), *Mídia, eleições e democracia* (São Paulo: Scritta), pp. 159–89.

Featherman, David, Jones, L., Lancaster, F. and Hauser, Robert (1975) 'Assumptions of Social Mobility Research in the U.S.: The Case of Occupational Status,' *Social Sciences Research*, vol. 4, pp. 329–60.

Felix, João Baptista de J. (2000) 'Chic Show e construção de identidade nos bailes black paulistanos,' dissertação de mestrado, Pós-Graduação em Antropologia da USP.

Fernandes, Florestan (1955) 'A luta contra o preconceito de cor,' in *Relações Raciais entre Brancos e Negros em São Paulo* (Unesco-Anhembi).

Fernandes, Florestan (1964) *A integração do negro na sociedade de classes*, vol. 2 (São Paulo: FFCL/USP).

Fernandes, Florestan (1974) *A revolução burguesa no Brasil: ensaio de interpretação sociológica* (Rio de Janeiro: Zahar Editores).

Argelina Maria Cheibub Figueiredo, *Democracia ou reformas? Alternativas democráticas a crise política, 1961-1964* (Sao Paulo, 1993).

Figueiredo, Argelina C. (2000) 'Government Performance in a Multiparty Presidential System: The Experiences of Brazil,' paper prepared for the XVIII World Congress of Political Science, IPSA, Québec, 1–5 August.

Figueiredo, Argelina C. (2000) 'Institutional Power and the Role of Congress as a Mechanism of Horizontal Accountability: Lessons from the Brazilian Experience,' paper prepared for the conference 'Institutions, Accountability and Democratic Performance in Latin America,' University of Notre Dame, Kellogg Institute for International Studies, 8–9 May.

Figueiredo, Argelina C. and Limongi, Fernando (1999) *Executivo e Legislativo na nova ordem constitucional* (Rio de Janeiro: Fundação Getúlio Vargas/FAPESP).

Figueiredo, Argelina C. and Limongi, Fernando (2000) 'Presidential Power, Legislative Organization, and Party Behaviour in Brazil,' *Comparative Politics*, vol. 32, no. 2.

Figueiredo, Argelina C. and Limongi, Fernando, 'Executivo e legislativo na formulação e execução do orçamento federal,' paper presented at II Encontro da Associação Brasileira de Ciência Política, São Paulo, 22-25 November.

Figueiredo, M. (1998) 'From Collor de Mello to Cardoso: The Media and Electoral Politics in Brazil,' communication presented at the Conference 'The Media in Latin America and Spain: Opportunities, Influence and Constraints,' Institute of Latin American Studies, University of London, March 16–17.

Figueiredo, R. (org.) (2000) *Marketing político e persuasão eleitoral* (São Paulo: Fundação Konrad Adenauer).

Foweraker, J. and Landman, T. (1997) *Citizenship Rights and Social Movements: A Comparative and Statistical Analysis* (New York: Oxford University Press).

Freedom House (1994) *Freedom in the World: The Annual Survey of Political Rights and Civil Liberties* (New York: Freedom House).

Freedom House (1994), *The Annual Survey of Political Rights and Civil Liberties*, 1993–94. Statistical Abstract of Latin America (1996), p. 32.

Freyre, Gilberto (1933) *Casa Grande & Senzala: formação da família brasileira sob o regime da economia patriarcal* (Rio de Janeiro: Schimidt).

Freyre, Gilberto (1936) *Sobrados e mucambos* (Rio de Janeiro: Editora Nacional).

Freyre, Gilberto (1956) 'A escravidão, a monarquia e o Brasil moderno,' *Revista Brasileira de Estudos Políticos*, vol. 1, no. 1 (December), pp. 39–48.

Fritsch, W. and Franco, G. (1991) *Foreign Direct Investment in Brazil: Its Impact on Industrial Restructuring* (Paris: OECD).

Fuller, B. and Habte, A. (eds.) (1992) *Adjusting Educational Policies: Conserving Resources While Raising School Quality*, World Bank Discussion Paper 132 (Washington DC: World Bank).

Fundação Getúlio Vargas (FGV) (2000) *Conjuntura Econômica*, October.

Fundação Instituto de Pesquisas Econômicas (1997) 'Reformas: o custo do atraso,' *Revista da Indústria*, Edição Especial (São Paulo, June).

Fundação SEADE (1983–97) *Anuário estatístico de São Paulo* (São Paulo: Fundação SEADE).

Fundação SEADE (1999) *Pesquisa de condições de vida 1988* (São Paulo: Fundação SEADE).

Fundescola (2000) *Boletim Técnico*, vol. V, nos. 37, 40.

Furtado, C. (1965) 'Political Obstacles to Economic Growth in Brazil,' lecture delivered to the Royal Institute of International Affairs, London, February.

Gambiagi, Fabio et al. (1999) *A economia brasileira nos anos 90* (BNDES).

Ganzenboom, Harry B.G., Luijkx, Ruud and Treiman, Donald (1989) 'Intergenerational Class Mobility in Comparative Perspective,' *Research in Social Stratification and Mobility*, vol. 8, pp. 3–84.

Garretón, M.A. (1988) 'Evolução política do regime militar chileno e problemas da transição para a democracia,' in G. O'Donnell, P.C. Schmitter and L. Whitehead (eds.) *Transiçoes do regime autoritário: América Latina* (Sao Paulo: Vértice, Editora Revista dos Tribunais), pp. 140–85

Garretón, M.A. (1992) 'From Authoritarianism to Political Democracy: Democratic Transition that Needs Rethinking?' in L. Albala-Bertrand (ed.), *Democratic Culture and Governance: Latin America on the Threshold of the Third Millennium* (UNESCO), pp. 19–21.

Gaviria, A. and Pagés, C. (1999) 'Patterns of Crime Victimization in Latin America,' Inter-American Development Bank, mimeo, November.

Goldthorpe, John H. (1982) 'On the Service Class: Its Formation and Future,' Anthony Giddens and G. Mackenzie (eds.), *Social Class and the Division of Labour* (Cambridge: Cambridge University Press).

Goldthorpe, John H. (1985) 'On Economic Development and Social Mobility,' *British Journal of Sociology*, vol. 36, pp. 549–73.

Goldthorpe, John (with Catriona Llewellyn and Clive Payne) (1987) *Social Mobility and Class Structure in Modern Britain* (Oxford: Clarendon Press).

Goldthorpe, John H. and Marshall, Gordon (1992) 'The Promising Future of Class Analysis: A Response to Recent Critiques,' *Sociology*, vol. 26, pp. 381–400.

Gomes-Neto, J.B. and Hanushek, E.A. (1996) 'The Causes and Effects of Grade Repetition,' in N. Birdsall and R.H. Sabot (eds.) (1996) *Opportunity Foregone: Education in Brazil* (Washington DC: Inter-American Development Bank/Johns Hopkins University Press), pp. 425–60.

Gonzalez, Lélia (1982) 'O movimento negro na última década,' in L. Gonzalez and C. Hasenbalg, *Lugar de negro* (Rio de Janeiro: Marco Zero).

Graham, D. (1972) 'The Growth, Change and Reform of Higher Education in Brazil,' in R. Roett (ed.), *Brazil in the Sixties* (Nashville: Vanderbilt University Press), pp. 275–324.

Graham, Richard (1990) *Patronage and Politics in Nineteenth Century Brazil* (Stanford: Stanford University Press).

Grindle, M. (2001) 'Despite the Odds: The Political Economy of Social Sector Reform in Latin America,' paper presented at the conference on *Exclusion and Engagement: Social Policy in Latin America*, Institute of Latin American Studies, University of London, March 22–23.

Guimarães de Castro, M.E. (1998) *Avaliação do sistema educacional brasileiro: tendências e perspectivas* (Brasília: MEC/INEP).

Guimarães, Antônio Sérgio Alfredo (1999), 'Classes Sociais,' in S. Miceli (ed.), *O que ler nas ciências sociais brasileiras (1970-1995) (vol. II – Sociologia)* (São Paulo: Editora Sumaré).

Guimarães, C. and Amaral, R. (1988) 'Brazilian television: a rapid conversion to the new order', in Elizabeth Fox (ed .), *Media and Politics in Latin America* (London: Sage), pp. 125-136.

Gurr, T.R. (1985) 'Das conseqüencias do conflito violento,' in T.R. Gurr (ed.), *Manual do conflito político* (Brasília: Editora Universidade de Brasília), pp. 273–334

Haddad, W., Carnoy, M., Rinaldi, R. and Regel, O. (1990) *Education and Development: Evidence for New Priorities* (Washington, DC: World Bank).

Hahner, June (1991) *Emancipating the Female Sex. The Struggle for Women's Rights in Brazil, 1850-1940* (Durham, NC: Duke University Press).

Hall, A. (2001) *Evaluation of UNDP Support to the Northeast Basic Education Project BRA/95/013* (Brasília: UNDP).

Hallin, D. and Papathanassopoulos, S. (2002) 'Political Clientelism and the Media: Southern Europe and Latin America in Comparative Perspective,' *Media, Culture and Society*, vol. 24, no. 2, pp. 175-95.

Hamburger, E. (1999) 'Politics and Intimacy in Brazilian Telenovelas,' PhD dissertation, The University of Chicago.

Hammergren, Linn (1998) 'Fifteen Years of Judicial Reform in Latin America: Where We Are and Why We Haven't Made More Progress,' unpublished paper available on http://darkwing.uroegon.edu/~caguirre/papers.htm.

Hasenbalg, C.A. and Silva, N.V. (1988) *Estrutura social, mobilidade e raça* (Rio de Janeiro: IUPERJ/Vértice).

Hasenbalg, Carlos (2000), 'Estado social da nação: fatos e percepções,' projeto apresentado à FAPERJ, mimeo.

Helleiner, Eric (1994) *States and the Reemergence of Global Finance* (Ithaca and London: Cornell University Press).

Herscovitz, H. (2000) 'Social and Institutional Influences on News Values and Routines in Brazil: From Military Rule to Democracy,' paper presented at the 50th Annual Conference of the International Communication Association, Acapulco, Mexico, June 1–5.

Hertz, D. (1987) *A história secreta da rede globo* (Porto Alegre: Tche).

Hochstetler, K. (2000) 'Democratizing Pressures from Below? Social Movements in the New Brazilian Democracy,' in Peter Kingstone and Timothy Power (eds.), *Democratic Brazil* (Pittsburgh: University of Pittsburgh Press), pp.167–82.

Hoffmann, R. (2000) 'Desigualdade e pobreza no brasil no período 1979-99,' UNICAMP, mimeo.

Holanda, Sérgio B. (1936) *Raízes do Brasil* (Rio de Janeiro: José Olympio).

Hout, Michael (1988) 'More Universalism, Less Structural Mobility: The American Occupational Structure in the 1980s,' *American Journal of Sociology*, vol. 93, pp. 1358–1400.

Hout, Michael (1989) *Following in Father's Footsteps* (Cambridge, Mass.: Harvard University Press).

Hout, Michael and Hauser, Robert (1992) 'Symmetry and Hierarchy in Social Mobility: A Methodological Analysis of the CASMIN Model of Class Mobility,' *European Sociological Review*, vol. 8, pp. 239–66.

Huber, John D. (1996) *Rationalizing Parliament* (Cambridge: Cambridge University Press).

Human Rights Watch (1998) *Behind Bars in Brazil* (New York: Human Rights Watch).

Humana, C. (1992) *World Human Rights Guide* (New York: Facts on File Publications).

Huntington, S. (1994) [1991]) *A Terceira onda: a democratização no final do século XX* (São Paulo: Ática).

Huntington, S. (1996) 'Democracy for the Long Haul,' *Journal of Democracy*, vol. 7, no. 2, pp. 3–13.

IBGE (2001) *Síntese de indicadores sociais 2000* (Rio de Janeiro: Instituto de Geografia e Estatística).

IMF (2000) *Brazil: Selected Issues and Statistical Appendix.*

Inglehart, R. (1997) *Modernization and Postmodernization: Cultural, Economic and Political Change in 43 Societies* (Princeton, NJ: Princeton University Press).

Jaguaribe, H., Iglésias, F., Santos, W.G.d., Chacon, V. and Comparato, F. (1985) *Brasil, sociedade democrática* (Rio de Janeiro: José Olympio Editora).

Jarquin, E. and Carrillo-Flóres, F. (2000) 'The Complexity of Anticorruption Policies in Latin America,' in Joseph Tulchin and Ralph Espach (eds.), *Combating Corruption in Latin America* (Baltimore: Woodrow Wilson Centre Press), pp. 193–201.

Jesus, D.E. (org.) (1986) 'A face oculta da ação policial,' in *Seminário Crime e Castigo* (Rio de Janeiro: Ciência Hoje).

José, E. (1996) *Imprensa e poder: ligações perigosas* (São Paulo: Hucitec).

Juaguaribe, H., Valle e Silva, N. do, Paiva Abreu, M. de, Bastos de Ávila, F. and Fritsch, W. (1989), *Brasil: reforma ou caos* (Rio de Janeiro: Paz e Terra).

Karl, T.L. (1988) 'Petróleo e pactos políticos: a transição para a democracia na Venezuela,' in G. O'Donnell, P.C. Schmitter and L. Whitehead (eds.), *Transiçoes do regime autoritário: América Latina* (Sao Paulo: Vértice, Editora Revista dos Tribunais), pp. 297–329.

Kelly, R.W. (1993) *Estratégias de resolução de problemas para o policiamento comunitário*, translation of: *Problem Solving Strategies for Community Policing – A Practical Guide* (Rio de Janeiro. Publicado pelo departamento de polícia de Nova York, PMERJ).

Kerr, Clark, Dunlop, J.T., Harbison, F.H. and Myers, C.A. (1960) *Industrialism and Industrial Men* (Cambridge, Mass.: Harvard University Press).

Kinzo, Maria D'Alva G. (1980) *Representação Política e Sistema Eleitoral no Brasil* (São Paulo: Editora Símbolo).

Kinzo, Maria D'Alva (1988) *Legal Opposition Politics under Authoritarian Rule in Brazil – the Case of the MDB, 1966-79* (London: Macmillan).

Kinzo, Maria D'Alva (1993) *Radiografia do Quadro Partidário Brasileiro* (São Paulo: Fundacao Konrad-Adenauer-Stiftung).

Kinzo, Maria D'Alva (1996) 'A eleição presidencial de 1994 no Brasil: Fernando Henrique Cardoso e o Plano Real,' in Céli Regina Pinto and Hugo Guerrero (orgs.), *América Latina: o desafio da democracia nos anos 90* (Porto Alegre: Editora Universidade/UFRGS), pp. 97–112.

Kinzo, Maria D'Alva G. (forthcoming) 'Democratization through Transition: The Case of Brazil,' in E. Newmann and M.A Garretón (eds.) *Democracy in Latin America* (United Nations University Press).

Koerner, Andrei (1999) 'Debate sobre a reforma judiciária,' *Novos Estudos CEBRAP*, July No. 54.

Kornberg, A. and Clarke, H. (1992) *Citizens and Community: Political Support in a Representative Democracy* (New York: Cambridge University Press).

Kornblith, M. and Levine, D. (1995) 'Venezuela: The Life and Times of the Party System,' in S. Mainwaring and T. Scully (eds.), *Building Democratic Institutions: Party System in Latin America* (Stanford: Stanford University Press), pp. 37–71.

Kucinski, B. (1998) *A síndrome da antena parabólica: ética no jornalismo brasileiro* (São Paulo: Editora Fundação Perseu Abramo).

Kume, H. (1996) *A política de importação no Plano Real e a estrutura de proteção efetiva* (IPEA).

La Pastina, A. (1999) 'The Telenovela Way of Knowledge: An Ethnographic Reception Study Among Rural Viewers in Brazil,' PhD Dissertation, University of Texas at Austin.

Laakso, Markku and Taagepera, Rein (1979) 'Effective Number of Parties: A Measure with Applications to West Europe,' *Comparative Political Studies* vol. 12, pp. 3-27.

Lamounier, Bolívar (1968) 'Raça e classe na política brasileira', *Cadernos Brasileiros,* vol. 47, 39–50.

Lamounier, Bolívar (1980) 'A representação proporcional no Brasil: mapeamento de um debate,' *Revista de Cultura e Política,* no. 7, pp. 5–42.

Lamounier, Bolívar (1985) 'Apontamentos sobre a questão democrática brasileira,' in Alain Rouquier et al. (org.), *Como renascem as democracias* (São Paulo: Ed. Brasiliense).

Lamounier, B. (1990) 'Brazil: Inequality Against Democracy,' in L. Diamond, J.J. Linz and S.M. Lipset (eds.) *Politics in Developing Countries: Comparing Experiences with Democracy* (Colorado: Lynne Rienner Publishers, Inc.), pp. 87–134.

Lamounier, B. and Marques, A. (1992) 'A democracia brasileira no final da década perdida,' in B. Lamounier (ed.), *Ouvindo o Brasil: uma análise da opiniao pública no Brasil hoje* (São Paulo: Editora Sumaré), pp. 137–58

Lamounier, B. and Meneguello, Rachel (1986) *Partidos políticos e consolidação democrática* (São Paulo: Brasiliense).

Lamounier, Bolivar and Moura, Alkimar (1986) 'Economic Policy and Political Opening in Brazil,' in Jonathan Hartlyn and S. Morley (eds.), *Latin American Political Economy: Financial Crisis and Political Change* (Boulder: Westview Press).

Lamounier, Bolivar and Muszynski, Judith (1993) 'Brasil,' in Dieter Nohlen (ed.), *Enciclopedia electoral latinoamericana y del Caribe* (San José: Instituto Interamericano de Derechos Humanos).

Lamounier, B. and Souza, A. (1991) 'Democracia e reforma institucional no Brasil: uma cultura política em mudança,' *DADOS,* vol. 34, pp. 311–48.

Larvie, S.P. and Muniz, J. (1995) 'Identifying Problems and Selling Priorities: Results of a Year-Long Evaluation Study of a Community Policing Programme in Rio de Janeiro, Brazil,' paper presented to the International Police Conference, Rio de Janeiro, December.

Lattman-Weltman, F., Carneiro, J.A. and Ramos, P. (1994) *A imprensa faz e desfaz um presidente* (Rio de Janeiro: Nova Fronteira).

Lau, L.J., Jamison, D.T., Liu, S. and Rivkin, S. (1996) 'Education and Economic Growth: Some Cross-Sectional Evidence,' in N. Birdsall and R.H. Sabot (eds.) (1996) *Opportunity Foregone: Education in Brazil* (Washington DC: Inter-American Development Bank/Johns Hopkins University Press), pp. 83–116.

Lauvaux, Philippe (1998) *Parlementarisme rationalisé et stabilité du pouvoir executif — quelques aspects de la réforme de l' État confrontés aux expérienced étrangères* (Bruylant, Bruxele: L' Université Libre de Bruxelles).

Lavareda, Antônio (1991) *A democracia nas urnas: o processo partidário-eleitoral brasileiro* (Rio de Janeiro, IUPERJ/Rio Fundo Editora).

Leal, V. N. (1978) *Coronelismo, enxada e voto* (São Paulo: Alfa-Ômega).

Leite, A. (1997) *A energia do Brasil (Brazil's Energy)* (Nova Frontera).

Lemgruber, J. (1986) 'Polícia, direitos humanos e cidadania: notas para um estudo,' in *Seminário crime e castigo*, Rio de Janeiro, Ciência Hoje, vol. 2.

Lieberson, S. (1992a) 'Eistein, Renoir and Greeley: Some Thoughts about Evidence in Sociology,' *American Sociological Review*, pp. 1–15.

Lieberson, S. (1992b) 'Small N's and Big Conclusions: An Examination of the Reasoning in Comparative Studies Based on a Small Number of Cases,' in C. Ragin and H. Becker (eds.), *What is a Case? Exploring the Foundations of Social Inquiry* (Cambridge: The Press Syndicate of the University of Cambridge), pp. 105–18.

Lima Junior, O. Brasil de. (1983) *Os partidos políticos brasileiros: a experiência federal e regional* (Rio de Janeiro: Edições Graal).

Lima Jr, Olavo Brasil (1993) *Democracia e instituições políticas no Brasil dos anos 80* (São Paulo: Editora Loyola).

Lima, R.K. (1989) 'Cultura jurídica e práticas policiais: tradição inquisitorial,' *Revista Brasileira de Ciências Sociais. ANPOCS*, vol. 10, no. 4 (São Paulo), pp. 65–84.

Lima, R.K. (1995), *A polícia da cidade do Rio de Janeiro: seus dilemas e paradoxos* (Rio de Janeiro: Forense), 2nd edition.

Lima, V.A. de (1988) 'The State, Television, and Political Power in Brazil,' *Critical Studies in Mass Communication*, vol. 5, no. 2, pp. 108–28.

Lima, V.A. de (1993) 'Brazilian Television in the 1989 Presidential Campaign: Constructing a President,' in Thomas Skidmore (ed.), *Television, Politics, and the Transition to Democracy in Latin America* (Baltimore: The Johns Hopkins University Press), pp. 97–117.

Lima, V.A. de (1998) 'Os mídia e a política,' in Maria das Graças Rua and Maria Izabel V. de Carvalho (orgs.), *O estudo da política* (Brasília: Paralelo 15), pp. 209–30.

Lima, V.A. de and Guazina, L. (1998) 'Politica eleitoral na TV: Um estudo comparado do Jornal Nacional (JN) e do Jornal da Record (JR) em 1998,' trabalho apresentado ao XXII Encontro Anual da Associação Nacional de Pós-Graduação e Pesquisa em Ciências Sociais (ANPOCS), Caxambu/MG, 27 a 31 de outubro.

Limongi, Fernando and Figueiredo, Argelina (1995) 'Partidos políticos na Câmara dos Deputados: 1989–1994,' *Dados – Revista de Ciências Sociais*, vol. 38, no. 3, pp. 497–525.

Limongi, Fernando and Figueiredo, Argelina (2000) 'O presidencialismo brasileiro pós-1988: fusão de poderes e representação política,' trabalho apresentado na I Conferência sobre Federalismo Cooperativo, Globalização e Democracia, Brasília, 9–11 de maio.

Lins da Silva, C.E. (1993) 'The Brazilian Case: Manipulation by the Media?,' in Thomas Skidmore (ed.), *Television, Politics, and the Transition to Democracy in Latin America* (Baltimore: The Johns Hopkins University Press), pp. 137–44.

Lins e Silva, Evandro (1997) 'A reforma do poder judiciário,' *Justiça e Democracia*, no. 3 (1997), pp. 43–72.

Lins da Silva, C.E. (2000) 'Journalism and Corruption in Brazil,' in Joseph Tulchin and Ralph Espach (eds.), *Combating Corruption in Latin America* (Baltimore: Woodrow Wilson Centre Press), pp. 173–92.

Linz, J. (1970) 'An Authoritarian Regime: Spain,' in E. Alladart and S. Rokkan (eds.) *Mass Politics: Studies in Political Sociology* (New York, NY: The Free Press), pp. 251–84.

Linz, J. (1978) *The Breakdown of Democratic Regimes: Crisis, Breakdown and Reequilibration* (Baltimore: Johns Hopkins University Press).

Lipset, S.M. (1981) *Political Man* (Baltimore: Johns Hopkins University Press).

Lopes, Juarez Brandao (1971) *Sociedade industrial no Brasil* (Sao Paulo: Difusao).

Mackie, T. and Rose, R. (1991) *The International Almanac of Electoral History* (London: The Macmillan Press), 3rd edition.

Mainwaring, S. (1991) 'Politicians, Parties and Electoral Systems: Brazil in Comparative Perspective', in *Comparative Politics*, vol. 24, no. 1, pp. 21–43.

Mainwaring, Scott P. (1992) 'Brazilian Party Underdevelopment,' *Political Science Quarterly*, vol. 107, no. 4.

Mainwaring, Scott P. (1993) 'Brazil: Weak Parties, Feckless Democracy,' in Scott P. Mainwaring and Timothy R. Scully (eds.), *Building Democratic Institutions: Parties and Party Systems in Latin America* (Stanford: Stanford University Press).

Mainwaring, Scott (1995) 'Brazil: Weak Parties, Feckless Democracy,' in S. Mainwaring and T.R. Scully (eds.), *Building Democratic Institutions: Party Systems in Latin America* (Stanford: Stanford University Press).

Mainwaring, Scott (1999) *Rethinking Party Systems in The Third Wave of Democratization: The Case of Brazil* (Stanford: Stanford University Press).

Mainwaring, S., O'Donnell, G. and Velenzuela, A. (1992) *Issues in Democratic Consolidation: The New South America in Comparative Perspective* (Notre Dame, IL: University of Notre Dame).

Mainwaring, Scott and Liñan, Anibal P. (1998) 'Disciplina Partidária: O Caso da Constituinte,' *Revista Lua Nova*, no. 44, pp. 107–36.

Mair, P (1997) *Party System Change – Approaches and Interpretations* (Oxford, Clarendon Press).

Malloy, J. and Connaghan, C. (1996) *Unsettling Statecraft, Democracy and Neoliberalism in the Central Andes* (Pittsburg: Pittsburg University Press).

Manning, P. (1977) *Police Work* (Cambridge, Mass: Cambridge University Press).

Marçal Brandão, Gildo (1997) *A esquerda positiva* (São Paulo: Hucitec).

Marques de Melo, J. (1992) 'Mass Media and Politics in Brazil: The Collor Phenomenon,' *Brazilian Communication Research Yearbook*, March, pp. 122–39.

Marshall, T.H. (1964) *Class, Citizenship and Social Development* (New York: Doubleday & Co., Inc).

Martins, José de Souza (1999) 'Reforma agrária – o impossível diálogo sobre a história possível,' in *Tempo Social – Revista de Sociologia da USP*, vol.11, no. 2, pp. 97–128.

Martins, Luciano (1986) 'The "liberalisation" of authoritarian rule in Brazil,' in Guillermo O'Donnell, Philippe C. Schmitter and Laurence Whitehead (eds.), *Transitions from Authoritarian Rule: Latin America* (Baltimore: Johns Hopkins University Press).

Martins, L. (1988) 'A "liberalização" do regime autoritário no Brasil,' in G. O'Donnell, P.C. Schmitter and L. Whitehead (eds.) *Transiçoes do regime autoritário: América Latina* (Sao Paulo: Vértice, Editora Revista dos Tribunais), pp. 108–39.

Mattenheim, K. and Malloy, J. (1998) 'Introduction,' K. Mattenheim and J. Malloy (eds), *Deepening Democracy in Latin America* (Pittsburgh: University of Pittsburgh Press).

Mcclosky, H. (1964) 'Consensus and Ideology in American Politics,' *American Political Science Review*, vol. 58, pp. 361–82.

Mello e Souza, A., Crespo, M. and Soares, J.F. (1998) 'Implementing a World Class Educational Assessment System: An External Appraisal of the SAEB Project,' mimeo (Brasilia: UNDP).

Melo, Carlos Ranulfo F. (2000) 'Por que mudam de partidos os deputados brasileiros?' *Teoria e Sociedade*, no. 6, pp.122–77;

Mendes, A. and Venturi, G. (1994) 'Eleição presidencial: o Plano Real na sucessão de Itamar Franco,' *Opinião Pública*, vol. II, no. 2, pp. 39–48.

Mesquita, P. (1998) 'Policiamento comunitário: a experiência em São Paulo,' *Relatório feito para o NEV/USP* (São Paulo), September.

Miguel, L.F. (1997) 'Mídia e discurso político nas eleições presidenciais de 1994,' *Comunicação & Política*, vol. IV, no. 1 (1997), pp. 80–96.

Miguel, L.F. (1999) 'Mídia e eleições: a campanha de 1998 na Rede Globo,' *Dados*, vol. 42, no. 2, pp. 253–76.

Miguel, L.F. (2000) 'The Globo Television Network and the Election of 1998,' *Latin American Perspectives*, vol. 27, no. 6, pp. 65–84.

Minguardi, G. (1992) *Tiras, gansos e trutas. Cotidiano e reforma na polícia civil* (São Paulo: Página Aberta).

Moisés, J.A. (1995) *Os brasileiros e a democracia: bases sócio-políticas da legitimidade democrática* (São Paulo: Editora Atica).

Motter, P. (1994a) 'A batalha invisível da constituinte: interesses privados versus caráter público da radiodifusão no Brasil,' dissertação de Mestrado, Universidade de Brasília.

Motter, P. (1994b) 'O uso político das concessões de rádio e televisão no governo Sarney,' *Comunicação & Política*, vol. 1, no. 1, pp. 89–115.

Muller, E. and Seligson, M. (1997) 'Civic Culture and Democracy: The Question of Causal Relationships,' *American Political Science Review*, vol. 88, no. 3, pp. 635–52.

Müller, L.D. (1986) *América Latina: relaciones internacionales y derechos humanos* (Ciudad de México: Fondo de Cultura Econômica).

Munck, G. (1994) 'Democratic Transitions in Comparative Perspective,' *Comparative Politics*, vol. 26.

Munck, G. and Leff, C.S. (1997) 'Modos de transição em perspectiva comparada,' *Lua Nova*, vol. 40, pp. 69–96.

Muniz, J., Musumeci, L., Larvie, S.P. and Freire, B. (1997) 'Resistências e dificuldades de um programa de policiamento comunitário,' *Tempo Social. USP* (São Paulo), vol. 9, no.1, pp. 197–213, May.

Musumeci, L. (coord.) (1995) *Policiamento comunitário em Copacabana: monitoramento qualitative*, Relatório parcial (Rio de Janeiro: NPE/ISER), fevereiro.

Naím, Moises (1995), 'Latin America the Morning After,' *Foreign Affairs*, vol. 74, no. 4, July/August.

Nascimento, Abdias et al. (1950) *Relações de raça no Brasil* (Rio de Janeiro: Quilombo).

Nascimento, Abdias (1968) *O negro revoltado* (Rio de Janeiro: G.R.D).

Nicolau, Jairo (1996) *Multipartidarismo e democracia: um estudo sobre o sistema partidário brasileiro (1985-94)* (Rio de Janeiro: Editora FGV).

Nicolau, Jairo M. (1997) 'As distorções na representação dos estados na Câmara dos Deputados Brasileira,' *Dados*, 40, no. 3, pp. 441–64.

Nicolau, Jairo (1998) 'A volatilidade eleitoral nas eleições para a Câmara dos Deputados Brasileira (1992-1994),' unpublished paper, XXII Encontro Anual da ANPOCS, Caxambu, outubro.

Nicolau, Jairo Marconi (ed.) (1998a), *Dados eleitorais do Brasil* (1982-1996) (Rio de Janeiro: Editora Revan).

Nisbett, R.E. and Cohen, D. (1996) *Culture of Honor: The Psychology of Violence in the South* (Colorado: Westview Press, Inc., A Division of Harper Collins Publishers, Inc).

Nogueira da Cruz, H. and Da Silva, M.E. (1997) 'Industry and Technology,' in M. Williamson and E. Giannetti da Fonseca (eds.), *The Brazilian Economy: Structure and Performance in Recent Decades* (Miami: North-South Centre Press).

Nohlen, Dieter (ed.) (1993) *Enciclopedia electoral latinoamericana y del Caribe* (San José: Instituto Interamericano de Derechos Humanos).

Nohlen, D. (1995) *Elecciones y sistemas electorales*, 3rd edition (Venezuela: Editorial Nueva Sociedad).

Nunes, M.V. (1998) 'Rádio e política: do microfone ao palanque. Os radialistas políticos em Fortaleza (1982-1996),' trabalho apresentado ao XXII Encontro Anual da Associação Nacional de Pós-Graduação e Pesquisa em Ciências Sociais (ANPOCS), Caxambu/MG, 27 a 31 de outubro.

O'Donnell, G. (1986) *Contrapontos: autoritarismo e democratização* (São Paulo: Vertice).

O'Donnell, G. (1988) 'Introduçao aos casos latino-americanos,' in G. O'Donnell, P.C. Schmitter and L. Whitehead (eds.) *Transiçoes do regime autoritário: América Latina* (São Paulo: Vértice, Editora Revista dos Tribunais), pp. 17–36.

O'Donnell, G. (1994) 'The State, Democratization and Some Conceptual Problems,' in William C. Smith, Carlos H. Acuña and Eduardo A. Camara (eds.), *Latin American Political Economy in the Age of Neoliberal Reform* (New Brunswick).

O'Donnell, G. (1996) 'Illusion About Consolidation,' *Journal of Democracy*, vol. 7, no. 2, pp. 34–51.

O'Donnell, Guillermo (1998) 'Accountability horizontal e novas poliaquias,' *Lua Nova*, no. 44, pp. 27–54

O'Donnell, G., Schmitter, P.C. and Whitehead, L. (1986) *Transitions from Authoritarian Rule: Comaparative Perspectives* (Baltimore: The Johns Hopkins University Press).

O'Neil, P. (ed.) (1998) *Communicating Democracy: The Media and Political Transitions* (Boulder: Lynne Rienner Publishers).

Orpinas, P. (1999) '¿Quién es violento? Factores asociados con comportamientos agresivos en ciudades seleccionadas de América Latina y España,' *Revista Panamericana de Salud Publica*, vol. 5, nos. 4/5.

Osiel, Mark J. (1995) 'Dialogue with Dictators: Judicial Resistance in Argentina and Brazil,' *Law and Social Inquiry*, vol. 20, no. 2 (1995), pp. 481–560.

Ouvidoria da Polícia do Estado de São Paulo (1997) *Relatório anual de prestação de contas da Ouvidoria da Polícia do Estado de São Paulo* (São Paulo).

Ouvidoria da Polícia do Estado de São Paulo (1998) *Relatório anual de prestação de contas da Ouvidoria da Polícia do Estado de São Paulo* (São Paulo).

Paes de Barros, R et. al. (2000) 'A establidade inaceitavel: desigualdade e pobreza no Brasil,' in Ricardo Henriques (ed.), *Desigualdade e pobreza no Brasil* (IPEA).

Paixão, A.L. (1982) 'A organização policial numa área metropolitana,' *Dados – Revista de Ciências Sociais*. IUPERJ (Rio de Janeiro), vol. 25, no.1, pp. 63–85.

Paixão, A.L. (1988) 'Crime, controle social e consolidação da democracia: as metáforas da cidadania,' in F.W. Reis and G. O'Donnell (eds.) *A democracia no Brasil dilemas e perspectivas* (São Paulo: Vértice, Editora Revista dos Tribunais), pp. 168-199

Paixão, A.L. (1995), *O Problema da polícia: violência e participação política no Rio de Janeiro*, Rio de Janeiro, Série Estudos, IUPERJ, p. 91.

Paixão, A.L. and Beato F., C. (1997) 'Crimes, vítimas e policiais,' *Tempo Social. USP* (São Paulo), vol. 9, no. 1, May, pp. 233–48.

Pandolfi, Dulce Chaves et al. (eds.) (1999) *Cidadania, justiça e violência* (Rio de Janeiro: Fundação Getúlio Vargas).

Panebianco, Angelo (1988) *Political Parties: Organisation and Power* (Cambridge: Cambridge University Press).

Parsons, T. (1951) *The Social System* (New York: The Free Press).

Pastore, Jose (1981) *Inequality and Social Mobility in Brazil* (Madison: University of Wisconsin Press).

Pastore, Jose and Silva, Nelson do Valle (2000) *Mobilidade social no Brasil* (Sao Paulo: Makron).

Patrinos, H. and Araisingam, D.L. (1997) *Decentralization of Education: Demand-Side Financing* (Washington DC: World Bank).

Paul, J.J. and Wolff, L. (1996) 'The Economics of Higher Education,' in N. Birdsall and R.H. Sabot (eds.) (1996) *Opportunity Foregone: Education in Brazil* (Washington DC: Inter-American Development Bank/Johns Hopkins University Press), pp. 523–54.

Pedersen, Mogens (1990) 'Electoral Volatility in Western Europe: 1948-1977,' in Peter Mair (ed.), *The West European Party System* (Oxford: Oxford University Press).

Pereira, Anthony W. (1998), '"Persecution and Farce": The Origins and Transformation of Brazil's Political Trials, 1964–1979,' *Latin American Research Review*, vol. 33, no. 1 (1998), pp. 43–66.

Pereira, Carlos (2000) 'What are the Conditions for Presidential Success in the Legislative Arena?: The Brazilian Electoral Connection,' unpublished doctoral dissertation (New York: New School University).

Pereira, Carlos and Mueller, Bernardo (2000) 'Uma teoria da preponderância do poder executivo: o sistema de comissões no legislativo brasileiro,' *Revista Brasileira de Ciências Sociais*, vol. 15, no. 43 (June), pp. 45–68.

Pereira, João Baptista B. (1982) 'Parâmetros ideológicos do projeto político de negros em São Paulo,' *Revista do Instituto de Estudos Brasileiros*, USP, vol. 24, pp. 53–61.

Peres, Paulo S. (2000) 'Sistema partidário, instabilidade eleitoral e consolidação democrática no Brasil,' II Encontro Anual da Associação Brasileira de Ciência Política (ABCP), mimeo.

Pinheiro and Cabral (1998) *Mercado de crédito no Brasil: o papel do judiciário e de outras instituições*, RJ, Ensaios BNDES no. 9.

Pinheiro, A. and Almeida, G. (1994) *Padrões setoriais de proteção na economia brasileira* (IPEA).

Pinheiro, Armando Castelar (2000) *Judiciário e economia no Brasil* (São Paulo: Editora Sumaré).

Pinheiro, P.S. et al. (1991), Violência fatal: conflitos policiais em SP (81-89),' *São Paulo. Revista da USP.* USP, no. 9, pp. 95–112.

Pinheiro, P.S. (1997) 'Autoritarismo e transição,' *Revista USP*, março, abril, maio, vol. 9, pp. 45–64.

Pinheiro, P.S. (1997) 'Violência, crime e sistemas policiais em países de novas democracias,' São Paulo, *Tempo Social*, USP, vol. 9, no.1, pp. 43–52, maio.

Pinheiro, Paulo Sérgio (1991) 'Police and Political Crisis: The Case of the Military Police,' in Martha Huggins (ed.), *Vigilantism and the State in Modern Latin America: Essays in Extra-legal Violence* (Westport CT: Praeger).

Pinheiro, Paulo Sérgio (1994) 'The Legacy of Authoritarianism in Democratic Brazil,' in Stuart S. Nagel (ed.), *Latin American Development and Public Policy* (New York: St Martins Press).

Pinto, C. (1996) 'Uma ordem no caos: o discurso político na eleição presidencial de 1994,' in Céli Regina Pinto and Hugo Guerrero (orgs.), *América Latina: o desafio da democracia nos anos 90* (Porto Alegre: Editora Universidade/UFRGS), pp. 157–65.

Piquet Carneiro, L. (1999) 'Para medir a violência,' in Dulce Pandolfi et all., *Cidadania justiça e violência* (Rio de Janeiro: FGV).

Plank, D.N., Sobrinho, J.A. and Ressurreição Xavier, A.C. da (1996) 'Why Brazil Lags Behind in Educational Development,' in N. Birdsall and R.H. Sabot (eds.) (1996), *Opportunity Foregone: Education in Brazil* (Washington DC: Inter-American Development Bank/Johns Hopkins University Press), pp. 117–45.

PNAD96 – CD Rom (1996) Instituto Brasileiro de Geografia e Estatística.

Pocock, J.G.A. (1975) *The Machiavellian Moment* (Princeton: Princeton University Press).

Porto, M. (1994) 'As eleições municipais em São Paulo,' in Heloiza Matos (org.), *Mídia, eleições e democracia* (São Paulo: Scritta), pp. 133–57.

Porto, M. (1996) 'A crise de confiança na política e suas instituições: os mídia e a legitimidade da democracia,' in Marcello Baquero (org.), *Condicionantes da consolidação democrática: ética, mídia e cultura política* (Porto Alegre: Ed. Universidade/UFRGS), pp. 41–64.

Porto, M. (1998a) 'Globo's Evening News and the Representation of Politics in Brazil (1995-1996),' paper delivered at the 48th Annual Conference of the International Communication Association (ICA), Jerusalem, Israel, July 20-24.

Porto, M. (1998b) 'Telenovelas and Politics in the 1994 Brazilian Presidential Election,' *The Communication Review*, vol. 2, no. 4, pp. 433–59.

Porto, M. (2000a) 'Making Sense of Politics: TV News and Audiences' Interpretation of Politics In Brazil,' paper delivered at the Annual Meeting of the Latin American Studies Association (LASA), Miami, USA, March 16–18.

Porto, M. (2000b) 'Telenovelas, política e identidad nacional en Brasil,' *Ecuador Debate*, no. 49, pp. 205–34.

Porto, M. and Guazina, L. (1999) 'A política na TV: o horário eleitoral da eleição presidencial de 1994,' *Contracampo*, no. 3, pp. 5–33.

Posthuma, A. (1999) 'Introdução: transformações do emprego no Brasil na decade de 90,' in *Abertura e ajuste do mercado de trabalho no Brasil* (Editora 34 Ltda).

Powell, G.B. (1982) *Contemporary Democracies: Participation, Stability and Violence* (Cambridge: The President and Fellows of Harvard College).

Power, T. and Roberts, T. (2000) 'A New Brazil? The Changing Sociodemographic Context of Brazilian Democracy,' in Peter Kingstone and Timothy Power (eds.), *Democratic Brazil* (Pittsburgh: University of Pittsburgh Press), pp. 236–62.

Powers, Daniel A. and Xie, Yu (2000) *Statistical Methods for Categorical Data Analysis* (New York: Academic Press).

Prado Junior, Caio (1965) [1937 1st Edition] *A formação do Brasil contemporâneo, Colônia*, Brasiliense.

Prandi, Reginaldo (1996) 'Raça e voto na eleição presidencial de 1994,' *Estudos Afro-Asiáticos*, no. 30.

Prillamen, William (2000) *The Judiciary and Democratic Decay in Latin America: Declining Confidence in the Rule of Law* (Westport CT: Praeger).

Przeworski, A. (1986) 'Some Problems in the Study of the Transition to Democracy,' in G. O'Donnell, P.C. Schmitter and L. Whitehead (eds.) *Transitions from Authoritarian Rule: Comparative Perspectives* (Baltimore: The Johns Hopkins University Press), pp. 47–63.

Przeworski, A., Alvarez, M., Cheibub, J.A. and Limongi, F. (1997) 'O que mantém as Democracias?' *Lua Nova*, nos. 40/41, pp. 113-136.

Psacharopoulos, G. and Woodhall, M. (1985) *Education for Development: An Analysis of Investment Choices* (London: Oxford University Press).

Pye, L. (1990) 'Political Science and the Crisis of Authoritarianism,' *American Political Science Review*, vol. 84, pp. 3–19.

Rae, Douglas W. (1975) *The Political Consequences of Electoral Laws* (New Haven, Yale University Press), 2nd edition

Ramos, A. Guerreiro (1957) 'Patologia social do "branco brasileiro"; "o negro desde dentro"; "política de relações de raça no Brasil",' in *Introdução Crítica à Sociologia Brasileira* (Rio de Janeiro: Andes).

Ramos, L. and Vieira, M. (2000) 'Determinantes da desigualdade de rendimentos no Brasil nos anos 90,' in Ricardo Henriques (ed.), *Desigualdade e pobreza no Brasil* (IPEA).

Ramos, M.C. (1985) 'O papel dos meios de comunicação de massa na abertura política brasileira,' in José Marques de Melo (org.), *Comunicação e transição democrática* (Porto Alegre: Mercado Aberto), pp. 246–63.

Reis, E.P. and Cheibub, Z.B. (1995) 'Valores políticos das elites e consolidação democrática,' *DADOS* 38, pp. 31–56.

Reis, F.W. (1988) 'Consolidação democrática e construção do estado – notas introdutórias e uma tese,' in F.W. Reis, and G. O'Donnell (eds.), *A democracia no Brasil dilemas e perspectivas* (São Paulo: Vértice, Editora Revista dos Tribunais), pp. 11–12.

Reis, Fábio Wanderley and O'Donnell, Guillermo (eds.) (1988) *A democracia no Brasil: dilemas e perspetivas* (São Paulo: Vértice).

Ribeiro, Paulo Jorge and Strozenberg, Pedro (eds.) (2001) *Balcão de direitos: Resoluções de conflitos em favelas do Rio de Janeiro, imagens e linguagens* (Rio de Janeiro: MAUAD Editora).

Risério, Antonio (1981) *Carnaval Ijexá* (Salvador: Corrupio).

Rocha, S. (2000) *Pobreza e desigualdade no Brasil: o esgotamento dos efeitos distributivos do Plano Real* (Brasília: IPEA), TD 721.

Rodrigues, Nina (1933) *Os africanos no Brasil* (São Paulo).

Romero, A. (1997) 'Rearranging the Deck Chairs on the Titanic: The Agony of Democracy in Venezuela,' *Latin American Research Review*, vol. 32, pp. 7–36.

Rosenn, Keith S. (1998) 'Judicial Reform in Brazil,' *Nafta Law and Business Review of the Americas*, vol. 4, no. 2, pp. 19–37.

Rouquié, A. (1986) 'Demilitarization and the Institutionalization of Military-Dominated Polities in Latin America,' in G. O'Donnell, P.C. Schmitter and L. Whitehead (eds.), *Transitions from Authoritarian Rule: Comparative Perspectives* (Baltimore: The Johns Hopkins University Press), pp. 108–36.

Rouquié, A. (1994) *Guerras y paz en América Central* (Ciudad de México: Fondo de Cultura Económica).

Rubim, A.A. (1999) *Mídia e política no Brasil* (João Pessoa: Editora Universitária/UFPB).

Rule, J.B. (1988) *Theories of Civil Violence* (California: The Regents of the University of California).

Sadek, Maria Teresa A. (1995b) *O judiciário em debate* (São Paulo: Editora Sumaré).

Sadek, Maria Teresa A. (1995a) *A justiça eleitoral e a consolidação da democracia no Brasil* (São Paulo: Konrad Adenauer Stiftung Serie Pesquisas), vol.4.

Sadek, Maria Teresa A. (ed.) (2000) *Justiça e cidadania no Brasil* (São Paulo: Editora Sumaré).

Sadek, Maria Teresa (2001a) (ed.) *Reforma do judiciário* (São Paulo: Fundação Konrad Adenauer).

Sadek, Maria Teresa (2001b) 'Controle externo do poder judiciário,' in Maria Teresa Sadek (ed.) *Reforma do judiciário* (São Paulo: Fundação Konrad Adenauer).

Sallum Jr, Brasilio (1996) *Labirintos – dos generais à Nova República* (São Paulo: Hucitec/Sociologia-USP).

Sallum Jr, Brasilio (1999) 'O Brasil sob Cardoso: neoliberalismo e desenvolvimentismo,' *Tempo Social. Revista de Sociologia da USP*, São Paulo, vol. 11, no. 2, pp 23–47 (October).

Sallum Jr, Brasilio (2000) 'Globalização e desenvolvimento: a estratégia brasileira nos anos 90,' *Novos Estudos Cebrap*, no. 58 (November).

Sampson, R. and Winson, W.J. (1995) 'Toward a Theory of Race, Crime and Urban Inequality,' in J. Hagan and R.D. Peterson (eds.) *Crime and Inequality* (Stanford: Stanford University Press), pp. 37–54.

Samuels, David (1998) 'Ambition and its Consequences: Federalism, Elections and Policy-Making in Brazil,' PhD Disseration, Univ of California, San Diego.

Santos, Joel Rufino dos (1985) 'O movimento negro e a crise brasileira,' in *Política e Administração* (Rio de Janeiro) vol. 2, no. 2 (July–September), pp. 287–307.

Santos, W.G.d. (1985) 'A pós-revoluçao brasileira,' in H. Jaguaribe, F. Iglésias, W.G.d. Santos V. Chaconand F. Comparato, *Brasil, sociedade democrática* (Rio de Janeiro: José Olympio Editora).

Santos, W.G.d. (1993) *Razões da desordem* (Rio de Janeiro: Rocco).

Sartori, Giovanni (1987) *Theory of Democracy Revisited* (Chatham: Chatham House), p. 206

Scalon, Maria Celi (1999) *Mobilidade social no Brasil: padrões e tendências* (Rio de Janeiro: Revan-Iuperj-UCM).

Schedler, Andreas, Diamond, Larry and Plattner, Marc F. (eds.) (1999) *The Self-Restraining State: Power and Accountability in New Democracies* (Boulder: Lynne Rienner).

Schiefelbein, E. (1992) *Redefining Basic Education for Latin America: Lessons to be Learned From the Colombian Escuela Nueva* (Paris: UNESCO, International Institute for Educational Planning).

Schmitt, R., Carneiro, L. and Kuschnir, K. (1999) 'Estratégias de campanha no horário eleitoral em eleições proporcionais,' *Dados*, vol. 42, no. 2, pp. 277–301.

Schultz, T.W. (1961) 'Investment in Human Capital,' *American Economic Review*, March, pp. 1–17.

Schumpeter, Joseph (1976) *Capitalism, Socialism and Democracy* (London: George Allen & Unwin), 5th ed., p. 269.

Schwarcz, L. Moritz (1993) *O espetáculo das raças; cientistas, instituições e questões raciais no Brasil (1870-1930* (São Paulo: Companhia das Letras).

Seyferth, Giralda (1990) *Imigração e cultura no Brasil* (São Paulo: Brasiliense).

Shanin. T. (1978) 'The Third Stage: Marxist Historiography and the Origins of our Time,' *Journal of Contemporary Asia*, vol. 6, no. 3.

Shugart, Matthew and Carey, John M. (1992) *Presidents and Assemblies: Constitutional Design and Electoral Dynamics* (Cambridge: Cambridge University Press).

Silva, Carlos B. Rodrigues (1995) *Da terra das primaveras às ilhas de amor. Reggae, lazer e identidade cultural* (São Luis: Edufma).

Silva, Nelson V. and Soares, Gláucio (1985) 'O charme discreto do socialismo Moreno,' *Dados*, Rio de Janeiro, vol. 28, no. 2, pp. 253–73.

Simkus, A.A., Jackson, J., Yip, K.-B. and Treiman, D. (1990) 'Changes in Social Mobility in Two Societies in the Crux of Transition: A Hungarian-Irish Comparison, 1943–1973,' *Research in Social Stratification and Mobility*, vol. 9.

Skidmore, T. E. (1976) *Preto no branco, raça e nacionalidade no pensamento brasileiro* (Rio de Janeiro: Paz e Terra).

Smith, P. (1993) 'La economia política de las drogas: cuestiones conceptuales y opciones de política,' in P. Smith (ed.) *El combate de las drogas en America* (México: Fondo de Cultura Econômica), pp. 37–56.

Soares, M. (2000) 'Veja e a construção do CR-P nas eleições presidenciais de 1998,' in Antônio Albino Rubim (org.), *Mídia e eleições de 1998* (Salvador: UFBA/Editora Universitária), pp. 89–102.

Sobel, Michael E. (1983) 'Structural Mobility, Circulation Mobility and the Analysis of Occupational Mobility: A Conceptual Mismatch,' *American Sociological Review*, vol. 48, pp. 721–27.

Sola, L. and Kugelmas (1996) 'Statecraft, instabilidade economica e incerteza política: o Brasil em perspectiva comparada,' in Eli Diniz (org.), *Anais do seminário internacional: o desafio da democracia na América Latina* (Rio de Janeiro: Iuperj), pp. 398–414.

Sorokin, Pitirim ([1927] 1959) *Social and Cultural Mobility* (New York: Free Press).

Souza, Amauri de (1971) 'Raça e política no Brasil urbano,' *Revista de Administração de Empresas*, vol. XI, Oct.-Dec.

Souza, P.R. (1999) ' Introdução: Um modelo de educação para o século XXI,' in J.P. dos Reis Velloso and R. Albuquerque (eds.) (1999), *Um modelo para a educação brasileira no século XXI* (Rio de Janeiro: José Olympio Editora), pp. 7–13.

Stadnik, C. (1991) 'A hipótese do fenômeno do "coronelismo eletrônico" e as ligações dos parlamentares federais e governadores com os meios de comunicação de massa no Brasil,' unpublished manuscript.

Stepan, Alfred (1973) *The Military in Politics – Changing Patterns in Brazil* (Princeton: Princeton University Press).

Stepan, A. (1986) 'Paths toward Redemocratization: Theoretical and Comparative Considerations,' in G. O'Donnell, P.C. Schmitterand L. Whitehead (eds.) *Transitions from Authoritarian Rule: Comaparative Perspectives* (Baltimore: The Johns Hopkins University Press), pp. 64–84.

Stepan, Alfred (ed.) (1989) *Democratising Brazil: Problems of Transition and Consolidation* (New York: Oxford University Press).

Straubhaar, J. (1996) 'The Electronic Media in Brazil,' in Richard Cole (ed.), *Communication in Latin America* (Wilmington: SR Books), pp. 217–43

Straubhaar, J. (1989) 'Television and Video in the Transition from Military to Civilian Rule in Brazil,' *Latin American Research Review*, vol. 24, no. 1, pp. 140–154.

Straubhaar, J. Olsen, O. and Nunes, M.C. (1993) 'The Brazilian Case: Influencing the Voter', in Thomas Skidmore (ed.), *Television, Politics, and the Transition to Democracy in Latin America* (Baltimore: The Johns Hopkins University Press), pp. 118–36.

Sullivan, J., Pierson, J. and Marcus, G. (1982) *Political Tolerance and American Democracy* (Chicago: University of Chicago Press).

Summers, L. (1994) *Investing in All the People: Educating Women in Developing Countries*, EDI Seminar Paper 45 (Washington DC: World Bank).

Taylor, C.L. and Jodice, D. (1983) *World Handbook of Political and Social Indicators III*. 3rd edition (New Haven: Yale University Press).

Thompson, M., Ellis, R. and Wildavsky, A. (1990) *Cultural Theory* (San Francisco: Westview Press).

Tilly, C. (1993) *European Revolutions, 1492–1992* (Massachusetts: Blackwell Publishers Ltd).

Todaro, M. (2000) *Economic Development* (Harlow: Addison-Wesley).

Touraine, Alain (1995), 'Democracy: From a Politics of Citizenship to a Politics of Recognition,' in Louis Maheu (ed.), *Social Movements and Social Classes – The Future of Collective Action* (London: Sage/ISA).

Tsebelis, George (1995) 'Decision-Making in Political Systems: Veto Players in Presidentialism, Multicameralism, and Pluripartism,' *British Journal of Political Science*, vol. 25, pp. 289–325.

UN Commissariat for Human Rights (1994) Report; chapter 2; *Factors and Difficulties Affecting the Application of the Covenant.*

UNESCO (2000) '181 Governments Adopt Framework for Action at the World Education Forum,' *Press Release*, 28 April.

UNICEF (1999) *The State of the World's Children 1999: Education* (New York: UNICEF).

UNICEF (2000) *The State of the World's Children 2000* (New York: UNICEF).

United Nations Economic and Social Council (2001) *Report of the Special Rapporteur on Torture: Visit to Brazil* E/CN.4/2001/66/Add.2 (Geneva: United Nations).

Uprimny, R. (1993) 'Narcotráfico, régimen político, violencias y derechos humanos en Colombia,' in Anonymous, *Bogotá Hoy* (Bogota).

Valenzuela, A. (1990) 'Chile: Origins, Consolidation, and Breakdown of a Democratic Regime,' in L. Diamond, J.J. Linz, and S.M. Lipset (eds.) *Politics in Developing Countries: Comparing Experiences with Democracy* (Colorado: Lynne Rienner Publishers, Inc.), pp. 39–86

Velasco e Cruz, Sebastião and Estevam Martins, Carlos (1983) 'De Castello a Figueiredo: uma incursão na pré-história da "abertura",' in Bernardo Sorj and Maria H. Tavares (eds.), *Sociedade e política no Brasil pós-64* (São Paulo: Ed. Brasiliense).

Velloso, J.P. dos Reis and Albuquerque, R. (eds.) (1999), *Um modelo para a educação brasileira no século XXI* (Rio de Janeiro: José Olympio Editora).

Venturi, G. (2000) 'Imagem pública, propaganda eleitoral e reeleição na disputa presidencial de 1998,' in Antônio Albino Rubim (org.), *Mídia e eleições de 1998* (Salvador: UFBA/Editora Universitária), pp. 103–24.

Vianna, Hermano (1988) *O mundo funk carioca* (Rio de Janeiro: Zahar).

Vianna, Luiz Werneck et al. (1999) *A judicialização da política e das relações sociais no Brasil* (Rio de Janeiro: Revan).

Vianna, Magalhães and Silveira, Tomich (2000) *Carga tributária direta e indireta sobre as unidades familiares no Brasil: Avaliação de sua incidência nas grandes regiões urbanas em 1996* (Brasília, IPEA, TD 757).

Waisbord, S. (1997) 'The Narrative of Exposés in South American Journalism: Telling the Story of Collorgate in Brazil,' *Gazette*, vol. 59, no. 3, pp. 189–203.

Waisbord, S. (2000) *Watchdog Journalism in South America* (New York: Columbia University Press).

Waiselfitz, J. (2000) *Dirigentes municipais de educação: um perfil* (Brasília: UNESCO, UNDIME, Ford Foundation).

Wattenberg, Martin (1998) *The Decline of American Political Parties, 1952-1996* (Cambridge, Mass.: Harvard University Press).

Weber, M.H. (1990) 'Pedagogias de despolitização e desqualificação da política brasileira: as telenovelas da Globo nas eleições presidenciais de 1989,' *Comunicação & Política*, no. 11, pp. 67–83.

Whitehead, Laurence (1993) 'On "Reform of the State" and "Regulation of the Market",' *World Development*, vol. 21 no. 8, pp 1371–93

World Bank (1986) *Financing Education in Developing Countries* (Washington, DC: World Bank).

World Bank (1990) *Primary Education: A World Bank Policy Paper* (Washington, DC: World Bank).

World Bank (1995) *Priorities and Strategies for Education: A World Bank Review* (Washington DC: World Bank).

World Bank (2000) *Projeto Nordeste: Borrower Completion Report* (Washington, DC: World Bank).

Xie, Yu (1992) 'The Log-Multiplicative Layer Effect Model for Comparing Mobility Tables,' *American Sociological Review*, vol. 57, pp. 380–95.

Yashar, D. (1995) 'Civil War and Social Welfare: The Origins of Costa Rica's Competitive Party System,' in S. Mainwaring and T. Scully (eds.) *Building Democratic Institutions: Party System in Latin America* (Stanford: Stanford University Press), pp. 72-99.

Zini, Alvaro (1993) *Taxa de cambio e politica cambial no Brasil* (São Paulo: EDUSP).

Printed in the United States
69376LVS00004B/172-192